Writing Marxist History

For Anne, Patrick, Andrew and Kate

That they may remember their great grandfather
Algernon (Charlie) Neale 1864—1953

Writing Marxist History

*British Society, Economy & Culture
since 1700*

R. S. Neale

Basil Blackwell

© R. S. Neale 1985

First published 1985

Basil Blackwell Ltd
108 Cowley Road, Oxford OX4 1JF, UK

Basil Blackwell Inc.
432 Park Avenue South, Suite 1505,
New York, NY 10016, USA

British Library Cataloguing in Publication Data

Neale, R. S.
Writing Marxist history: British society
economy and culture since 1700.
1. Great Britain — History
I. Title
941.07   DA470
ISBN 0-631-14051-4

Library of Congress Cataloging in Publication Data

Neale, R. S.
Writing Marxist history.
Includes index.
1. Great Britain—Social conditions. 2. Great
Britain—Economic conditions.   I. Title.
HN385.N43   1985   306'.0941   84-28379
ISBN 0-631-14051-4

Typeset by Pioneer, East Sussex
Printed in Great Britain by
Bell & Bain Ltd, Glasgow

Contents

Acknowledgements

On the day I received the contract for this book I also heard that Emeritus Professor Jim Belshaw had only a few months to live. He died before the book was finished. As Professor of Economics at the University of New England, Jim Belshaw brought me into the university world in 1964. In 1969, almost single-handedly, he brought into being a Department of Economic History, separate from Economics. These circumstances made possible my work over the last 20 years, and created the environment, especially favourable over the last five years, in which most of this book was written. My debt to Jim is beyond redeeming. He and his yesterdays he shared with me, making them mine, have been present in my mind throughout the last three months of my writing. He is mixed in this book in many ways. Without him it could never have been written.

Time, too, has been important to me. I thank the Trustees of the Huntington Library in California for a Visiting Fellowship in January and February 1982, and I thank Professor Eugene Kamenka and the Australian National University for two periods as Visiting Fellow, from November 1980 to February 1981, and in June 1984, in the History of Ideas Unit at the Australian National University. The Council of the University of New England is also to be commended (and thanked) for maintaining a substantial programme of study leave in the face of opposition from the Commonwealth Government of Australia, and for granting me leave within this programme at a time most valuable for the completion of this book.

It gives me very great pleasure to express my thanks to three of my students; Ian Harriss, Peter Burn, and Margaret Moussa. Ian's criticism and sharply analytical mind have contributed much to my understanding of *Mansfield Park* and *Moll Flanders*, and to my presentation of them in chapters 5 and 10. Chapter 10 has also benefited from several discussions with Peter and Margaret. In fact, Peter kindly lent me one of his sentences. The editors of *Social History* also concentrated my mind, although I have put back a section of the chapter originally removed for reasons of space. Chapter 6 was much improved through being read by and discussed with Bob Cage, a colleague in the Department of Economic History. Bob, too, lent me some of his own work. Although the design and writing of chapter 9 is mostly mine, the hard work of collecting and processing the minutiae on which it is based was done by Gael Ramsay and Shirley Fisher, and Graydon Henning provided a critical appraisal and a knowledge of sources unrivalled in Australia. The original article in the *Australian Economic History Review* is jointly authored by the four of us, colleagues in the Department of Economic History. I thank them all for their permission to reprint it. Chapter 11 has been much talked over, over a long time with my wife Margaret. As my severest critic she also read the Introduction, and chapters 7 and 11, and they are better for her critical attention and comment. Chapter 3 is a much revised version of my inaugural lecture delivered at the University of New England in 1976.

Chapter 4, 'The Bourgeoisie, Historically, Has Played a Most Revolutionary Part' first appeared in Eugene Kamenka and R. S. Neale (eds), *Feudalism, Capitalism and Beyond*, ANU 1975. Chapter 7, 'Class and Urban History, and the Historian's Task', was commissioned by Routledge and Kegan Paul for inclusion in a book to be called *The Making of Urban Society*, which has yet to be published. Chapter 9, 'Life and Death in Hillgrove, 1870—1914' first appeared in *The Australian Economic History Review*, September 1981. Chapter 10, 'Cultural Materialism: a critique: first appeared in abbreviated form in *Social History*, May 1984. I would like to thank the editors and publishers of these journals and books for their permission to republish those chapters and essays as chapters in this book, and, at the same time to thank the following for their permission to reproduce illustrations: The Trustees of the British Museum for 'Tristram Shandy's Story', and William Blake, *Albion Rose or Glad Day*; The Whitworth Art Gallery, University of Manchester for William Blake, *God Creating the Universe*; John Harris IFL for *Orgreave, Lesley Boulton*; the Parker Gallery, London for R. Caton Woodville RA, *The Charge of the Light Brigade*; The Historical Resources Centre, CAE Armidale, NSW, for *Empire Day, Hillgrove, NSW, 1908*; The Detroit Institute of Arts for *The Nightmare* (1781), by Henri Fuseli (Swiss, 1741—1825), oil on canvas 101.6 × 127 cm, accession 55.5 A, gift of Mr and Mrs Bert L. Smokler and Mr and Mrs Lawrence A. Fleischman, copyright © 1984 Founder Society Detroit Institute of Art; *Crawlers* by John Thomson is reproduced by kind permission of Sotheby's. The appendix to chapter 8 reproduces pp. 489—96 of Karl Marx, *Grundrisse: Foundations of the Critique of Political Economy*, translated by Martin

Nicolaus; Translation and Foreword copyright © Martin Nicolaus, 1973; reprinted by permission of Penguin Books Ltd and Random House Inc.

I would also like to thank the librarians, archivists and staff of the following libraries and record offices for their unstinting help and cooperation: The Dixson Library UNE, Armidale, NSW; The National Library, Canberra; The Court House, Armidale, NSW and the office of the Registrar General, NSW; The Huntington Library and Art Gallery, San Marino, California; Cambridge University Library; The Reference Library, Bath; City of Bath Archive's Office; The Archives section, Lambeth Libraries; The Record Office, Gloucester; Norfolk Record Office, Norwich; and Somerset Record Office, Taunton.

Finally my thanks, to Judith Dodd, Naomi Bell, Cathy Ward, Peg Leask and Jenny Weissel for typing and word-processing innumerable versions of different parts of the book. Without them there would be no book.

I AM now beginning to get fairly into my work; and by the help of a vegitable diet, with a few of the cold seeds, I make no doubt but I shall be able to go on with my uncle Toby's story, and my own, in a tolerable straight line. Now,

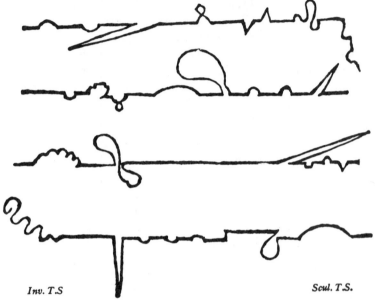

Inv. T.S   *Scul. T.S.*

These were the four lines I moved in through my first, second, third, and fourth volumes.—In the fifth volume I have been very good,—the precise line I have described in it being this:

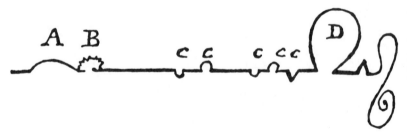

Tristram Shandy's Story (Laurence Sterne, 1759—67)

Introduction

My discovery of economic and social history in 1947 was my beginning, the obituary of Charlie Neale my first publication. As a student of economic and social history a few years earlier I had begun to learn that while my family had scarce any yesterdays, my class did. And I had come to know my grandfather when I realized he, too, was part of the history I studied. Without that experience of economic and social history from 1947—52, I would never have reached back to him. When he died in 1953 I wrote:

MR. A. NEALE

On Sunday, Mr. A. Neale, who first came to Southall about 1905, died at his home at 16, Leamington-road, Southall. He was 88, a retired woodworking machinist and cabinet maker.

His father, who attended his place of work in frock coat and top hat, was a royal coach builder who built for Prince Albert.

Mr A. Neale could remember striking for three weeks for an extra ½d an hour to bring the rate to 9½d an hour, and when living at Battersea in the 1880's he was active in the political movements of his day. He attended lectures by Hyndman, founder of the Social Democratic Federation and knew Tom Mann and Ben Tillett at the time of the strike for the "Dockers' Tanner." He also knew well Annie Besant, of match girl fame and Mr. and Mrs. Aveling. Mrs Aveling's maiden name was Eleanor Marx and she was the daughter of Karl Marx.

Mr. Neale's connexions with the past extended beyond his own immediate experience and he could, in conversation, take his listener with his wife's grandparents back to the Gold Rush in Australia, paint a picture of his wife's parents' coal and grocery business or tell of his father's two years in France learning his craft.

Mr. Neale began life as the son of a small successful business man. Depression brought ruin and he started work at the age of nine, married the daughter of a London grocery and coal merchant, and became a foreman woodworking machinist. His sons, following his example, became carpenters and joiners — a tradition maintained into a further generation through two grandsons.

He leaves ten great grand-children.

When I returned from his funeral to teach liberal studies to a class of apprentices on day-release from industry at Bath Technical College, I was full of memory and history. Many of the apprentices in class that morning were particularly obtuse. They always resented my presence in their lives. They wanted, they said, to be engineers; liberal studies and English would not make them better workers. And I wept. I raged at them for the memory of my grandfather and my class. I raged at the lack of connection, of memory, of yesterdays and at my impotence as a scholarship boy made good — or at least made into a teacher. What use was I? What hope was there for creating a lineage of the best of working-class life, ideas and of action? What good was my job?

So, in a piecemeal fashion, I set about the private task of recovering my past. As teacher, as an external post-graduate student, and tentatively as a history writer, I tried to weave myself and the people around me into a pattern of relationships giving significance to their ordinary lives. Unless I did so I would be lost. This sensation is a very powerful one; I never feel at home in a place unless I believe I know something of the past of its people and share their lives. For that reason, I think, I am not a good tourist. And, for sure, it never ceases to surprise me that people seem to find their way around their present world without maps of the past to help them. The map I used was drawn by Marx. In those early days it was given to me in the two-volume edition of *Selected Works* and the first volume of *Capital*. What I read there matched my experience and justified my twelve years teaching liberal studies. But there were other influences at work.

Although I was introduced to economic and social history under the localist, utopian, agriculturalist influence of W. G. Hoskins, and was inspired as a student of social history by the aging R. H. Tawney, the young E. J. Hobsbawm, and Maurice Dobb's *Studies in the Development of Capitalism*, the mainstream of the subject had an insidious effect. It was objectivist, positivist, empiricist, and economistic, weighed down by interest in economic growth, business cycles, long swings, rates of interest and high economic policy. Then there were all the structures and inhibitions of language as they came to me through my scholarship education. No more dropped aitches, no more glottal stops, no more me and you, no more no bleetn fear, no more nuvink; no more. As they knocked out of me the language of ordinary people (much admired, so they say, by historians), 'Be creative,' they said, 'more energy needed', 'Use your imagination!' 'Use proper language'. And I never could. Consequently, in my search for the class conditions of my yesterdays, there were many false starts, dead ends and detours. (For some unaccountable reason I allowed my first history writing on Bath to be structured by Gayer, Rostow, and Schwarz, *The Growth and Fluctuations of the British*

Economy 1750—1850, in two volumes. A book I doubt, sometimes, that anyone else has ever read.)

As I read more of Marx, and some twentieth-century Marxists, I understood more of the complexities of the materialist conception of history and its problems. Its structure appeared to me to be neither linear nor historicist. The determination of the mode of production it asserts, which is not the same as economic determinism, actually relates structure to agency in interactive 'un-determined' ways. And the system places at the centre of its discourse human agency of a powerfully creative kind. It also suggests ways of exploring relationships between modes of production in circumstances of uneven economic development. It employs an empirical mode of enquiry, does not provide automatic (or dogmatic) answers to social and historical problems, and it does not generate models for utopia — they are for people to *make.* Then, it seemed to me, Marx's assertion about the three principal elements that should be represented in any historical construction, in the *Eighteenth Brumaire of Louis Bonaparte,* still challenges the dominant mode of history writing today. Consequently, my reading of Marx strengthened my native prejudice against narrative as *the* proper form for constructing a work of history.

About the same time, I finally realized that the use of the third person, the first person plural, the passive voice — 'it appeared to be the case that . . .', 'as we can see . . .', 'as the evidence shows . . .', the past tense, and all the Ph.D. paraphernalia of the objectivist, distancing mode of writing history was no guarantee of objectivity, truth, scholarship, or readable writing, and inhibited commitment. I decided against it, although I sometimes use it.

Certainly my search for my yesterdays and tomorrows has not been linear nor uncommitted. It could not have been. And the outcome of that search does not exist in my mind in linear or narrative form, and I can never call upon it as a holistically constructed edifice to aid my understanding. I can only reply to those who challenge my Marxist formulations; 'they are merely "necessary" but not "sufficient"'; 'and what would I say about *Emma,* and Michelangelo, and Islam, and the Moghul Empire?' that I have not been able to do everything or describe everything, that I recognize that my 'necessary' is never 'sufficient' (but neither is theirs), and, were I to wait upon 'sufficient', I would be dumb through all eternity, and my yesterdays would never be tomorrows. So, the chapters in this book, more or less structured by chronology and using narrative, are not *a* narrative. And they are never complete. They could as well be read from end to front as front to end, or in any sequence the reader prefers. They are images of yesterday, fragments of memory, variously formed at moments of intellectual and emotional danger, historical diversions (from a straight line) with theoretical and descriptive points to make about writing Marxist history, because, as Walter Benjamin wrote:

To articulate the past historically does not mean to recognize it 'the way it really was' (Ranke). It means to seize hold of a memory as it flashes up at a moment of danger. Historical materialism wishes to retain that image of the past which unexpectedly appears to man singled out by history at a moment of danger. The danger affects both the content of the tradition and its receivers. The same threat hangs over both: that of becoming a tool of the ruling classes. In every era the attempt must be made anew to wrest tradition away from a conformism that is about to overpower it. The Messiah comes not only as a redeemer, He comes as the subduer of Antichrist. Only that historian will have the gift of fanning the spark of hope in the past who is firmly convinced that *even the dead* will not be safe from the enemy if he wins. And this enemy has not ceased to be victorious.[1]

And there are gaps. They are part of the nature of images. Consequently this is *not* the definitive Marxist history of British society, economy, and culture since 1700. It is a book of images. Although I link each one to its neighbours, I rely upon what the reader retains in the retina of his or her mind to provide a connected and moving picture. If the images also move, so much the better. Although they lack Laurence Sterne's wit I like to think of this collection of images as something a *Life and Opinions of Tristram Shandy* (in proper history-writing) might look like.

Laurence Sterne was a profound critic of history writers when he wrote:

Could a historiographer drive on his history, as a muleteer drives on his mule, — straight forward; — for instance, from Rome all the way to Loretto, without ever once turning his head aside either to the right hand or to the left, — he might venture to foretell you to an hour when he should get to his journey's end; — but the thing is, morally speaking, impossible: For, if he is a man of the least spirit he will have fifty deviations from a straight line to make with this or that party as he goes along, which he can no ways avoid. He will have views and prospects to himself perpetually soliciting his eye, which he can no more help standing still to look at than he can fly; he will moreover have various
    Accounts to reconcile;
    Anecdotes to pick up;
    Inscriptions to make out;
    Stories to weave in;
    Traditions to sift;
    Personages to call upon;

[1] Walter Benjamin, *Illuminations* (London, 1970), p. 257.

Panegyrics to paste up at this door;

Pasquinades at that: — All which both the man and his mule are quite exempt from. To sum up all; there are archives at every stage to be looked into, and rolls, records, documents, and endless genealogies, which justice ever and anon calls him back to stay the reading of: — In short, there is no end of it; — for my own part, I declare I have been at it these six weeks, making all the speed I possible could, — and am not yet born: — I have just been able, and that's all, to tell you when it happened, but not how: — so that you see the thing is yet far from being accomplished.[2]

Sterne's accomplishment, mocked in his 'Chapter Forty', is a proper caution, a cautionary tale and an enchanting one.

CHAPTER FORTY

I AM now beginning to get fairly into my work; and by the help of a vegitable diet, with a few of the cold seeds, I make no doubt but I shall be able to go on with my uncle Toby's story, and my own, in a tolerable straight line. Now,

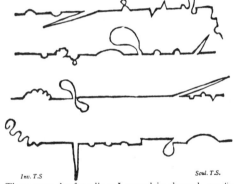

Inv. T.S   *Scul. T.S.*

These were the four lines I moved in through my first, second, third, and fourth volumes.—In the fifth volume I have been very good,—the precise line I have described in it being this:

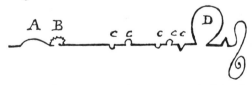

By which it appears, that except at the curve, marked A where I took a trip to Navarre. — and the indented curve B, which is the short airing when I was there with the Lady Baussiere and her page, — I have not taken the least frisk of a digression, till John de la Casse's devils led me the round you see marked

---

[2] Laurence Sterne, *The Life and Opinions of Tristram Shandy* (London, 1967), Vol. 1., p. 64.

D. — for as for c c c c c they are nothing but parentheses, and the common *ins* and *outs* incident to the lives of the greatest ministers of state; and when compared with what men have done, — or with my own transgressions at the letters A B D — they vanish into nothing.

In this last volume I have done better still — for the end of Le Fever's episode, to the beginning of my uncle Toby's campaigns, — I have scarce stepped a yard out of my way.

If I mend at this rate, it is not impossible — by the good leave of his grace of Benevento's devils — but I may arrive hereafter at the excellency of going on even thus;

---

which is a line drawn as straight as I could draw it, by a writing-master's ruler, (borrowed for that purpose) turning neither to the right hand or to the left.

This *right line* — the path-way for Christians to walk in! say divines —

— The emblem of moral rectitude! says Cicero —

— The *best line*! say cabbage planters — is the shortest line, says Archimedes, which can be drawn from one given point to another, —

I wish your ladyships would lay this matter to heart, in your next birth-day suits!

— What a journey!

Pray can you tell me, — that is, without anger, before I write my chapter upon straight lines — by what mistake — who told them so — or how it has come to pass, that your men of wit and genius have all along confounded this line, with the line of GRAVITATION?[3]

A key concept (not to be confounded with the line of gravitation) shaping the images in this book and repeatedly pushing my own deviations and parentheses into a tolerable straight line, is the mode of production. Although I have something to say about it in chapters 8 and 10, in this Introduction I want to indicate my understanding of Marx's formulation of the notion, and to state as sharply and abstractly as possible the articulation of modes of production in the eighteenth and early nineteenth centuries.

Marx's most concise statement on the mode of production is in the *Preface to the Critique of Political Economy.* He wrote:

In the social production of their life, men enter into definite relations that are indispensable and independent of their will, relations of production which

[3] Ibid, Vol. VI., p. 453.

[4] Karl Marx, *Preface to the Critique of Political Economy,* Marx/Engels *Selected Works* (Moscow, 1949), Vol. 1, p. 329.

correspond to a definite stage of development of their material productive forces. The sum total of these relations of production constitutes the economic structure of society, the real foundation on which rises a legal and political superstructure and to which correspond definite forms of social consciousness. The mode of production of material life conditions the social, political and intellectual life process in general.[4]

Marx concluded this statement with the only determinist proposition in his formulation of the concept, 'It is not the consciousness of men that determines their being, but, on the contrary, their social being that determines their consciousness.'[5] When this extract is read and understood in conjunction with the argument circulating around the 'Four Moments' in *The German Ideology* and the opening paragraph of the *Eighteenth Brumaire of Louis Bonaparte*, the concept may be 'imaged' in the following way, rather than in the crude (or sophisticated) architecturally derived model of base-superstructure, as foisted on us by those who look only or mainly at Marx's *Preface*, believe that words are signals, and that the discussion should focus on the analogy rather than the substance of the perception struggling to be born. Marx, too, rarely wrote in straight lines.

My understanding of Marx is as follows. The world is constituted by people with physical and created needs interacting with nature (rather like animals), but endowed with (or developing) a capacity to satisfy those needs through labour as an imagined and constructed, rather than as a random and instinctual activity, and through language. These people are organized in social groups. These groups of people satisfy their needs through their labour, and facilitate and understand their productive activity through language. This labour and productive activity is necessarily social. It always takes place within definite sets of socially produced property relations. These property relations grant powers of control and decision-making and, therefore, of appropriation of the social product. Property relations, whether they be familial, communal, national, co-operative, corporate, absolutist, communist or private, and as they generate class relations, determine what can be produced and when, and how much, and who gets what and when, and how much. They both structure societies and create conditions for conflict within and between them over power, and over control and appropriation of the social product. One cannot envisage a human society apart from these crucial structures and relationships.

As each cohort of people enters into the pre-existing set of propertied and class circumstances they also, in satisfying their needs through

---

[5] Ibid.

labour, produce and make themselves, and shape their language. They are also always constrained by the tradition of their dead generations. They work out their own destinies using and developing the range of symbolic forms, including language, available to them. Marx also believed (as I attempt to show in chapter 7) that national conflicts are basically conflicts over territory, therefore conflicts over property rights, and that their theoretically indeterminate results have great importance for changes in and development of property rights. Nationalism is itself a symbolic form. The conflicts and struggles people enter into, structured by property rights and encrusted by tradition and symbolic forms, sometimes lead to social structural change, sometimes nowhere, and sometimes to the destruction of the society or societies involved. Consciousness and cultural production, although imbricated in the whole productive process, immersed in relations of production, are shaped by it — there are no innate ideas, no gods, except people make them, no spirits of the age, except historians conjure them up, no 'arts' apart from human definition of them; yet everywhere there is creativity, conscious human labour, trapped and liberated by relations of production. However, how consciousness, creativity and class struggle are manifested in a real world crowded with people in their millions, sometimes striving for the freedom and autonomy they come to believe is theirs by right, is a matter for empirical enquiry. Marxist yesterdays while shaped by theory are not given by it.

Therefore, although the following description of the economic and social structure of Britain in the eighteenth and early nineteenth centuries, couched in terms of modes of production, is highly abstract, it should not be concluded too readily that empirical material has been stuffed into an *a priori* schema, like feathers into a pillowcase. This abstract account is the result of attempts to organize a mass of material, already empirically as well as theoretically apprehended, into a coherent, complex, yet shifting pattern of economic and social structures. Nor would it be appropriate to conclude, because the analysis identifies that which is 'necessary' but not 'sufficient', that it has no status and no greater merit than other claims, such as that which asserts that trees were also 'necessary' to eighteenth-century economic and social change and cultural production. If anyone wishes to produce a 'tree' description and analysis of that society and culture, they are free to do so. And free to show that it would provide a better basis for the construction of images of reality than what follows. The proof of the pudding . . . .

It is my contention that Marx's concept 'mode of production', freed from the technological determinism of vulgar marxism, is a powerful aid in organizing thought about the basic components of all economic systems. The abstraction is a way of thinking about reality rather than an attempt to represent or mimic it within the limited compass of the words actually used; a way of imaging the period while acknowledging a fuzziness and blurring in the image it seeks to evoke. (The empirical data may be rearranged with every plump of the pillow that changes its shape yet leaves it recognizably a pillow of a certain shape and size and not a heap of feathers.) Therefore, while the characteristics of and differences between modes of production and sub-sets of modes of production are never as sharp in reality as in the words I use, I use the words as sharply as I do to be clear and economical, at least at the outset; the fuzziness and blurring complexity will come later.

Social structure in England in the first half of the eighteenth century was a product of the articulation of its several modes of production, some of which were sub-sets of the dominant agrarian-capitalist mode of production. Each mode of production had distinctive forms of property relationships (including work relationships), and distinctive methods whereby those with property appropriated surplus value and distributed the total product and, thereby, set boundaries to the realization of the productive potential of the forces of production. The agrarian-capitalist mode of production had at its economic centre the legally enforceable, complex and flexible, contractual relationships characteristic of a society built on private property in land, which had evolved from the property relationships of feudal society. Thus, these contractual relations were a modern set of legal relations bearing, paradoxically, the hallmark of the benefit of England's legal and political backwardness in the seventeenth century. The economic and social structure of this mode of production consisted of rentier landlords, capitalist tenant farmers, and wage labourers; a very distinctive set of relations of production and of appropriation relations in Europe at the time. These property and appropriate relations, and the way they intermeshed with and affected other modes of production, were central to the process of economic and social structural change in our period. They were particularly important for the creation and maintenance of a class of 'free' wage labourers.

The agrarian-capitalist mode of production was the dominant mode of production. Historically, its actors had turned land into capital and productive work into wage labour — a key element in its legal relations was the wage contract. However, the agricultural sector was not wholly agrarian-capitalist. In many regions capitalist landowners and farmers, and their wage labourers, lived cheek by jowl with copyholders, lifeholders and small freeholders, whose tenures signified the tenacity of relations of production characteristic of pre-capitalist modes of production. However, it is also true to say, that in the immediate hinterland of some towns these pre-capitalist tenancies had come into the hands of people already integrated into the dominant mode of production.

Within the agrarian-capitalist mode of production, economic and political advantage sometimes lay with the beneficiaries of entailed estates who were able to augment their share of the agricultural surplus through winning property rights in place at court and gaining appointments as functionaries in the growing administrative branches of the crown, mainly in London. In these circumstances political rights, such as those held by closed corporations and the proprietors of rotten boroughs, also stood out as property rights.[6] Thus many agrarian-capitalists were also parasitic on the crown and dependent on residual but resilient pre-capitalist relations of production for their ability to appropriate an even greater share of the surplus product. Competition structured by this mélange of pre-capitalist property relations was to be a source of division within the ranks of the propertied classes throughout the eighteenth and early nineteenth centuries, although these divisions declined in intensity as capitalist relations of production, including those of industrial capitalism, spread.

Next, there was the rural/urban manufacturing mode of production. This, too, had two elements. First, the capitalist sector characteristic of the putting-out industries. In these industries capitalist entrepreneurs controlled raw materials, stocks of goods, warehouses and assorted tools and machines, and employed wage labour, as in great segments of the west country woollen industry. Secondly there was the sector characterized by petty production. In this sector artisans and independent producers owning tools, frequently worked on their own account or in small workshops, as in shoemaking, tailoring and building, and in the woollen industry in the West Riding of Yorkshire. In these trades there was a blurring of distinction between masters and journeymen. However, even in these trades, whenever market conditions were favourable, capitalist relations tended to oust pre-capitalist relations of production.

In some industries, in the early decades of the eighteenth century, relations of production characteristic of developed industrial capitalism could be found; in mining, in the metal, glass and fulling industries, and

---

[6] Wade's *Black Book*, first published in periodical parts, is a detailed account of the material gains made by those able to supplement revenues from property with incomes derived from place at court and the exploitation of political property rights. Wade's account of the activities of Lord Huntingtower in Ilchester, between 1802 and 1820, shows the extent to which contemporaries failed to distinguish political from property rights. The *Black Book*, A New Edition (London, 1828), Vol. I, pp. 12—91, Vol. II, pp. 172—3. See also Norbert Elias, *The Civilizing Process* (Basel, 1939), for what, one might call, the deferential rights of the landowning elites, and their role in the development of manners.

in shipbuilding. Nevertheless, the industrial capitalist mode of production did not become dominant in England until the second half of the nineteenth century — uneven economic development remained a major characteristic of the economy.

In cities such as Bristol, Norwich, and Glasgow, but especially in London, where international as well as local market conditions were favourable, the urban manufacturing mode of production was embedded in a mercantile mode of production characterized by large capitals, frequently of a joint stock nature. In this mode of production, merchant capitalists generated surpluses through the exploitation of price and cost differences as well as through the appropriation of surplus labour in the production process.

Then there was the monied interest, also concentrated in London. Its members were the finance capitalists of their day. As products of the military role of the state, which served the interests of the oligarchy at the head of the agrarian-capitalist mode of production, they were a sub-set of that mode of production. The key instruments in their appropriation of a substantial portion of the domestic agricultural surplus were; the national debt, intricate networks of international and national credit, and taxation, behind which lay the coercive powers of the state. These coercive powers also protected the links between the dominant mode of production and the world economic system; additional sources of surplus for the oligarchy of agrarian capitalists and the monied interest were colonialism (as in Ireland and India) and slavery. In terms of personnel, the monied interest was not easily distinguished, either from the great agrarian-capitalists, or from those with place at court, or from those engaged in the mercantile mode of production. A fact which highlights the problem contemporaries had in comprehending the significance and desirability of this financial mode of production.

It was, perhaps, this financial aspect of the capitalist mode of production in England, spanning agrarian and mercantile capitalism, yet dependent upon the military and administrative role of the state, in a country surrounded by a predominantly politically absolutist and economically feudal world, that gave England its edge in the race to accumulate the wealth of the nation. In *Class in English History*, I refer to this period, as the heroic age of primitive accumulation; it should also be emphasized that it was a period of uneven economic development. Therefore, as I wrote in *Class in English History*, English society may be characterized as: 'neither pre-industrial nor industrial, neither feudal nor industrial capitalist, neither classless nor multi-class, neither order-based nor class-based, neither one thing nor another although dialectically it was both. . . . Consequently, the late seventeenth and early eighteenth centuries were socially complicated. It is not to be wondered at that men were confused and uncertain.'[7]

Not until there were significant developments in technology, notably in the application of steam power to production and transport, was it possible for the industrial capitalist mode of production to become dominant; but it grew to dominance slowly and unevenly. Furthermore, because the key to productivity increases, even with the new technology, still rested with skilled manpower, industrial capitalism in Britain in the early nineteenth century, was marked by relations characteristic of pre-industrial capitalist modes of production. Thus, even in the first four or five decades of the nineteenth century, when Britain's economy was overwhelmingly capitalist, it was not industrial; the articulation of the various modes of production was still complex. Scotland, for example, was only beginning to 'enjoy' the advantages of economic backwardness. The significance of this complexity and uneven economic development for class consciousness and class struggle, creativity and cultural production, were considerable. The chapters in this book are about some of the incidents and issues that would have to be included in a work on these questions of a much larger compass. They point a general direction, identify diversions, suggest some parentheses, take in some views and prospects (more or less pleasing to the eye), call upon personages, decipher inscriptions, reconcile accounts, pick up some anecdotes, tell a few stories, sift some traditions, and paste up panegyrics and pasquinades, but working all the while, like the man and his mule, to get from Rome to Loretto — from England in 1700, ruled by agrarian capitalists like the Duke of Chandos, to Charlie Neale in Camden Town in 1900, from thence to Southall, to get myself born. And they use various devices, from mode of production to autobiography, to haul the mule along.

I had thought to give a map of the journey to sketch the chapters' paths and tell what they are about, but decided against it. Not for me to deny the pain and pleasure of the journey to other muleteers. The odd rope bridge dangling across deep chasms between chapters will be my only aid. Whether they will be able to bear the weight of the mules some muleteers might wish to push and pull across them is another matter. You may have to build yourself another bridge, make your own diversions, or fly. On the other hand, you may not wish to get to Camden Town at all. And you may agree with Yorick.[8]

---

[7] R. S. Neale, *Class in English History 1680—1850* (Oxford, 1981), pp. 94, 99.

[8] If you wish to know what Yorick said about Laurence Sterne's 'history' you will have to read *Tristram Shandy*.

1

The Landlady, the Duke and the Banker:
Marx's 'Missing Link'

In the spring of 1726, the Duke of Chandos, probably the richest man in England, and his second wife Cassandra, took the waters at Bath, he with a 'twitching upon his nerves [which] still continues troublesome', she suffering from 'hysterick fits'.[1] While they were in the city they stayed in Anne Phillips's lodging house close to the Cross Bath. Chandos's experience in this Bath lodging house had three important consequences for English history. First, it resulted in Chandos's employment of John Wood in one of the earliest schemes of urban redevelopment in Bath, and set in train a sequence of events crucial for the building of Bath as the most beautiful city in England. Second, Chandos's venture into urban redevelopment provides convincing evidence of the entrepreneurial role of two women in a sector of the economy of pre-industrial England, the keeping of lodging houses, not mentioned by Alice Clark for the seventeenth century nor by Ivy Pinchbeck for the eighteenth century. Third, this same evidence, the minutiae of daily practice dealing with items ranging from the price of three skewers and a lark spit to the purchase of a job lot of close stools and pans, also reveals the intricate network of local, national, and even international systems of credit, which made that urban redevelopment possible, and locked women as well as men into the primitive accumulation phase of the capitalist mode of production. In short, Chandos's twitchings, Cassandra's fits, and Anne Phillips's lodgings lead willy-nilly to a key problem in Marxist historiography highlighted by Crouzet's opinion that there is a 'missing link' in Marx's argument about primitive accumulation.

I have already told the story of Chandos's connection with Wood in the development of Bath, and of the mediating role played by the London

[1] C. H. Collins Baker and Muriel Baker, *James Brydges, First Duke of Chandos* (Oxford, 1949), p. 299.

Bill of Exchange: drawn by Davies and Hodgett, glass manufacturers, on Walker, Leech, Cork and Bottle dealer, Bath, 18 May 1830

timber merchant Theobald, and I have no intention of repeating myself.[2] Nevertheless, in that story, the part played by the two lodging house keepers, Anne Phillips and Jane Degge, was mentioned rather than explored for its implications for English history and Marxist theory. This chapter is an attempt to recover the 'missing link' through their story. Anne Phillips and Jane Degge were, for a fleeting moment, actors in the drama of primitive accumulation in eighteenth-century England.

Chandos and Cassandra did not enjoy their stay in Bath. Anne Phillips's lodgings, built in the vernacular style above St John's Hospital, a much abused pauper charitable institution, were extremely uncomfortable. And they lacked privacy. According to Chandos, they were objectionable, 'to a person of fashion because they did not afford a dressing room and dining room besides the room he lyes in, especially if he has his lady with him.'[3] The furniture, too, was bad, and the windows inadequate. Not one could 'Keep out the least puff of wind'. They were 'old rotten lodgings'.[4] Their one redeeming feature was their favourable location. To the south-west they looked out across Kingsmead towards the tree-lined scarp of Beechen Cliff. On the town side they gave direct access to the Cross Bath. The Cross Bath was the most fashionable of the city's five baths. In its confined and steamy waters women wore calico shifts exposing their breasts, and bathed in the company of men who, 'presenting them with several antick postures, as sailing on their backs',[5] sank in rapture. As Defoe put it, Bath was a place where, 'men find a mistress sometimes, but rarely look for a wife',[6] and it was at the Cross Bath that there were, 'performed all the wanton dalliances imaginable'.[7] Chandos, however, had other things in mind. He thought to turn developer, to benefit from other people's fancies and their wish for good quality accommodation. And he had other plans for Anne Phillips.

In the first 40 years of the eighteenth century, argument for greater equality between the sexes was not as muted as it might seem at first glance. Women were active as playwrights, at least up to 1720. Novelists and many poets lamented the position of women.[8] Moreover, Defoe had

[2] R. S. Neale, *Bath 1680—1850: A Social History* (London, 1981), pp. 116—70.

[3] Baker and Baker, *James Brydges,* p. 299.

[4] Ibid., p. 299.

[5] Anon., *A Step to the Bath with a Character of the Place, 1700.*

[6] Daniel Defoe, *Moll Flanders* (Harmondsworth, 1978), p. 117.

[7] Anon., *A Step to the Bath.*

[8] Fidelis Morgan, *The Female Wits: Women Playwrights of the Restoration* (London, 1981), especially p. xi; John J. Ricketts, *Popular Fiction Before Richardson* (Oxford, 1969), pp. 119—210; *The Cupid: A Collection of Love Songs* (London, 1736).

written *Roxana*, presenting to the world a heroine who spurned marriage and acquired a fortune, subverting all the proprieties and props of society in the process. Then, in 1739, Lady Mary Wortley Montagu wrote a pamphlet entitled, *Woman Not Inferior to Man.*[9] In it she argued for equality between men and women in the most important areas of authority and decision-making she could identify: military command, and the highest public offices in law, medicine, philosophy and university teaching. As was to be expected from a woman of her class in the eighteenth century, she did not argue for equality in production, commerce, or trade. Production was a sphere of life beyond her ken, although she may have perceived it as a sphere in which equality of labour already existed. Certainly Chandos, 13 years earlier, had seen no barriers to entering into commercial agreements with several women in the matter of his venture into urban redevelopment in Bath. Thus, in the contract between himself and Anne Phillips, she was required to pay £300 per annum in rent. In return for this she was given the responsibility for furnishing the new lodgings and their subsequent management. According to Chandos's calculation, Anne Phillips would be able to let 40 rooms at 10s per week each, and seven kitchens and 17 garrets at 5s per week each. Therefore, for a twenty-week season she would be able to clear at least £100 a year. Lettings out of season would be all gain to Mrs Phillips. Costs of furnishings were to be charged, as capital items, to Chandos. Under this arrangement, Anne Phillips was to be responsible for the management of an enterprise generating earnings of between £400 and £450 per annum. Her own annual money income would be more than £100, then some 20 to 25 times the annual earnings of a domestic servant, and her accommodation was to be free.[10] According to Gregory King, in 1688, on a yearly income per head basis, a yearly income of £100 per head would have made Anne Phillips one of the wealthiest women in England.[11] (Chandos was almost certainly the wealthiest man.) Subsequently Chandos entered into a similar agreement with Jane Degge for her management of another part of the venture.

Chandos's accounts with Anne Phillips, between 1726 and 1730, and with Jane Degge, between 1729 and 1731 reveal much about the range of

[9] Lady Mary Wortley Montagu, *Woman Not Inferior to Man* (London, 1739).

[10] Chandos to Marchant, 6 Feb. and 6 April 1727, Brydges Correspondence, ST57, Huntington Library, California.

[11] Gregory King's Scheme of the income and expense of the several families of England calculated for the year 1688, in Peter Laslett, *The World We Have Lost* (London, 1971), pp. 36—7.

skills and competence exercised by these two single women.[12] For example, as they made payments for various services and goods, they were reimbursed by Chandos in two main ways. The two women either drew bills of exchange on Chandos and received payment from local 'discount houses', or they were paid out of various Bath rents payable to Chandos, which were either collected by or remitted to them. Between November 1726 and October 1730, Anne Phillips received payments as follows: her own rent payable to Chandos but retained by her, £850; other rents collected by her, £221 5s 3d; bills to tradesmen paid directly by Chandos, £145 10s 6d; cash for the sale of lead and brass from Wood's failed water closets, £31 2s 1d; bills of exchange drawn by Anne Phillips on Chandos and paid by three 'discount houses', £650. Of these bills, £550 was paid by Richard Marchant, a local Quaker, banker and member of the city's Company of Merchant Taylors. Marchant also made a cash payment of £50 to Anne Phillips. Between July 1729 and October 1731, Jane Degge received the following payments: rents collected £41; cash received, £191 9s 9d; rent for lodgings retained by her, £544 19s 1d; bills of exchange drawn by Jane Degge on Chandos, £470, £350 of which was paid by Marchant. The difference between these revenues and actual outlays, £1,963 4s 10d by Anne Phillips and £1,358 10s ½d by Jane Degge, were met by balances paid by Chandos's agent. As well, Jane Degge received a payment of £300 for her care of her house, the business not being as profitable as Chandos had expected, and both women received presents from Chandos, Anne Phillips £21 and Jane Degge £17.

Behind the bare facts of these accounts we can see Anne Phillips and Jane Degge well skilled in living in a world held together by credit, dealing with bankers and the intricacies of the credit system based on the bill of exchange, keeping detailed invoices, and handling large sums of money annually. The total of bills discounted with at least three separate discount men and generally at a rate of 3.25 per cent was £1,120, and to these we will return. These accounts show, too, that the two women could live with the notion that unpaid rent was income, and that they were acting as rent collectors.

But, these accounts, particularly those of Anne Phillips, show more than this. They show Anne Phillips acting as agent for Chandos: paying ground rents, land and window taxes, and poor, water, sewage and church rates; paying Mrs Tynte's annuity (a charge on the development

---

[12] All figures and calculations relating to Chandos's dealings with Anne Phillips and Jane Degge are based on four volumes of his accounts held by the Huntington Library, San Marino, California, ST12, Vols 1–4. Entries may be identified through the alphabetical index contained in each volume.

consequent on a loan made to Chandos); negotiating with assessors over the value of building materials; paying building tradesmen; and taking care of medical attention and funeral arrangements for Chandos's coachman. Furthermore, through these accounts, we can show connections between Chandos's speculation in urban development and a myriad of aspects of the economy of England in the third decade of the eighteenth century. We can see clearly the place of these two women in the economy.

In order to carry out their responsibility for equipping and furnishing the two houses, the women not only needed knowledge of the business of lodging house-keeping, but also knowledge of sources of supply of the goods they needed, and how best to deal with suppliers and tradesmen. Anne Phillips bought bottles from Bridgewater, probably from Chandos's new glass works there, and probably for bottling the Bath water. She also bought chairs and pewter from London, and bellows from Bristol. She imported Kidderminster stuff through Bristol and iron ware from Wolverhampton. One account from Wolverhampton lists: 6 stove grates, 24 brass fenders, 16 iron ones, 4 sets of shovels, tongs and pokers, and 3 dozen of knives and snuffers for £39 2s 6d. Carriage paid was 5s. According to these accounts, it cost Chandos, through Anne Phillips, about £135 to equip her kitchens. Jane Degge also bought iron ware from Wolverhampton, but she appears to have bought even more from John Greaves of Birmingham, to whom she paid £30 5s for one shipment. Apart from importing iron ware from Wolverhampton and Birmingham, Jane Degge seems to have dealt mainly with tradesmen in Bristol and Bath. She bought pewter, candlesticks, joinery, blankets and brass work in Bristol. Because her accounts were generally more specific than those of Anne Phillips, we can glimpse in even greater detail the responsibility placed on the two women, and the intricacies of the business they were in. (Other aspects of the importance of these accounts will become more apparent later in the chapter.) For example, Jane Degge's account with Churchman, a local blacksmith, in December 1729, lists the following items:

	£	s	d
Checking a pair of grates	0-	2-	6
2 scrapers	0-	2-	0
2 Dripping pan frames	0-	4-	0
A band for a stew/a fender	1-	1-	6
3 grates and 3 trippets at 3½ a piece	0-	9-	2
Windowbars 17½ at 3d yd	0-	5-	1

	£	s	d
A spit 13 lbs at 6d	0-	6-	6
Slice tongs and poker 19 lbs at 5½	0-	8-	9
Mending a lock	0-	0-	6
3 skewers and a lark spit	0-	1-	0
A gridiron	0-	3-	6
	3-	16-	6

In the same month she also settled an account for £9 18s 8d with Mr Axford, brazier of Bath — he was probably that Axford who was a member of Bath Corporation. This account included 1s for 'a tin-patty pan', but also listed:

6 London hard dishes, 3 doz. plates wt. 5oz at 14d	2-17-10
2 small soop dishes wt. 3 lb 2 ozs at 11d	0- 2-10
2 best hard dishes wt. 4 lb 3 ozs at 12d	0- 4- 2

Her biggest order for brass ware, however, was from Mr Randall of Bristol, to whom she paid £56 0s 10d for the following:

December 1729 To Mr Randalls Bill the Brazier at Bristol

12 hand candlesticks	0-19- 4
3 boylers	2- 0- 4
2 hash pans	1- 0-10
a copper frying pan	0- 8- 9
6 saucepans and covers	1-16- 5
a brass cullinder and a copper ditto	1- 4- 6
a basket	0- 0- 8
5 brass trippets	1- 4- 0
a brass kettle	0-13-10
2 fish kettles	3- 0- 2

	£	s	d
2 false bottoms to fish kettles	0-	5-	6
a fixt stove grate	0-	8-	7
a brass trippet wt 3 lb 5 oz	0-	6-	7
one ditto 2 lb 6 oz	0-	4-	9
2 stove grates	0-	15-	6
3 trippets wt. 6 lb 6 oz	0-	12-	5
3 warming pans	1-	10-	0
3 handles	0-	1-	6
a large copper pot 1 lb 15 oz	0-	4-	2
a stove grate	0-	9-	0
a tripet 3 lb 7 oz	0-	7-	0
a large kitchen grate and cranes	2-	7-	3
a stove grate	0-	7-	6
carriage paid	0-	8-	6
3 flower boxes and pepper	0-	4-	9
a skimmer	0-	2-	6
3 tripets	0-	16-	6
a stove grate 84 lb	1-	11-	6
one iron horse	0-	2-	6
4 tripets	0-	16-	6
a stove grate 23 lb	0-	8-	10
Another ditto of same weight	0-	8-	10
14 pair candlesticks	2-	9-	0
4 second hand spits	0-	10-	0
2 fenders	1-	1-	0
10 pair of standing candlesticks and sliders at 3-6 pr	1-	18-	0

oval tables	1- 9- 0
4 tripets wt. 11½	1- 3- 0
3 fenders	1-11- 6
3 snuffers and pans	0-12- 0
a boyler and mortar	0-11- 8
a copper pot with a cock	1-16- 8
2 pair of holders	0- 5- 0
3 bells and springs	0- 6- 6
a large plate warmer	1- 5- 0
2 four foot oval tables	1-10- 0
a dozen hat pins	0- 2- 6
6 looking glasses and a box	3- 5- 6
a large five foot and a half table	1- 0- 0
2 iron dripping pans	0-13- 8
a dish kettle	1- 1-10
a copper for broth	0-18- 6
a brass pot 6 lb 14 oz	0-10- 2
a brass cullinder	0-15- 3
5 saucepans and 4 covers	1- 6- 3
2 toss pans	0-15- 0
a saucepan	0-10- 6
a fender	0-10- 6
150 curtain rings	0- 4- 1
5 saucepans	1- 7- 1
2 hash pans	1- 5- 8
	56- 0-10

These accounts are sometimes overwhelming in their detail, but they are fragmentary and not consistent in their coverage. Consequently it is not possible to estimate the cost of equipping a suite of rooms in either of the two houses, except, perhaps, for the cost of Anne Phillips's kitchens. But they do indicate the cost of the largest and the smallest items, ranging from '3 skewers and a lark spit' at 1s to a wrought iron bed at £17 10s. Thus, Anne Phillips's upholsterer's bill was £201. She also spent £42 10s on Calico quilts and £5 10s on a feather bed, two pillows and a bolster. A pair of blankets bought in Bath market cost 16s, and she paid 10s 6d each for warming pans. About the same time Jane Degge paid £104 15s for feathers used in her house, and the 'ticken for beds' cost £46 16s. A close stool pan cost 3s 6d and a close stool box 9s. Chairs, on the other hand, were very cheap. Anne Phillips bought two dozen garret chairs for £1 12s, and Jane Degge a similar quantity for £1 5s. On another occasion she bought 'three dozen ordinary chairs at 15d/twelve twig at 10d'. Four looking-glasses cost £2 18s and two dozen snuffers 2s 2d.

The two women also employed labour. Anne Phillips paid two young women 2s 6d per week and paid another woman, 'for looking after the house and fires at 3s 6d per week'. Jane Degge also paid a 'workwoman' 3s 6d a week. Anne Phillips undertook yet more difficult management tasks connected with the building work itself. It happened thus. John Wood, Chandos's young architect and builder, had shown himself too dilatory and too incompetent a builder to suit Anne Phillips. She complained bitterly to Chandos about him. Chandos, too, had many an occasion to complain about him, particularly with regard to the water-closets Chandos had set his mind on as an important innovation in Bath lodging houses. This undertaking had proved too difficult for Wood's management and the skill of his workmen. After leaking and smelling, the water closets had to be removed. In November 1729 Chandos wrote to John Wood:

Mrs Phillips is so exceedingly unwilling to have you have anything to do about hers [her house], that I cannot decline gratifying her in it, and therefore the remaining Business you have to do will be so much the less for I would not have you meddle with any part of her house except the Stone Steps which ought to have been finished long ago. . . . I cannot blame her for desiring to have nothing more to do with you. It was this Resolution I had once taken myself.[13]

Although James Theobald, the London timber merchant, persuaded Chandos to keep Wood on as his builder, Anne Phillips was adamant. She refused to have any further dealings with him. Instead, she employed

---

[13] Chandos to Wood, 23 Nov. 1729, Brydges, *Correspondence*. The full story of Chandos's relations with Wood is in R. S. Neale, *Bath 1680—1850*, pp. 116—70.

several local tradesmen to finish the work about the house, charging their accounts to Chandos. Emes, the mason, stopped the water-closets and paved the street. Morris, the Smith, put iron grates over the kitchen window. Robins, the tyler, repaired the roof, 'stoping it from raining in', and other tradesmen cleaned the sewer, finished off the interior joinery work and completed the house by painting and liming. The bill for putting to rights Wood's bad workmanship was £257 3s 2d. Some of this extra cost was recouped by selling the lead and brass works of the water-closets for £31 2s 1d. Against that Anne Phillips had to offset £18 15s 6d for the purchase of 'Pipes, Close Stools and Pans etc.'. All of which, in the end, was chargeable to Chandos. As far as one can judge by the accounts alone and by the absence of recrimination by Chandos, for this stage of the work, Anne Phillips seems to have proved herself a better and more efficient manager than John Wood. But Wood, himself, maintained the righteousness of his position and his actions right up to the end. Chandos's firm response to him, two days before the final settlement of their account, in August 1730, brings all the threads of the story together, and sets the background to Anne Phillips's own resignation from the venture.[14]

Cannons 29th Aug. of 1730

Mr Wood Architect

Mr Theobald had delivered me in the Account you sent him to lay before me. I find it consists of several so extravagant and unreasonable Demands that at first I intended to have given no answer at all to it, but upon second thoughts, lest you should interpret it as an unwillingness to close the Account with you and a design to keep you out of the mony that is justly your due I think it more advisable to acquaint you out of hand with the Resolution I am come to, and it is this. The amount of what you claim £4,904-1-2¾, out of which I deduct what you charge for House Rent, for a pretended promise upon finishing Mrs Degge's house, and for the return of several sums of money to Bath, amounting to £171-3-6, and there remains (including three Guineas I am willing to allow you for your Journey to Rickford) £4,736-0-8¾; which sum of £235-12-11¾ you may receive whenever you sign a General Discharge and give a Receipt in full of all Debts, Dues and Demands whatsoever. As to your Demand of £120 which you say I promised you upon finishing Mrs Degge's House including your own House Rent, I remember nothing of it; but had I made any such promise nobody can imagine I intended it otherwise than on Condition that the House had been finished in a good workmanlike manner. How insufferably ill this has been done is but too

---

[14] Chandos to Wood, 29 Aug. 1730, Brydges' Correspondence.

notorious to every lodger who has been in either of the Houses and the vast expense I have been put to in mending your bad works, and doing that in a workmanlike manner which ought to have been done by you according to the Tenure of that Covenant is too notorious and heavy a truth. As for your Demands of allowance for the return of mony to Bath I do not find by the Articles that I am obliged to pay it thence, but if it should be so, you dispensed with that Covenant yourself by giving a letter of Attorney to Mr Theobald to receive it in mony and writing to me to desire to pay it. I cannot but wonder at your making any Demands on account of Mrs Phillips House. You know very well all that Account has been long since settled and I have your Discharge in full upon it, nor will I suffer it to be opened again. The other Articles relating to Mrs Degge's and Mrs Robertson's Houses which without making any Demand you leave to me to make some Allowance for I do not see any reason to take the least notice of them. If there has been anything done in them more than what was stipulated for in the Articles there is infinitely less done in many others, and it is the Opinion of almost everyone who has seen them and especially who have lodged in them that no two houses have been worse finished and in a less workmanlike manner by anyone who pretended to be an Architect and had any regard for his own Reputation or the interest of the Person who was his Benefactor and imployed him. I conclude with repeating what I have said above that when you are ready to give a General Release up on the foot of the Account, the £235-12-11¾ shall be paid to you.

I am

yours etc.

Although the two women, especially Anne Phillips, had demonstrated their importance to Chandos and shown their competence over a number of years, the venture seemed doomed from the outset. As well as Woods' prolongation of the building work and his bad workmanship, all of which was upsetting to lodgers already sick, Chandos clearly over estimated the attractions of the site and the rate of return on his capital. Especially damaging was the other new building going on in the city, particularly Wood's own work on Queen Square, which was shifting the location of high quality accommodation outside the confines of the town walls, and to the north and west of the old city. Then, too, in demanding water-closets from John Wood, Chandos was in advance of his time and John Wood's competence. And John Wood was over-extended, particularly after 1728 in Queen Square. It is not surprising, therefore, that Anne Phillips had 'always been uneasy and perpetually complaining'.[15] She intimated to Chandos that she intended to leave at Midsummer in 1729. But, she

---

[15] Chandos to Tynte, 2 June, 1729, Brydges' Correspondence.

stayed, apparently persuaded by Chandos. The accounts show her paying rent up to Christmas 1730, and still making payments in October of that year. Thereafter she disappears from the historical record. By 1734, when Chandos sold the whole development, now known as Chandos Buildings, to a London man at a considerable loss to himself, both women had been replaced as tenants by Mary Whittington and Elizabeth Davies.[16]

So to return to the 'missing link' in Marx's concept, 'primitive accumulation'.

Francois Crouzet, in a much-used survey of the sources of capital during the period of the Industrial Revolution, touches upon the secondary aspect of Marx's concept of primitive accumulation.[17] He does so in order to refute it. Indeed, through his discussion of the concept as it appears in the writings of John Saville and Maurice Dobb, he believes he disposes of it as of no account for serious economic historians. At the same time, and although he qualifies almost everything he writes, Crouzet seeks to reaffirm a number of propositions about sources of capital during the Industrial Revolution, which, whether intentionally or not, collectively support the notion that capital accumulation during the eighteenth century, like property in Locke, was 'clean'. This is to say that it had its own unique origins in the industriousness and thriftiness of small producers. As owners of capital accumulated out of savings, these entrepreneurs had a moral as well as a legal title to it, and to the profit it is alleged to have generated. This title was justified by labour and thrift. Crouzet writes:

Altogether retained profits were seen as the greatest single source of long term capital, and the role played by 'external' capital, supplied by landowners, overseas traders, banks, etc. was rather played down. The Industrial Revolution would have involved the creation of new savings and new outlets to absorb them rather than the tapping of traditional types of savings.

Broadly speaking, these conclusions seem to remain valid.[18]

In connection with the role of landowners in urban development he writes: 'The development of urban sites was done generally through building leases to speculators who built at their own expense.'[19] Elsewhere

---

[16] Opinion of William Hamilton, 15 Nov. 1734, St Brydges Legal Papers, 2 Boxes, 1675–1759, Huntington Library, California.

[17] François Crouzet, *Capital Formation in the Industrial Revolution* (London, 1972), especially pp. 57–9.

[18] Ibid., p. 44.

[19] Ibid., p. 55.

he adds: 'The London capital market did not make . . . any significant direct contribution to capital formation.'[20] Furthermore, although Crouzet admits that existing banks did engage in short-term lending to industrial enterprises and in discounting bills for financing variable capital, and, although he reports that some historians have argued, therefore, that 'The banks financed not only the movement of goods and the holding of stocks, not merely commodity sales, but also commodity production',[21] he also emphasizes, in his view, that the integration of the national financial system implied by such developments, especially the emergence of bill brokers and the London discount market, was achieved only in the late eighteenth century. Therefore, he reasserts the view that 'The English banking system was largely a response to industrialization rather than a causal factor, the banks were capital-servicing rather than capital-forming institutions'.[22]

In short, Crouzet's argument emphasizes a significant discontinuity between the sources of loanable funds and financial institutions in pre-industrial capitalism and those characteristic of and produced by the industrial capitalist mode of production, which began to appear in the last quarter of the eighteenth century. Thereby, he also acclaims the novelty and thriftiness of industrial capital, and appears as an advocate of the heroic model of capital accumulation during the eighteenth century.

On the other hand, the secondary aspect of Marx's notion of primitive accumulation emphasizes significant continuity and evolution between these two phases in the development of capitalism, and points out the unsavoury origins of capital. According to Marx, a stock of loanable funds accumulated by Western European nations through colonialism, slavery, war, the national debt and taxation, especially in England, was crucially important in creating favourable financial conditions for the development of capitalism in eighteenth-century England. Marx's argument, therefore, emphasizes a complex relationship between trade, overseas expansion, war, state power, and national and international networks of credit for the generation of and freeing-up of funds, which eventually found their way into industrial production. Marx drew attention to the importance of the 'monied interest' in this process. In his inimitable fashion, he expressed it thus: 'capital comes into the world soiled with mire from top to toe, and oozing blood from every pore.'[23] Crouzet's comment upon this Marxian notion is that it lacks empirical evidence of direct conversion of either

---

[20] Ibid., p. 51.
[21] Ibid., p. 48.
[22] Ibid., p. 49.
[23] Karl Marx, *Capital* (Everyman's Library edition), Vol. II, p. 843.

agricultural or commercial wealth into industrial capital. There is, says Crouzet, a 'missing link' in Marx's analysis.

Nevertheless, Crouzet does seem to accept views put forward by Pollard, Dickson, Pressnell, Cameron, Chapman and others, who, collectively, emphasize the importance of short-term bank credit, discounting of bills, lending on mortgage, the growth of government finance, and the intricacy and development of a money market during the early stages of England's economic development in the eighteenth century. And he seems to accept Pollard's view that: 'This web of credit should be placed near the centre of the exposition of the accumulation of capital.'[24] Yet, at the same time Crouzet seems unaware of the fact that Pollard's view undermines his own position on Marx. This is so because Marx's argument about the generation of wealth as potentially loanable funds in pre-industrial society, funds which become available for use in employing labour in commodity production, does not depend upon evidence of observed shifts in investment from the agricultural and commercial sectors to industrial production, even though such shifts can be shown to have taken place. (The argument here is similar to that relating to the main part of Marx's concept of primitive accumulation, the development over several hundred years of 'free' wage labour. This development also does not depend upon observed shifts of people from the agricultural sector into factory industry and urban areas, even though such movements can be identified.) Therefore, since Marx's argument is more intricate than his opponents, such as Crouzet, frequently allow, it is appropriate, before taking up again the theme of the Duke, the landladies and the banker, to set out a rather more expanded version of it than is generally available in substantive texts on English economic history.[25]

The concept 'primitive accumulation' emphasizes the historical development of a propertyless workforce and the emergence of capitalist relations of production, 'free' wage labour, in the agricultural sector. Its secondary aspect focuses attention upon the monetization of the economy and the development of a set of conditions favourable to the accumulation of monetary wealth (wealth in a mobile form) in England by the end of the seventeenth century. However, in spite of Crouzet, the next step in the argument does not depend upon evidence of direct transfers of wealth from the agricultural to the industrial sector. Marx is explicit:

[24] Ibid., p. 45, quoting Pollard.
[25] However, see Karl Marx, *Capital,* pp. 832—3 and the discussion in Eugene Kamenka and R. S. Neale, *Feudalism, Capitalism and Beyond* (London, 1975), pp. 22—5. And Enclosure and Population Change, *Our History,* Pamphlet No. 7, Autumn 1957.

The monetary wealth which becomes transformed into capital in the proper sense, into industrial capital, is rather the mobile wealth piled up through usury — especially that practised against landed property — and through mercantile profits. . . . It is inherent in the concept of capital, as we have seen — in its origin — that it begins with *money* and hence with wealth existing in the form of money. It is likewise inherent in it that it appears as coming out of circulation as the *product* of circulation. The formation of capital thus does not emerge from landed property . . . but rather from merchant's and usurer's wealth.[26]

However, these last two developments have to be understood not merely in a local context. Marx argues that 'The conditions for capital have to be developed not only locally but on a grand scale.'[27]

Hence, he emphasizes the growth of the international market, the development of wage labour, the dependence of wage labour on money purchases, and all those developments, such as money and the construction of roads, which reduce circulation time and transaction costs. Given these conditions, Marx states:

Capital proper does nothing but bring together the mass of lands and instruments which it finds on hand. It agglomerates them under its command. . . . There can therefore be nothing more ridiculous than to conceive this *original formation* of capital as if capital had stockpiled and created the *objective conditions of production* — necessaries, raw materials, instruments — and then offered them to the worker, who was bare of these possessions.[28]

Rather, command over these conditions of production was granted by the formation of money wealth already referred to, which was brought about during 'the prehistory of the bourgeois economy. Usury, trade, urbanization and the treasury rising with it play the main roles here.'[29] Therefore 'The only stockpiling presupposed at the origin of capital is that of *monetary wealth*, which, regarded in and for itself, is altogether unproductive, as it only springs up out of circulation and belongs exclusively to it.'[30]

---

[26] Karl Marx, *Grundrissse* (London, 1973), p. 504.
[27] Ibid., p. 505.
[28] Ibid., p. 508.
[29] Ibid., p. 509.
[30] Ibid., p. 512.

The link between this monetary wealth and capital proper is credit. Indeed, according to Marx, it was credit alone which ensured the continuity of the production process under capitalism. Since Marx's explanation of this is clear and cogent I quote him in full:

It is clear from everything said above that circulation appears as an essential process of capital. The production process cannot be begun anew before the transformation of the commodity into money. The *constant continuity* of the process, the unobstructed and fluid transition of value from one form into the other, or from one phase of the process into the next, appears as a fundamental condition for production based on capital to a much greater degree than for all earlier forms of production. On another side, while the necessity of this continuity is given, its phases are separate in time and space, and appear as particular, mutually indifferent processes. It thus appears as a matter of chance for production based on capital whether or not its essential condition, the continuity of the different processes which constitute its process as a whole, is actually bought about. The suspension of this chance element by capital itself *is credit*. (It has other aspects as well; but this aspect arises out of the direct nature of the production process and is hence the foundation of the necessity of credit.) Which is why *credit* in any developed form appears in no earlier mode of production. There was borrowing and lending in earlier situations as well, and usury is even the oldest of the antediluvian forms of capital. But borrowing and lending no more constitute *credit* than working constitutes *industrial labour or free wage labour*. And credit as an essential developed relation of production appears *historically* only in circulation based on capital or on wage labour. (*Money* itself is a form for suspending the unevenness of the times required in different branches of production, to the extent that this obstructs exchange.) Although *usury* is itself a form of credit in *its bourgeoisified* form, the form *adapted to capital*, in its pre-bourgeois form it is rather the *expression of lack of credit*.[31]

So far Marx's exposition is clear and uncomplicated. It might even be thought of as commonplace and too general because it lacks any account of the transfer mechanism — Crouzet's 'missing link'. But, in *The Grundrisse,* in his discussion of the problem of the suspension of circulation time, which is the time that must elapse between the initial act of production and the realization of its product in the form of money, Marx does refer to a transfer mechanism. He claims that the problem of circulation time can be overcome and the production process maintained in two ways. However, he explains only one of these ways; credit. His account of how credit works to facilitate both production and consumption,

31 Ibid., p. 535.

which consists of a description of the process involved in the generation and discounting of a bill of exchange, is also an account of such a transfer mechanism. He assumes an institutional structure and the prior existence of what he calls a 'creditman' with control over a stock of money.[32] What he describes is the key financial instrument in the web of credit described by Pollard. Certainly it is difficult to believe, without Marx's 'creditman' and the men behind him, and without the bill of exchange, that the circulation of commodities and the conditions for their production and the accumulation of capital could have developed in the way they did in eighteenth-century England.

Yet, even as the web of credit facilitated production, consumption, and accumulation of capital in its fixed or constant form, it obscured the sources of that capital accumulation. The web is also a veil of credit.

In my earlier account of the activities of the Duke of Chandos, the London timber merchant, James Theobald, and some 30 or so London brokers, international discount houses and local creditmen, I showed how monetary wealth accumulated through war, the national debt, taxation, slavery and stockjobbing was transferred into industrial development in Somerset and Staffordshire and into urban development in Bath. I showed how capital sums required for the purchase of building materials and the payment of wages was made available by means of the bill of exchange, and how the funds used to discount those bills arose out of an intricate network of international, national and local systems of credit.[33] I now claim that the story I have told about Anne Phillips and Jane Degge, through the minutiae of their daily lives, shows the extent to which the bill of exchange — the web and veil of credit — penetrated the remotest corners of economic life in the 1730s. Their story shows how capital requirements for equipping the two lodging houses, for paying the very substantial earnings of the two women themselves, and for paying the wages of tradesmen and servants were met by and within this same network of credit. Thus, bills of exchange eased the transfer of some £1,120 of Chandos's monetary wealth from their original sources into the two lodging houses. In the process, and in conjunction with some £1,657 of urban rents remitted by Chandos, these bills helped to stimulate industrial production and pay wages in the iron, brass, glass, pewter, timber and textile industries in Birmingham, Wolverhampton, Bridgwater, Bristol, Bath, London and Kidderminster. Furthermore, my demonstration of the familiarity with the bill of exchange and the business of discounting shown by Anne Phillips and Jane Degge, reveals how widespread the use of the bill of exchange must have been.

[32] Ibid., p. 549.
[33] R. S. Neale, *Bath 1680—1850*, pp. 116—70.

Finally, there is Richard Marchant, Quaker, banker, and member of Bath's Company of Merchant Taylors. Through his activity in discounting bills drawn on Chandos and providing cash when it was most needed by the two women, he, too, played a most important role in overcoming the problem of circulation time, in helping the urban redevelopment to go ahead, and in facilitating the general economic activity mentioned above. The one remaining question in this story is, where did Marchant get the funds which alone enabled him to fulfil his role in the business of economic development, and to function as part of the 'missing link'?

Marchant made his money in many ways: buying and selling land, expunging communal property rights, dealing in fire insurance and property development, lending to landowners, developers and builders on mortgage, discounting bills of exchange, and making profits from industrial enterprises. When he died, in 1774, he held a £6,000 share in the Bristol Brass Company![34] As the key 'credit man' facilitating urban redevelopment and its associated economic activities in this instance, Marchant was clearly instrumental in transferring money from the agricultural and commercial sector into urban and industrial development, even though a merely positivist approach to the question of capital accumulation would not identify him as an industrial or urban entrepreneur, except, perhaps, for his share-holding in the Bristol Brass Company. And that, too, poses a nice problem. Given that Marchant made some of his money by discounting Chandos's bills at 3.25 per cent, we have additional evidence that Chandos's ill-gotten wealth turns up in another arena of industrial production. As I have said, the web *is* a veil of credit.

When economic historians finally face up to the intricate ramifications and implications of the bill of exchange in the history of economic change in eighteenth-century England, they might do justice to Marx's insight about the nature of that economic change. They might come to realize that the real 'missing link' is the absence of all but positivist economic theory in the structures of their minds, and their consequential preferences for the appearance rather than the substance of the phenomena into which they enquire. I claim for this story of the Duke, his two landladies and their banker, theoretically interpreted, that it shows the relevance of Marx's insight about the secondary aspect of 'primitive accumulation'. Like the evidence for capital accumulation itself it points to a remarkable continuity in the slow process of economic change in eighteenth-century England, a process involving women as well as men, drawing a veil over the web of credit, and obscuring the real sources of capital.

[34] Fuller details of Marchant's career are in ibid., pp. 56—63.

God Creating the Universe: 'Jehovah, the Creator . . . formed golden Compasses And began to explore the Abyss' (William Blake, 1794/1824, Whitworth Art Gallery, University of Manchester)

2

A Mere Reasoning Machine

The Duke of Chandos was born James Brydges at Dewsall in Herefordshire in 1674 of a marriage between the eighth Baron Chandos, the head of a minor family of landed gentry newly created in 1554, and the daughter of a Turkey Merchant. He was (almost literally) a product of that union between the agrarian capitalist mode of production and the mercantile mode of production characteristic of the turn of the century. After attempting to make his own way in the world in the 1690s, through haunting the ante-rooms of leading politicians, he got himself elected MP for Hereford in 1698 and never looked back. He immediately became active against the Junto, and in 1701 carried to the Lords the articles of impeachment against Halifax. In 1702 he was chosen as commissioner of accounts to serve on what was, perhaps, the Commons key committee in its control over expenditure. In the same year he became Surveyor-General to The Board of Ordnance. In 1703 he was appointed one of the Commissioners of the Admiralty. In 1705 he became Paymaster General to the Forces Abroad, in which position he laid the foundation of his fortune. He is the very model of the monied interest, with its dependence on an intricate network of relations between Commons, political manoeuvring, knowledge of government dealings in money, place at court and handling government monies, taxation and the interests of the class of agrarian capitalists who ran the country. He may usefully be regarded as an exemplar of the power, needs and achievement of property (both movable and fixed) in the first three decades of the eighteenth century.

Brydges' career contrasts strongly with that of Samuel Clarke. Clarke was born the year after Brydges, on the other side of the country, in Norwich — the second city in England and, probably, its only provincial capital with a cultural life of its own. A one-time aspirant for the see of Canterbury, Clarke may be regarded as an exemplar of the role of the Church and religion in a materialistic world structured by the economic activities of men such as Brydges. His life is also interesting as an example of the way in which the rural/urban manufacturing mode of production shed able people to meet the need for moral order in a society based on the power of property and absolute self-interest. Almost a true burgher, Clarke in serving God, served well the dominant class of agrarian capitalists. Brydges and Clarke, with careers in money and property, and in morality respectively, were keel and bulwark of English society, economy and culture at the turn of the seventeenth and eighteenth centuries. Controllers and guardians of Britain's 'free' wage labourers, I see them as two of Sterne's mules of history starting us on circuitous and intertwining routes through the next 300 years, and, the 310 pages of this book.

*   *   *

Samuel Clarke was born in 1675 into a family of worsted weavers already well established in the rural/urban manufacturing mode of production in Norwich and East Anglia. His father, Edward Clarke, was a leading member of the merchant oligarchy of the city; he was Alderman and Mayor, and, in 1701, an MP in the Whig interest. His mother Hannah was the daughter of Samuel Parmenter, also a worsted weaver and member of the same merchant oligarchy in Norwich. Little is known about Clarke's early life except that he was educated at the Free School in Norwich and went up to Caius College in 1691. In 1695 he took his BA degree with an outstanding defence of one of Newton's principles. Two years later he published a new Latin translation of the principal Cartesian text then in use in Cambridge, Rohault's *Physics.*[1] According to an earlier biographer, Clarke annotated his translation according to the principles of Newtonian physics in order to 'lead the young men insensibly, and by degrees, to other and truer notions than what could be found there'. As this biographer noted: 'this certainly wás a more prudent method of introducing truth unknown before, than to attempt to throw aside this treatise entirely, and write a new one instead of it. . . . He may justly be stated a great benefactor to the University, in this attempt. For, by this means, the true philosophy has without any noise prevailed.'[2] This translation of Clarke's was still the main text in Cambridge in the 1730s.

On graduation, Clarke was appointed by John Moore, the latitudinarian

---

[1] Biographical details based upon: Hoadly's preface to Clarke's 2nd edn, 1730; W. Whiston, *Historical Memoirs of the Life of Dr Samuel Clarke,* London, 1730; the entry in the DNB; Cozens-Hardy and Kent, *The Mayors of Norwich, 1403—1835* (Norwich, 1938); Millican, *Freeman of Norwich 1548—1712* (Norwich, 1934).

[2] Samuel Clarke, *Sermons,* Vol. I, p. v. According to Whiston the idea for this translation was put to Clarke by Whiston himself at a coffee house in Norwich in 1697. W. Whiston, *Historical Memoirs of the Life of Dr Samuel Clarke* (London, 1730), p. 5.

Bishop of Norwich, as his chaplain, and rewarded with the rectory of Drayton near Norwich and a parish in the city. During his 12 years as chaplain he married Katharine Lockwood, daughter of the rector of Little Massingham near Norwich, by whom he had seven children. He also published several religious works of a practical kind. Then, Tenison, Archbishop of Canterbury, probably unaware that at Drayton Clarke had read the Athanasian Creed but once (and that by mistake) chose him to save the Church from the materialists; he invited Clarke to deliver the Boyle lectures of 1704.

The Boyle lectures had been instituted by Robert Boyle's will in 1691, and had as their object, 'Proof of the Christian Religion against notorious Infidels, viz., Atheists, Theists, Pagans, Jews, and Mahometans, not descending lower to any controversies that are among Christians themselves'.[3] According to Margaret Jacob, they were the principal vehicle used by latitudinarian divines, such as Tenison, to popularize Newtonian natural philosophy for religious and political purposes, thereby developing it into the ideology of an emerging bourgeoisie. Whatever the truth of this claim, Clarke's lectures were to be an important, perhaps a crucial factor in protecting the property and interests of the ruling oligarchy of agrarian capitalists and its attendant monied interest. (The year after Clarke gave the Boyle lectures, Brydges became Paymaster General.) I have more to say about them later. Following the brilliant success of Clarke's lectures the Bishop of Norwich, having decided to 'bring him to town', found for him the Rectory of St Bennett's, Paul's Wharf. There, in 1706, Clarke translated Newton's *Optics*, 'into that pure and intelligible Latin, which has sent it all over Europe in a plainer and less ambiguous style, than the English language will sometimes permit'.[4] Clarke's reputation as a Newtonian was beyond reproach.

Within a few years of his arrival in London, Clarke was appointed chaplain to Queen Anne and Rector of St James, Westminster, where he preached from the most prestigious pulpit in England. It was in his capacity as chaplain to the Queen, in 1715, that Clarke defended Newton's system against the scathing attack of Leibniz, sparking off a controversy about gravity, time and space that is still of concern to philosophers and historians of science, if not to scientists themselves. Indeed, the Queen so valued Clarke that she had a bust of him placed in the Hermitage alongside those of Boyle, Locke and Newton. One might have thought

---

[3] W. Derham, *Physico-Theology or, A Demonstration of the Being and Attributes of God,* 5th edn (London, 1720), p. 3. See also E. S. De Beer (ed.), *Diary of John Evelyn* (Oxford, 1955), Vol. 5, p. 88.

[4] Samuel Clarke, *Sermons,* Vol. I, p. xx.

that Clarke was heading for the highest honours the state and Church could bestow. But Clarke had one glaring fault.

In 1709 Clarke took his DD, defending the two propositions that, (a) no article of the Christian faith delivered in the Holy Scriptures, is disagreeable to right reason; and (b) without the liberty of human actions there can be no religion. Then, following the precept laid down in proposition (a), he wrote *The Scripture Doctrine of the Trinity*. It was clear from this work that Clarke favoured Arian, anti-Trinitarian views. Because 1712, the year of publication, was a sensitive time for both the Whig Ministry and the Anglican Church, the Lord Treasurer, Godolphin sought to dissuade Clarke from publishing, but to no avail. After publication Clarke was brought to account before Convocation. In response to great pressure from some of the bishops, Clarke appeared to recant. He agreed to believe the following: '[The] Son of God eternally begotten by the eternal incomprehensible power and will of the Father and that the Holy Spirit was likewise eternally derived from the Father, by or through the Son, according to the eternal incomprehensible power and will of the Father.'[5] Whether, with these words, he had recanted in fact was for others to decide.

Clarke had many sympathizers. Among those of his readers who were persuaded to reject the doctrine of the Trinity was James Peirce, a presbyterian preacher in Exeter. Peirce's consequential expulsion from his ministry provoked the Salter's Hall conference of Dissenters in 1719, the outcome of which was that about 60 preachers refused to subscribe to the doctrine of the Trinity. This set back the cause of Dissent for many years.

Subsequently, churchmen accused Clarke of preaching a disguised deism. Deists criticized him for retaining orthodox, that is, revelatory, phraseology. The former criticism is reflected in the story told by Voltaire that Gibson, Bishop of Norwich, prevented Clarke's preferment to the see of Canterbury by telling the Queen that while Clarke was the most learned and honest man in her dominions, he had one defect — he was not a Christian.[6] After the controversy, Clarke spent his remaining years at St James, Westminster, working on an annotated translation of Homer's *Iliad*.

Clearly, Clarke was an important intellectual in a civil society in which

---

[5] W. Whiston, *Historical Memoirs,* p. 45. The main evidence for the pressures brought on Clarke and for the support he received is in a collection of letters in Cambridge University Library, Add. 7113, especially two letters dated 4 July 1714, from the Bishops of Bristol, Asaph and Lincoln. See also, W. Whiston, pp. 25.

[6] DNB entry, also Voltaire, *Letters Concerning the English Nation,* 1st edn (London, 1733), pp. 48—9.

few people perceived any contradiction between religion and science, and between belief and reason, at least at the highest level of thought. In this civil society reason was the day labourer of belief, and science and religion, both rooted in the work of reason, were twin pillars supporting the economic and social structure. It may have been this aspect of Clarke's life and thought that Voltaire sought to identify when he referred to Clarke as among the first 'artists of reason' and 'a mere reasoning machine'.[7] Yet these terms may also be thought to identify Clarke as a man without belief and feeling, a man symptomatic of the post-Newtonian separation between thought and feeling, which some historians find characteristic of the eighteenth century. If the latter is the case then Voltaire's judgement may contribute to the masking of relationships between religion and science, between belief and reason, which, in turn, helped to mask relationships between economy, society and ideas in the early eighteenth century. If we can find religious belief using reason for its own ends, masquerading as science, we might well claim that science was ideological. We might also be able to trace out more clearly the sources of continuities in prophetic and millennialist ideas in the eighteenth and nineteenth centuries.

The invitation to deliver the Boyle lectures was Clarke's great chance. He was to be so successful, that after Locke died in 1704 it was said 'for the next quarter of a century Clarke was generally regarded as the first of English Metaphysicians.'[8]

The 1704 series of lectures, dealing with the being and attributes of God, was aimed directly at Hobbes and Spinoza. But there can be little doubt that the hidden enemy was the mechanical, materialist system of Descartes. In this system, in which there was a plenum rather than a void, matter was deemed to be necessarily existing and itself active. According to Clarke, this was nonsense. As he attacked Descartes, he attacked all materialists; the dead, the living and the as yet unborn.

As he set out to prove that God, as the self-existent and original cause of all things, was eternal, intelligent, free, infinitely powerful and wise, and fit to be the supreme governor and judge of the world, Clarke appealed to Lockeian notions of the process of human understanding and to Newtonian natural philosophy. He claimed that man's physical, intellectual and spiritual experience of the world proved the existence and intelligence of God. Thus, men apprehended God from 'the constitution, order,

---

[7] Voltaire, *Letters,* p. 48, and *Traité de Mataphysique,* Chapter 2, *Oeuvres,* Vol. XXXI, p. 20ff.

[8] DNB entry.

beauty, and harmony of the several parts of the world; in the frame and structure of our own bodies, and the wonderful power and faculties of our soul; in the unavoidable apprehension of our own minds, and the common consent of all other men.'[9] In short, men apprehended God through, 'everything within us, and everything without us'.[10]

The significance of Newtonian natural philosophy in this mode of apprehension was that it placed God in the foreground rather than in the background of knowledge. The Newtonian universe depended upon an agent not only to set it going, but repeatedly to intervene to keep it on course; God had to prevent the fixed stars falling on each other, correct irregularities in the motion of the planets because of disturbance caused by other planets, and maintain constant the amount of motion in the universe. In short, the Newtonian system required God's repeated intervention. Clarke wrote:

If the supreme cause be not a free and voluntary agent; then in every effect, (for instance, in motion) there must have been a progression of causes in infinitum, without any original cause at all. For if there be no liberty anywhere; then there is no agent; no cause, mover, principle, or beginning of motion anywhere. Everything in the Universe must be passive, and nothing active: everything moved and no mover: everything effect and nothing cause.[11]

This notion, that everything was effect and nothing cause, was, according to Clarke, the logical conclusion of Spinoza's system, and it was to be the initial major issue in Clarke's debate with Leibniz. Such a notion made God, at least a Christian God with the will and capacity to intervene in the world, redundant. This was patently absurd. It was also contrary to natural philosophy. Secure in his easy familiarity with Newtonian natural philosophy, Clarke wrote:

As that opinion [that everything was effect and nothing cause] is impious in itself, so that late improvements in mathematics and natural philosophy have discovered, that, as things now are, that scheme is plainly false and impossible in fact . . . Seeing matter is utterly uncapable of obeying any laws, the very original laws of motion themselves cannot continue to take place, but by something superior to matter, continually exerting on it a certain force or power . . . and . . . that most universal principle of gravitation itself, the spring

---

[9] Samuel Clarke, *A Discourse Concerning the Being and Attributes of God,* 8th edn (London, 1732), p. 127.

[10] Ibid., p. 127.

[11] Ibid., p. 70.

of almost all the great and regular inanimate motions in the world answering not at all to the surface of bodies (by which alone they can act one upon another) but entirely to their solid content cannot possibly be the result of any motion originally impressed on matter, but must of necessity be caused . . . by something which penetrates the very solid substances of all bodies, and continually puts forth in them a force or power entirely different from that by which matter acts on matter. Which is, by the way, an evident demonstration, not only of the worlds being made originally by a supreme intelligent cause; but moreover that it depends every moment on some superior being, for the preservation of its frame; and that all the great motions in it, are caused by some immaterial power, not having originally impressed a certain quantity of motion upon matter, *but perpetually and actually exerting itself every moment in every part of the world.*[12]

Although Clarke was himself clear that God was not corporeal, a position emphasized by his Arian belief, and certain that faith was an act of will determined by reason, his use of the latest developments in natural philosophy, as indicated in the previous quotation, helped to fix the idea of an anthropomorphic God as transeunt cause into the minds of his congregation and readers. It must have seemed to many of them — his lectures went to nine editions by 1739 — that Clarke spoke and wrote of God as if 'he' *was* an interventionist personally concerned with the fate of the world. Indeed, it was this notion of God as an external power intervening at will in the affairs of the universe that lay at the heart of Clarke's debate with Leibniz. Thus, Leibniz's wholly rational God had acted once at the creation. With total foresight and knowledge he had built all possible courses of action, including beneficient remedial action into the universe. But, Newton's and Clarke's God was still a God of pure will, actively intervening in his creation, and ready at any moment, if it so pleased him, to intervene in such ways as to bring any part of it to an end, or miraculously, to subvert his own laws of nature. Certainly this was how the dispute appeared to Leibniz. 'The question is', wrote Leibniz to Clarke, 'whether God does not act in the most regular and most perfect manner? Whether his machine is liable to disorders, which he is obliged to mend by extraordinary means? Whether the will of God can act without reason? Whether space is an absolute being? Also concerning the nature of miracles; and many such things, which make a wide difference between us.'[13] And he charged against Clarke and Newton, that 'the Newtonian

---

[12] Ibid., pp. 160–1, my italics.
[13] A. G. Alexander (ed.), *The Leibniz—Clarke Correspondence* (Manchester, 1956), p. 29.

universal attraction of matter . . . is either miraculous or absurd.'[14] Clarke's reply to Leibniz indicated that he agreed with the principal distinctions Leibniz made between their opposing positions. 'It was', Clarke avowed, 'no impossibility for God to make the world sooner or later than he did: nor is it at all impossible for him to destroy it sooner or later than it shall actually be destroyed.'[15] Accordingly, Clarke's general position was that God's production of disorder was no more miraculous than his creation of order. Both were evidence of God's will and of the superiority of Clarke's God over Leibniz's, because 'God's acting in the world upon everything after what manner he pleases, without any union [between God and the world]; shows plainly the difference between an omnipresent governor, and an imaginary soul of the world. . . . There is no union between God and the world.'[16] In private correspondence Clarke was even more forthright. He wrote:

of Carte's absurd hypothesis concerning a Plenum of matter, and his endeavouring to ascribe all the effects of Nature to mechanical causes; whereas, in truth, almost all the motions, on which the effect of Nature depend, are purely arbitrary: Nor can it possibly proceed from anything but intelligence, power, and will, that Gravitation (on which it all depends) is as the square of the distance, rather than in any other equally possible proportion. No miracle if (in truth) a strict proof of the Being of God, than are the principal works of Nature, which require the very same power to effect them, as any miracle does; and 'tis nothing but mere custom and careless inattentiveness, which makes men think *continual* works not to be the effect of a great Power as occasional ones.[17]

[14] *The Correspondence of Isaac Newton* (Cambridge, 1976), Vol. VI, p. 356.

[15] A. G. Alexander, *Leibniz — Clarke Correspondence*, p. 49.

[16] Ibid., p. 51.

[17] Letters to Dr Samuel Clarke, Add. 7113, Cambridge University Library. These holograph letters are catalogued as, Letters to Dr Samuel Clarke. However, a close reading of the text of this first letter and the letter quoted below shows them to have been written on behalf of Clarke by way of comment upon several letters written to him. The following letter also makes clear the religious importance of his objection to Leibniz's notion of space and time and of his conviction that both space and time were absolute.

The order of synchronal things is not space but the *order* or situation of things *in space;* and the order of successive things is not *time,* but the order of things in time. For the *order or succession* may be the very same, and yet the *interval of time* may be very different. God may create matter, and annihilate it all again, and create *new matter* either *immediately* after the *annihilation of the first Universe,* or after a very long interval. . . . All the difference between us, seems to depend upon this question, whether *space* be the *mere order and relation of bodies,* or be entirely independent (sic) on the Will (Letter, 31 Dec. 1715).

Clearly, God as sole cause of the world (as well as cause of the Son and the Holy Ghost) was separate from the world and, therefore, separate from man — a true God exercising real power.

However, these charges of Leibniz were in the future. For the present, in 1704, Clarke had made a name for himself. His reasoning and argument were seen as impeccable if not sublime. Consequently, Tenison invited him to deliver a second series of lectures, which was to be entitled *A Discourse Concerning the Unchangeable Obligations of Natural Religion and The Truth and Certainty of Christian Revelation.* Because these lectures reveal an aspect of Clarke's thought not generally considered by historians, I will spend more time discussing them than I have spent on the 1704 series.

Clarke's principal target in the 1705 series of lectures was Hobbes. Having, in 1704, proved the existence of God as an intelligent, free and external cause of all things, as pure will, his purpose now was to demonstrate man's consequent moral obligations, and the truth of God's revelation of himself to man.

He approached his first task from the proposition that as it was God's will to act only with justice, equity, goodness and truth, all subordinate rational beings ought to act according to the same rules. But, he added, these moral obligations were made more urgent through a system of rewards and punishments. He wrote:

there must at some time or other be such a revolution and renovation of things, such a future state of existence of the same persons, as that by an exact distribution of rewards and punishments therein, all the present disorders and inequalities may be set right; and that the whole scheme of providence, which to us who judge of it by only one small portion of it, seems now so inexplicable and much confused; may appear at its consummation, to be a design, worthy of infinite wisdom, justice and goodness.[18]

Although this view, with its millennialist undertones, was as plain as a pikestaff to men of sound reason, Clarke believed that many people — such as atheists and deists — were so corrupt, degenerate and obdurate that a divine revelation was necessary to convince men of the truths of reason. But God was not obliged to grant it. That he did so, in the form of scripture, was simply additional evidence of God's mercy. Men ignored it at their peril.

Since the central argument for revelation focused upon the observable fulfilment of scriptural prophecy (a position consistent with Clarke's view

[18] Samuel Clarke, p. 153.

that God possessed total foreknowledge), prophecy and the fulfilment of prophecy were central to Clarke's argument for revealed religion. Furthermore, the rational comprehension of fulfilled prophecy was a measure of man's ability to approach the infinite nature of God at least as worthy of man's rational attention as was Newton's attempt to comprehend the infinite nature of God in the heavens. Accordingly, Clarke argued that the creation, the flood, the granting of law to the Jews, and God's sending his son into the world 'which all the ancient prophecies had determined', and as set down in scripture, were instances of divine revelation. Indeed, the innumerable prophecies and miracles which scripture show to have been fulfilled and performed were all evidences of God's freedom as a causal, interventionist and all-knowing agent. Clarke wrote: 'The proof of the Divine authority of the Christian Revelation, is confirmed and ascertained, by the exact completion both of all those prophecies that went before concerning our Lord, and of those that he himself delivered concerning things that were to happen hereafter.'[19] He claimed, therefore, the truth of prophecies about a physical resurrection, expressed the view that God could give supernormal powers to men just as he saw fit, and argued that the apparently orderly course of nature was but the 'Arbitrary will and pleasure of God'.[20] Also, he conceded that God, by revelation and tradition, may 'have given some further degree of light, to such as are sincerely desirous to know and obey him; so that they who will do his will, may know of the doctrine whether it be of God. As our natural knowledge of moral and religious truths in fact is, so revelation possibly may further be, as it were, a light shining in a dark place.'[21]

It is not surprising, therefore, that this series of lectures, illuminated by such mystical and antinomian as well as by prophetic allusions, and shaded with millennialist undertones, ended with a long and equivocal survey of 'the possibilities of the predicted series [of prophecies] *for the future*; for several thousands of years'.[22] In these prophecies, mainly in Daniel and the Revelation of St John, said Clarke, God indicated that 'Truth and Virtue should finally prevail, should prevail over the Spirit of Error and Wickedness, of Delusion and Disobedience.'[23] Carried away by his own rhetoric, Clarke turned the final 50 pages of the second series of lectures into a compendium of millennialist texts. Had they been included in the

---

[19] Ibid., p. 388.
[20] Ibid., p. 379.
[21] Ibid., p. 394.
[22] Ibid., p. 395.
[23] Ibid., p. 395.

lectures as originally delivered in St Paul's Cathedral, they would have had a most remarkable effect. Even so, in the lifeless black and white of the printed text, they give the lie to the superficial notion that Clarke was a mere reasoning machine. Here were included, as if for easy access, references to Shiloh, New Heavens and New Earth, the Thrones cast down and the Antient of days, the woman clothed with the sun and the moon under her feet, the opening of Graves and the Land of Israel. All presented within the context of an argument about their general rather than their particular historical meaning. For example, on the subject of the return of God's people to Israel seeking the Lord their God and fearing the Lord and his goodness in the 'Latter days', but concerning his own times, Clarke wrote:

These predictions therefore necessarily belong to that age, when the times of gentiles shall be fulfilled and the fulness of the gentiles become in. And that, through all the changes which have happened in the Kingdom of the Earth, from the days of Moses to the present time, which is more than 3,000 years: nothing should have happened, to prevent the POSSIBILITY of the accomplishment of these prophecies; but on the contrary, the state of the Jewish and Christian nations at that day, should be such as renders them easily capable, not only of a figurative, but even of a literal completion in every particular, if the will of God be so; this (I say) is a miracle, which hath nothing parallel to it in the phenomenon of nature.[24]

Following this passage, and in the context of the notion that the Revelation of St John related to the present, Clarke wrote about Babylon the Great, the Mother of Harlots drunken with the Blood of the Saints and with the Blood of the Martyrs of Jesus, and so on. Then he speculated:

And, if there be not now such a power actually and conspicuously exercised in the world; and if any picture of this power, drawn after the event, can now describe it more plainly and exactly, than it was originally described in the words of the prophecy: Then may it with some degree of plausibleness be suggested, that the prophecies are nothing more than enthusiastic imaginations.[25]

---

[24] Ibid., p. 436. According to Whiston, Clarke derived his interpretation of Scripture prophecies from Newton and, 'did . . . sometimes speak of such interpretations without telling their true author'. Whiston also expressed the view that both Clarke and Newton were guided in their actions by belief in prophecy. Whiston, *Historical Memoirs,* Clarke's correspondent, John Jackson, also wrote to him about the political significance of prophecy. Add. 7113, 28 Dec. 1714.

[25] Ibid., p. 437.

But would any Englishman, Brydges for example, in 1705, only 20 years after the revocation of the Edict of Nantes and a mere 12 months after Marlborough's great victory over the agent of Anti-Christ, have doubted the soundness and truth of such a prophecy? The Mother of Harlots drunken with the Blood of Saints and with the Blood of the Martyrs of Jesus had been resoundingly defeated, the protestant cause and the property of the oligarchy of agrarian capitalists preserved.

Yet my defence of Clarke against a merely superficial characterization of him as devoid of feeling and belief does not rest only on the second series of Boyle lectures. Clarke's published sermons show that his interest in miracles and prophecy, including their importance for revealed religion, was no passing fancy. He included in his sermons eight texts from Daniel and 43 from the Revelation of St John. He was particularly taken with the prophecy about the Antient of Days and, quoting it in full, wrote of: 'The Prophet Daniel, in the sublime prophetick style', foretelling the final judgement. Furthermore, his discussion of the spiritual nature of the Gospel reads very like an exposition of the Behmenist everlasting gospel. On one occasion he became quite mystical, seeming to suggest, contrary to his expressed view, that there was in fact a union between God and the world, and that God was a personal God. Speaking of the presence of God, he said: 'Where ever we are, he is always with us, and surrounds us with his boundless presence; he includes and penetrates every part of our substance, sees into our inmost thoughts and purposes, and searches the most secret recesses of our hearts and souls with his unerring and all-seeing Eye.'[26] In his sermon on the nature and design of the holy communion he revealed clearly the symbolic, spiritual and irrational nature of his religion, and his personal relationship with his God. He wrote:

One principal reason why men in these latter ages of the world, who profess themselves Christians, are yet so loose and sensual, so careless and indifferent in matters of religion, so cold and lifeless in their devotion, and so little affected with things spiritual and of a heavenly nature, is because they seldom allow themselves time from the cares and businesses and pleasures of the world, to recollect their thoughts, and meditate seriously upon the great motives and arguments of religion.[27]

Communion, he said, should be one such occasion.

[26] Samuel Clarke, *Sermons,* Vol. I, p. 256.
[27] Ibid., Vol. IV, p. 131.

Doing this in remembrance of Christ, is declaring publickly to the world our faith in him; and endeavouring to continue down the memory of his love to all generations. . . . We here profess publicly our faith in his death; and declare solemnly to the world, that we expect remission of our sins, only through the virtue of his blood shed for us. We commemorate his unspeakable love to Mankind; and extol and magnify in our praises those great acts which were the effects of that inestimable love. We rehearse and proclaim the benefits he has procured for us . . . and make known to all men the glory of his love and power.[28]

Further, 'the sacrament of the Lord's Supper was to be a declaration of our communion one with another; a declaring, that, according to the apostles' expression, we, being many, are one bread and one body, signified by our being all partakers of that one bread.'[29] Yet, in an age fraught with faction, Clarke was also clear that the spiritual should serve a practical end.[30]

It is clear, I think, that Clarke, speaking and writing about the existence, nature and power of God, did not distinguish the weight of argument from natural philosophy from the weight of argument from revealed religion. As far as I recall, neither did Paley 70 years later.

In short, Clarke may properly be regarded as the exemplar of the latitudinarian position in all its complexity in the first 30 years of the eighteenth century. He was a man of sound reason. He was familiar with the natural philosophy of Descartes, Hobbes and Spinoza, as well as with the Newtonian system he advocated and defended against Leibniz. He was acutely conscious of the social and political implications of the systems he analysed, and conscious, too, of their dangerous implications for the Church to which he belonged. He combined Newtonian natural philosophy with traditional evidence for revealed religion to keep the idea of an interventionist God in the forefront of intellectual thought — his God was with him every moment of his day. He also accepted scriptural evidence about prophecy and miracles, and lived comfortably with the idea of gravity *and* the idea of the Flood; both were evidences of God's free intelligence and will. Because of the importance to him of 'The Truth and Certainty of the Christian Revelation', he was led willy nilly into a flirtation with interpretations of millennialist prophecies. Indeed, Clarke's published writings reveal the truth of Manuel's observation that 'the true prophet was a supremely rational man, a man worthy of receiving a

---

[28] Ibid., pp. 137—8.
[29] Ibid., p. 166.
[30] Ibid., p. 167.

message from the Divine Reason through the agency of the prophetic spirit',[31] and that a careful and rational analysis of the Book of Daniel and the Revelation of St John was a fit and proper activity only for the most rational and skilled of natural philosophers. (It is in this sense that Voltaire was correct — Clarke like Newton reasoned about the irrational.)

There can be little doubt that Clarke, through his sermons and the nine editions of his lectures by 1739, was an important, perhaps a central intellectual link between the scientific/prophetic latitudinarians of the late seventeenth century, and Anglican and other divines who aligned themselves with prophetic and millennialist movements throughout the eighteenth century; more important in this respect than Newton, whose work, *Observations Upon the Prophecies of Daniel, and the Apocalypse of St John*, was only published posthumously in 1733.

However, Clarke was a controversial figure in his own day and I would like to ensure there is no misunderstanding of my position. Although I claim that Clarke in his discussion of revealed religion was led to argue a case for fulfilled prophecy and to hover on the millennialist brink, and, moreover, in his defence of gravity against Leibniz brought Leibniz's charge against himself and Newton, that gravity is either miraculous or absurd, I do not claim that he was a mystic, an enthusiast, nor yet a believer in salvation by faith as popularly understood. If anything Clarke was touched by Arianism and Socinianism. He perceived God as an undivided spirit and understood his attributes through reason. Nevertheless, and this cannot be emphasized too strongly, revelation at least had equal status with reason. Indeed, the true comprehension of revelation was accessible only through reason; reason *was* the day-labourer. Thus, for Clarke, revelation and reason, feeling and thought were as tightly bound to each other as capital and labour were for Marx.

My position is as follows. Clarke was held in very high esteem in Church circles and he was the Church's intellectual. He was one of the few Church divines who understood Newton's system, and he was instrumental in educating generations of Cambridge men in its truth. He was so persuaded of the power of reason that he came close to Socinianism. He was the most intellectual of churchmen preaching from St James Westminster, the most prestigious pulpit in the country. Nevertheless, as is shown in his Boyle lectures, his sermons, and his correspondence with Leibniz, while he may have perceived God as a unified deity he also saw

---

[31] F. E. Manuel, *The Religion of Isaac Newton* (Oxford, 1974), pp. 87–104. For a short, clear contemporary exposition of the link between revelation, prophecy and miracles, see John Leland, *A View of the Principal Deistical Writers* (London, 3rd edn 1757, Vol. II, pp. 360–71.

him as an interventionist, present at every moment in the world. Indeed, Clarke went out of his way to argue the necessity of God's intervention and the necessity of revealed religion; divine revelation would be the death of deism. Because of the central place of prophecy and miracles in Christian revelation his theology was necessarily touched by prophetic and millennialist thought.

A result of this was that Clarke's theology did not in principle forbid millennialist systems, such as Burnet wrote about in his *Sacred Theory of the Earth*. Another was that it incorporated miracles as proper objects of study. Consequently, as far as I can judge, Clarke perceived no incompatibility between scientific and theological modes of thought. There was none. The unifying theme was God as transeunt cause as demonstrated in the book of nature and in the book of religion, and as comprehended through reason. Surely, if Clarke as well as Newton could live in these two worlds and reason their unity, lesser men could also be expected to live comfortably in them. In short, as Clarke's works so clearly show, a conflict between belief and reason, revelation and reason, prophecy and science was not evident in England in the first 30 or 40 years of the century. I doubt that it was present in any hegemonic sense thereafter.

The perceived compatibility between belief and reason in the 1730s, as exemplified in the thought of Samuel Clarke, meant that scarcely anyone would have been surprised at the re-publication of several prophetic works in the second decade of the century; Burnet's *Sacred Theory of the Earth*, 1719, Sir John Floyer's *An Exposition of the Revelation*, 1718, which predicted the millennium in 1898, and *Nixon's Cheshire Prophecy at Large*, originally published in the reign of James I and going through seven editions between 1715 and 1718. Nixon had foretold: 'The Civil Wars, the death of King Charles I, the Restoration of King Charles II, the Abdication of King James II, and the flourishing state of the Kingdom afterwards. . . . and, that whoever shall pretend to disturb the peace of our flourishing Church and State, under George and the son of George, shall bring the most terrible ruin on themselves and their posterity for ever.'[32] In short, because of the all-pervasiveness of revelation in Christian theology, the prophetic and millennialist mode of thought was enmeshed in the intellectual tradition of the Church in the 1720s and 1730s, however rational that tradition might seem to be. Hoadly, the Bishop of Salisbury, for example, in recommending Clarke's sermons to the reading public was in no two minds about the necessity of revealed religion justified by reason. He assured his readers that

---

[32] *Nixon's Cheshire Prophecy at Large,* 6th edn (London, 1719), pp. 27—31.

Every christian in this country, in which they [Clarke's sermons] first saw the light, ought to esteem them as his treasure; as they contain the true strength not only of natural, but of revealed religion: which, if ever it be removed from such a foundation; or separated from such an alliance with Reason and uncorrupted nature, will not long subsist in the belief of understanding persons, after such a separation. And therefore, what God hath joined together, let no man put asunder.[33]

Because of the importance the argument from revelation placed on miracles and prophecy, prophetic and millennialist notions were endemic in Christian theology. What historians observe, on some occasions, is that these notions become epidemic and even pandemic. Accordingly, in the latitudinarian period, and in the period of Clarke's intellectual life from 1695—1729, the miraculous and prophetic mode of thought was inevitably present in religious intellectual thought, although in a subdued and muted form. When it became epidemic, as in the enthusiasm of the French Prophets, as well as in the writings of Burnet, Floyer and Nixon, mentioned earlier, it was, in spite of appearances and contemporary fears, essentially conservative. For example, the messages for men in the early eighteenth century in *Burnet's Sacred Theory of the Earth* were not much different from those in Clarke's Boyle lectures. (Burnet's *Sacred Theory* was republished in 1719, 1722 and 1726.) They were: first, that far from there being any incompatibility between natural philosophy and natural religion, natural philosophy was reassuring and strengthening about belief in a God who planned the unreasonableness as well as the reasonableness of earthly life, and who could intervene at will. Within the context of knowledge at the time, Burnet certainly rescued the idea of the Flood, and presented a plausible account of paradise. He strengthened the claims of revealed religion. One wonders how many lay readers could have distinguished Clarke and Burnet on prophecy! Secondly, his book, like Clarke's work, showed that there was no incompatibility between rational theological discourse and the prophetic and millennialist mode of thought. Thirdly, this prophetic millennialist tradition was reaffirmed in such a way as to make it perfectly clear, to the French Prophets and other enthusiasts, for example, that the millennium could not occur tomorrow on this earth. Rather, this earth and all upon it had first to be destroyed, and destroyed not by man but by God, before a morally regenerate people could be brought to inhabit the New Heaven and the New Earth. (This idea, that God could act in such an arbitrary way was central to Clarke's

---

[33] Samuel Clarke, *Sermons,* Vol. I, p. xv.

theology.) In this way, the English translation of *The Sacred Theory of the Earth* ruptured the connection between the millennialist and revolutionary traditions of the seventeenth-century sects.

In short, the message of Burnet's book complemented at the quasi-intellectual level the thoroughly conservative message of the more popular *Nixon's Cheshire Prophecy at Large* and of Floyer's *Revelation,* as well as of Clarke's own intellectual writing. It did so at a period when the ruling classes, still insecure following the Revolution of 1688, had been badly shaken by the Sacheverell affair in 1709/1710, the Jacobite rising of 1715, and the Atterbury plot of 1722.

What then does this account of Clarke's thought suggest about the connection of religious belief, reason and science with the economic and social structure of England in the first three decades of the eighteenth century? What generalizations does it permit?

If one concedes the possibility that people may be judged according to their public face, and as far as Samuel Clarke is concerned that seems to be the only face there is, then it is true to say that Clarke saw the universe and man's place in it as a single, unified and intelligible structure under God. Not only had God created the world in its law-like relations to the other planets, he had placed man on it as a free and rational imitation of himself so that his (God's) achievement would not pass unrecognized. So marvellous were God's powers, he not only regulated and controlled his creation by universal laws, but also reserved his right to intervene to break those laws should another set of laws, his universal moral laws, be broken or ignored by man as a free agent. In fact God intervened continually. God also possessed total foreknowledge. Through scripture he had given man ample advice of these moral laws, but, more importantly, he had also warned of the consequences of deviations from them. These warnings were in the prophetic books. Like the laws of nature these clues to the working out of God's moral system were decipherable only by rational men who, through acts of will (reason), had accepted evidence for the being and attributes of God. When they had mastered the laws of nature — including an understanding of God's capacity to break those laws — and the moral laws, together with God's prophetic warnings and promises about those laws, then, and only then, would men be able to feel themselves at one with God, and to be clear in their minds about the relationship of that oneness to their life on earth.

As far as I can judge from the tenor of Clarke's language and the intentisy of his dialogue with God — his sermons strike me as occasions on which Clarke argued the grounds of his own belief before an audience which was not essential to his purpose — he was as passionate about his belief in reason, and as passionate about what it meant to be truly human as any Ranter. Thus, while the structure of Clarke's world was as classically formal as John Wood's Bath, like it, it was the product of a creative passion with deep religious roots.[34] Clarke's passion, like Wood's, was the passion expressed by Handel in the Chandos Anthems. In brief, he was passionate about reason, and passionate about the single, unified and intelligible view of the structure of the world which reason had created.

There was one problem. The real world upon which Clarke built his intellectual universe, like the world in which Wood built Bath, was neither singular nor unified, although it may still have been intelligible. The fact was, it was a world in turmoil. A mere 20 years before Clarke's birth it had been turned upside down by Arians, Socinians, Anabaptists, Fifth Monarchy men, Sensual Millenaries, Behmenists, Familists, Seekers, Antinomians, Ranters, Sabbatarians, Muggletonians, Sweet Singers, and Quakers like James Nayler who, in 1656, took Bristol by storm. Nayler entered the city riding an ass led by a bareheaded Quaker and preceded by three women — one of whom he had raised from the dead — spreading their handkerchiefs before him and singing 'Holy, holy, holy is the Lord God of Hosts. Hosannah in the highest. Holy, holy, holy is the Lord God of Israel.'[35] As Thomas Tenison, Archbishop of Canterbury and co-trustee of the Boyle lectures caustically observed, such sects as 'these may associate in a caravan, but cannot join in the communion of a church.'[36]

At the turn of the century, the world was still not free of such enthusiasts. They remained part of Clarke's universe and remained a threat to his unified and intelligible structure of the world. A threat clearly expressed for him at the start of his intellectual life by Richard Baxter in 1696. Commenting on his ministry in Kidderminster, Baxter had written:

And I must add this to the true information of posterity, that God did so wonderfully bless the labours of his unanimous faithful ministers that had it not been for the faction of the Prelatists on one side that drew men off, and the factions of the giddy and turbulent sectaries on the other side . . . England had been like in a quarter of an age to have become a land of saints and a pattern of holiness to all the world, and the unmatched paradise of the earth. Never were such fair opportunities to sanctify a nation lost and trodden underfoot as have been in this land of late. Woe be to them that were the causes of it![37]

---

[34] R. S. Neale, *Bath 1680—1850: A Social History,* chapter 6.

[35] William Sewel, *The History of the Christian People called Quakers,* 3rd edn (New Jersey, 1774), p. 161.

[36] DNB, Vol. XIX.

As Clarke passed into his early teens, the Anglican faith of his burgher parents was further threatened by Catholic and absolutist monarchs, both at home and abroad; by Cartesian science imported from France and the Netherlands; and by the after-effects of the Revolution of 1688. This latter event in turn led to the exclusion from the Church of divines who could not accept the legitimacy of the succession. They, too, threatened the unity of Clarke's world.

Then, in his maturity, he would have experienced constant reminders of all these threats and disturbances. They were the long continued war with France, the popularity of Shaftesbury's deism, his own debate with Leibniz, the escape to England of the French Prophets carrying enthusiastic millennialism in their knapsacks, attacks on the Church by non-juring divines, the antics of Dr Sacheverell, and a succession of Jacobite plots in 1695, 1708, 1715, 1719 and 1722.[38]

Whether Clarke would have perceived behind all this a great swell of change moving through the economy, creating great landed and monied wealth on the one side, a dissatisfied gentry on the other, and between and beneath both, an urban patriciate at odds with both and in increasing conflict with a mass of masterless men, is a question I cannot answer. It is sufficient to say, I think, that Clarke was clear that the instability of his times called for a rational and determined effort to hold society together to maintain it as a functioning whole under the auspices of Christian morality. This was to be done by consensus, by minimizing merely procedural

[37] Richard Baxter, *Autobiography,* London, 1931, p. 84. First published in 1696 under the title, *Reliquiae Baxterianae.* See also, Shaftesbury, Anthony, Earl of, A Letter concerning Enthusiasm, 1707, in *Characteristicks of Men, Manners, Opinions, Times,* 4th edn (London, 1727), Vol. I, pp. 3—55.

[38] See, John Leland, *A View of the Principal Deistical Writers* (London, 3rd ed, 1957) Vol II, pp. 48—83; Stanley Creon, *Shaftesbury's Philosophy of Religion and Ethics* (Ohio, 1967); Geoffrey Holmes, *The Trial of Dr Sacheverell* (London, 1973); Hillel Schwartz, *The French Prophets in England,* Ph.D. (Yale, 1974); A. G. Alexander (ed.) *The Leibniz—Clarke Correspondence* (Manchester, 1956); and the following trials: Sir Richard Grahme and John Ashton, 1690; Sir William Parkins, 1695/6; Robert Charnock, Edward King, Thomas Keyes, 1695/6; Francis Francia, 1716; Earl of Wintoun, 1716; Christopher Layer, 1722, and *A Report from the Lords Committees,* 1723. For a discussion of a possible link between Newton and the French Prophets in the person of Fatio De Duillier, see F. E. Manuel, *A Portrait of Isaac Newton* (Harvard, 1968), pp. 206—12. For discussion of the political instability of the period, see J. H. Plumb, *The Growth of Political Stability in England, 1675—1725* (London, 1967), and chapter 3. below.

differences between the Church and the sects, and between the sects, by rooting out enthusiasm, by accommodating Christian belief to the Newtonian branch of natural philosophy, by emphasizing the wilful and interventionist nature of God as compatible with that branch of natural philosophy, and by upholding a Christian moral code based on rewards and punishments. Clarke's thought was ideological.

In setting the whole corpus of his thought in a revelatory context, which emphasized God's total foreknowledge and God's wilful nature, Clarke also necessarily preserved the prophetic and millennialist mode of Christian thought, however conservatively it was interpreted. But this was no accident. The compatibility between revelation and reason, so clearly perceived by Clarke, was also perceived by Hoadly, the Bishop of Salisbury, as essential to the stability of Church and state in circumstances of disorder. Remember what Hoadly wrote about revelation and reason: 'And therefore, what God hath joined together, let no man put asunder.'

When Clarke died in 1729 there seemed no good reason, at least on the surface of things, why this marriage between revelation and reason should end in divorce. Newton was in the heavens and in the text books at Cambridge, the deists and the French Prophets were in full retreat, the sects, arguing over the Trinity, were in disorder, William Law had scarcely begun to publish the results of his conversion by Boehme, and John Wesley was but a lecturer in Greek and a priest of a year's standing, new yet to the writings of William Law. One might have thought that the latitudinarian achievement was assured; belief and reason, revelation and reason, prophecy and science lay comfortably side by side, religious ideological conflict had been contained, the millennium domesticated, and enthusiasm and the passion of self-interest held in check by an interventionist God. Further, the prophecies of Daniel and the Revelation of St John were about to be fulfilled in the liberality of the protestant succession. Utopia in England, — properly lopped and bound — as well as in Bath, seemed just around the corner. Thus, while Samuel Clarke might have died embittered over his failure to get preferment (although his rejection of the Mastership of the Mint, worth £1,200 per annum, suggests that he did not), he must surely have died content with his part in building a sort of stability in England. With his passionate conviction in the necessary unity of revelation and reason, and the steps he had taken to bind them together, he could safely leave posterity to look after itself. Or so he must have thought, not knowing what the Voltaires of the world would do with reason, nor what the William Laws and the evangelicals, entering through the back door, and the new social classes would do with revelation. And not knowing what changes would be wrought in men by that growing swell of economic change, which was itself the very condition of his own position in the world, and the hidden basis of his own search after order even if not the source of his preferred solution. A solution rooted firmly in the unity of revelation and reason. A solution in which he bound thought to feeling and perpetuated belief in miracles and prophecy as only a Newtonian could. Clarke argued for this solution throughout his life. Were he to be resurrected with the saints during Burnet's millennium, I doubt that he would recognize himself as a mere reasoning machine pitting reason against Christian revelation.

'Some of the Principal Inhabitants of ye Moon': Royalty, Episcopacy and Law
(William Hogarth, 1724)

3

The Wealth of Nations: the Expenses of the Sovereign or, Private Vices, Publick Benefits?

Having started us on our journey, in 1726, with the landlady, the Duke, and the banker, in their comings and goings over three skewers and a larkspit, and again in 1675 with the birth of a 'mere reasoning machine', I start once more in 1688, with the Battle of Wincanton. In that battle, according to report, some 40 of the ordinary men in England were killed in a dispute about who should wield power over them. James Brydges and Samuel Clarke, who were to wield economic and moral power over other ordinary men, were then fourteen and thirteen years old respectively, more shaped by than shaping the circumstances in which they would try to make their own histories. This chapter brings their two interests together in a most unlikely context, and pushes our history forward by about 100 years.

With echoes of chapter 1 on the role of credit and the legal conditions for the bill of exchange during the phase of primitive accumulation, and, therefore, in all subsequent development of the rural/urban manufacturing and industrial-capitalist modes of production, this chapter explores some aspects of the role of the state in those developments. It shows how, in the production of the wealth of the nation in the eighteenth century, the 'expenses of the sovereign' played a role without which the private vices of agrarian-capitalist and other entrepreneurs, such as Chandos and Wood and Marchant and Clarke's parents, would have produced few of the public benefits claimed for them. Indeed, the role of the state (including its military and coercive role) was a necessary (but not sufficient) condition for the success of their activities as entrepreneurs. And I show how Adam Smith, allegedly the father of the myth of *laissez-faire*, was in fact a characteristically benevolent eighteenth-century man, full of wisdom and virtue (just like Samuel Clarke), wishing to contain the private vices of civil society within a rigid moral framework for the better protection of civil society. He also shared Samuel Clarke's opposition to 'enthusiasm'. In short, Smith, like Clarke, Shaftesbury and Wood, felt and expressed the fearfulness of property owners in a world of the propertyless.

*   *   *

One of the most persistent myths about our period in English history, which saw the birth of the modern world with its complex articulation of modes of production (some portion of which has a special place in the minds of millions under the title 'The Industrial Revolution'), is that this birth took place without the help or intervention of governments, and in spite of the actions of the dominant class in the agrarian capitalist mode of production. According to this myth, what Adam Smith called the 'Expenses of the Sovereign' were negligible, and Western peoples' entry into their present abundant estate and the industrial capitalist mode of production, was brought about by the spontaneous effort and enterprise of a new 'middle class' of men. These men, allegedly the product of the protestant ethic, are said to have moved peacefully and freely, but restlessly, about their business, rather like individual atoms or monads, but in reality as agents of a benevolent, man-centred, hidden hand. And they worked wonders; according to a contemporary of theirs, Bernard Mandeville, even their private vices resulted in public benefits.

In the nineteenth century, historians gave a title to this myth. It was *laissez-faire*. Authorship of it was attributed to Adam Smith for, did he not write:

The natural effort of every individual to better his own condition, when suffered to exert itself with freedom and security, is so powerful a principle, that it is alone, and without any assistance, not only capable of carrying on the society to wealth and prosperity, but of surmounting a hundred impertinent obstructions with which the folly of human laws too often incumbers its operations.[1]

Since then, in spite of much questioning of the myth and its authorship, various bowdlerized and pirated versions continue to appear and the myth persists.

This would not matter except for two related phenomena. First, although most people do not look to history writing for the truths it might offer

---

[1] Adam Smith, *An Inquiry into the Nature and Causes of the Wealth of Nations* (London, 1947), Vol. II, p. 40.

(these truths might be unpleasant and disturbing), humankind does have a kind of curiosity about the past. But this curiosity is all too easily satisfied and manipulated. As a result, most people make decisions about the present, therefore about the future, according to the myths (the history) they carry in the pockets of their minds, ready for use like the pocket calculators they carry in their other pockets. Accordingly the myth of *laissez-faire* appears in popular form as a guide to action in the most unlikely places. For example, it appeared captured in the headlines of an advertisement in Murdoch's newspaper, the *Australian*, which read: 'Capitalism and Freedom. Without one you can't have the other.'[2] Secondly, and more alarmingly for history writing and the truth its practitioners seek to promulgate, a post-war generation of consciously ideological historians and economists, among them Professors Hayek and Ashton, organized in the Mont Pélèrin Society, offered themselves as musketeers of free enterprise, and refurbished the myth. They argued that economic individualism alone not only generated economic growth in the past but also, and necessarily, caused all personal and political freedoms. They claimed that this was an observed truth falsifiable only by false history. Unfortunately, they said, most economic and social history written before the mid-1950s *was* false. Therefore, said the men of Mont Pélèrin, history should be rewritten and the truth proclaimed.[3] And it came about that an ideological misreading of Adam Smith's representation of his world and its history was turned back upon the past from which it came, to enable historians and others to argue that that was how it really was, and to celebrate that alleged mimicry — myth became history and history the myth. (Here is our 'moment' of danger.) Therefore the truth of this contemporary cultural production — the myth with its alleged source in the cultural production of Adam Smith — and the relationship of Adam Smith's cultural production to the mode of production, merit our close attention.

THE BATTLE OF WINCANTON

I begin at a beginning which is Adam Smith's as well as mine, 1688. On 20 November 1688 a party of the King's Horse rode into Wincanton, a small market town about 25 miles south of Bath on the road between Exeter and Salisbury. They were ambushed at the eastern approaches of

[2] *The Australian*, 12 Oct. 1974.
[3] F. A. Hayek, *The Road to Serfdom* (London, 1944), F. A. Hayek (ed.), *Capitalism and the Historians* (London, 1954).

the town by an advance party from William's invading army. About 40 men were killed that day before the King's men broke off the engagement and retreated towards Salisbury.[4] I tell the nub of this untold story to remind you that the English sovereigns of the late seventeenth and eighteenth centuries were illegitimate, placed in power by a disaffected landowning class, a rebellious officer corps, and an invading army at a time when the rank and file of the King's army remained loyal, and the bourgeoisie, if bourgeoisie there was, slept comfortably in their beds. I also tell it to remind you of other attempts, some successful, some not, to secure by means of violent and civil conflict the right to command the English nation. Rebellion and civil war, 1642—6, regicide and republic to 1660, the march of General Monk and the Restoration, 1660, the Exclusion Crisis, 1678—81 followed by the Rye House plot to assassinate the King in 1683; the Argyll and Monmouth Rebellions in 1685 and their ruthless suppression; the landowner inspired and Dutch-led coup in 1688; the suppression of the Irish in 1691; the Turnham Green plot to assassinate the King in 1696; and the Jacobite invasions, risings and plots of 1708, 1715, 1719, 1722, and 1745.

In 1745 Adam Smith was already twenty-two years old. It is difficult to believe that he was unaffected by the violence of his time and unaware that the '45 had inspired such a dread in the English Government that it rapidly passed legislation to allow it to stage the treason trials in London and not, as would otherwise have been the case, in the counties where the treasonable offences occurred, and at Inverness to pour £200,000 into the biggest single building project in Scotland before the great building of Edinburgh 15 years later. The result was Fort George. It stands today as Europe's best example of an eighteenth-century artillery fort, and a permanent reminder of the political insecurity of the sovereign in the first half of the eighteenth century, and of the expenses of the sovereign. That its batteries have never fired a shot in anger simply serves to contrast the difference between the nineteenth century which read Adam Smith, and the early eighteenth century which bred him.

Indeed, we do not have to speculate upon Adam Smith's acquaintance with these events. He well knew about them and the wastes they involved.

---

[4] The History of the Desertion, in *Collection of State Tracts* (London, 1705), Vol. 1, pp. 78—9. Other versions of the skirmish place the number of dead at 15 including only four on the King's side. However, the fact that 30 of the prince's force fired at least four volleys almost point blank into the ranks of 120 horses packed into a narrow lane suggests that the number killed must have been substantially more than four. I am indebted to the Rev. J. Everett of Wincanton for supplying me with a copy of G. Sweetman, *Wincanton During the Civil Wars.*

In fulminating about the expense of government it was to the costs of rebellion and war that he referred. But there was nothing remarkable about the remarks he made, they were the stock in trade of all eighteenth-century opponents of national debts and taxation. He wrote:

Thus, in the happiest and most fortunate period of them all, that which has passed since the restoration, how many disorders and misfortunes have occurred, which, could they have been foreseen, not only the impoverishment, but the total ruin of the country would have been expected from them? The fire and the plague of London, the two Dutch wars, the disorders of the revolution, the war in Ireland, the four expensive French wars of 1688, 1702, 1742, and 1756, together with the two rebellions of 1715 and 1745.[5]

As Adam Smith observed, these events were responsible for a national debt of over £200,000,000. These expenses of the sovereign were truly great and had immense significance for England's future as an economic and world power.

THE SOVEREIGN

The landowners, generals, and bishops had engineered and welcomed the revolution of 1688 as a revolt against absolutism and strong government. But William's interest was not theirs. He wanted to throw England's strength into the war against the hegemony of absolutist France in Europe and thereby in the world. As he and his successors succeeded in this design, England was involved in 25 years of warfare. The military machine which England built to fight those wars led to the frustration of many of the hopes of the 16,000 landed families who owned the land and governed it. Having fought or at least conspired against or objected to a domestic absolutism, many of them became its victims. The army and navy grew apace and the bureaucracy expanded. There took place a great reform of government finance which resulted in the creation of the national debt. The debt, 35 per cent of which, in the period 1700—9, was serviced by revenues from the land tax, transferred a considerable portion of the surplus produced in agriculture out of the hands of landowners and placed it in the pockets of stockjobbers and speculators, government functionaries, military men and placemen, those whom the Tories of the time called 'the monied interest'. We have Gregory King's calculations at the end of the seventeenth century to show that the Government took at least 15 per

---

[5] Adam Smith, *the Wealth of Nations*, Vol. 1, p. 308. For Fort George see Iaian MacIvor, *Fort George*, HMSO, 1983, p. 8.

cent of the annual national income,[6] while other evidence shows that by 1722 the total debt at £53 million was rather more than the gross national product. By 1750 it had risen to nearly £79 million. This debt was generally serviced by a land tax at 4s in the pound, and customs and excise, and much of it was in Dutch hands. English landowners protested about the purposes and levels of taxation. One of them wrote:

We have lived to see our ancient constitution in a manner dissolved, and the most important articles of our new contract settling the protestant succession evaded, suspended, or set aside: the wealth and strength of the kingdom exhausted in foreign acquisitions, and the very nation itself sold to make purchases abroad and to enrich strangers.

We have lived to see the first honours of the Peerage bestowed to dignify prostitution, the freedom of the people, the most inestimable article of their freedom, the freedom of elections destroyed with one breath of their own representations, so that all the most precious parts of our liberty may be said to be stabbed by its own guard.

We have lived to see more persons illegally seized, whipped, fined, pilloried, imprisoned, impeached, attainted, and executed in the space of one year than our Histories can show us in 300 before.

We have lived and we yet live to be tramped upon by the vilest, the most ignominious of all tyrannies, the tyranny of Ministers, the tyranny of fellow subjects raised from the dirt by faction, supported by senates chosen and directed by corruption.[7]

For almost 50 years, disgruntled landowners, mostly of the lesser sort, who shared these sentiments, fought a losing battle against the encroachments of a strong executive, and single party government. They were the democrats of their time, not the monied interest nor the city merchants who, while they may not have sought their fortunes at the cannon's mouth, drew, like James Brydges, a goodly substance from the exigencies of an armed state, which, for a time at least, with 200,000 men under arms and under Marlborough was the most powerful in Europe. (As James Brydges' accounts as Paymaster General to the Forces Abroad

---

[6] Gregory King, *Natural and Political Observation on the Population of England and Wales,* 1697, Kashnor Collection, Australian National Library. See also, PGM. Dickson, *The Financial Revolution in England 1688—1786* (London, 1967); and W. R. Ward, *The English Land Tax in the Eighteenth Century* (London, 1953).

[7] *Letter from a Nobleman to the Right Honourable the Lord Viscount Townsend,* 8 May 1725, Kashnor MS1458, Australian National Library. Written on the back of the letter is, Lord Bolingbroke.

show, in the period 1705—13 the land war outside England cost at least £24 million.[8] Indeed, it does seem that the only recompense that landowners got for a 4s land tax was military victory. As one contemporary wrote, Marlborough's stunning victory at Blenheim made, 'a pleasing spectacle to the generality of people, being more victory for 4s in the pound than ever they yet saw'.[9]

Yet, the English did get more than Blenheim for their 4s. Winston Churchill, for example, celebrated the period of the War of the Spanish Succession as the greatest in English history. Even if one allows that Churchill was no economist, not even an economic historian, and that he had a family interest in the period, he was probably not far off the mark. In any case, he writes about it in language which it is difficult to match:

In ten years England rose to the leadership of Europe. She gained the mastery of the seas, including the control — never since lost — of the Mediterranean. The ocean roads to trade and empire in the New World were opened. Her soldiers according to her enemies, were the best in Europe. Her wealth and prosperity seemed for a while to rise upon the tide of war. By the union with Scotland the island became one. The might of France was abated, and a balance was established in Europe to correct her exorbitant power. The Dutch ally, crippled in the long war, ceased to be a rival at sea, and, weakening under the financial strain, soon ceased to be a rival in trade.

The foundations were laid of that power which fifty years later enabled Lord Chatham by the victories of Wolfe and Clive to drive all challengers alike from America and India.[10]

All this and more was the work of the sovereign personified for a time in the person of the Duke of Marlborough. When in 1776, after innumerable invasion scares, Adam Smith reserved defence as one of the powers of the sovereign, and described the protective provisions of the Navigation Acts as the wisest of all commercial regulations in England, he well knew that the world-wide offensive defence practised by Marlborough was the very condition of England's existence as a modern and growing economic power. Further, when he argued for the superiority of a standing army over a militia for the purpose of state defence and the defence of wealth, he took sides on what has been described as the 'first

[8] S. T. S. Brydges, James, First Duke of Chandos, Paymaster General's Accounts, 1705—13. Huntington Library, California.

[9] Quoted in W. R. Ward, *The English Land Tax*, p. 24.

[10] Sir Winston S. Churchill, *Marlborough His Life and Times* (London, 1934), Vol. II, p. 44.

genuine political issue to divide politics since the reign of Anne'.[11] This was the controversy over the Militia Bills of 1757 and 1762. Adam Smith devoted 16 pages of what is generally considered a wholly economic tract to this issue of standing armies. In his discussion he makes clear his views about the nature of the state and the crucial role he thought it should play in civil society.

This armed state or sovereign of the early eighteenth century, admired by Adam Smith, was neither bourgeois, democratic, nor free. It was a military and ministerial bureaucracy which impinged greatly upon England's political and economic community to protect property and restrict freedom. For example, measured in terms of the extent of the franchise and the frequency of contested elections, England was much less democratic after the Reform Act of 1832 than it had been in 1688.[12] And it was Marx rather than other nineteenth- and twentieth-century historians who saw that this state was illiberal and coercive. He wrote of this period in English history, 'Force is the midwife of every old society pregnant with a new one. It is itself an economic power.'[13] In foreign affairs the force used by the sovereign was military; in domestic affairs it was the force of law backed by ministerial control of patronage: statute law, common law, equity courts, and all the crafts of the lawyers were used by landowners to protect their property by surrounding them with a mass of legally binding contracts. At the same time, lifeholders, copy holders, and those with merely customary rights were picked off one by one, and leasehold tenures and individual wage contracts became the norm. Where corporate powers were needed, as they were by river improvement companies, turnpike trusts, canal companies and water supply and sewerage companies, parliament created corporate powers of compulsory entry and of purchase of land subject only to a jury's determination on the value of compensation. Then there was the criminal law. The Black Act of 1723, for example, was passed to expedite the penal treatment of those who offended against property; it added 50 capital offences to the list of offences against property. The evidence is clear enough. It points to the existence of a political and legal superstructure serving the interests of large landowners both as individuals and as members of the dominant class in the agrarian-

[11] Correlli Barnett, *Britain and Her Army 1509—1970* (Harmondsworth, 1974), p. 172. Also J. R. Western, *The English Militia in the Eighteenth Century* (London, 1965).

[12] See, for example, J. H. Plumb, *The Growth of Political Stability in England 1675—1725* (London, 1967); and J. H. Plumb, 'The Growth of the Electorate in England from 1600—1715', in *Past and Present,* No. 45, Nov. 1969.

[13] Karl Marx, *Capital,* Everyman end (London, 1962), Vol. 2, p. 833.

capitalist mode of production. These men were secure in their possession of absolute property, newly won in 1660 with the abolition of military tenures, and reaffirmed subsequently through the outcome of the Revolution in 1688 (and the Battle of Wincanton). Certainly Adam Smith, like John Locke before him, saw a necessary and inextricable connection between the rights of property and the need for civil government. He wrote:

The acquisition of valuable and extensive property, therefore, necessarily requires the establishment of civil government. [But] Civil government, so far as it is instituted for the security of property, is in reality instituted for the defence of the rich against the poor, or of those who have some property against those who have none at all.[14]

HUMAN NATURE

The century of economic change and political conflict, which gave birth to this ministerial bureaucracy and a warlike state as an economic power, also brought about a philosophical and political debate about the nature of society and government. The problem facing Englishmen, who had twice abolished absolute monarchy and, as it were, twice shown in practice that they rejected arguments for absolutist government, whether they derived from notions about the divine right of kings or the Hobbesian state of nature, was how to contain the self-regarding and potentially socially disruptive forces of a society recognizably based on private property. Their political or philosophic problem, like Clarke's religious one, was how to justify a framework of legitimate authority in such a society in ways which would place emphasis on the notion of a moral commonwealth, and prevent the disintegration of society. It was clear that absolute

[14] Adam Smith, *The Wealth of Nations*, Vol. II, pp. 199 and 203. When I gave this lecture, on 8 March 1976, I added a parenthesis at this point, I said:

There was and is no end to the powers sought by government in relation to wage contracts. Indeed, almost at this very minute the Government of New South Wales is seeking to remove even the residual protection granted to employees of this university by the wage contract and, against the wishes of the Council of the University, wishes to grant statutory powers to Council to do what it chooses to and with its employees.

Subsequently, as a result of strong opposition from all the New South Wales universities and their staff associations, the offending clause was dropped. I record this in a footnote for future historians to note.

monarchy was unacceptable. There remained the Lockeian notion of conditional authority granted by men of property which appeared to have been achieved in the Glorious Revolution of 1688, but, as we have seen, that, too, was rejected. Almost before the ink on the Bill of Rights was dry the contract was dishonoured. The political alternatives were further confused by the fact that the nature of governments was seen to be determined by the nature of the men who were to live under them, and arguments about government and society were also arguments about the nature of human nature.

THE THIRD EARL OF SHAFTESBURY AND BENEVOLENCE

It was in this context that Anthony Ashley Cooper, Third Earl of Shaftesbury, published a series of essays subsequently republished in 1711 under the title of *Characteristicks of Men, Manners, Opinions, Times*, a work which went through nine editions by 1749 and had great influence on the thought of the first half of the eighteenth century. The Professor of Moral Philosophy at Glasgow, Hutcheson, who was Adam Smith's predecessor and teacher, was greatly influenced by him, and Mandeville, the author of *The Fable of the Bees* and of the other half of my title in this chapter, made Shaftesbury his prime target. Shaftesbury wrote:

A PUBLICK Spirit can come only from a social Feeling or *Sense of Partnership* with human kind. Now there are none so far from being *Partners* in this *Sense,* or Sharers in this *common Affection*, as they who scarcely know *an Equal,* nor consider themselves as subject to any Law of *Fellowship* or *Community.* And thus Morality and good Government go together. There is no real Love of Virtue, without the knowledge of *Publick Good.* And where absolute Power is, there is no PUBLICK.[15]

Shaftesbury's point was that a political contract between parties with unequal power was no contract. Further, that a government could only be justified and supported if it reflected a public spirit and was based on Virtue. By Virtue he meant a love of order, harmony, proportion and beauty in society. This love of order and beauty he considered a natural phenomenon existing in that state of nature which preceded civil society. It derived from the herding or affective impulse, had its origins in God, and was perceived by reason. The novelty of his definition of Virtue was that it denied the dominant rigorist doctrine which claimed there was only

---

[15] Anthony Ashley Cooper, *Characteristicks of Men, Manners, Opinion, Times,* 4th edn (London, 1727), Vol. I, pp. 106—7.

Virtue where there was self denial. According to Shaftesbury, men were innately virtuous and innately capable of looking to the public as distinct from their own private interest. He also argued that there was no Virtue in a vicious act which unintentionally resulted in public good. Actions were only to be considered good if they arose from an intent to achieve the public good. Merit could only consist in, 'a real Antipathy or Aversion to *Injustice* or *Wrong*, and in a real Affection or Love towards *Equity* and *Right*, for its own sake, and on account of its own natural Beauty and Worth.'[16]

Shaftesbury also believed that this innate capacity to perceive and pursue Virtue was unevenly distributed throughout society, and was more likely to be found in the educated and cultivated social class to which he belonged. Nevertheless, he did believe that Virtue as he perceived it was a precious thing to be cherished and cultivated by a virtuous administration. Only if it was so cherished would

a people rais'd from Barbarity or despotick Rule, civiliz'd by Laws, and made virtuous by the long Course of a lawful and just Administration; if they chance to fall suddenly under any Misgovernment of unjust and arbitrary Power, they will on this account be the rather animated to exert a stronger Virtue, in opposition to such Violence and Corruption. And even where, by long and continu'd Arts of a prevailing Tyranny, such a People are at last totally oppres'd the scattered Seeds of Virtue will for a long time remain alive, even to a second Generation; ere the utmost force of misapply'd Rewards and Punishments can bring them to the abject and compliant State of long accustom'd Slaves.[17]

If I remind you that Shaftesbury wrote this in 1699, when the power of the bureaucratic military state was in the ascendant, producing a burgeoning monied interest seen to be battening on the wealth of men of property in the agricultural sector, you will appreciate the real political danger he saw in a political system based on the notion that private self-seeking would produce the public benefit. You may also discern the ideological nature of Shaftesbury's thought. However, since the social class for whom he spoke was under threat from within as well as without that social class, his thought also had utopian characteristics.[18] This utopian ideology, which he shared with many of his class, was firmly

---

[16] Ibid., Vol. II, p. 42.

[17] Ibid., Vol II, pp. 63—4.

[18] The concepts 'Ideology' and 'Utopia' are defined in Karl Mannheim, *Ideology and Utopia* (London, 1972), p. 36.

backward looking, rooted in the classical world. His ideal type was the cultivated man of landed property who believed that property should not be used for self-aggrandisement, but for the benefit of the community in which he was a citizen. Generally, men in the eighteenth century called Shaftesbury's Virtue 'benevolence'. (Fielding, drawing upon his experience of Ralph Allen, one of Bath's favoured sons, bestowed immortality on this ideal in the person of Squire Allworthy.) So strongly was the ideal canvassed in the first three-quarters of the century, that it is not surprising that a Professor of Moral Philosophy should have endorsed it. Adam Smith wrote:

And hence it is, that to feel much for others and little for ourselves, that to restrain our selfish, and to indulge our benevolent affections, constitutes the perfection of human nature; and can alone produce among mankind that harmony of sentiments and passions in which consists their whole grace and propriety.[19]

Paradoxically, those who embraced the Shaftesburian Virtue, either plain or in its benevolent disguise, were generally those very men who through their actions did much to destroy the Virtue they themselves desired and loved.

To find out more of this, let us, as did the ruling classes in the eighteenth century, return to Bath.

BATH, AGAIN, AND JOHN WOOD

In the early years of the eighteenth century Bath was 'a valley of pleasure, and a sink of iniquity'.[20] It was also the place where the English county first learned to forgo the wearing of high-topped riding boots when dancing, and the wearing of swords — the mark of the county's right to resist — when walking. It was to become the most beautiful of English cities. Most of eighteenth-century Bath was built in Adam Smith's lifetime, and much of it by one John Wood, born the son of a mason in 1705. As a young man, Wood worked as a surveyor in London and Yorkshire. In 1726 he entered into a contract for digging dirt in the Twerton cut on the Avon navigation near Bath, and he worked for the Duke of Chandos. Two years later, as a speculating builder without capital, he began building Queen Square as part of his 'Roman' city and according to the rules of

[19] Adam Smith, *The Theory of Moral Sentiments,* 1869 edn London p. 24.
[20] Anon, *A Step to the Bath with a Character of the Place* (London, 1700).

Vitruvius as brought to England in 1721 in Andrea Palladio's *Four Books of Architecture*. When he died in 1754, at the start of his greatest work, the King's Circus, he had planned and initiated property development with a capital value of £200,000 and was himself worth £1,200 per annum in ground rents alone. He was the very model of the new middling class of men in the eighteenth century. By dint of individual industry and application he lifted himself from obscurity to esteem and wealth in his own time and to immortality in ours. But, while Wood built for profit in one of the most buoyant sectors of the consumer market of his day — real estate — and built successfully, what he built he intended as a negation of the frivolous, vicious, self-interested values of his clientele. He built to glorify God, a God who was the divine architect of all things, in whose work, wrote Wood: 'we find nothing but perfect figures consisting of the utmost Regularity, the sweetest harmony, and the most delightful Proportion.'[21]

I have shown elsewhere that as Wood worked to assemble his contribution to Bath as a total symbol of his vision of a Roman but Christian utopia, he used an array of religious symbols consisting of circles, squares, Vitruvian figures, tabernacle windows, and the orders of columns. He used all of these harmoniously to express the idea of unity in diversity. In short he aimed to put a frame rather like a proscenium arch around the urban environment of civil society, with the purpose of enhancing man's awareness of God and of Virtue. For example, on the effect of piling the orders; Doric, Ionic, and Corinthian, one upon the other, a device he used in the King's Circus, Wood wrote: 'as the orders advance towards virginal beauty and elegance, the columns increase in their altitude, and thereby one order receives a majesty above the other, even in miniature upon paper, which words can scarcely describe!'[22] When one reads Wood on the orders of columns one can almost imagine the impossible and believe that he had not only seen Botticelli's *The Birth of Venus*, and equated Venus with the Corinthian order, but also understood Botticelli's portrayal of divine or transcendent love. Certainly, no one who looks at Wood's Bath, knowing the language of the polemic signs incorporated in his building, can ever again look at the piled orders

---

[21] John Wood, *The Origin of Building — or, The Plagiarism of the Heathens Detected,* London and Bath, 1741, frontispiece. See also, R. S. Neale, Bath: Ideology and Utopia, 1700—1760, in R. F. Brissenden and J. C. Eade (eds), *Studies in the Eighteenth Century,* Vol. III, Canberra, 1976, pp. 37—54, and R. S. Neale, *Bath 1680—1850: A Social History* (London, 1981).

[22] John Wood, *A Dissertation Upon the Orders of Columns,* London, 1750, p. 27.

of columns and see merely pillars. He should at least see Venus or the Three Graces, and pretend he can see God.

With the co-operation of landowners and a complex system of building leases sub-leases and mortgages, Wood ensured that others carried out the work according to his intent. For, entrepreneur though he was, he was also a thoroughly Shaftesburian man. In building the King's Circus in the midst of the corruption of civil society and in its interest, he worked to glorify God by writing the *Whole Duty of Man* in stone.

John Wood's son, who completed the King's Circus for his father, financed his building with the help of loans from local Quakers who had close ties with the West Indian sugar and slave trades. In this manner, Wood's ideological and 'virtuous' utopia, like capital in Marx, came into the world, 'soiled with mire from top to toe and oozing blood from every pore'.

Wood's life-story and his life's work illustrate the paradox and problem of Adam Smith's England. For, while it is true that Virtue and benevolence were everywhere in Adam Smith's world, so was property and power, civil conflict and war, luxury and self-interest. The spokesman for self-interest was Bernard Mandeville. Mandeville, born in Rotterdam in 1670 was a man of parts, specialist in 'hypochondriack and hysteric passions', successful London physician, when physic was even closer to magic than it is today, and author in the style of La Fontaine. In this style he published in 1705, possibly as an election pamphlet defending Marlborough's policies, a piece of doggerel called *The Grumbling Hive; or Knaves Turn'd Honest.* This was subsequently included in *The Fable of the Bees: or Private Vices Publick Benefits.* It was not until he incorporated an essay *A Search into the Nature of Society* in the 1723 edition that his work attracted much attention. When it did, it went through a total of nine editions by 1772.

In the essay on the nature of society, Mandeville attacked Shaftesbury's notion of Virtue, and argued that all ostensible public acts sprang in fact from motives of self-interest. There were no benevolent or altruistic actions. Furthermore, he said, a nation could not be wealthy and powerful and also virtuous. It could be either, but not both. He wrote,

> Bare Vertue can't make Nations live
> In Splendour; they, that would revive
> A Golden Age, must be as free
> For Acorns, as for Honesty.[23]

---

[23] Bernard Mandeville, *The Fable of the Bees: or, Private Vices, Publick Benefits,* Pelican edn (Harmondsworth, 1970), p. 76.

One modern philosopher has taken great pains to show that Mandeville did not recommend that self-interest should be the guide to action, and to prove that he was simply a man with a tragi-comic vision of the eighteenth century. However, in his attack on Shaftesbury, Mandeville *did* set out to prove Shaftesbury wrong, and to demonstrate that natural Virtue was not and could not be the basis and bond of a wealthy society like England. Indeed, Mandeville argued that while man was not naturally virtuous, he *was* naturally slothful and pleasure seeking, fearful and peace loving. Consequently he believed that man was self-seeking but in a fearful sort of way, and only moved to vigorous action by the deliberate exploitation of one or more of his selfish or self-liking passions or vices. Thus, he argued, the virtue of the soldierly man of honour was the product of the vices of pride and of flattery, and, therefore, that it was not Virtue. In economic affairs, he argued that it was a mixture of conspicuous consumption, prodigality, pride, emulation, flattery, and deception, all vices subsumed and castigated by eighteenth-century moralists under the notion of 'luxury', which was the creator of wealth, and not any plan or intent of a virtuous administration. For those who have a fancy for the protestant ethic part of the myth of *laissez-faire*, I give you Mandeville's comment as an early critical version of it. The extract captures the flavour of his style and emphasizes his view about the importance of consumption, or the vice of luxury:

I protest against Popery as much as ever Luther or Calvin did, or Queen Elizabeth herself, but I believe from my heart, that the Reformation has scarce been more instrumental in rendering the kingdoms and states that have embraced it, flourishing beyond other nations than the silly and capricious invention of hoop'd and quilted petticoats.[24]

For pleasure (and good measure) here is Mandeville's satirical comment about the one certain road to Virtue which was then, as it is today, the stock-in-trade of conservative moralists:

Would you banish Fraud and Luxury, prevent Profaneness and Irreligion, and make the generality of the People Charitable, Good and Virtuous, break down the Printing Presses, melt the Founds and burn all the books in the Island, except those at the Universities, where they remain unmolested, and suffer no Volume in private hands but a Bible.[25]

---

[24] Ibid., p. 358. The most recent discussion of Mandeville is in, H. Monro, *The Ambivalence of Bernard Mandeville* (Oxford, 1975).

[25] Ibid., p. 241.

As we shall see, Adam Smith also held universities in low esteem.

Because Mandeville wrote in a vein which appeared to recommend vice as the guide to action, his contemporaries, including Berkeley, Hutcheson, the Middlesex Grand Jury, and the authorities in France, who ordered his writings to be burned by the common hangman, took him seriously. So must the historian. For just as *Virtue* represented Shaftesbury's attempt to define the social nexus, so, too, did *Private Vices, Publick Benefits* represent Mandeville's.

But, Mandeville's utopia was not to be the product of unrestrained vices competing with each other for their share in producing the public benefit, because all people and all vices were not equal. And it was to be the function of Adam Smith's 'sovereign' to determine which ones should be allowed free rein. He wrote:

> So Vice is beneficial found,
> When it's by Justice lopt, and bound.[26]

Mandeville's first 'lopping and binding' involved dividing up the communal land and the creation of private property rights. He wrote: 'Let Property be inviolably secured, and Priveledges equal to all Men: Suffer nobody to act but what is lawful, and everybody to think what he pleases.'[27] Accordingly theftbote was to be declared illegal. Theftbote was the market economy taken to its competitive limits. It was organized stealing of important although often valueless articles, such as a tradesman's shopbook, made with the purpose of resale to their owners through a network of receivers. Theftbote was to be made a capital crime. Further, because of the public expense involved in maintaining felons convicted for other crimes against property, and before Australia was invented, Mandeville recommended that they be used to redeem European slaves held on the Barbary coast. Such an exchange would save those who, 'were labouring for the safety, the wealth, and glory of their country'. More importantly it would, 'rid without slaughter, or probability of return, the country of the vermin of society, that perpetually nibbling at our property, destroy the comforts of secure and undisturbed possession'.[28] Mandeville wrote this after the Black Act of 1723, but made no attempt to estimate the cost to the sovereign of such an operation!

---

[26] Ibid., p. 76.

[27] Ibid., p. 201.

[28] Bernard Mandeville, *An Inquiry into the Causes of the Frequent Executions at Tyburn* (London, 1725), p. 52.

In like manner and for the good of mankind he argued for the abolition of private and the introduction of public prostitution. Public stews, he wrote: 'will regulate this affair so precisely, and with such critical exactness, that one year with another, we shall not have one woman employed in the Public Service more than is absolutely necessary, nor one less than is fully sufficient.'[29] Again he made no attempt to estimate the expense to the sovereign of such a planned operation.

In a third area of social policy, education, Mandeville *was* opposed to public intervention, even to private charitable intervention. He argued that Shaftesburian benevolent men who supported the charity school movement were misguided. Any successes they might achieve in education would cause workers to become insolent and lazy. This would lead to demands for higher wages and undermine the economic basis of civil society. Therefore, the benevolent would be better advised to look to their own self-interests and oppose charity schools.[30]

Because Mandeville wrote in this way about the capital/labour relationship, that is, without hypocrisy, Marx described him as, 'an honest and clear sighted man'[31] by which he meant an honest and clear-sighted bourgeois. But Mandeville has to be seen as a bourgeois apologist for a consuming and trading view of the world, a mercantilist view, rather than as an advocate for a productive, industrial *laissez-faire* one. The exemplar he recommended to those virtuous Englishmen who longed for a wealthy nation was Holland, and his secret ingredient for success was consumption, or that which the eighteenth century knew as luxury and, therefore, as vice. Mandeville did not recommend capital accumulation, improved technology, increased labour productivity in agriculture, nor hard work as necessary for the production of the wealth of a nation. That is, he did not recommend any of the productive virtues admired by nineteenth century men (and women), and allegedly liberated by *laissez-faire,* as necessary (and almost sufficient) for the creation of our modern world. Moreover, he had no doubts about the central role of the state in setting the conditions for, and the exploitation of, those vices which he approved as conducive to the public benefit. They were those which, properly lopped and bound, worked in the interests of the existing owners of property.

Hence, just as Shaftesbury's ideology was utopian, Mandeville's utopia,

[29] Bernard Mandeville, *A Modest Defence of Public Stews: or An Essay upon Whoring* (London, 1724), p. 63.

[30] Bernard Mandeville, *An Essay on Charity and Charity Schools,* included in *The Fable of the Bees.*

[31] Karl Marx, *Capital,* Vol ii, p. 678.

like Wood's, was ideological. This is not surprising. These eighteenth-century men were grappling with the same problem, the problem of the place and role of men and their government under capitalism. And, they were doing so with a dearth of concepts. Men did not know what was upon them and did not talk or write with the aid of concepts such as capitalism, stratum, class, class-consciousness, and class conflict. Like Shaftesbury they thought in terms of men, manners, opinions, characteristics and times. But they *were* aware of the novelty of what they called civil society, and of the passion of self-interest, divisions within society and social disruption that went with it. While they never came to grips with these life problems (the constantly recurring 'moment' of danger), they did seek to contain the socially divisive consequences of private property and the passion of self-interest within a framework of law, institutions, and manners to restrict social and political change, with their associated dangers, to the barest minimum. Consequently their utopias, like those of our own time, and like Bath, were all rooted in the past. There can be little doubt that Mandeville, for all his apparently vicious and anarchic views, was as concerned to determine the shape of civil society as was Shaftesbury.

THE EXPENSES OF THE SOVEREIGN

And so it was with Adam Smith. His interest in setting out conditions for increasing the wealth of nations was political. Writing of the benefits of commerce and manufactures, he argued that they

gradually introduced order and good government, and with them, the liberty and security of individuals, among the inhabitants of the country, who had before lived almost in a continual state of war with their neighbours and of servile dependency upon their superiors. *This, though it has been the least observed, is by far the most important of all their effects.* Mr Hume is the only writer who, so far as I know, has hitherto taken notice of it.[32]

In this respect, at least, the myth is right. Adam Smith did hold that liberty was the product of increasing wealth. Yet 'liberty' in the eighteenth century was not 'democracy' or 'freedom' as we in the twentieth century might like to think of it. Furthermore, Adam Smith was not consistent. He *also* argued that wealth itself was the product of power, power over labour arising from the power of some to appropriate the product of the labour of the rest. Consequently, on many occasions, he argued that the

---

[32] Adam Smith, *The Wealth of Nations*, Vol. I, p. 363 (my italics).

political and legal institutions a country possessed, which alone could embody this power, were reasons for economic failure as well as keys to the piling up of wealth. This was true of China, India, the Ancient World, Spain, Portugal, and North America. In the case of England, the best of all cases, he traced the wealth of the nation to its source in its legal system, which gave full protection to private property and, therefore, to the Revolution of 1688. And to that we have already referred. The sequence he identified was: servile dependency and war followed by revolution, the confirmation of absolute property in the Lockeian sense and, finally, the growth of manufactures. In fact, Smith's views about the conditions for and influences on the wealth of nations, particularly in relation to the role of the state in fixing and protecting property rights, is not fundamentally opposed to the picture of the course of events outlined under the section on the Battle of Wincanton. It is one little reckoned with in conventional accounts of the economic development of England. In the next chapter I will show that a property law, which embodied and projected a concept of property as something increasingly flexible and functional, had developed in England by the second half of the seventeenth century. I will argue that this law provided the legal and a good deal of the institutional framework which alone made possible the development of the industrial capitalist mode of production in England.[33] I simply note here my agreement with Adam Smith that the events of 1688 *were* vital to early stages in that development.

PROPERTY RIGHTS, COSTS AND BENEFITS

Unfortunately the economic costs to the sovereign of instituting and maintaining these property rights has never been calculated. Nevertheless, given that the wars arising out of the revolution are part of that cost, Gregory King does provide some evidence that the real economic cost was substantial. In 1695 he calculated that between 1688 and 1695 it had cost £13 million, and was likely to cost a further £10.5 million between 1695 and 1698. He also showed that the only country to gain out of the wars was Holland. King calculated that in 1695 England's national income had declined by 11s per head, compared with a rise in Holland of 7s 7d per head and a decline in France of 8s 10d.[34] I also remind you of Adam Smith's own view that the full cost of war and revolution, over a one

---

[33] Eugene Kamenka and R. S. Neale (eds), *Feudalism, Capitalism and Beyond* (Canberra and London, 1975), pp. 95—102.
[34] Gregory King, *National and Political Observations.*

hundred year period, measured in terms of the National Debt, was of the order of £200 million. If, however, one chooses to disregard these estimates, some account should be taken of the 10,000 lawyers, some 0.2 per cent of the population who, according to Gregory King, received annually nearly 4 per cent of the national income at an absolute cost of £1.5 million, exclusive of the costs of law-courts, gaols, army and militia.[35]

The fact is the expenses of the sovereign in maintaining property rights and in protecting, as the Bristol merchants put it 'Liberty and Merchandise at Home and Abroad'[36] were out of all proportion to the income generated, at least in the short term. Nevertheless, property *was* the key to the wealth of the nation, and Englishmen believed it to be inextricably connected with the protestant succession. They paid for it at 4s in the pound.

Property was the key to wealth since it gave to some the right to appropriate the product of the labour of others. And Adam Smith knew this to be so. Consequently, and in spite of his protestations to the contrary, he knew that civil society was a divided society. He also knew that 'to indulge our benevolent affections constitutes the perfection of human nature.' What he was not sure about was his belief that private interest, if not private vices, would override divisions in society to generate the public benefit. So it was that he came up against the issue which John Trenchard had identified in 1698 when he wrote 'It is certain that every man will act for his own interest; and all wise Governments are founded upon that Principle: so that the whole mystery is only to make the interest of the Governors and the Governed the same.'[37]

In resolving this mystery (his attempt to push away the 'moment' of danger) Adam Smith indulged his benevolent affections. Like all the British living in the age of Church and King, Adam Smith summoned tradition to his side. To do what the passion of self-interest could not be relied upon to do by itself he called for help from God, puritan morality, fear of the last judgement, and the sovereign. In so doing he proposed such a profound interference with 'liberty' as we would understand it, that it is not surprising that, like the 'Battle' of Wincanton, it is a part of the story which remains untold. The telling of it will show how far the powers if not the expenses of the sovereign were to be used by Adam Smith to guarantee the Wealth of Nations. It has to do with education. Adam Smith argued:

[35] Gregory King, in Charles Davenant, *Essays upon the Probable Methods of Making People Gainers in the Ballance of Trade* (London, 1699).

[36] John Wood, *A Description of the Exchange of Bristol* (Bath, 1740), p. 14,

[37] John Trenchard, *Short History of Standing Armies* (London, 1698), preface.

There are no public institutions for the education of women, and there is accordingly nothing useless, absurd, or fantastical in the common course of their education — Every part of their education tends evidently to some useful purpose; either to improve the natural attractions of their person, or to form their mind to reserve, to modesty, to chastity, and to economy; to render them both likely to become the mistresses of a family, and to behave properly when they have become such — It seldom happens that a man, in any part of his life, derives any conveniency or advantage from some of the most laborious and troublesome parts of his education.[38]

Surprisingly Adam Smith did not conclude from this observation that public education should cease. He simply thought it should be different and differently provided. Indeed, he favoured mass education to reduce the intellectually and socially harmful effects of the division of labour, and to provide the basis for social harmony. This was to be achieved by imposing upon:

almost the whole body of the people the necessity of acquiring those most essential parts of education, by obliging every man to undergo an examination or probation in them before he can obtain the freedom in any corporation, or be allowed to set up any trade either in a village or town corporate.[39]

He also turned to education to achieve a much greater measure of social control over the already educated. His purpose was to combat the rigorist and unsocial morals of the enthusiastic sects which had sprung up like so many weeds during the seventeenth and eighteenth centuries and seemed like to turn into Liberty Trees. Adam Smith does not name these enthusiastic sects, but the historian can have little difficulty in identifying them as: Quakers, Baptists, Moravians, the Baptist New Connection, Methodists, Sandemanians, the Countess of Huntingdon's Persuasion, even Unitarians and deists and, maybe, the French Prophets. (Adam Smith was as fearful as Samuel Clarke.) Indeed, 1776 was a good year for enthusiasm and for Liberty Trees. In that year the deist, Tom Paine, welcomed the American Revolution with words with which Adam Smith would have agreed, at least as far as they related to merely economic affairs: 'Society is in every state a blessing, but government, even in its best state is but a necessary evil; in its worst state an intolerable one. . . . Government like dress, is the badge of lost innocence; the palaces of kings are built on the ruins of the bowers of paradise'.[40]

---

[38] Adam Smith, *The Wealth of Nations,* Vol. II, p. 263.
[39] Ibid., p. 267.
[40] Tom Paine, *Commonsense,* 1776.

In the same year the Unitarian, Dr Price, who was to deliver a sermon welcoming the French Revolution, published his *Observations on Civil Liberty*, and sold 60,000 copies; Major Cartwright published the first version of what the nineteenth century came to know as the *Charter*; the Sandemanian, Thomas Spence was expelled from the Newcastle Philosophical Society for advocating equal rights to property in land; while, across on the other side of Scotland, the Professor of Humanity at Aberdeen, Willian Ogilvie, was preparing the first draft of his *Essay on The Right of Property in Land,* in which he argued that all men had a birthright in land. In an agrarian law designed to give effect to that birthright, he declared 'that every citizen aged twenty one years or upwards may, if not already in possession of land, be entitled to claim from the public a certain portion, not exceeding forty acres, to be assigned to him in perpetuity for residence and cultivation.'[41] Clearly the world which Adam Smith sought to prop up with his moral economic ideology already showed signs of coming apart in reality as well as in thought. To ensure that it would hold together in reality as well as in thought, Adam Smith proposed two further educational remedies. First, encourage, 'the frequency and gaiety of public diversions',[42] in order to undermine the moral rigorism of the sects. Second, compel all members of the middling and higher ranks of society to subject themselves to a study of science and philosophy. He wrote:

The state might render [this] almost universal among all people of middling or more than middling rank and fortune; not by giving salaries to teachers in order to make them negligent and idle, but by instituting some sort of probation, even in the higher and more difficult sciences, to be undergone by every person before he was permitted to exercise any liberal profession, or before he could be received as a candidate for any honourable office of trust or profit. If the state imposed upon this order of men the necessity of learning, it would have no occasion to give itself any trouble about providing them with proper teachers. They would soon find better teachers for themselves than any whom the state could provide for them. Science is the great antidote to the poison of enthusiasm and superstition; and where all the superior ranks of people were secured from it, the inferior ranks could not be much exposed to it.[43]

By 'enthusiasm', Adam Smith indicted the sects and their radical connections, and of these we have already spoken. In 'superstition' he

---

[41] William Ogilvie, *An Essay on the Right of Property in Land* (London, 1782), pp. 93—4.

[42] Adam Smith, *The Wealth of Nations,* Vol. II, p. 278.

[43] Ibid., pp. 277—8.

must have included Roman Catholicism. Its political corollary, Jacobitism, the fear of which dogged Walpole all his political life, was so alive and active as recently as 1758, that, according to reports, the militia at Southwold were said to have toasted James III! The point is that even though Adam Smith favoured some greater decentralization of economic decision-making, he could not tolerate equal freedom for apparently irrational ideas and beliefs. These were things to be feared. Therefore, like Mandeville, he wanted the state to 'lop and bind'. But, what the criminal law and a standing army could repress (in the last instance) might be better educated out by compulsory education in science and philosophy!

THE WISE AND VIRTUOUS MAN

Adam Smith does not go so far as to add a booklist for his proposed courses in science and philosophy, but we can guess that, had there been one, his own *Theory of Moral Sentiments* and *An Inquiry into the Nature and Causes of the Wealth of Nations* would have headed the list. And why? Because he had no doubt that the new science and the method of rational inquiry could demonstrate that reason (or the Divine Being) stood revealed in what he described, and that in consequence he *knew* what was best for other men. He wrote:

The wise and virtuous man is at all times willing that his own private interest should be sacrificed to the public interest of his own particular order of society. He is at all times willing, too, that the interest of this order of society should be sacrificed to the greater interest of the state or sovereignty, of which it is only a subordinate part. He should, therefore, be equally willing that all those inferior interests should be sacrificed to the greater interest of the universe, to the interest of that great society of all sensible and intelligent beings, of which God himself is the immediate administrator and director.[44]

Adam Smith, like Samuel Clarke, was undoubtedly a wise and virtuous man, a typically benevolent eighteenth-century man, a Shaftesburian man, more interested in 'liberty' than 'freedom', and more convinced of the importance of Church and King and of the expenses of the sovereign for the preservation of that 'liberty' than a good many of his contemporaries. For example, he viewed Mandeville's system as, 'in almost every respect erroneous',[45] but like John Wood he sought to contain civil

[44] Adam Smith, *The Theory of Moral Sentiments,* p. 209.
[45] Ibid., p. 273.

society within a rigid moral framework. The chief difference was that John Wood saw God as architect, while Adam Smith thought of him as administrator and director of that moral framework. Their works served the same ends and contain the same contradiction. The proper place to read *The Wealth of Nations* is in Queen Square and the King's Circus, sitting next to Samuel Clarke, on a Sunday morning with the sound of the Hallelujah Chorus from Handel's *Messiah* blowing in the wind from Bath Abbey!

4

'The Bourgeoisie, Historically, Has Played a Most Revolutionary Part'

The route from Queen Square and the King's Circus on a Sunday morning, around 1776, to the bourgeoisie and their alleged revolutionary role, might be thought a tortuous path from the sublime to the profane. Yet it will be worth following. Although some familiar ground will be covered, travellers' eyes will be constantly drawn to the other side of primitive accumulation, that is to notice the creation, within the agricultural sector, of a mass of 'free' wage labour, undeniably necessary, even if not sufficient for the development of the industrial capitalist mode of production. In this process, the role of the landowning class will be seen as crucial. Their role in the development of law (relations of production) favourable to the development of capitalist modes of production other than the agrarian-capitalist mode, will also be seen to be necessary (and almost sufficient). As in Bath, these conditions for creating disorder, at least as far as the ruling class were concerned, crept in by the back door, even as the Hallelujah Chorus was under way. On the other hand, while the traveller will glimpse a variety of entrepreneurs at work in the economy of the second half of the eighteenth century; traders, merchants, independent artisans and small producers, it will be difficult to spot the allegedly ubiquitous 'middle class', and virtually impossible to discover a bourgeois, in Marx's sense, worth talking to or about in the whole journey. Consequently, it will not be possible to transfer the burden of changes in British society, economy and polite culture from the Brydges and Clarkes to the mulish backs of a bourgeoisie, in order to be forced into a straight line all the way to Camden Town. All that might be required is an increase in the number of mules.

*　　　*　　　*

My text for this chapter is the sentence from the *Communist Manifesto*:

Marriage A-la-Mode (William Hogarth, 1745)

'The bourgeoisie, historically, has played a most revolutionary part',[1] and my reason for attempting to approach our subject in this indirect way is to try to avoid the dangers of reification inherent in all discussions of feudalism, traditional society, capitalism, industrialism, and so on, and to remind us, as Marx frequently did his contemporaries, that capital and capitalism necessarily imply the existence of a human capitalist — a bourgeois. But, when I came to put my thoughts in order, there seemed to be as much difficulty with the term bourgeoisie as with the concept capitalism. Works of reference were no help. The 1971 edition of the *Encyclopaedia of the Social Sciences* is very abrupt. Under bourgeoisie, it says: 'In Great Britain and the US bourgeoisie had nearly disappeared from the vocabulary of political writers and politicians by the mid twentieth century.' This is in contrast to the *Encyclopaedia Britannica* of 60 years earlier, which was confident that the bourgeoisie was 'the trading middle class of any country'. It is also in contrast to the usage of historians. There can be very few commentators on modern English history who do not use the term bourgeoisie, even if only to point out that before the mid-nineteenth century England never had one, and that there is no English word to describe the concept. Others use it implicitly when they endorse or oppose the validity of the notion of the embourgeoisement of the working class. However, most historians, even Marxist ones, use the term as a synonym for middle class or, as I have already done, for a class of capitalists. For example Book 2 of Morazé's *The Triumph of the Middle Classes* (original title *Les Bourgeois Conquérants*) is called *The Bourgeois Revolution 1780–1840*, and it has a sub-section on England called 'The Middle Classes Take Over'. E. J. Hobsbawm, too, moves easily between several terms to express this single concept. According to these and other historians the 'bourgeoisie' was *the* dynamic group leading the development of the modern world. Further, when bourgeois is used as an adjective as in 'bourgeois ideology' we tend to nod sagely as if we all understand and agree on what this ideology is, and that what it is can be, perhaps, must be, exclusively attributed and attached to the bourgeoisie.

Although we might press historians to choose their words with care and to formulate, with greater verbal precision, any explanatory apparatus they might use, we are unlikely to meet with much success, at least in the short term. So, in order to get closer to the concept beneath the words, I would like to highlight what the Marx of the *Communist Manifesto* had to say in elaboration of the text with which I started. Marx recognized that the bourgeoisie he eulogized was 'itself the product of a long course of development, of a series of revolutions in the modes of production and of

---

[1] K. Marx and F. Engels, *Selected Works*, 3 vols (Moscow, 1969), Vol. i, p. 111.

exchange'[2] and that it had taken a variety of forms in the process of its evolution until 'the place of manufacture was taken by the giant, Modern Industry, the place of the industrial middle class, *by industrial millionaires, the leaders of whole industrial armies, the modern bourgeois.*'[3] It seems that what Marx meant by bourgeois was the modern bourgeois about 1850, the big (millionaire) industrial bourgeois and, according to *Capital*, a bourgeois for whom 'the increasing appropriation of abstract wealth is the sole motive of his operation.'[4] This was the revolutionary bourgeoisie which in less than 100 years, from about 1750, 'has created more massive and more colossal productive forces than have all preceding generations together'.[5] Yet, as Marx agrees, this bourgeoisie was itself a result as well as a cause of this expansion. The paradox is only partially resolved by praxis, the big bourgeoisie was not its own product. In Marx's own model, big bourgeois came from little ones, but little ones grew from serfs who created towns anew with the break-up of feudalism consequent on the growth of markets and world trade; that is, they were new men outside the agricultural sector.

In this *Communist Manifesto* and *German Ideology* model of Marxist history, it appears that men can only make or transform themselves outside the rural sector and in response to exogenous forces, in this case the extrusion of serfs and, in particular, the growth of international trade following the discovery of the Americas and the rounding of the Cape. At the heart of this model lies the notion that the pre-industrial agricultural societies of Western Europe, whatever one chooses to call them, could not change themselves without the emergence of a sector and a class outside the agricultural one. As Sweezy said in a review of Dobb's alternative Marxist model: 'Dobb has not succeeded in shaking that part of the commonly accepted theory which holds that the root cause of the decline of feudalism was the growth of trade.'[6]

Behind *this* notion of the rigidity of agricultural societies there lies the nineteenth-century bourgeois antagonism to conservative agriculturalists and powerful landowning aristocracies. Marx frequently commented on

---

[2] Ibid., p. 110.

[3] Ibid., p. 110. My italics. For discussion of the origin of the term see Shirley Gruner, 'The Revolution of July 1830 and the Expression "Bourgeoisie" ', *Historical Journal,* 11 (3), 1968. For the symbolism in Marx's usage see Robert Tucker, *Philosophy and Myth in Karl Marx* (Cambridge, 1961).

[4] *Capital,* Everyman edn, p. 138.

[5] K. Marx and F. Engels, *Selected Works,* Vol. 1, p. 113.

[6] P. M. Sweezy, M. Dobb et al., *The Transition from Feudalism to Capitalism* (New York, 1963), p. 7.

the antagonism between town and country and considered it a necessary condition for the separation of capital from landed property, that is, as 'the beginning of property having its basis only in labour and exchange'[7] without which capitalism could not be said to exist. In the *Grundrisse*, for example, he comments that 'it was a great step forward when the industrial or commercial system came to see the source of wealth not in the object but in the activity of persons, viz. in commercial and industrial labour.' Marx also praised the physiocratic system as a further step forward since it considered a certain form of labour, namely agricultural labour, as the source of wealth, not in the disguise of money, but as 'product in general'. Nevertheless, according to Marx, this physiocratic view was still a limited one. The 'product in general' was still only a natural product and land was regarded as the source of production *par excellence*. Marx then went on to say:

It was a tremendous advance on the part of Adam Smith to throw aside all the limitations which mark wealth-producing activity and to define it as labour in general, neither industrial nor commercial nor agricultural, or one as much as the other. Along with the universal character of wealth-creating activity we now have the universal character of the object defined as wealth, viz. product in general, or labour in general, but as past, objectified labour.

That is, Capital.

Marx went on to say: '*How difficult and how great was the transition is evident from the way Adam Smith himself falls back from time to time into the physiocratic system*'.[8] As far as I know, Marx, unlike Ricardo, never committed this physiocratic error and always attacked those bourgeois theorists who were inclined to slip back into physiocratic-type arguments. Consequently he was critical of the pessimism of Malthus as well as the optimism of the systematic colonizers. For Marx, the key to productivity and the forward movement of the economy was always capital and capital accumulation, and all capital was objectified labour. It is true that Marx, in discussing primitive accumulation in *Capital*, regarded the early development of capitalist agriculture in Britain as important. It was a major factor creating wage labour and supplying labour to the developing manufacturing sector. Further, it provided a market for manufactured goods and was a source of primary funds necessary to set labour to work in manufacturing. Nevertheless, according to Marx, there

[7] K. Marx and F. Engels, *The German Ideology* (Moscow, 1968), p. 66.

[8] All extracts are from David McLellan, *Marx's Grundisse* (London, 1971), 87—8. My italics.

was a continuing tendency for peasant agriculture to re-establish itself such that capitalist agriculture could not develop and solidify into a capitalist mode of production without the prior development of industrial capitalism, 'Not until large-scale industry, based on machinery, comes, does there arise a permanent foundation for capitalist agriculture.'[9] Thus, the principal human agents or mediators remained the capitalists — the big industrial bourgeois of the *Communist Manifesto.*

It seems that one of the components of Marx's concept of capitalism, and of the revolutionary role he attributed to the bourgeoisie, was his critique of the ideas of the physiocrats and the class for whom they spoke. Another was a conviction, shared with the eighteenth-century historians of civil or bourgeois society, that the bourgeoisie was necessarily progressive. A corollary of this was that although he considered the economic and social structure of western Europe to constitute a progressive mode of production, he was also caught up in the belief that the agricultural 'feudal' societies of that part of the world could not have changed without the development of the bourgeoisie — men, perhaps, of his own kind. Certainly the greater their achievement, the greater would be the final achievement of the proletariat; they would be giant-killers indeed, fully entitled to hail the emancipation of man, 'by the crowing of the Gallic cock'. Marx, deriving his 'model' from his Prussian experience in the second quarter of the nineteenth century, was led to formulate a late-comers growth model. In it, massive capital accumulation was regarded as central to the problem of economic and social change as well as the key to the proletarian emancipation of society. Such massive capital accumulation would have appeared impossible to achieve within the agricultural sectors of early nineteenth-century Prussia. Hence the need for a new sector and new men. Marx then applied this 'model' in an attempt to explain the first successful case of industrialization, and the actual experience of England.

I think it true to say that, since then, similar notions have for long been implicit and generally explicit in Western bourgeois thought. For example, they can be found in one form or another in the work of thinkers as

---

[9] *Capital*, Everyman edn Vol. II, p. 830. However in *The Grundrisse*, Pelican Marx Library, 1973, pp. 252—3. Marx wrote:

> It is, therefore, precisely in the development of landed property that the gradual victory and formation of capital can be studied. . . . The History of landed property, which would demonstrate the gradual transformation of the feudal landlord into the landowner, of the hereditary, semi-tributary and often unfree tenant for life into the modern farmer, and of the resident serfs, bondsmen and villeins who belonged to the property into agricultural day-labourers, would indeed be the history of the formation of modern capital.

diverse in time and place as Weber and Hirschman, and they are all certainly implicit if not explicit in the work of many modern economic historians. Thus, W. W. Rostow in his anti-communist-manifesto growth model[10] defines traditional society, roughly the equivalent of Marx's feudalism, as incapable of change, and postulates the need for exogenous shocks to terminate each of its first two stages: 'traditional society' and 'pre-conditions for take-off'. He also emphasizes the crucial importance of a sharp upward shift in investment preceded or accompanied by the emergence of a new entrepreneurial and political elite. In this connection the most recent survey of the role of capital in the industrial revolution, that by Crouzet,[11] takes to task those economic historians who, in the recent past, have argued that capital and enterprise were derived from all sectors and sections of English society and that entrepreneurs were not a class (that is bourgeois) but a type. Although Crouzet recognizes that the capital requirements in England during the period of industrialization were relatively slight, he argues that the evidence does show that there was an increase in accumulation and that the main providers of capital for productive, that is factory, investment were first, the industrialists themselves, and, second, those engaged in commerce. On the other hand, he considers the part played in industrialization by landed capital and landowners to have been 'very small'. The point is that recent work in economic history appears to give some support to the notion that industrialization was mainly the work of newcomers, whether one calls them bourgeois or not. However, unless we are prepared to equate these small industrial and commercial investors, adding perhaps 1—2 per cent of national income to investment in the industrial sector from the 1780s, with the Marxist bourgeoisie, the question of the revolutionary role of the bourgeoisie during the crucial period of industrialization in the eighteenth and early nineteenth century must remain an open and two-part one.

The first question is whether a bourgeoisie as envisaged by Marx had an objective existence as a class in itself. The second is, did it exist as a class for itself? As a class for itself it certainly did not exist. English industrial capitalists or entrepreneurs (we must call them something) were either too busy making their economic fortunes, or spending them to gain entrée to the landowning and aristocratic class, to be conscious of themselves as a class in opposition to their rulers. As a class in itself it is also unlikely that it existed. It is true that there was a variety of small capitalists in the trading, manufacturing and industrial sectors in the economy, in civil

[10] W. W. Rostow, *The Stages of Economic Growth* (Cambridge, 1960).
[11] François Crouzet, *Capital Formation in the Industrial Revolution* (London, 1972).

society, but as yet they were only an embryonic bourgeoisie — they were certainly not the big industrial millionaires identified by Marx. On the other hand really great wealth, and the power which went with it, was still landed wealth supplemented by wealth derived from government office and financial speculation for capital gains rather than for productive purposes. For example, the wealthiest man in mid-eighteenth-century England was the First Earl of Bath. He is reputed to have left a fortune of £1.6 million in 1764, and, in 1737, opposed a reduction in the interest on the national debt because his wife's very considerable fortune was invested in government stock. Then there was the Duke of Chandos. Between 1705 and 1713 the Duke made £600,000 out of the office of paymaster at a time when only four of London's aldermen, after a lifetime of effort, possessed wealth estimated at over a quarter of a million pounds.[12] By the 1740s he was a millionaire.

According to Harold Perkin, a recent commentator on the modernization of England, it was landed wealth and landowner consumption as well as aristocratic land-based power which provided the key to the modernization of Britain in the eighteenth and early nineteenth centuries, rather than any activity by a bourgeoisie. Moreover, according to J. H. Plumb, this landed aristocracy increased its grip on power during the eighteenth century, while according to Perkin and myself, there was little or no pressure from the big bourgeoisie to challenge that power. In my view, the politically revolutionary force in the early nineteenth century was neither a Marxist bourgeoisie nor a proletariat, but a middling class. Perhaps I might emphasize that there seems to be little doubt that the major component in the radical movements of the eighteenth and early nineteenth centuries was a sense of loss of liberties and political rights; consequently these movements were pervaded by a strongly anti-aristocratic rather than anti-bourgeois bias. The fact that at the end of the seventeenth century 4.7 per cent of the population exercised a franchise, compared with only 4.2 per cent after the 1832 Reform Bill, shows that there were real rather than imagined grounds for radical opposition to the increasing power of the aristocracy throughout the eighteenth century. Guttsman has also demonstrated beyond all doubt that the landowning aristocracy retained a virtual monopoly of political power throughout

[12] Richard Grassby, 'The Personal Wealth of the Business Community in Seventeenth-Century England', *Economic History Review*, Second Series, 23 (2), Aug. 1970. See also W. D. Rubinstein, 'The Victorian Middle Classes: Wealth, Occupation, and Geography', *Economic History Review*, Second Series, Vol. XXX, No. 4, Nov. 1977, pp. 602—23, and Men of Property: *The Very Wealthy in Britain Since The Industrial Revolution* (London, 1981), p. 261.

most of the nineteenth century in England, and many historians find no difficulty in accepting the fact that the Anti-Corn Law League was more symptomatic of the failure of the bourgeois challenge to aristocratic power than of a bourgeois political maturity.[13] So much then for the negative aspect of my argument. But who should replace the bourgeoisie?

Earlier in this paper I referred to Dobb's alternative Marxist model and I would like now to say a little more about it as a preliminary to putting forward an explanation of eighteenth-century economic change which relegates the embryonic bourgeoisie to a minor role in relation to the more important part played by landowners, the agricultural sector and the aristocracy. First of all consider what Dobb had to say:

Regarding the 'conservative and change resisting character of Western European feudalism', which needed some external force to dislodge it, and which I am accused of neglecting, I remain rather sceptical. True, of course, that, by contrast with a capitalist economy, feudal society was extremely stable and inert. But this is not to say that feudalism has no tendency within it to change. To say so would be to make it an exception to the general Marxist law of development that economic society is moved by its own internal contradictions. Actually, the feudal period witnessed considerable changes in technique; and the later centuries of feudalism showed marked differences from those of early feudalism. Sweezy qualifies his statement by saying that the feudal system is not necessarily static. All he claims is that such movement as occurs 'has no tendency to transform it'. But despite this qualification, the implication remains that under feudalism class struggle can play no revolutionary role. It occurs to me that there may be a confusion at the root of this denial of revolutionary and transforming tendencies. *No one is suggesting that class struggle of peasants against lords gives rise, in any simple and direct way, to capitalism. What this does is to modify the dependence of the petty mode of production upon the feudal overlordship and eventually to shake loose the small producer from feudal exploitation. It is then from the petty mode of production (in a degree to which it secures independence of action,*

---

[13] Harold Perkin, *The Origins of Modern English Society, 1780—1880* (London, 1969); J. H. Plumb, 'The Growth of the Electorate in England from 1600—1715', *Past and Present*, 45 Nov. 1969; R. S. Neale, *Class and Ideology in the Nineteenth Century* (London, 1972); W. L. Guttsman, *The British Political Elite,* (London, 1963); Carl B. Cone, *The English Jacobins,* (London, 1968). See also the work of D. C. Moore, 'Concession or Cure: The Sociological Premises of the First Reform Act', *Historical Journal,* 9 (1), 1966; Social Structure, Political Structure and Public Opinion in Mid-Victorian England; in R. Robson (ed.), *Ideas and Institutions of Victorian Britain* (London, 1967); and 'The First Reform Act: A Discussion', *Victorian Studies,* 14 (3), 1971.

D

*and social differentiation in turn develops within it) that capitalism is born.
This is a fundamental point to which we shall return.*[14]

The essence of Dobb's view, as it is of the Marxist approach to history, is
that economic society is moved by its own internal contradictions,
consequently exogenous factors and a prior creation of a new elite
(bourgeoisie) were not necessary for the emergence of capitalism.

What Dobb argues, and what a good deal of recent research shows, is
that because of various peculiarities in English agriculture and society
capitalism and capitalists developed within the rural sector. Certainly
recent work has shown that by the early sixteenth century English
agriculture was largely a specialized and market-orientated agriculture,
literally dominated in parts of the west country by large-scale capitalist
farming. Over the next 200 years the agricultural sector — by far the
largest sector in the economy and the source of the bulk of wealth —
experienced a series of changes mostly generated in response to
developments internal to that sector, although by this time there were
close interconnections between the urban and the rural sectors of the
economy and society. The changes I have in mind were legal,
organizational, and technological. First, in the sixteenth century there
was the legal shift from copyhold to leasehold, and the parallel and
continuing shift from long leases for life to leases for short terms of years,
both of which developments accompanied the growth of the large landed
estate. Organizationally, there was the consolidation of holdings, achieved
largely through enclosure by agreement. Technologically, the most
important development was the introduction and spread of convertible
husbandry from the 1560s to the mid-eighteenth century. It is a further
pointer to the degree to which commercial attitudes and the production of
exchange values had penetrated English agriculture, that the practice of
convertible husbandry was not dependent on the spread of enclosure, but
was easily and readily introduced into open-field farming.[15]

This technological change was itself contingent upon the commercializa-
tion of agriculture. In conjunction with the relative stagnation of

---

[14] Sweezy, Dobb, at al., *Transition,* pp. 22—3. My italics. Since this chapter was
first written the question of the development of capitalism within the agricultural
sector has been re-opened by Robert Brenner, 'Agrarian Class Structure and Economic
Development in Pre-Industrial Europe' in *Past and Present,* No. 7, Feb. 1976,
pp. 30—75, and in subsequent extended discussion. Brenner's position is essentially
an improvement upon and extension of Dobb's. Also, J. V. Beckett, 'The Pattern of
Landownership in England and Wales, 1660—1880', *Economic History Review,*
Second Series, XXXVI, No. 1, Feb. 1984, pp. 1—22, emphasizes the continuous slow
process, in the period, whereby landownership became concentrated by 1880.

population growth at the end of the century, it was both cause and effect of a fall in agricultural prices. This price decline increased the real incomes of those outside the agricultural sector. At this point the landowner class made a significant, albeit unconscious, contribution to the maintenance of demand by keeping up farm incomes through accepting widespread defaults in rents and pumping into agriculture income earned elsewhere in the economy. As Perkin has noted, they also increased their own consumption expenditures and created conditions favourable to consumer emulation. The biggest and clearest surviving example of the consequences of these expenditures is the city of Bath. This was built in a matter of 70 years at a total capital cost of some £3 million, an amount roughly equivalent to the fixed capital invested in the cotton industry by the end of the eighteenth century. But landowners and the aristocracy did more than consume, they also invested in crucial sectors. They invested widely in mineral extraction, timber production, and iron manufacture, and they made the bulk of investment in the turnpike system, contributed about one-third of the investment in canal construction, and played a vital role in urban developments in the eighteenth century. Above all, perhaps, they subscribed to the funds and then taxed themselves to build and maintain a navy which, in a militarily competitive world, was a piece of infrastructure without which the one or two per cent of national income invested in the industrial sector could never have paid off. Further, the landowner-dominated parliament and county administrations were responsible for legislative and administrative decisions which encouraged the expansion of the small industrial sector; they strove to protect wool and effectively protected cotton, they maintained the navigation laws and allowed a great range of restrictive practices to fall into disuse. They made possible the Enclosure Acts and invested heavily in enclosure itself. In doing so they made a contribution to increasing agricultural output without which the recurring bread riots of the eighteenth century could have turned into revolution, and, in so far as they shared in the 'moral economy' of the eighteenth century, they also contributed to reducing the sharpness of the impact of market conditions.[16]

It is in this long, slowly moving history of the agricultural sector that one can see how the small producer was shaken free from direct exploitation as a serf, how nominally 'free' labour and the petty mode of production

[15] Joan Thirsk (ed.), *The Agrarian History of England and Wales*, Vol. IV, 1500–1640 (Cambridge, 1967); Eric Kerridge, *The Agricultural Revolution* (London, 1967); E. L. Jones, *Agriculture and Economic Growth in England 1650–1815* (London, 1967).

generated capitalistic modes of production within the agricultural sector itself without the need for, or example of, even the embryonic bourgeoisie, and long before the coming into existence of the big bourgeoisie of the *Communist Manifesto*. I think that what we need to understand about the actual growth of capitalism and the process of industrialization, in England in particular, is that the English landowner and capitalist farmer experienced a substantial dose of embourgeoisiement well before the bourgeoisie existed, and before the emergence of the concept, at least as Marx envisaged it.

What I have argued so far is that landowners and the landed aristocracy, within a commercialized agricultural sector, led the transformation of England in the eighteenth century. Since it was they who wielded political, economic, and social power it is inconceivable, in the absence of revolution, that the case could have been in any way different. I have denied that the variety of small investors and capitalists in civil society were a class or that they constituted a bourgeoisie in Marx's sense. I have described the landowning class as having experienced a degree of embourgeoisiement. In much of what I have said I am in full agreement with Harold Perkin in his *Origins of Modern English Society*. But I wish now to press the argument further; to consider the extent to which the changing needs of landowners led to significant changes in law and economic institutions; to show how this changing law was also a necessary pre-condition for the development of a capitalist society and for the industrialization of England, and a pre-condition for the clarification of notions of capital without which the concept of capitalism itself could not have emerged.

When historians make their rare comments on relationships between law, the economic transformation of England, and the growth of capitalism, they generally do so from only one point of view: that of the contribution of law to the development of economic liberalism. They discuss *Davenant* v. *Hurdis*, and *D'Arcy* v. *Allein*, to point out how the one effectively challenged the monopolist powers of corporate bodies and the other the powers of the crown. They might also consider the Statute of Monopolies, mention the Bubble Act, and look at the falling into disuse and eventual repeal of a mass of restrictive legislation. More sophisticated

---

[16] Some of the sources for these views are to be found in: Perkin, *Modern English Society;* William Albert, *The Turnpike Road System in England 1663—1840* (Cambridge, 1972); Crouzet, *Capital Formation;* G. E. Mingay, *English Landed Society in the Eighteenth Century* (London, 1963); J. T. Ward and R. G. Wilson, *Land and Industry* (London, 1971); C. W. Chalkin, 'Urban Housing Estates in the Eighteenth Century', *Urban Studies,* 5 (1), Feb. 1968.

versions, like that of Harold Perkin, will interpret Locke in order to emphasize the emergence, at the end of the seventeenth century, of a concept of absolute private property.[17] However, although property is clearly a matter for the courts, Perkin and others have not discussed concepts of property in connection with any legal decisions in regard to land or property. Yet I would expect an examination of land law and property law to reveal more about the beliefs and attitudes of society in respect to property than the writings of more well-known polemicists.

I do not wish to underestimate the importance of economic liberalism or the development of a concept of absolute private property for the emergence of capitalism. In so far as they facilitated the shaking loose of the petty producer and the property owner from collectivist restraints, they did make a contribution to the transformation of England. However, to set producers and property owners 'free' as compulsorily independent agents, and then to endow them with a concept of private property as something 'absolute, categorical and unconditional' could have produced a legal and conceptual framework for a merely fragmented society of petty producers. That is, while these developments may set producers free, they do not make it legally possible for them to do anything much with that freedom. Therefore, I would like to look at some aspects of the development of land and property law in order to show two things. First, that a property law, which embodied and projected a concept of property as something increasingly flexible and functional, rather than absolute and categorical, had developed in England by the second half of the seventeenth century, and had developed out of the changing demands of the class of landowners rather than out of the needs or because of the ideology of a bourgeoisie. Second, that it was this aristocratic/landowning property law and concept of property which provided the legal, and a good deal of the institutional framework which alone made possible the development of industrial capitalism in England. If I can make good this claim then it seems to me that one can fairly say that not only was the bourgeoisie not its own product, but that it really was the creature of the aristocracy — a sort of Balfour's Poodle in reverse!

The first thing that has to be said about land law in England after the Conquest is that it was centrally administered and relatively uncomplicated, there were no allods as on the continent, and all land was held on tenure, that is by contract.[18] Neither common law nor equity recognized absolute titles. The next thing that has to be said is that almost from the very

---

[17] Perkin, *Modern English Society,* pp. 51–3; C. B. Macpherson, *The Political Theory of Possessive Individualism* (Oxford, 1962).

beginning (after the Conquest) property was inheritable and lords sought powers to alienate freely and at will, mainly to avoid the heavy burden of feudal incidents and to found a dynasty. This led to a development in law which was peculiarly English, the use. This effectively divided property between the trustees with seisin and the beneficiary or *cestui que use*. Here already was a sophisticated breakdown of rights in property in land; the crown had some rights, the grantor and trustees others, and the *cestui que use* yet others. As a consequence, there was a continuing struggle between all interested parties, highlighted in the modern period by the Statute of Uses, 1535—6, and the problems which it produced. By not executing all uses, this statute recognized some uses but, for the most part, turned use into possession. Subsequently the Statute of Wills, 1540, reversed some of the conditions of the Statute of Uses and compounded further the problem of clarifying titles to land. The main battleground was Chancery and so hard fought was the battle that by the mid-seventeenth century, uncertainty about who held legal title was such that Lord Chief Justice Hale, after a purchase of land, is reported to have said that he would gladly pay another year's purchase in order to be sure of his title! Much of the ground for uncertainty about title was removed with the final abolition of military tenures and the abolition of the crown's prerogatives in regard to land in 1660. But, even though landowners had secured their titles against the claims of the crown, and, through their attack on customary tenures, copyholds and long-lifehold leases, against the claims of the peasantry, the use in the form of the settled estate, persisted, with the result that about half of nominal landowners had only qualified title to property. In fact the secret of the classic settlement was to turn every possessor into a life tenant. This device contributed greatly to clarifying and consolidating titles, but it also placed severe restrictions on the freedom of action of the possessor. As a result of these developments, by

---

[18] The following comments on law are based on work on several hundred leases, building leases, conveyances and mortgages in the Guildhall Archives of the City of Bath and the Somerset County Record Office, Taunton and on the work of legal historians: Sir William Holdsworth, *Historical Introduction to the Land Law*, and *A History of English Law*; A. W. B. Simpson, *An Introduction to the History of Land Law* (Oxford, 1961); D. E. C. Yale, *Lord Nottingham's Chancery Cases*, Selden Society (London, 1961); E. W. Ives, 'The Genesis of the Statute of Uses', *English Historical Review*, 82 (325), Oct. 1967; Mary Cotterell, 'Interregnum Law Reform: The Hale Commission of 1652', *English Historical Review*, 83, Oct. 1968 and private communication on the Hale Commission; B. Coward, 'Disputed Inheritances: Some Difficulties of the Nobility on the late Sixteenth and early Seventeenth Centuries', *Bulletin of the Institute of Historical Research*, 44, Nov. 1971. See also Wolfgang Friedmann, *Law in a Changing Society*, 2nd edn (London, 1972), pp. 93—101.

the last quarter of the seventeenth century, the courts recognized at least three types of rights or powers in landed property: the rights of the original devisor or grantor of an estate; the rights of the trustees appointed by him; and the rights of the beneficiary. With the growth of the mortgage and the elaboration of equity of redemption, both of which were by-products of the stability of the settled estate, the courts recognized a fourth right, that of mortgagees and their executors to a share in the income from land. As landowners developed their lands, for example, when building was carried out on leashold lands as in Bath and elsewhere, rights in land and property became even more divided; landlords retained rights to fee farm rents, but developers gained rights to ground rents, and builders to house rents, and all had powers to sell or mortgage their respective rights, but only without detriment to the property rights of the others.

The rights of beneficiaries, and the claims arising from ground rents are interesting since in neither instance was there any absolute right to property as an object, that is land, only legal titles to the money income from property. As mortgages developed, following the elaboration of rules in regard to equity of redemption by Lord Nottingham in the 1670s, and although they could only ensure rights to income and not to land, they began to take on many of the characteristics of property. As Lord Hardwicke put it in 1738:

An equity of redemption is considered as an estate in land; it will descend, may be granted, devised, entailed, and that equitable estate may be barred by a common recovery. This proves that it is not considered as a mere right, but as such an estate, whereof, in the consideration of this court, there may be a seisin for without such a seisin, a devise could not be good.[19]

Since ground rents could be mortgaged as well as sold, it is clear that the law had arrived at a very sophisticated and flexible concept of property, at least as early as 1700. My own work on building in the city of Bath in the eighteenth century leaves me in no doubt that this concept of property was part of popular culture, and I would go so far as to say that the great achievement of the developers of Bath depended upon this fact. It is also worth noting that titles to ground rents and building mortgages represented titles to exchange values (property) arising from the application of labour and/or capital (objectified labour) to land.

Thus, whatever the notions in regard to property held by economic and political theorists at the turn of the seventeenth and eighteenth centuries,

[19] Simpson, *History of Land Law,* p. 228.

society and the law recognized the divisibility of property titles and recognized legal titles to present and future income as property, thus giving legal form to the notion that property was the product of labour and capital as well as the product of land and of all three together. Other paper titles that, like mortgages, were regarded as property in the early eighteenth century were bills of exchange. While the importance of the bill of exchange for the finance of a vast range of transactions and thereby for the financing of industry is now generally recognized, the importance of the mortgage on land for similar purposes is now only being discovered. It is also worth noting that the courts permitted penalty rates on unpaid interest and made it possible to charge a little more than the legal maximum. All these developments flowed from the changing needs of landowners, and they point to the existence of a world in which credit, like the English weather, was a fact of life — credit was property.

Further, the Lockeian notion that property meant freedom to use to the extent of destroying[20] was not applicable to landed property. Titles to land were so intermixed with the titles of others that few property owners had anything approaching that kind of power. The restrictions on life tenants on settled estates have already been alluded to, but even land held in fee simple rarely gave the possessor absolute title or power. But the last word on this should be allowed to the lawyer author of *Tenants Law* who, with a wealth of experience and judgement of men, wrote:

A man that is seized in land or tenements to hold to him and his heirs forever, is said to be tenant in fee simple; and such an estate is called Feodum Simplex. And indeed fee simple is the most pure holding; that is, being unmixed or intangled in itself. But as the whitest colour will soon be tainted, so is this pure tenure most subject to be spotted and involved in troubles above any other; which the law calls incumbrances.

If a man was to deal as purchaser with a tenant in fee simple, he hath a happy bargain if he meets with a simple tenure and a simple tenant; I mean the one free from incumbrances, and the other from deceit; which many have found it a difficult thing to obtain.

I shall therefore, by way of caution, set down the several troubles and incumbrances this pure tenure, called fee simple is subject unto.

Fee simple may be incumbered with several judgements, statutes merchant, and of the staple, recognizances, mortgages, wills, pre-contracts, bargains and sales, feoffments, fines, amerciament, jointures, dowers, and many other feudal conveyances if a knave once possess it; and last of all, may be quite forfeited for treason, or felony which incurs forfeitures.

---

[20] John Locke, *Two Treatises of Government* (Cambridge, 1963), p. 203.

But fee simple being free from any of the above mentioned incumbrances, is the most free, absolute and ample estate of inheritance that any man can have; and therefore a tenant in fee simple is said to be seized in his domain as of fee.[21]

Thus, whatever the state of theory about property, the law and society worked with a fee simple tenure so spotted that the quantity of spots changed the quality of the beast. As the Duke of Portland discovered in 1767 the beast could be a very nasty one. What he had believed to be a grant of land in fee simple from the crown was, according to his political enemies, an estate tail which the crown had no powers to alienate. His estate in the Forest of Inglewood was resumed by the crown and granted to Sir James Lowther.[22]

So to the second point I wish to make. The key to most of these encumbrances, as it was also the key to the flexibility of property law, was the use or the trust, which seems to me to have been also the legal embodiment of the moral position that the liberty of the property-owner ought to be circumscribed by familial and dynastic considerations, as well as by the legitimate claims of others. The trust, according to Holdsworth, has

played a part in the development of our public law, larger and more direct than that played by contract. They [trusts] have peopled our state with groups and associations which have enabled the individual persons who have created or have composed them to accomplish much more than any single individual composing them could have accomplished.

This was also Maitland's opinion: 'If I were asked', he said, 'what is the greatest and most distinctive achievement performed by Englishmen in the field of jurisprudence I cannot think that we should have any better answer than this; namely the development from century to century of the trust idea.'[23]

As I have already argued, these trusts grew out of the dynastic ambition of landowners and out of their struggle with the crown for the right to alienate freely — a right fully achieved only in 1660. The paradox was that while each landowner sought the right to alienate for himself, he

---

[21] *Tenants Law*, 17th edn (London, 1777), p. 4.

[22] James Adair, *Observations on the Power of the Crown* (London, 1767).

[23] W. Holdsworth, *A History of English Law*, 3rd edn (London, 1945). Vol. IV, pp. 407—80 (quote p. 408); F. W. Maitland, 'Trust and Corporation', *Collected Papers* (London, 1911), Vol. III, pp. 356—403.

sought it with the purpose of denying it to his heirs, hence the great growth of the trust and the settled estate, particularly after the work of a number of eminent conveyancers like Sir Orlando Bridgman at the end of the seventeenth century. By the early eighteenth century many of these settled estates functioned like joint stock companies; through the creation of life tenancies ownership was distinguished from management and use, the claims of investors (mortgagees) were given preferences, while the claims of all beneficiaries put pressures on salaried estate managers and agents to maximize the income from the undertaking. Any policy changes had to be discussed by what was in fact a board of trustees. When the issue was complex, recourse had to be made to parliament to alter the terms of the settlement by statute, for only in this way could the restrictions on life tenants be removed — there is increasing evidence to show that enterprising landowners did seek new powers. For example, William Johnstone Pulteney, husband of the heir of the Earl of Bath, persuaded the trustees of his wife's estate in Bathwick, near Bath, to secure an act of parliament in 1769 to permit the exploitation of that estate for building development. Under the Act, the number of trustees was increased to four, and they were given powers to: build a bridge (to link Bathwick with Bath), raise £3,000 on mortgage, grant 99-year building leases, buy or exchange land with any corporate body, convey three springs of water to Bath, and charge all costs to the estate. The bridge-building project proved more costly than was envisaged. It became necessary to obtain two more acts of parliament to raise mortgages to finance a total investment of £11,000. By the end of the century, however, this initial investment had made possible a further £300,000 investment in real estate, and produced an estimated three-fold increase in income to the family.[24]

As legal historians are aware, the trust was adapted to a variety of purposes. It was, for example, the legal instrument which enabled 'bourgeois' dissenting groups to hold property and build meeting houses. It provided the legal basis for the turnpike trust which in 1706 began to replace the old justice trust. It is also worth noting that the earliest of the turnpike trusts were all in rich agricultural areas, while the fourth of them, in 1707, was the Bath Trust, designed to facilitate the flow of wealthy and largely aristocratic consumers to what was described as 'a valley of pleasure and a sink of iniquity'. The trust, in the form of the equitable trust, has also been traced in financing the fulling, brass, insurance, flour-milling and building industries as well as in the big American land companies in the eighteenth century. It was a form of

[24] Based on the Pulteney Estate Papers deposited in Bath Reference Library.

financial organization which made possible what the Bubble Act expressly prohibited. In the most developed trusts the trust had a corporate existence, ownership was separated from management, there was limited liability and transferability and sale of shares. Indeed, in the course of the eighteenth century limited liability came to be written into the policies of unincorporated insurance companies, thereby demonstrating the degree of public confidence in the trust form.[25] It is worth remembering that the trust developed in response to the needs and as a result of the power of landowners — the embryonic bourgeoisie of the eighteenth century merely borrowed it almost intact. Further, since the analogies we use reflect our own perception of the world, we would do well to consider the possibility that when Locke wrote his *Two Treatises of Government* he might have had the image of a settled estate or trust in mind rather than that of a joint stock company. To change the analogies we use is to alter the concept we wish to express.

I began with the text 'The bourgeoisie, historically, has played a most revolutionary part' and I have ended with the notion that what passed for a bourgeoisie in the period preceding the transformation of the economy in eighteenth-century England was more caused by than cause of that transformation. On the other hand I have sought to emphasize the 'revolutionary' role of landowners and the aristocracy, with regard to not only their objective contribution to things like industrial investment, agricultural improvement, urban development, and consumption, but also their crucial contribution to developing an ideology, law and institutions favourable to that transformation and helping them to maximize their appropriation of the available surplus. The basic point I wish to make is that the landowning and political elite in England — like the later bourgeoisie and proletariat — also made and changed themselves in the course of economic development. There was no need for a new elite, and no new elite in fact, until perhaps the twentieth century. Further, without such revolutionary praxis, which was particularly marked in the late seventeenth and early eighteenth centuries, the industrial capitalist mode of production could not have emerged when, where, and in the form it did.

[25] C. A. Cooke, *Corporation Trust and Company* (Manchester, 1950); Albert, *The Turnpike Road System;* R. S. Neale, 'An equitable Trust in the Building Industry in 1794', *Business History,* 7 (2), July 1965; L. E. Davis and D. C. North, *Institutional Change and American Economic Growth* (Cambridge, 1971).

The Nightmare (Henry Fuseli, 1781: the Detroit Institute of Art)

5

Zapp Zapped: Property and Alienation in *Mansfield Park*

'Not social history', said a journal of social history; 'Not literary criticism', said a journal of literary criticism about this chapter. 'Trespassers will be prosecuted!' And the journey brought to a halt. Yet *Mansfield Park* buzzes with murmurs and echoes of all the themes and fancies of my first four chapters. After all, it is only a short step across the park from the material and monied world of the Duke of Chandos and the moral universe of Dr Clarke to Mansfield Park. The Duke would have been very much at home (although a little cramped) in Sir Thomas Bertram's billiard room turned theatre. The good Doctor would have found Fanny Price a congenial (even an adoring) pupil. And Bath was always there to escape to.

Mansfield Park, read within the context of the materialist conception of history, expresses a perception of the plight of the dominant class under threat, which offers (perhaps, only could offer) an ideological solution to the problem it poses. It is a 'cultural' image of harmony containing its own negation; a dialectical image of economy and society at the turn of the eighteenth and nineteenth centuries. Rather than 'A book about the difficulty of preserving true moral consciousness amid the selfish manoeuvering and jostling of society', it is a plea to halt what many saw as the moral degeneration consequent upon the economic and social development of England. A plea for the renewal of a rational moral order derived from revealed religion. Also, it offered to women in the middling and upper classes, in especially dark times, a moral heroine with whom they could identify, as they fretted at the bonds of property and the restricted position of women.

And the bourgeoisie are nowhere in sight. There are no proletarians either, only a shadowy press of people waiting to be impressed into awe-ful quiescence by the physical structures and political dimension of property.

*   *   *

Morris Zapp is one of the principal characters in David Lodge's *Changing Places*. He is professor of English at one of America's leading universities, with an ambition to write a series of commentaries on Jane Austen's novels

saying absolutely everything that could possibly be said about them. The idea was to be utterly exhaustive, to examine the novels from every conceivable angle, historical, biographical, rhetorical, mythical, Freudian, Jungian, existentialist, Marxist, structuralist, Christian—allegorical, ethical, exponential, linguistic, phenomenological, archetypal, you name it; so that when each commentary was written there would be simply *nothing further to say* about the novel in question. The object of the exercise, as he had often to explain with as much patience as he could muster, was not to enhance others' enjoyment and understanding of Jane Austen, still less to honour the novelist herself, but to put a definitive stop to the production of any further garbage on the subject.[1]

I have read only some dozen explanations of the 'real' meaning of *Mansfield Park*, and I sympathize with Zapp's sentiments. But they will not prevent me from pressing on in the manner of Laurence Sterne's muleteer, straight forward all the way to Loretto, my own explanation; one man's garbage may be another man's dinner.

Property and the legal and social relationships surrounding it and arising from it, were the basis of eighteenth- and early nineteenth-century society. I will argue that property, private property in land, structured the very conditions for and the possibility of the creative act, *Mansfield Park*, and that at its centre lies a complex relationship between property, propriety and alienation. In part this explanation rests on the view that property is explicitly the material basis of *Mansfield Park*. However, even if property was not explicitly the material basis of the novel, it would not matter for my explanation of its meaning. This is because eighteenth-century civil society, based on property, generated a hegemonic ideology which permeated every level of that society, from which sprang the creative act, *Mansfield Park*, and the novel's concepts and language are saturated with allusions to property. Fortunately there *is* much about property in the novel, which is invested by Jane Austen with, to use Duvignaud's terminology, polemic significance; this will make my task that much easier.

Discussion about the expressive meaning of *Mansfield Park* sometimes

---

[1] David Lodge, *Changing Places* (London, 1975), p. 35.

merges with and leads to discussion of the documentary meaning of the novel. When it does, the discussion often starts with the question of Jane Austen's intention in writing so uncharacteristically about a character such as Fanny Price. It then proceeds to examine the relationship of the character of Fanny Price to what some claim to be Jane Austen's only explicitly stated intent in writing the novel, namely, her wish to write a book about 'ordination'. As the argument unfolds it generates two contradictory opinions about Fanny. The first opinion is that Fanny may be regarded as 'a monster of complacency and pride',[2] and the novel objected to because, as Lionel Trilling observed: 'there is scarcely one of our modern pieties that it does not offend.'[3] According to this opinion, Fanny is morally cold and *Mansfield Park* an abomination. As the students of the Open University are told: 'The process [of moral affirmation in Jane Austen's writing] leaves Fanny and Edmund stripped of feeling and purpose, naked in the cold wind of casuistry. The larger misfortune is that *Mansfield Park* and, for the time being, Jane Austen herself are there beside them.'[4] It was probably his awareness of this opinion which led Zapp to wake sweating from nightmares in which students paraded around the campus carrying placards declaring: FANNY PRICE IS A FINK.

According to the second opinion, Fanny Price may be regarded as a Christian heroine (who never calls upon God), and the instrument of Jane Austen, herself an agent of 'the Terror which rules our moral situation [which leads us] to put our lives and styles to the question, making sure that not only in deeds but in décor they exhibit the signs of our belonging to the number of the secular spiritual elect.'[5] In accordance with this view Tony Tanner's verdict is that 'if Fanny Price is [Jane Austen's] least popular heroine, it is arguable that *Mansfield Park* is her most profound novel (indeed to my mind it is one of the most profound novels of the nineteenth century).'[6] Nevertheless, whatever the opinion, it seems to be agreed that Fanny *is* Jane Austen's least attractive and least popular heroine, and that, as Trilling said: 'Nobody has ever found it possible to like the heroine of *Mansfield Park*.'[7]

It is in the context of this almost universal abhorrence of Fanny Price — at least within the ranks of recent observers — that critics draw our

[2] *Mansfield Park,* Tony Tanner (ed.) (Penguin Books), 1966, quoting Kingsley Amis, Introduction, p. 8.

[3] Lionel Trilling, *The Opposing Self* (London, 1955), p. 210.

[4] Marvin Mudrick, 'The Triumph of Gentility', from Arnold Kettle (ed.), *The Nineteenth Century Novel* (London, 1972), p. 107.

[5] Lionel Trilling, *The Opposing Self,* p. 228.

[6] Tony Tanner (ed.), *Mansfield Park,* p. 8.

[7] Lionel Trilling, *The Opposing Self,* p. 212.

attention to our alleged liking for the individualistic values and self-interested moral stance of Henry and Mary Crawford. Both Crawfords are inhabitants of London, which is described as 'the world of liberty, amusement, fashion'. No one, we are told, doubts Henry's sincerity. He shows no condescension to Fanny about her lack of position or fortune and he is generous with his favours. As for Mary she is described as 'downright, open, intelligent, impatient. . . . She is all pungency and wit.' Above all she has 'a *free* tongue and a *free* mind . . . she has her *own free*, high spirited ideas about sex.'[8] This libertarian and *free* world of the Crawfords is then strongly contrasted with the apparently authoritarian morality of Sir Thomas Bertram and Fanny Price. Sir Thomas's principles are described as 'negative, a code of thou-shalt nots: the code of a system striving to affirm itself against the as yet unaroused majority of outsiders. The goal becomes, not the happiness or fulfilment of individuals but the fortification of a privileged world.'[9] It is this negative world of *Mansfield Park* which conditions and produces Fanny as Jane Austen's anti-heroine. She is held to be 'totally lacking in vivacity and all but lacking in wit, she appears incapable of making any effort of friendship with those about her, she is self effacing, silent and above all passive.'[10]

Thus, the central issue in the novel is seen to circulate around the contrast between material worlds, one of which, London, is perceived to generate freedom and liberty, while the other, Mansfield Park, for all its arcadian attractiveness, is perceived as unfree. Accordingly the novel is admired or rejected because of the value choice it seems to offer, or it is appreciated because it presents to us the dilemma of choice. Indeed, Trilling, aware of the Hegelian dialectical duo, appearance and reality, took himself to the very edge of arguing that Fanny Price is an existentialist heroine, making a free, conscious choice. That he did not and perhaps could not, rests, I think, on the fact that, like most commentators on Jane Austen, he explored the meaning of *Mansfield Park* almost exclusively at the level of values and attitudes, that is, at the level of ideology. He did not take cognizance of the fact of property in eighteenth- and early nineteenth-century England, nor its central significance in the novel itself. Property was excluded from the concepts he employed, and the material basis of Fanny's position eluded him.

However, Trilling did contrast the material worlds of Mansfield Park, London and Portsmouth as they appear in the novel, and he considered their symbolism. Subsequently his views about these three worlds have

---

[8] Marvin Mudrick, 'The Triumph of Gentility', p. 92 (my emphasis).

[9] Ibid., p. 104.

[10] *Mansfield Park,* John Lucas (ed.) (Oxford, 1970), p. viii.

been repeated with greater or lesser emphasis by many other writers. Thus, Tanner argued that the full meaning of the various characters and incidents in the novel can only be grasped by understanding these worlds of the novel, and the differences in life in Portsmouth, London, and Mansfield Park. Mudrick, too, pointed to the importance of the contrasts between what he called 'proletarian Portsmouth, fashionable London and Mansfield Park'.[11] But no critic has related these worlds with all their values, beliefs, attitudes, moralities — ideological and utopian — to property. Consequently it is never clearly seen or stated, that while the Crawfords and the individualistic world they inhabit appear to be free, they are not free, and, that while the world inhabited by Fanny Price is unfree and she appears to be unfree, Fanny Price *is* free; she of all the women in the novel, her mother excepted, refuses to sell herself to property. Yet, as I shall argue, in her 'freedom' Fanny, too, is unfree. It is my view that *Mansfield Park* is about the unfreedom of property whether it be in London or Mansfield Park.

In order to elaborate this point, to locate it theoretically and in time, I must step sideways, suspending in memory what I have said so far about *Mansfield Park.*

In 1821 Hegel published his major work in political theory, the *Grundlinien der Philosophie des Rechts oder Naturrecht und Staatswissenschaft in Grundrisse*, known in English as *Hegel's Philosophy of Right.* In this work, Hegel set out his account of the nature and evolution of the modern state as the realization of the Absolute Idea on earth. According to Hegel, the state was the only body able to adjudicate disinterestedly on matters of class interest in civil society. The agents of the disinterested state were the bureaucracy. Its members were held to have no interests of their own, and their aims were said to be identical with those universal or disinterested aims of the state; thus, the bureaucracy was a universal class. Its task was to administer the institutions and laws which collectively reconciled the particularism of the interests within the separate classes in civil society, notably the corporation of burghers and the system of entailed landed property governed by primogeniture. These institutions and laws, themselves rooted firmly in the institution of the family, particularly the landed family, were the guarantors of political stability and of freedom: 'Accordingly, the institution of primogeniture within the substantial estate, like the corporation within the acquisitive estate, is a

---

[11] Tony Tanner, *Mansfield Park,* Marvin Mudrick, 'The Triumph of Gentility', p. 87. Also, Ann Banfield, 'The Moral Landscape of Mansfield Park' and A. M. Duckworth, *Mansfield Park* and Estate Improvements: Jane Austen's Grounds of Being', both in *Nineteenth Century Fiction,* Vol. 26, 1971–2, pp. 1–48.

force of socio-political unity: it mediates between the egoistic spirit of civil society and the public spirit of political life.'[12] Such a mediation, administered by a universal class, Hegel regarded as essential for 'freedom' and for the further evolution of what was socially and politically beneficial in civil society. Although a somewhat mystical explanation of the benefits of landed property and its attendant institutions and laws, Hegel's explanation is reminiscent of the Augustan notion of 'Virtue', and of the idea that landed property conferred a political independence on its owners. Hegel's argument is not unlike that expounded by Shaftesbury in *Characteristicks of Men, Manners, Opinion, Times*, more than 100 years earlier, and justified by Locke, probably as early as 1683, in his *Two Treatises of Government*. According to Locke, large landed property justified by acquisition, occupation, labour, and the invention of money, was the condition of liberty in a state. The essence of this notion was that property created liberty. As a self-evident truth this idea penetrated every facet of the hegemonic culture, and permeated all levels of eighteenth-century society.

In 1843 Marx wrote a systematic critique of paragraphs 261–313 of Hegel's work. This has subsequently been published under the title, *Critique of Hegel's Philosophy of Right*. The importance of this work for the development of Marx's thought is that it shows how Marx arrived at his notion of alienation, essentially a state of unfreedom, through his criticism of Hegel's argument about the relationship between the entailed estate, primogeniture, and freedom.

Marx's views about objectification, alienation, and reification in relation to capital are probably generally well known. Fewer people, I think, know that, in his discussion of Hegel's views about landed property, Marx also stood Hegel right way up with his feet firmly on the ground; he simply demonstrated the unfreedom, that is, the alienation of property. His comments arose from considering the facts of the entailed estate, that form of land-holding which came to prevail in England in the eighteenth century, and which effectively overrode common law preference for primogeniture and the barring of perpetuities. Marx wrote:

It is also consistent to say that where private property, landed property, is inalienable, universal freedom of will (to which also belongs free disposition of something alienable, like landed property) and ethical life (to which also belongs love as the actual spirit of the family, the spirit which is also identified with the actual law of the family) are alienable. In general then, the inalienability of private property is the alienability of universal freedom of will and ethical life. Here it is no longer the case that property is in so far as I put my will into it, but rather my will is in so far as it is property. Here my will does not own but is owned.

Thus, landed property like capital was a non-human force derived from human activity, that is, labour, which stood outside and above men and women, and was as hostile as it was necessary to them. Thus the relation of landowners and their families to landed property was one of alienation; and their consciousness was determined by their relation to property.

In general this was certainly the case in England. In the entailed estate the nominal occupier was merely tenant for life. As such, he was subject to the will of trustees, prohibited from action damaging to the estate, obliged to meet interest payments on mortgages as a first charge on the estate, and prevented from exploiting the estate for the maximizing of its revenues. In these circumstances marriage was a business arrangement, and family law, love, and moral relationships were all determined by, and subject to the needs of property.

What was true of the relationship of men to property was also true for women. Furthermore, while men might have the illusion of freedom, women, except they were widows, never could. William Alexander wrote, in 1779:

As the possession of property is one of the most valuable of all political blessings, and generally carries the possession of power and authority along with it; one of the most peculiar disadvantages in the condition of our women is, their being postponed to all males in their succession of the inheritance of landed estates, and their being generally allowed much smaller shares than the men, even of the money and effects of their fathers and ancestors. . . . By the laws of this country, the moment a woman enters into the state of matrimony, her political existence is annihilated, or incorporated into that of her husband . . . and she who, having laid a husband in the grave, enjoys an independent fortune, is almost the only woman among us who can be called free. . . . Thus excluded almost from everything which can give them consequence, they derive the greater part of their power which they enjoy,

---

[13] Ibid., p. 101. Recent work, for example, Lloyd Bonfield, *Marriage Settlements 1601—1740* (Cambridge, 1983) and J. V. Beckett, 'The Pattern of Landownership in England and Wales, 1660—1880', *Economic History Review*, Second Series, Vol. XXXVII, No. 1, Feb. 1984, pp. 1—22, confirms the importance of the entailed estate in the lives of the landowning class, at all levels. *Mansfield Park* was written when the practice of the strict settlement was operating effectively and opposition to it was beginning to rise to a crescendo (J. V. Beckett, p. 11).

from their charms; and these, when joined to sensibility, often fully compensate, in this respect, for all the disadvantages they are laid under by law and custom.[14]

In short, all family relationships, marriage, love and morality were determined by and the servants of, property; they were facets of total alienation. There can, I think, be no gloss on this for the eighteenth century. After all there were only two ladies of Llangollen and one Mary Wollstonecraft at a time when William Paley's *Principles of Moral and Political Philosophy,* preached just such a gospel in 17 English editions between 1785 and 1809, and in 11 American editions before 1825. Property *was* the material basis of civil society, and its alienating consequences constituted the network of its social relationships. Consequently, according to this view, the appearance of freedom in the lives of the Crawfords, like the roles acted out in *The Lover's Vows,* is also an illusion.

In this larger world of property the value stance expected of women may be encapsulated in the word, 'propriety'. One might say that among the landed classes, propriety was to women as property was to men. And, while Paley seems not to have used the word, 'propriety', Hannah More gave it currency in 11 editions of her *Strictures on the Modern System of Female Education*, between 1799 and 1811. 'Propriety', she said:

is to a woman what the great Roman critic says action is to an orator; it is the first, the second, the third requisite. A woman may be knowing, active, witty, and amusing; but without propriety she cannot be amiable. Propriety is the centre in which all the lines of duty and of agreeableness meet. It is to character, what proportion is to figure, and grace to attitude. It does not depend on any one perfection, but it is the result of general excellence. It shows itself by a regular, orderly, undeviating course; and never starts from its sober orbit into any splendid eccentricities; for it would be ashamed of such praise as it might extort by any deviations from its proper path.[15]

According to Hannah More, propriety in women was to be the chief defence against subversion from inside, and threat of revolution from outside the boundaries of civil society in England; only propriety could protect property.

It seems likely that Jane Austen meant by propriety much the same as Hannah Moore; propriety meant knowing what was proper to be done and

[14] William Alexander, *The History of Women* (Dublin, 1779), Vol. II, pp. 421–39.
[15] Hannah More, *Strictures on the Modern System of Female Education,* 12th edn (London, 1826), Vol. 1, p. 6.

when, and it meant knowing the conventions that maintained order in society. As Jane Austen expressed it, propriety would keep everyone in his right place and ensure that everything would be done as it ought to be.[16] Indeed, Jane Austen's awareness of the convergence of all the elements in propriety, as they related to property, is clearly shown in the incident in *Sense and Sensibility* in which Willoughby shows Marianne over his aunt's house, Allenham. In this incident, Willoughby drives Marianne at breakneck speed through the countryside to Allenham, where they spend a long time walking about the house and the garden, alone, but knowing that Willoughby's aunt was at home. Later, news of this visit spreads, and Marianne is exposed to suggestive remarks from Mrs Jennings. When Elinor hears of the visit, she condemns it absolutely for its impropriety. The visit is seen by Elinor as tantamount to trespass; it offended against all rights of property, against seisin and entail, and against those delicate relations between the sexes, which pertained to marriage and the inheritance of property. Elinor is so angry at Marianne's spirited defence of her own impropriety, that she cuts her off in mid-sentence to say firmly and authoritatively: 'If they [the house and grounds] were one day to be your own Marianne, you would not be justified in what you have done.'[17] Clearly the proprieties, whether they pertained to relationships within families, or to those between families and between social classes, were expected to work to protect a society based on private property in land. Their task was particularly important when society seemed under the threat of dissolution. In *Mansfield Park* this threat of dissolution has its economic roots in the financial crisis that sends Sir Thomas to Antigua, and appears personified in the characters of Henry and Mary Crawford; the need to reaffirm the proprieties is made especially urgent by the effect they have on all around them.

Propriety is a key word at two crucial points in the development of the drama of *Mansfield Park*. Jane Austen uses it three times in its negative form to describe the impropriety of the theatrical performances, and twice to contrast the 'elegance, propriety, regularity, harmony' of Mansfield Park with the 'noise, disorder and impropriety' of the house at Portsmouth.[18] The association between property and propriety and its associated virtues in these passages is striking.

[16] *Mansfield Park,* John Lucas (ed.) (Oxford, 1970), Vol. III, ch, VIII, p. 354. All quotations are from this edition.

[17] *Sense and Sensibility,* Claire Lamont (ed.) (Oxford, 1970), Vol. I, ch. XIII, p.59.

[18] *Mansfield Park,* Vol. I, ch. XVI, p. 138; Vol. II, ch. II, p. 169; Vol. III, ch. VIII, p. 354; Vol. III, ch. X, p. 364.

But, it is not only in association between concepts that one may deduce Jane Austen's consciousness of the determining nature of property relations in the lives of women. She makes this clear on the first page of the novel. There the fates of the three equally handsome sisters, Maria, Frances and Miss Ward, are settled by their different relationships to property. Maria becomes the Lady of Mansfield Park and settles into somnolence. Miss Ward, who might have expected better things, has to wait six years before marrying with scarcely any fortune, and she lives a bitter parasitical life on the fringes of Mansfield Park as the wife of the Revd. Mr Norris. Frances 'disobliged her family', marrying a lieutenant of Marines without education, fortune, or connections. She breeds rapidly and leads a deprived existence. The significance of her life in Portsmouth and its warning to Fanny is not that it is proletarian and uncomfortable, but that it teaches the lesson of impropriety; the lesson of the relationship between propriety and property.

The Crawfords, too, symbols of the London world of mobile property, are identified in terms of that property, although Henry is also identified in terms of landed property. The first we hear about the Crawfords from Jane Austen is that 'They were young people of fortune. The son had a good estate in Norfolk, worth £4,000 per annum the daughter twenty thousand pounds.'[19] With twenty thousand pounds, probably invested in government stock, Mary Crawford possesses a fortune almost three times as large as that of Lady Bertram when she entered into a baronetcy. With such a fortune Mary Crawford was, according to Webster, in the fifth rank of households properly entitled to four servants. In the marriage market she could have bought herself an earldom. Instead she toys with the idea of marrying for love! Even so the determining character of property remains true for Mary Crawford. For all the 'freedom' of her mind and her 'free' ideas about sex, and for all that she excuses her brother's adultery, she is no Mary Wollstonecraft; she never once bucks the system, never once tries to seduce Edmund, and never, to our knowledge, takes a lover. On the other hand, we may well agree with Avrom Fleishman that 'Mary, far from being the Romantic heroine manqué, is portrayed as the over-sophisticated protagonist of aristocratic decadence.'[20] Certainly if, in this context, aristocratic decadence is allied to flirtation with radical ideas, and accompanied by mere talk about them, Fleishman came close to the truth. Mary *is* all talk. And while Fanny Price may be thought of as a fink, Mary Crawford stands out as a fraud! But,

[19] Ibid., Vol. I, ch. IV, p. 35.
[20] Avron Fleishman, 'Mansfield Park in its Time', *Nineteenth Century Fiction,* Vol. 22, June 1967, p. 11.

why should she challenge the system? It provides her with £20,000 and grants her the semblance of choice. And in her choice, made with regard to the proprieties, she approaches Edmund not as lover, but as a prospective wife (as Jane Austen writes: 'Matrimony was her object'). The arguments she uses to convince herself of the suitability of the match are calculated in utilitarian terms and shaped by her concern for property. For example, when Henry describes to Edmund what could be done to improve the parsonage at Thornton Lacey, another 'place' in the novel much neglected by critics, which Edmund will occupy on a mere £700 a year, and which Mary contemplates as her home also, she shows great enthusiasm. However, Henry's arguments refer above all to appearance and improvement, and it is to such arguments that Mary positively responds. In Henry's view, Thornton Lacey could almost become another Sotherton. Accordingly, Mary is encouraged to see herself as the (married) lady of the manor:

The place deserves it, Bertram [says Crawford] You talk of giving it the air of a gentleman's residence. *That* will be done by the removal of the farmyard, for independent of that terrible nuisance, I never saw a house of the kind which had in itself so much the air of a gentleman's residence, so much the look of a something beyond a mere Parsonage House, above the expenditure of a few hundreds a year. . . . it is a solid, roomy, mansion-like looking house, such as one might suppose a respectable old country family had lived in from generation to generation, through two centuries at least, and were now spending from two to three thousand a year in. . . . By some such improvements as I have suggested . . . you may give it a higher character. You may raise it into a *place*. From being the mere gentleman's residence, it becomes, by judicious improvement, the residence of a man of education, taste, modern manners, good connections. All this may be stamped on it; and that house receive such an air as to make its owner be set down as the great land-holder of the parish.[21]

Mary urges Edmund to agree with her brother's plans, because in this way she could marry a poor ordained parson — for love — and still have all the appearance of property. This means, I think, that Mary is so much the victim of property, £20,000 worth of which allows her to choose, that her 'free' preferential choice would make her the servant, not of the reality of property, but its illusion. The fact that she does not achieve her illusory objective is not the result of any deliberate action on her part. Thus, Mary, too, is unfree; despite appearances she, too, is a victim of the hegemonic values of a society rooted in landed property and held together by propriety.

[21] *Mansfield Park,* Vol. II, ch. VII, p. 219.

Then there is Maria Bertram. She, longing to be free from the solemn restraint of her father, engages herself to the doltish Mr Rushworth and his extensive property at Sotherton. When the Crawfords appear on the scene she hopes to capture the attention of Henry Crawford, the most eligible bachelor to come her way, but piqued by the independence of his departure for Bath, she quickly marries Rushworth. Trapped by property, the victim of its hegemonic values, there is no real choice for her to make; she acts with propriety. Moreover, the novel also shows that Maria can only exercise her 'freedom' through committing the worst offence against property open to a woman. She commits adultery. In her 'freedom' she is destroyed by the very system which was the whole condition of her existence, and which she willingly embraced. Thus, for Maria, as for her mother, her aunts, her sister and all women of her class, there is no freedom. Women can be only what property makes them. Hence Fanny, in thinking over the consequences of Maria's discovered adultery, concludes 'that as far as this world alone was concerned, the greatest blessing to every one kindred with Mrs Rushworth [Maria] would be instant annihilation.'[22]

Nevertheless, throughout the novel, the relationship between property and propriety is frequently inverted, and there does seem to be a rough calculus according to which propriety brings its own (propertied) reward. Hence alienation in Jane Austen's world is sometimes effectively masked.

It is in relation to Henry Crawford's proposal of marriage to Fanny Price that the alienation of *all* the characters in the novel, except Fanny herself, may best be shown.

A climacteric of the novel occurs about three-quarters of the way through it, in the scene in which Henry proposes and is refused by Fanny, and in the scene in which Fanny reiterates her refusal to Sir Thomas Bertram. These two scenes are the culmination of all that has gone before, and to which Jane Austen directs the plot slowly and deliberately. (The contrast between the dramatic intensity of Fanny's affirmation of an inner conviction at this point is such as to ridicule the merely trivial melodrama of *The Lover's Vows*.)

Moreover, these two scenes are a powerful piece of theatre. At the peak of the climacteric, everything crowds in upon Fanny. The pressures become unbearable. Henry, enamoured of his own presence, persists in pressing upon Fanny the propriety of his claims. Sir Thomas is angry in a manner never before apparent. Fanny is terrified. After the scene between Sir Thomas and Fanny, everything rushes downhill to the final denouement. Perhaps I should elaborate.

---

[22] Ibid., Vol. III, ch. XV, p. 403.

During the long climb towards the climacteric the story unfolds. The role of women in a system of property is carefully delineated, and the dilemma and consequences of choice and of impropriety are highlighted in the ways I have suggested. Henry Crawford is introduced as a most attractive and engaging marriage partner, and *all* the women in the novel, and some outside it, flutter around him to capture his attention. Moreover, in spite of what is frequently said about him, he is not to be seen, and, I believe, is not presented as a threat to the existing system of property, nor to values as exemplified by Mansfield Park. He is neither an overt nor an intentional destroyer. On the contrary, in the name of property and in its interest he is an improver. Also, he takes care to present himself as a benevolent landowner, anxious to avoid being put upon by a grasping land agent, and watchful that his tenants should be honest men rather than hard-hearted, griping fellows whose only interest is in exploiting the land for merely short-term gains. As shown by his views about Thornton Lacey, he talks about improving property the better to impress on the land and its people the appearance of the power and authority of property. And he acknowledges the importance of ancient property and power. It is difficult to see Crawford as any less intent on the preservation and proper improvement of his heritage than Sir Thomas Bertram. That what he sometimes advocates, and always does, works to undermine an economic system based on landed property, is a dialectical not an objective contradiction;[23] it is no different in this respect from Sir Thomas Bertram's involvement in commercial affairs in the West Indies. In short, within the novel and in the context of the system, Henry Crawford is the best possible case that Jane Austen can make for any man as a prospective husband. Hence his attractiveness and the attractions of the milieu of London, Bath, and Brighton he inhabits. Such is his standing in property and his understanding of the proprieties, that Sir Thomas can find nothing in him to object to. Even Fanny is almost captivated by him.

So to Fanny Price. Hers is the worst possible case that Jane Austen can make for any woman within the system; she is physically weak, she is neither beautiful (at the outset), nor brilliant, she lacks accomplishment and conversation, she is penniless and the creature of charity. Fanny lives in a constant state of terror with a mind 'which had seldom known a pause in its alarms or embarrassments'.[24] As Lady Bertram said, who would

[23] For an alternative view that Henry Crawford is an improver in an innovative and, therefore, an intentionally destructive sense see A. M. Duckworth, '*Mansfield Park* and Estate Improvements: Jane Austen's Ground of Being'; Duckworth claims that Crawford represents, 'those intent on destroying a culture' rather than those, 'who will preserve and properly improve their heritage', *Nineteenth Century Fiction*, Vol. 26, 1971—2, p. 48.

[24] *Mansfield Park*, Vol. I, ch. IV.

invite her? Ineligible as she is, she is also continually reminded by Mrs Norris of her dependent position, and made aware of the cost to a woman of placing herself outside or on the fringe of the system, by the knowledge that her mother, in disobliging her family and acting with impropriety, condemned herself to a social limbo. Hence the importance of Portsmouth. It is not so much the symbol of the proletarian world as the limbo of impropriety, a place where people wait, either coming in or going out, either pushed out by force of circumstance or pulled out by the attraction of new worlds. It is probably no accident that Jane Austen made Fanny's mother reside in Portsmouth rather than in some Midland town. It was certainly a place to reawaken all the dread that is in Fanny. But, there is, for Fanny, a chance of redemption and a chance of becoming safely integrated into the system. It comes to her through Henry Crawford; and, according to the established relationship between property and propriety, should be mediated by her propriety and passivity. Yet she is, as Trilling observed, a Christian heroine; consequently her passivity, which should prove her material salvation, proves her undoing. This is because her passivity, like Christian passivity generally, is of an active kind. As she said to Crawford: 'We have all a better guide in ourselves, if we would attend to it, than any other person can be.'[25] Furthermore, as a Christian, she has actively to place herself in a condition to receive grace; and hers is a positive, almost aggressive passivity. These characteristics give to her propriety an externally derived moral dimension, which leads her into impropriety.

In the affair of the play, Fanny's insistent propriety offends the role players, she is their conscience. But on this occasion her inner strength is supported by her knowledge that Sir Thomas shares her moral principles, and that he will return. She is not alone and, young as she is, she resists Tom's bullying, Mrs Norris's nagging, Mary's persuasion and Edmund's equivocation — or, almost. Even Fanny does not hold out completely; the milieu is too overpowering and she is only human. She helps with the props, takes part in rehearsals — it is she who brings Rushworth up to scratch with his two and forty speeches — and is prepared to be part of the audience. The importance of this for understanding the novel, is that we should not be too impressed by what goes on stage. That, too, is an illusion. What really matters in theatre is what Marx referred to as 'Darstellung', the whole stage machinery and management which enables the play to proceed at all. (And that, it seems, is what Jane Austen describes in all its mystifying complexity in *Mansfield Park* — the machinery of relationships which, in a society based on landed property,

---

[25] Ibid., Vol. III, ch. XI, p. 376.

permits the actors to play their parts with that degree of the appearance of freedom the system requires in order to continue functioning.) If we also note Fleishman's point that the play, *Lover's Vows*, was seen by some of Jane Austen's contemporaries to embody continental political radicalism, expressed in the convention of sentimental comedy[26] — it denounces the aristocracy as a class as villainous — then the play is an illusion within an illusion, and the message of the novel at this point is complex indeed. It shows Fanny uneasily linked to two facets of the system of landed property. On the one hand, she is shown not to be the freely acting moral agent her subsequent resistance to Crawford's proposal makes her appear to be. On the other hand, it suggests that her moral stance, apparently concerned with sexual propriety, is actually an unrecognized defence of landed property and existing political conditions. But that, as I have already said, is what propriety does for property. Therefore, in so far as Fanny contributes to the preparations for the play's performance, she, like the others, may be thought of as guilty of undermining the system of landed property. Fortunately, she and all the rest are rescued from their theatrical folly by something like divine intervention: Sir Thomas returns. Order is restored. Fanny is saved. Fanny is vindicated. And from this point she gains enormously in moral strength and seems to be rewarded with a great leap forward in physical beauty.

So now back to the scenes of the climacteric in which Fanny expects, but in fact receives no support. She is isolated. She is alone. On this occasion the impropriety of her wilfulness is emphasized by the case that Jane Austen makes for Henry Crawford as a husband, and the initial case she makes for Fanny as the most ineligible of spinsters. Consequently everyone, including Mary Crawford, expects Fanny to accept Henry without more ado, and they react uncomprehendingly to her refusal. Even the generally somnolent Lady Bertram is provoked by it and becomes, for the only time in the novel, quite animated. For the first time she sees Fanny as an attractive marketable commodity, like all the women in the family, and gives her the only piece of advice in eight and a half years. 'You must be aware, Fanny', she says, 'that it is every young woman's duty to accept such a very unexceptionable offer as this.'[27] This advice astounds Fanny into silence. Yet, compared to the social chatter of Lady Bertram, the reaction of Sir Thomas overwhelms her with its violence. The scene of Sir Thomas's judgement upon her possesses a dramatic quality matched nowhere else in the novel.

Hitherto in the novel, Fanny has rarely spoken other than when spoken

---

[26] Avrom Fleishman, 'Mansfield Park in its time', p. 8.
[27] *Mansfield Park,* Vol. III, ch. III, p. 302.

to, and then cautiously and apologetically, except, perhaps, at the point of her objection to the play. But, in this scene, she not only declares her refusal to marry Henry Crawford in a torrent of words that leaves her breathless, she contradicts Sir Thomas. The experience bemuses Sir Thomas. He says, in a voice of calm displeasure, "This is very strange! There is something in this which my comprehension does not reach."[28] Then, as he attacks Fanny for her wilfulness, self-conceit, and independence of spirit, 'which in young women is offensive and disgusting beyond all common offence', his calmness gives way to stern coldness; he becomes threatening:

You have now shown me that you can be wilful and perverse, that you can and will decide for yourself, without any consideration or deference for those who have surely some right to guide you. . . . The advantage or disadvantage of your family . . . never seems to have had a moment's share in your thoughts. . . . How they might be benefited . . . is nothing to you. You think only of yourself . . . let me tell you, Fanny, that you may live eighteen years longer in the world, without being addressed by a man of half Mr Crawford's estate, or a tenth part of his merits.[29]

By the time his four-page tirade is over, Fanny is reduced to bout after bout of tears until she is utterly wretched, her mind 'all disorder. The past, present, future, everything was terrible. But her uncle's anger gave her the severest pain of all. Selfish and ungrateful! to have appeared so to him! She was miserable for ever.'[30] Since Edmund, also, supports her marriage to Henry Crawford in a way which shows that he, too, has failed in his understanding of her, she is, as I have said, utterly alone; for the first time in her life. And free. For, of all the women in the novel, she alone refuses to see herself as a marketable commodity, she refuses to sell herself to landed property or its semblance; if she cannot marry Edmund she will marry no one. Without doubt hers is an exercise of will — the impropriety of propriety — beyond the comprehension not only of Sir Thomas but of the Crawfords, too, and all the Bertrams. That it is beyond their comprehension is because of their total integration into a system of property; their consequent alienation, and their narcissism. Even after her Portsmouth experience she remains firm in her refusal. It is as if she has taken to heart the cynical message of Bernard Mandeville in *The Fable of the Bees* that,

---

[28] Ibid., Vol. III, ch. I, p. 285.
[29] Ibid., Vol. III, ch. I, pp. 287—8.
[30] Ibid., Vol. III, ch. I, p. 290.

they that would revive
A Golden Age, must be as free
For Acorns, as for Honesty.

In modern terms she seems an existential heroine driven by an active moral principle not attributable to circumstance (after Hypatia, Fanny Price should be the patron saint of the women's movement); while in the early nineteenth century, it is little to be wondered at that so many of Jane Austen's contemporaries found Fanny a most delightful and sympathetic character.[31] Then, she touched upon a tender nerve to which so many women could respond, particularly if they sympathized with the moral message of Lady Pennington's *An Unfortunate Mother's Advice to Her Absent Daughters*, first published in 1761, and going through eight editions by 1790, and reprinted again in 1827, 1844 and 1872.

On the face of things, Lady Pennington's advice did not contradict the family morality of Paley, nor Hannah More's propriety. But in pushing the argument about female virtue or propriety to its logical conclusion, she advocated a female Christian doctrine, which in principle was far more subversive of a society based on landed property than any merely self-interested attitude of the Crawfords could ever have been. Lady Pennington, herself a divorcee, wrote:

The being united to a man of irreligious principles, makes it impossible to discharge a great part of the proper duty of a wife. To name but one instance; that of obedience will be rendered impracticable, by frequent injunctions inconsistent with, and contrary to the higher obligations of morality. . . . All commands repugnant to the laws of Christianity it is your indispensable duty to disobey; all requests that are inconsistent with prudence, incompatible with that rank and character you ought to maintain in life, it is your interest to refuse. A compliance with the former would be criminal, a consent to the latter highly indiscreet, and subject you to a general censure.[32]

Women, she said, would do their whole duty to society if they were to do what appeared to them right. They should aim at perfection and 'Be religious without hypocrisy, pious without enthusiasm, [and] Endeavour to merit the favour of God, by a sincere and uniform obedience to whatever you know or believe to be his will.'[33]

[31] B. C. Southam (ed.), *Jane Austen, The Critical Heritage* (London, 1968), pp. 48—51.
[32] Lady Pennington, *An Unfortunate Mother's Advice to Her Absent Daughters,* in *Instructions for a Young Lady* (Edinburgh, 1770), p. 56.
[33] Ibid., p. 82.

What better description could there be of the actions of Fanny Price, and what better proof of the dilemma posed by Lady Pennington's advice than the isolating consequences for Fanny of those actions — the impropriety of propriety. The problem was — what was God's will and how was it to be known? Was it God's or man's will that Fanny should engage herself to a man she felt to be a poseur, a man she knew she could not obey with propriety? And, now that Sir Thomas and Edmund had turned away from her, how was she to know? How was any Christian woman to know? That an answer was yet to be found outside the bounds of formal Christianity, and that Fanny Price was not a prototype of Elizabeth Sharples, simply serves to illustrate the limitation of Jane Austen's vision, as does the way she ties up all the strands in the story. As is well known, Tom Bertram has a drunken accident but survives a sick man to promise better in the future. Maria, oppressed by her alienation, commits adultery and is destroyed, condemned to Mrs Norris forever. Julia marries Yates and is returned to the system. Mary Crawford retires from it and despairs of re-entering it. Henry Crawford becomes a non-person. Fanny, once having stood alone, is vindicated. She is more than a fit wife, even in Lady Pennington's terms, for Edmund, now an ordained clergyman and fully recovered from his aberration; Fanny, too, re-enters the system victorious. Furthermore, by her marriage to Edmund, when Tom is so sickly, she seems set to inherit Mansfield Park. In any case she is assured of Thornton Lacey and the Mansfield Parsonage, and her moral virtue seems likely to be its own reward. Property and propriety would seem to be reconciled, but are they?

Mansfield Park, Jane Austen's polemic sign pointing to a system of landed property and its proprieties, is also a fictional embodiment of the alienation of humanity. It has its main roots deep in the English countryside and feelers spreading out towards London — the world of the Crawfords — but it has also sent out economic tap-roots to the West Indies. And I suggest, that in sending Sir Thomas to Antigua to restore the estate which supports life at Mansfield Park, Jane Austen offers another polemic sign of place recognizable by Jane Austen's generation, if not by our own. *Mansfield Park*, set in the late eighteenth and early nineteenth centuries, was written in 1811, only three years after the appearance of Clarkson's book on the history of the abolition of the slave trade, which was brought about largely at the instigation of evangelical Christians, although themselves the product of those changing economic conditions which made their ideas acceptable. Since, throughout this period, an estate in Antigua could only have been based on the exploitation of slave labour, Jane Austen places her Christian heroine Fanny and her ordained husband, and for that matter, all her readers, in a nice situation — she confronts us all, almost throughout the whole course of the novel, with our own alienation. (The West Indian property is introduced in the second paragraph of the book.) Life at Mansfield Park depends on commercial, slave-based wealth, as well as on ancient landed property. It is, therefore, rooted in slavery and is morally degenerate, at least in early nineteenth-century evangelical terms.

In the novel neither Fanny nor Edmund perceive that this creates conditions in which there is a problem or a choice to be made. Indeed, when Sir Thomas returns from Antigua, his business having been 'prosperously rapid',[34] Fanny endears herself to him by listening avidly to all he has to say. Yet to talk about business in the West Indies in the early nineteenth century without mention of slavery would be to talk about *Hamlet* without the prince, and Jane Austen did make Fanny Price ask Sir Thomas about the slave trade. She 'could listen to him for more than an hour together' on the topic. Indeed, Jane Austen may even have known, after the abolition of the slave trade in 1807, that Antigua became a net exporter of slaves to other places in the West Indies.[35] Nevertheless, in the novel, the moral dilemma posed by a system of landed property bolstered by the exploitation of slave labour and the slave trade, is not recognized. It is as if it is beyond Fanny's comprehension, just as her resistance to the impropriety of a marriage based on deference to property — the slavery of marriage — is beyond the comprehension of Sir Thomas. As far as Fanny is concerned there is no moral problem. This may be so because the concepts of property and propriety as employed in the eighteenth century left a determinate remainder, propertylessness. Propertylessness carried with it a wide range of moral problems. Except that these problems were resolved in terms of charity, poor relief and prisons, and glossed over by the concept propriety, the landed elite of eighteenth-century England took little cognizance of propertylessness and none at all of the propertylessness of slave labour in a system of landed property. Accordingly, it was only as slavery became uneconomic that the abolitionists were able to establish their case and influence the legislature. Thus, Fanny, as a beneficiary of landed property secured by slavery and the slave trade, is an alienated

---

[34] *Mansfield Park,* Vol. II, ch. I, p. 160.
[35] Thomas Clarkson, *The History of the Abolition of the African Slave Trade* (London, 1808), Vol. II, p. 552. See also, R. B. Sheridan, 'The Rise of a Colonial Gentry: A Case Study of Antigua, 1730—1775', EHR., Vol. XIII, No. 3, Apr. 1961, pp. 342—57, and D. Eltis, 'The Traffic in Slaves between the British West Indian Colonies, 1807—1833', EHR, Vol. XXV, No. 1, Feb. 1972, pp. 55—64. The problem facing Sir Thomas Bertram is illustrated by the fact that between 1799-1807, 65 plantations in Jamaica were abandoned, 32 sold for debt and, in 1807, suits were pending against 115 others.

victim of property, and Mansfield Park is a prison from which there is no escape, least of all through the practice of the moral values of the Crawfords, because they, too, are rooted in a system of landed and mobile property, and saturated with notions of bourgeois right. Just as there is no escape through the impropriety of propriety exemplified by Fanny Price. Maria, for example, is linked by Jane Austen to the caged starling in Sterne's *Sentimental Journey*, where it chatters 'I can't get out — I can't get out', and Fanny Price's room in this prison is described as 'a nest of comforts'.[36] For her it is a happy prison.

Clarkson's comment about the moral of the history of the abolition of slavery can be taken as a contemporary measure of the degree of Fanny's alienation. The history of the abolition of slavery, he wrote:

has proved what a creature man is! how devoted he is to his own interest! to what length of atrocity he can go, unless fortified by religious principle! But as if this part of the prospect would be too afflicting, it has proved to us, on the other hand, what a glorious instrument he may become in the hands of his Maker; and that a little virtue, when properly leavened, is made capable of counteracting the effects of a mass of vice![37]

---

[36] *Mansfield Park*, Penguin, 1966, pp. 27, and 174.

[37] Thomas Clarkson, *The History of the Abolition of the African Slave Trade*, Vol. II, p. 582. Avrom Fleishman in A *Reading of Mansfield Park*, Minneapolis, 1967 and 'Mansfield Park in its time', has drawn attention to the importance of the state of landed property and of Antigua for understanding the novel. Yet his standpoint and purpose are not mine. His purpose is to argue that, 'the economic peril of the gentry is an underlying tension in Mansfield Park.' His evidence is the fall in agricultural prices after 1812 and the depression of 1816, coupled with the decline of the West Indies. However, there was no sustained fall in agricultural prices until after 1817 and the yield on Schedule A tax on rent of land and real property rose 34 per cent between 1806 and 1815. Nevertheless, although the novel was probably completed in 1811, Fleishman's argument from the dates 1812 and 1816, is that Mansfield Park was set at a turning point in the gentry's fortunes. Hence he sees the novel as a mirror of a doubt about the survival of the gentry as a class and its theme, the possibility of and conditions for connection. My point is, the continuing hegemony of the ideology of property, whoever its class bearers happened to be, and the persistence of alienation. This, and the reality of the effects of property relations on people, cast doubt on the possibility of really human connection. Thus the beliefs people had about the possibility of human connection, generally couched in religions and moral terms, were illusory. I do not deny the existence of tensions within the novel itself, my argument identifies some of them. But I also claim that the existence of Antigua, off stage as it were throughout the novel, points to an even greater tension, particularly for evangelical minds, in the first two decades of the nineteenth century. The chief difference between Avrom Fleishman and myself is that while he sees Mansfield Park as a reform school I see it as a prison.

Fanny, in accepting the morally inferior Edmund with the accompanying landed property, with Antigua clearly in the background, failed to express even that little virtue. On Antigua, it seems she was as passive as ever! She observed the proprieties and was alienated. Fanny Price was not free.

It may be, of course, that Jane Austen was as blind as Fanny Price, and her sending of Sir Thomas to Antigua an accident without intentional significance. And it may be argued, therefore, that we can forget Antigua. Even if one concedes this argument, it is still true to say that the significance or meaning of cultural products cannot be settled merely by reference to their authors' intentions. There remains the problem of the unconscious and the structuralist position, which suggests that the way people see themselves and their intentions may not actually represent the reality of their existence and their behaviour. In which case *Mansfield Park* may yet be seen as an ideological product, as an image of, rather than a comment upon society in which Jane Austen was herself a prisoner. A distorted image, perhaps, in which the illusion, propriety/property replaced the reality, property/propriety. That is, a dialectical image in which the expression of an harmonious idea (propriety/property) contains its own negation (property/propriety) from beginning to end and through its spoken silences. (There are nine references to Antigua or the West Indies before Sir Thomas returns to break up the play.)

Yet it could be that Jane Austen was wholly aware of what she was about; she always invested places, and the placing of the smallest things in their places, with high moral significance. Her works are suffused with a sense of the nothingness of persons outside the little worlds in which she moved them, and with an awareness of the social pressures to which that fear of nothingness subjected them. And Fanny never was a paragon of virtue; she experiences jealousy and she lapses from propriety over the play — she *does* have her weaknesses. Then, too, Antigua *was* the occasion that triggered the fall from propriety of all the main characters in the novel, including, as I suggest, Fanny herself. It signals the dissolution of a system based on landed property (inherent in its own economic structure and development). Mansfield Park (the place) is, I suggest, the agrarian capitalist mode of production already corrupted by its connections with the urban/mercantile mode of production and its attendant monied interest. Had Mansfield Park, the place and family, remained firmly rooted in the English countryside (an historical impossibility), life there would have followed a more even course, and Fanny's 'nest of comforts' could have remained permanently shrouded in its veil of propriety. Therefore, unless one supposes that Jane Austen thought Antigua could be comprehended within a moral order different from the one with which she informs the rest of the novel, then it is not Jane Austen who is 'naked in the cold wind of casuistry', merely those of her critics who believe that

E

while her head is in heaven her feet are not upon the ground, and whose placing of and judgement upon cultural productions leaves out the mode of production, and the codes and signals in which domination is expressed. Like cultural production generally, *Mansfield Park* is washed by its critics in a sea of silence. Yet, while it is my view that *Mansfield Park* has its eloquent silences, written in by Jane Austen, a doubt remains about authorial intent, as it seems it always must. A dialectical image *is* dialectical, it embraces both ideology and utopia. So I leave you with a question. Is it Jane Austen or Fanny Price who speaks in the last paragraph? 'On that event [which I take to be Fanny's pregnancy] they removed to Mansfield, and the parsonage there, which under each of its two former owners, Fanny had never been able to approach but with some painful sensation of restraint or alarm, *soon grew as dear to her heart, and as thoroughly perfect in her eyes, as everything else, within the view and patronage of Mansfield Park, had long been.*'[38]

---

[38] *Mansfield Park,* Penguin, p. 457. My italics.

6

The Poverty of Positivism:
from Standard of Living to Quality of Life,
1780—1850

After our brief sojourn in Mansfield Park, with its delightful views and prospects, its personages and pasquinades, it is a hard task to get back on the road again, cluttered as it will be from now on by the swarming labouring population, properly excluded from Sir Thomas's domain. But there is serious work to do. What we have to decide is, whether the labourers we will meet were done good by all the things that were being done to them. Lindert and Williamson, two of the most determined muleteers I have come across (they can haul you across 150 years — and back again — in no time at all), assert that something called 'the Industrial Revolution' removed all the labouring population of England from Brydges' world, into one blessed by material progress. Their version of the *laissez-faire* argument claims that *all* the labouring population experienced great benefits (and negligible losses), as the industrial capitalist mode of production became dominant. Their march from Rome to Loretto is relentless and blinkered. They allow no turnings to the right or left, no *rencontres*. They do not stay to look around. And there are no people, no classes, no regions, no uneven economic development, and no time in their history.

This chapter calls a halt to their march. It brings women and domestic servants and handloom weavers and labourers in Bath, and workers in Glasgow, into the centre of the account, and it directs our journey more surely towards Camden Town.

The contrast between the last chapter and this one, their subjects and mode of discourse, their dissonance, as they run against each other, are reasons for writing their images next to each other. Martha Abraham in

Crawlers (John Thomson: reproduced by kind permission of Sotheby's)

1774 and Jane Austen in 1811 were both historic figures, and they meet in Bath. A history of British society should not separate them to suit the convenience of editors of 'scholarly' journals.

*   *   *

Peter H. Lindert and Jeffrey G. Williamson have proclaimed the final positivist solution to the problem of living standards in England in the period 1780—1850. There were, they say, 'impressive net gains in the standard of life: over 60 per cent for farm labourers, over 86 per cent for blue collar workers, and over 140 per cent for all workers'.[1] Confident in the precision of their scientism and the conclusions they reach, they challenge the world: 'why has this announcement not been made before?'[2]

My short answer is, the concept — the standard of living — they discuss is elusive. In their hands it slides from standard of living, through standard of life, material well being, hardships faced by workers, workers' net gains, to human gains and to quality of life (and back again). And there are such deficiencies in their data and argument, and in their methodology, that their sums and behaviourist Benthamite calculus do not describe, let alone account for, any discernible reality. These faults leave their proclamation devoid of human content, and with negligible significance for all other aspects of history writing. If they can be thought to have made any contribution to knowledge, it is only within the confines of the vaguely positivist epistemological paradigm in which they work, a paradigm with no special claim in the production of knowledge.[3]

My long answer is longer. It includes a detailed examination of the questions of earnings and unemployment, a comment upon some aspects of the quality of urban life, and a theoretical discussion of the way in which their paper misses the point of the Marxist critique of the capitalist mode of production.

EARNINGS

In their attempt to make concrete the elusive concept they seek to describe, Lindert and Williamson construct national price and wage indices

---

[1] Peter H. Lindhert and Jeffrey G. Williamson, 'English Workers' Living Standards during the Industrial Revolution: a New Look', *The Economic History Review*, Vol. XXXVI, No. 1, Feb. 1983. p. 24.

[2] Ibid., p. 12.

[3] See, Leslek Kolakowski, *Positivist Philosophy: From Hume to the Vienna Circle* (London, 1972), and my *Class in English History 1680—1850* (Oxford, 1981), ch. 2.

in order to fabricate a *national* real wage index for all workers for selected years. Their main innovation in this undertaking is the production of an index of full-time earnings using a 52-week year to turn selected daily and weekly wage *rates* into actual yearly *earnings*.[4] They claim for this index a national coverage and relevance. It lies at the heart of their proclamation about the 140 per cent gain in the standard of life for *all* workers. Yet, Lindert and Williamson's *national* real wage index, like all real wage indices, describes only what its method of fabrication permits it to represent. Consequently it does not, and, I submit, cannot, objectively represent a *national* human reality, either at any point in time or as it may have changed over time. This is so not only because of the theoretical, and therefore subjective basis of their methodology, which I discuss later on, but because of that which they leave out or exclude, even using their own methodology.

The main empirical problem is their index of earnings for *all* workers. Their class 'all workers' excludes all domestic servants and others engaged in personal services, all women workers, all handloom weavers, all boot and shoe makers, all tailors, all stockingers, and all wool combers. (But it does include a handful of judges, government lawyers, and paid officials.) They also use the wages of male cotton-spinners as a surrogate for the earnings of all other occupations in the textile trades. In short they omit direct wage data for some 44 per cent of the labour force (in 1841), including almost all of those in the worst paid and most vulnerable sectors of it. If we note that while they include the earnings of judges, they omit the earnings of some 300,000 farmers and graziers, and if we also note that their method of calculating the annual earnings of 'non-farm common labour' is also questionable, then it is clear that the 18 occupational groups they identify omit almost half of the labour force (in 1841) and, thereby, omit a much higher proportion in 1780. Their 'all workers' *earnings* index is simply a selection of daily and weekly wage rates from 18 male occupations. Their work is also deficient with regard to regional differences, unemployment, short-time and over-time earnings, life-time earnings, and family earnings. In short, their 'final solution' earnings index does not begin to address those problems that would have to be resolved to convert selected daily and weekly wage rates for male workers in 18 occupations into a measure of annual family earnings as an adequate measure of the material living standards of *all* workers. These are problems which inhibit the construction of anything more than the most tentative, regional and occupationally based indices of earnings. This is a view, following T. S. Ashton and after my experience of trying to construct an

---

[4] Lindhert and Williamson, 'English Worker's Living Standards', p. 3.

earnings index, I held 20 years ago.[5] After my encounter with Lindert and Williamson's cavalier approach to the problem, I hold this view even more strongly today. My reasons follow.

If any one thing is true about Britain's (and England's) economic and social structural development in the period 1780—1850, it is the marked unevenness of both. As I have already argued, the articulation of modes of production was complex.[6] Thus, the history of Lancashire is not the history of Dorset. The history of Dorset is not the history of East Anglia. And Birmingham was not Sheffield, nor Bath, nor London, nor Bradford-on-Avon, nor Manchester, nor Glasgow. Should we choose to discuss the question of living standards within wider, regional contexts,[7] then, it also becomes clear that the histories of the regions of England are not the history of Wales, of Ireland, or of Scotland, even though these regional histories are fragments of some larger history. Lindert and Williamson do know about the unevenness of economic development. They worry about it. In their minds, they seek to eliminate it. They employ various devices 'to capture the regional mix' they believe, will best eliminate difference, and reduce everything to a notional, national norm. For example, they arrive at their index of earnings for non-farm common labour (10.9 per cent of the work force in 1811, according to Lindert and Williamson, 20 per cent of the work force in Bath in 1831, according to me) in the following roundabout way. They adjust Phelps-Brown and Hopkins's index of earnings for skilled building workers to produce what they regard as the appropriate 'regional mix'. This has the effect of generating a steeper rise in earnings in the building trades up to 1797 than that

[5] R. S. Neale, 'The Standard of Living, 1780—1844: a Regional and Class Study', *The Economic History Review*, 2nd Series, Vol. XIX, (1966) pp. 590—606. See also, R. T. Gourvish, 'The Cost of Living in Glasgow in the early nineteenth century', *Economic History Review*, 2nd Series, XXV (1972), pp. 65—80; G. J. Barnsby, 'The Standard of Living in the Black Country during the nineteenth century', *Economic History Review*, 2nd Series, XXIV (1971), pp. 120—39; W. A. Armstrong, 'The Trend of Mortality in Carlisle between the 1780s and the 1840s: A Demographic Contribution to the Standard of Living Debate', *Economic History Review*, 2nd Series, XXXIV, (1981) pp. 94—114; R. A. Cage, 'The Standard of Living Debate: Glasgow, 1800—1850', *The Journal of Economic History*, Vol. XLIII, Mar. 1983, No. 1, pp. 175—82; and D. J. Oddy, 'Urban Famine in Nineteenth Century Britain: The Effect of the Lancashire Cotton Famine on Working-Class Diet and Health', *Economic History Review*, 2nd Series, XXXVI (1983), pp. 68—86.

[6] R. S. Neale (ed.), *History and Class: Essential Readings in Theory and Interpretation* (Oxford, 1983), pp. 277—81.

[7] Compare the titles to the two articles by Williamson under discussion.

reported in Phelps-Brown and Hopkins (1955), which was restricted to southern England only.[8] Then they apply the ratios of skilled to unskilled pay rates used by Phelps-Brown and Hopkins to their own reconstructed index of earnings of skilled workers, to generate their own index of earnings for non-farm common labour. According to this procedure, this fragment of their 'final solution' index is not based on any new observations of actual earnings by unskilled labourers, and is inflated, at least before 1797, by adjustments based on wage rates for skilled labour in northern England. Therefore, I have a non-rhetorical question to put to Lindert and Williamson. If they are so certain of the correctness of their procedures and the objective truth of their earnings index for non-farm common labour, should I abandon, as part of my construction of the reality of Bath, my own index of earnings for non-agricultural labourers in Bath? And should I pretend that the weighting they give to this component is appropriate for Bath?

Before Lindert and Williamson proclaim their solution to this question, I should restate briefly how the earnings index for non-agricultural labour in Bath was constructed. The annual figures in the Bath index are based on the average of the average actual weekly earnings (not daily or weekly wage rates) of all labourers employed on the Walcot highways in the first weeks of January, May and September of each year. (This represents 822 observations of labourers' *actual* weekly earnings for 42 years, an average of nearly 20 observations each year). I also calculated the actual yearly earnings of several individual labourers, and the life-time earnings experience of two labourers. In table 6.1, these totals are placed alongside my index of non-agricultural labourers' earnings recalculated on the 52-week year basis adopted by Lindert and Williamson throughout. For good measure table 6.1 includes figures for labourers in Glasgow.[9]

In table 6.2 I set out a new real wage index for Bath labourers, using the Bath earnings data and Lindert and Williamson's cost of living index, and their real wage index for non-farm common labour. Columns 2a and 2b of table 6.2 summarize the real wage experience of the best- and worst-paid labourers employed on the Walcot highways in two years, 1791 and 1841.

The main point to notice is that these new calculations still show that non-agricultural labourers in Bath in 1837 were not materially better off than their equivalents in 1781. On the other hand, Lindert and

---

[8] See Lindert and Williamson's Working Paper Series, No. 156, pp. 17—18.

[9] R. A. Cage, 'The Standard of Living Debate: Glasgow, 1800—1850', *The Journal of Economic History,* Vol., XLIII, March 1983, No. 1., pp. 175—82; and, Charles R. Baird, *On The General and Sanitary Condition of the Working Classes and the Poor in the City of Glasgow,* 1872, pp. 159—87.

Table 6.1   Estimates of annual earnings of non-agricultural labourers for selected years in England and Scotland 1781—1851 (one year = 52 weeks)

	National* Lindert and Williamson	Bath† (Neale)	Actual earnings ‡ (Neale)		Glasgow¶ (Cage)
	£ s	£ s	£ s	£ s	£ s
1781	23.13	19.06	(a)	(b)	
1791	—	22.53	19.66	17.06	
1796	—	22.31			
1797	25.09	—	(c)	(d)	
1804	—	24.70	23.33	19.97	
1805	36.87	—			
1809	—	24.26			
1810	43.94	—			28.60
1815	43.94	—			28.60
1816	—	22.31			28.60
1819	41.74	—			21.66
1827	43.65	—	(e)	(f)	
1835	39.29	19.71			
1837	—	19.71	18.20	20.80	31.20
1841	—	26.43	28.60	24.70	
1850	—	27.51	32.50	26.00	
1851	44.83	28.60	32.50	26.00	

(a) worked 50 weeks: 9 weeks of 5 days, 27 weeks of 6 days, and 14 weeks of 7 days.
(b) worked 44 weeks: 9 weeks of 5 days, 25 weeks of 6 days, and 10 weeks of 7 days.
(c) worked 51 weeks
(d) worked 51 weeks
(e) and (f) two labourers working from 1837 to 1851.

Sources:
*Economic History Review, Vol. XXXVI, No. 1. Feb. 1983, table 2, p. 4.
† R. S. Neale, Bath 1680—1850: A Social History, (London, 1981), pp. 416—17.
‡ R. S. Neale, Economic Conditions and Working Class Movements in the City of Bath, 1800—1880 (MA thesis, Bristol, 1961) pp. 35, 41.
¶Cleland, Statistical Tables Relative to The City of Glasgow; and Charles R. Baird, On The General and Sanitary Condition of the Working Classes and the Poor in the City of Glasgow (1872), pp. 159—87. I am indebted to R. A. Cage for these references.

Williamson's 'national' non-farm common labourers in 1835 had a real wage nearly 80 per cent higher than their equivalents in 1781. Bath non-agricultural labourers only experienced significant gains in real wages above the 1781 level in the 1840s. Furthermore, R. A. Cage's evidence

The Poverty of Positivism

Table 6.2   Real wages in 'England' and Bath, 1781—1850 (1850 = 100)

	1 COL (Lindert and Williamson)	2 Real Wage Non-agricultural labourer Bath (Neale)			3 Real Wage Non-farm common labourer (Lindert and Williamson)
			Best-paid labourer	Worst-paid labourer	
1781	118.8	58	—	—	43
1791	121.2	68	50	55	—
1796	159.5	51	—	—	—
1797	138.8	—	—	—	40
1804	160.2	56	—	—	—
1805	186.7	—	—	—	44
1809	204.9	43	—	—	—
1810	215.4	—	—	—	46
1815	182.6	—	—	—	54
1816	192.1	42	—	—	—
1819	182.9	—	—	—	51
1827	140.9	—	—	—	69
1835	112.8	64	—	—	78
1837	129.2	55	43	60	—
1841	133.3	72	66	71	—
1850	100.0	100a	100	100	100

a   Assumed earnings in 1850 as in 1851
Sources: As for table 6.1.

for labourers and 18 other occupations in Glasgow shows that in that city real wages for labourers were substantially lower in the 1840s than 25 or 30 years earlier.[10]

If the answer to my question about the use of the Bath earnings index is that it is to be preferred to Lindert and Williamson's in matters relating to Bath (and that Glasgow data is to be preferred in matters relating to

[10] R. A. Cage, Ibid. As well as these variations in earnings between regions there were variations of 20 to 50 per cent between contiguous or nearly contiguous parishes, even as late as the 1890s. See M. K. Ashby, *Joseph Ashby of Tysoe, 1859—1919* (Cambridge, 1961), p. 159.

Glasgow), it throws into doubt the value of Lindert and Williamson's fabrication, particularly when national income data could be thought to provide a more comprehensive aggregative approach. If the answer is that Lindert and Williamson's index of earnings for non-farm common labour is to be preferred to any regional and occupationally specific indices in matters of description or explanation, then economic and social historians are in cloud cuckoo-land (or in Orwell's 1984). Clearly, what is at stake here is the validity of differently constructed indices of annual earnings (and the data incorporated in them), and the appropriateness of studying regions, nations or regional groupings, and how best to relate regional data to national, and even to international or, wider regional developments. Some of the same issues are also at stake in Lindert and Williamson's use of the earnings of spinners as a surrogate for the earnings of all workers in the textile industries.

Table 6.3 summarizes the real wage experience of workers in 21 occupations in the woollen cloth industry in Gloucestershire in the period 1808 to 1838, and offers a comparison of that experience with the real wages of spinners as set out by Lindert and Williamson. Their C.O.L. index is used throughout.

According to Lindert and Williamson, spinners, therefore *all* textile workers, experienced a real wage increase of nearly 40 per cent between 1810/15 and 1835. Yet, as the evidence in table 6.3 shows, in Gloucestershire, only workers in seven male and one child occupation experienced a similar or greater rise in real wages. Furthermore, these rises were almost all in occupations employing very few hands, such as engineman, millman and rower (or rover). On the other hand, the highest real wage rise in women's trades was 26 per cent for markers and drawers. Most women workers, the majority of the work force, however, experienced either a small rise or a fall in real wages between 1808/15 and 1836/38. This different real wage experience for men and women reflects the fact that while, in 1808/15, women's rates were on average 55 per cent of men's rates, by 1838 they had fallen to 37 per cent of men's rates. These changes in relative rates over a 30-year period are sufficient to cast doubt on Lindert and Williamson's conclusion that 'the relative earning power of women did not decline. It may have stayed the same, or it may have risen.'[11] In Gloucestershire, it undoubtedly fell. Consequently, the earnings of spinners may not be used as a surrogate for the movement of earnings in all occupations in the textile trades.

An additional reason for this view is that Lindert and Williamson's textile index leaves out handloom weavers in both the worsted and cotton

[11] Lindert and Williamson, 'English Workers' Living Standards', p. 17.

Table 6.3 Real wages in 21 occupations in the woollen cloth industry, Gloucestershire, and of spinners, according to Lindert and Williamson, 1808–38

| Type of labour | | Yearly earnings | | | | Real wage change 1808/15 to 1836/38 |
| | | 1808/15 | | 1836/38 | | |
		£ s	Index [a]	£ s	Index [a]	Index [b]
Rowers or roughers	(men)	78.00	100	78.00	100	157
Millman	(men)	54.60	100	52.00	95.24	150
Brushers	(men)	39.00	100	36.40	93.33	147
Engineman	(men)	(1819 = 62.40)		62.40	–	(cf 1819 = 157)
Feeders to carders	(children)	10.40	100	9.10	87.50	138
Scourers	(men)	39.00	100	33.80	86.67	136
Sorters	(men)	39.00	100	33.80	86.67	136
Roller joiners	(children)	7.80	100	6.55	83.97	132
Slubber or abb Spinner	(men)	62.40	100	52.00	83.33	131
Mule spinner	(men)	(1819 = 65)		57.20	–	(cf 1819 = 138)
Mule piecer	(women)	–	–	13.00	–	–
Markers and drawers	(women)	26.00	100	20.80	80.00	126
Feeders to scribblers	(children)	10.40	100	7.80	75.00	118
Pressers and packers	(men)	46.80	100	33.80	72.22	114
Warpers	(women)	26.00	100	18.20	70.00	110
Beaters and pickers	(women)	20.80	100	14.30	68.78	108
Cutters	(men)	54.60	100	37.44	68.57	108
Master weavers	(men and women)	41.60	100	27.04	65.00	102
Burlers	(women)	26.00	100	15.60	60.00	94
Dyers	(men)	62.40	100	36.40	58.33	92
Jenny spinners	(women)	36.40	100	18.20	50.00	78
		Average 1810/15	100	1835		
Spinners (Lindert and Williamson)		72.91	100	64.56	88.55	139

a Index 1808/15 = 100

b Using Lindert and Williamson C. O. L. Index. Based on 1808/15 = 100, 1836/38 = 63.40.

Source: Report from Assistant Commissioners on Hand Loom Weavers 1839–41. Part V, p. 374 and Lindert and Williamson.

industries (188,000 in cotton alone in 1835). Yet wage data in *Reports from Assistant Commissioners on Hand Loom Weavers*, when used in conjunction with the Bath retail price index and the Schumpeter/Gilboy 'A' index, points to a fall in the real wages of worsted weavers in the West Riding of Yorkshire of more than 50 per cent between 1815 and 1838.[12]

Lindert and Williamson's omission of handloom weavers and women's trades from their index of earnings for textile workers is matched by their equally glaring omission of all domestic servants from their 'all workers' index of earnings: 1,143,000 domestic servants omitted in 1841 compared to the inclusion of a handful of judges, lawyers, and court officials. Yet, in 1841, domestic servants and other persons employed in supplying personal services were about 7 per cent of the male work force and 54 per cent of the female work force. Their wage experience, particularly that of women workers, cannot be determined by reference to the wage experience of other groups of workers. This much I have already argued. I now emphasize that Lindert and Williamson's claim about the unchanging or improving relativities between female/male earnings has no basis in evidence of earnings of female domestic servants. This is not surprising. There were many non-competing markets for domestic services, and domestic servants moved easily from employer to employer, not always in response to wage-related incentives. Consequently, standardized earnings of domestic servants, amenable to statistical manipulation, are not easy to come by.

The employment history of two domestic servants in Bath may be used to show some of the difficulties involved in ascertaining and attributing fixed annual earnings for female domestic servants. In 1774 Rachel Gunston was fifty-three, and an applicant for poor relief. She had begun work at eighteen. For three years she earned £8 per year, plus victuals and lodging. Subsequently she worked for two years for vails of the house, eight years at £4 per year, and eleven months at £4 4s per year. At fifty-three she was unemployed and, probably, unemployable. Martha Abraham was also an applicant for poor relief in 1774. She was twenty-eight years old. She started paid work at twenty. In eight years she had the following work experience; twelve months at £5 per year, nine months no work, two years at £6 per year, three years with no wages but board and lodging, nine months at £5 per year, fifteen months at £8 per year, three months two weeks at £7 per year. At twenty-eight she was pregnant by James Mullaway

[12] *Reports from Assistant Commissioners on Hand Loom Weavers*, Part III, p. 573; Elizabeth Boody Schumpeter, 'English Prices and Public Finance, 1660—1822', *The Review of Economic Statistics*, Vol. XX, No. 1, 1938, p. 35; and R. S. Neale, 'The Standard of Living'.

the wine merchant for whom she had worked at £8 per year. She was unemployed and a charge on the parish.[13]

In table 6.4, I list 140 observations of annual earnings paid to domestic servants in Bath between 1730 and 1865. In 1851, 63 per cent of the female work force and 25 per cent of all women in the city were domestic servants. When washerwomen are added to domestic servants, 75 per cent of employed women were in domestic service.

These observations in table 6.4 suggest that there was no clearly discernable change in the annual money wages received by female domestic servants in the City of Bath over the period 1730 to 1865. They certainly do not show the doubling in annual earnings, commensurate with Lindert and Williamson's index of earnings for farm labourers, over the period 1755 to 1851, that would be necessary to sustain their argument that the relative earning power of women 'may have stayed the same, or it may have risen'. For example, the figure, £8 per year, appears in; 1739, 1767, 1773, 1774, 1837, and in 1865 as the upper limit to the wage earned by more than 58 per cent of a sample of 89 servants. Like the relative earnings of non-agricultural labourers in Bath and Glasgow, of farm labour in the West Country, of female agricultural workers in southern and eastern England, and of hand-loom weavers everywhere, the relative earning power of women fell, probably substantially, in the textile industry in the West Country and in domestic service in Bath. As I argue in my book on Bath, it seems unlikely, at any time in the period 1781 to 1851, 'that many wives and daughters in labouring families could have contributed more than four or five shillings a week to the maintenance of the household to which they belonged'.[14] In good times, the most a girl or woman could earn was her own subsistence. When food prices were high, as they were in 1800—1, 1805—6, 1810—13, 1816—18, 1825, 1829, 1839—40, she could barely do that.[15] As nineteenth-century observers knew, and twentieth-century historians seem to have forgotten, it is family income that matters.

The implications for changes in family income of a relative decline in women's earnings, at least in textiles and in all forms of domestic service, and also in the millinery trades, coupled with declining participation in the paid work force by women, are considerable. These considerations suggest that descriptions of material living standards based on notional, national increases in the annual earnings of some male workers bear little relation to the real experiences of people. In what follows I do not pretend

---

[13] *Bath City Examination Book, 1758—1774,* Bath City Archives.
[14] R. S. Neale, *Bath 1680—1850: A Social History* (London, 1981), p. 279.
[15] Ibid., Appendix D.

*Table 6.4   Annual earnings of domestic servants in the city of Bath
1730—1865 (1730—1837 female servants only)*

1730	£6 10s ; £9 2s
1739	£5 0s ; £8 0s
1740	£10 0s
1750	£5 0s
1763	£5 0s
1766	£5 0s
1767	£4 0s ; £8 0s ; £12 12s
1768	£6 0s
1769	£6 0s
1770	Board and Lodging
1771	Board and Lodging ; £2 0s
1772	Board and Lodging ; £3 10s ; £7 7s
1773	£2 15s ; £5 0s ; £8 0s
1774	£3 10s ; £4 4s ; £7 0s ; £8 0s ; nursemaid, £10 0s
1799	£10 10s
1805	£2 10s
1806	£2 12s plus meat, drink, washing and lodging
1809	Cook, £10 0s
1810	£11 11s
1813	£2 12s ; £29 0s
1814	£5 0s
1815	£7 0s
1817	£5 0s ; £6 0s
1819	Upper Housemaid £12 12s plus tea and sugar
1823	£9 0s
1837	£8 0s
1865	Average of 89 servants £11 5s 9d. Range; 3 at £40 p.a. to 1 at £1 6s with board. Fifty-two earned less than £8; 9 earned £8 to £10; 28 earned more than £11 0s. (Note these figures include male domestic servants.)

Sources: Bath City Examinations Book 1758—74, Bath City Archives; St Michael's Examination Book 1811—20, Bath City Archives; St James Examination Book 1823, Bath City Archives; Walcot Examinations 1765—67 and 1816—19, Bath City Archives; St 12, Vols 1—4, Chandos's Accounts with Anne Phillips and Jane Degge, Huntington Library, San Marino, California; *Report of the Committee of Investigation of the Bath United Hospital 1866, Bath Pamphlets,* Vol. VI, Bath Reference Library; R. S. Neale, *Bath 1680—1850: A Social History,* pp. 264—300.

to be able to describe those real experiences, or changes in them over time. I merely indicate the magnitude of the problem.

The fact that the evidence in table 6.5 covers only a handful of families, in one industry, and in one year, does not detract from the point I think it makes, namely, that the material living standard of a male worker and his family was not determined by his own earnings. Rather, it was a function of the number of wage earners, women and girls as well as boys and men, in the family, and the size of family. As is shown in table 6.5, income per head was as much as four times higher in the most advantaged family, as in a family with only one wage earner and eight children. Lindert and Williamson have nothing to say about family income and changes in it over time. The problem, perhaps, lies neglected in their too hard basket.

This evidence: the original low level of women's earnings, the relative decline in women's earnings in the main women's occupations, and falling

Table 6.5　*The income of hand weaver's families in the West Riding of Yorkshire in 1838, according to size of family and number of workers in family*

No. in family		No. of workers in family	Family income	Income per head
12	(a)	4	26s	2s 2d
	(b)	4	20s	1s 8d
10	(a)	4	30s	3s
	(b)	4	28s	2s 4d
9	(a)	3	20s	2s 2½d
	(b)	3	15s	1s 8d
8	(a)	4	36s 6d	4s 6¾d
	(b)	2	14s	1s 9d
	(c)	1	10s	1s|3d
	(d)	1	12s	1s 6d
7	(a)	2	12s 11d	1s 10d
	(b)	1	10s	1s 5d
	(c)	1	11s	1s 7d
	(d)	2	14s	2s
6	(a)	2	17s 6d	2s 11d
	(b)	2	12s	2s
5	(a)	1	11s	2s 2½d
	(b)	3	20s	4s
4	(a)	2	21s 9d	5s 5d
3	(a)	2	12s 3d	4s ¾d
	(b)	3	16s 6d	5s 6d

Source:　Hand Loom Report, Part V, pp. 406–8.

participation by women in the paid work force,[16] when coupled with unchanging levels of expectation of life between 1826 and 1871, also leads to another aspect of the relationship between family income, material living standards, and aspects of the broader question of the quality of life; the question of widowhood and orphanage.

As early as 1842, Edwin Chadwick drew attention to the social cost of premature widowhood brought about by environmental conditions, and argued for making social savings on poor relief through urban improvements. His general conclusion was that 27,000 cases of premature widowhood and 100,000 cases of orphanage were avoidable.[17] But the point I wish to make is that the social costs of urban living, where they can be seen to be borne by one-parent families in circumstances of low and relatively declining earnings and declining employment participation rates for women, cannot be thought to be offset by apparent increases in the earnings of some male workers. This aspect of the standard of living debate is also ignored by its twentieth-century participants, even though it was emphasized as of crucial importance by earlier social commentators. For example, in 1899, Rowntree showed that 23 per cent of primary poverty in York (549 families) resulted from the death, illness, desertion or unemployment of the chief male wage earner. He showed further that only 367 out of the 549 families received any earned income, and that 71 per cent of the 367 income earners were either charwomen, washerwomen or dressmakers. Their notional 'annual' earnings in 1899 were £28 8s. The other 182 householders were dependent upon charity and poor relief.[18] The problem facing historians is that there are no comparable studies for earlier periods, and, seemingly, no way to compare the earnings experience of single-parent families over time.

These brief comments on family income suggest that historians may only *begin* to describe the material standard of life of *all* workers, and changes in it, when their calculus takes cognizance of the following: the absolutely low and relatively declining earnings of women, the low and

[16] Eric Richards, 'Women in the British Economy since about 1700: an Interpretation', *History*, Vol. 59, No. 197, Oct. 1974, pp. 337—57. See also, the very important article by K. D. M. Snell, 'Agricultural Seasonal Unemployment, the Standard of Living, and Women's Work in the South and East, 1690—1860', *Economic History Review*, 2nd Series. 1981 XXXIV, pp. 407—37. Snell argues for a decline in relative earnings and in participation rates for women.

[17] *Report on the Sanitary Condition of the Labouring Population*, 1842, p. 192.

[18] Seebohm Rowntree, *Poverty, A Study of Town Life*, 2nd edn. pp. 152—80. Also, F. A. Walker, *The Wages Question* (London, 1877), pp. 25—6; *Report on the Sanitary Condition of the Labouring Population of Great Britain*, 1842; *Report on the Condition of the Handloom Weavers*, 1840 Part V, pp. 406—8.

declining participation of women in paid employment, the number of wage earners in and size of family, and the varying incidence of single-parent families. Then their calculations must incorporate the real effects of unemployment.

UNEMPLOYMENT

Lindert and Williamson's treatment of unemployment for the period 1780—1850 is based on trade union data covering the period 1851—92, as reported by Mitchell and Deane, and taken at its face value. On the basis of general laws about relationships between unemployment rates for skilled workers in the engineering, metals and ship-building trades, and all other workers (based on these data and the experience of the 1920s and 1930s) they use regression analysis to calculate a notional national increase in unemployment of less than 7.37 per cent between the 1820s and 1850s. Throughout, Lindert and Williamson treat unemployment as a single, homogeneous, national fact(or) which can be subtracted from the notional, national gains in the real wage of *all* workers. Their claim, based on this method, is that unemployment could not have reduced real earnings by any great amount, between the 1820s and 1850s, because unemployment was not exceptionally high in the 1840s. In any case, they argue, unemployment may be discounted, at least in part, because of another general law which proclaims that time spent unemployed has value as leisure or non-market work. Needless to say, they do not supply the mathematically derived scale whereby workers in the 1840s may be thought to have discounted their own unemployment losses. They cannot. Their method excludes from their calculus the obsequiousness of the roundsman system, the humiliation of the workhouse, and for many, the loss of that independence and fellowship so clearly shown by Margaret Ashby in her description of unemployment in Tysoe.

It was in 1818 that the most intolerable entry was made. The Easter Vestry Meeting: 'unanimously agreed that all men and boys who are out of employ shall walk from the Coal Barn as far as the Red Lion Inn in Middle Tysoe, or stand in the gateway near the Barn the full space of ten hours on each day from the above date till Michaelmas next, and also it is agreed that if any person enter any house during the ten hours he or she shall receive no pay from the Parish'. The roundsman system had broken down: there were at that time 45 men and boys in receipt of relief, besides girls and women. It might be that the churchwardens and overseers — few but these had been at the meeting — were desperate, and for the moment had lost their wits, which they recovered on reaching home. Possibly they never mentioned their strange decision again, even to each other; there was no reference to it in later minutes. But deduct all that a kindly reader might, the words were a knell tolled after community had died. It scarcely added to a young reader's sense of calamity that in the same year, the overseers sent a number of small children from Tysoe in a wagon to a cotton factory at Guyscliffe, 20 miles away, to be apprenticed to the machines there, in a small building beside the picturesque Avon, the most romantic spot in Warwickshire.[19]

I make three main points about Lindert and Williamson's own calculations and conclusions. First, their unemployment series covering the period 1851—92 are unreliable even as measures of unemployment in the trades and period to which they refer. Secondly, the series for 1851—92, and relationships between unemployment rates in the engineering, metals and ship-building trades and other trades, derived from the 1851—92 and inter-war periods, do not predict actual levels of unemployment in the first half of the nineteenth century. Finally, unemployment is not the sort of optional extra Lindert and Williamson seem to regard it as, but is immanent in employment.

The first crucial step in Lindert and Williamson's argument is to show that unemployment amongst skilled workers in the engineering, metals and ship-building trades (EMS), in the period 1851—92, when related to unemployment in a selection of other skilled trades, is generally higher than other unemployment rates. Therefore, they argue: 'the 3.9 and 5.2 per cent EMS figures clearly overstate unemployment for the non-agricultural sector as a whole.'[20] But the truth of this statement is not a

[19] M. K. Ashby, *Joseph Ashby of Tysoe 1859—1919* (Cambridge, 1961), p. 282. See also Royden Harrison (ed.), *Independent Collier: The Coal Miner as Archetypal Proletarian Reconsidered* (Sussex, 1978). For a contemporary opinion with wide circulation see Thomas Carlyle, *Past and Present* (London, 1843), p. 181:

> And yet I will venture to believe that in no time, since the beginnings of Society, was the lot of those same dumb millions of toilers so entirely unbearable as it is even in the days now passing over us. It is not to die, or even to die of hunger, that makes a man wretched; many men have died; all men must die — the last exit of us all is in a Fire-Chariot of Pain. But it is to live miserable we know not why; to work sore and yet gain nothing; to be heart-worn, weary, yet isolated, unrelated, girt-in with a cold universal Laissez-faire: it is to die slowly all our life long, imprisoned in a deaf, dead, Infinite Injustice, as in the accursed iron belly of a Phalaris' Bull! This is and remains forever intolerable to all men whom God has made. Do we wonder at French Revolutions, Chartisms, Revolts of Three Days? The times, if we consider them, are really unexampled.

For the social consequences of long-term unemployment see Pilgrim Trust, *Men Without Work* (Cambridge, 1938); and Alan Bleasdale, *Boys from The Blackstuff* (BBC 1983).

[20] Lindert and Williamson, 'English Workers' Living Standards', p. 14.

matter of logic, statistical or otherwise. It is a question of the evidence that Lindert and Williamson choose not to scrutinize. For example, A. E. Musson's study of *The Typographical Association* shows that the unemployment figures for the printing and bookbinding unions, presented by Mitchell and Deane, and taken at their face value by Lindert and Williamson as an important part of their crucial assertion about the relationship of EMS unemployment rates to all other unemployment rates, have no status.[21] Writing of the 1849—1914 period Musson said:

Although the printing industry was rapidly expanding in this period and absorbing workers displaced by the new machinery, there was always a fairly large number of unemployed and casuals. Printing, in common with other industries, continued to suffer from periodic trade depressions. According to the Board of Trade's Abstracts of Labour Statistics, the lowest annual percentage returned as unemployed in the printing and allied trades was 1.3 (1873) and the highest 5.7 (1894), but in some months it rose as high as 8 or 9. Moreover, TA [Typographical Association] figures show that in slump periods about a quarter, or even a third, of the members were casually employed and that even in periods of good trade about a fifth to an eighth were casuals. Unemployment was, in fact, the greatest problem facing the Association.[22]

On the period before 1849, he wrote:

There were also sharp fluctuations in the printing industry even during years of general prosperity. The wage rates given above are apt, therefore, to present a misleading picture, when a large proportion of the trade was often out of work for long periods in each year. It was stated in the *Typographical Gazette* of May 1846 that 'more than half the journeymen are unemployed during a portion of the year', and trade union statistics invariably show between one-third and one-fifth of the members as out of work or casuals. Average wages, therefore, were a good deal lower than the established rates, sometimes as low as 10s or 15s per week, taking the whole year round.[23]

[21] B. R. Mitchell and Phyllis Deane, *Abstract of British Historical Statistics* (Cambridge, 1971), pp. 64—5.

[22] A. E. Musson, *The Typographical Association* (Oxford, 1954), p. 89. Unemployment in other trades much higher than those shown in the EMS figures is reported in P. J. Walker, *Democracy and Sectarianism: A Political and Social History of Liverpool, 1868—1939,* (Liverpool, 1981), p. 147.

Thus in 1894, unemployment among the Gasworkers and General Labourers Union was reported at 32.9 per cent while, in July, 4,000 out of 9,000 members of the Warehouse Porters' Union were unemployed.

[23] Ibid., p. 21, Lindert and Williamson, 'English Workers' Living Standards', p. 14.

In short, Musson claims that figures for the Typographical Association, a union covering some of the most highly skilled workers — men who referred to themselves as 'gentlemen' and their trade as a 'profession' — show that 12 to 20 per cent of its members were unemployed, even in good times, and that under-employment and unemployment, taken together, rose to 25 to 33 per cent of members in periods of depression. In 1846 half of all journeymen members were unemployed at one time or another. Therefore, Lindert and Williamson's assertion that the EMS figures overstate unemployment (3.9 and 5.2 per cent), is not valid even for the period to which their 'evidence' relates.

High levels of unemployment similar to those experienced by members of the Typographical Association in the mid-1840s, and not predicted by Lindert and Williamson's method, were to be found in other trades during periods of depression. Thus, while continuous employment of agricultural labourers may have become more common after the Poor Law Act of 1834, there is evidence to suggest that many labourers worked only a 40-week year, and that about 13 per cent of labourers were regularly stood down during the winter months.[24] In periods of depression, such as the early 1830s, and at times when new technology was introduced, unemployment, especially among women, would have been considerably greater. In the textile trades, local unemployment could be very high indeed; 60 per cent in Stockport in 1816; and in 1826, in two weaving townships above Burnley, 1,400 and 1,353 persons out of a total population of 1,500 and 1,611 respectively, were in receipt of poor relief. There was high unemployment and under-employment in textiles in 1826, 1829, 1837 and 1841—2.[25] In Bath, in the mid-1840s, about one-third of the population was in poverty, the result of low wages, unemployment and under-employment combined. In one parish this proportion was as high as 50 per cent. In Leeds, in 1842, after four years of depression, it was estimated every fifth person in the borough was a pauper — 16,000 individuals out of a population of 80,000 were existing solely on workhouse relief. In Liverpool, from 18 to 26 January 1847, over 173,000 persons were relieved — some 50,000 more than lived in the borough itself in 1851. In Ireland, 'employment' conditions were so bad they resulted in a million deaths from famine in the 1840s.[26]

It is possible to pile instance upon instance to show that Lindert and Williamson's solution to the problem of unemployment is no answer. To use regression analysis based on some dubious trade union unemployment

---

[24] F. A. Walker, *The Wages Question*, p. 32.
[25] Duncan Bythell, *The Handloom Weavers* (Cambridge, 1969), pp. 122—3, 238—9, 283.

rates for the second half of the century, and general laws, to produce a small notional percentage rise in unemployment, then to subtract that percentage rise from alleged real wage gains, inadequately calculated, misses the point. To incorporate the real effects of unemployment into a measure of material living standards based on family income, some attempt has to be made to measure unemployment as experienced by people in the work situation itself: as short-time working, in terms of days worked in the week and weeks worked in the year; as a cyclical phenomenon, wiping out real wage gains overnight; as a longer-term phenomenon resulting from changing capacity to labour over a life-time of manual work; and as structural change tied to the fact of uneven economic development. In short, unemployment must be understood as immanent in employment itself (as incorporated into my earnings index and annual earnings calculations for Bath labourers), not as a sort of optional extra.

QUALITY OF URBAN LIFE

The wider 'human gains' and 'quality of life' of Lindert and Williamson's elusive concept are added in (or subtracted) also on the basis of speculation and appeal to general laws. The authors use mortality rates as surrogates for what they refer to as 'urban disamenities'; and they assume that the 65 per cent 'wage gap' between Manchester and East Anglia was a rationally perceived compensation for a lower (urban) quality of life freely entered into by all workers in the urban, industrial world. Williamson also speculates about improvement in urban conditions on the basis of regression analysis in his 1981 paper. Only this time, he uses data collected in 1908 which relate to some urban conditions in 1905. On the basis of these data, the authors allow no more than a 2.5 per cent reduction in living standards because of 'urban disamenities' in the period 1781—1851. Therefore, I direct my comments to Williamson's 1981 paper.[27]

---

[26] R. S. Neale, *Bath,* p. 283. P. J. Walker, *Democracy and Sectarianism: A Political and Social History of Liverpool 1868—1939* (Liverpool, 1981), p. 8; and Anthony Sutcliffe, *Multi-Storey Living: The British Working Class Experience* (London, 1974), p. 54; B. M. Add. MSS 40, 612, quoted in Asa Briggs (ed.), *Chartist Studies* (London, 1959), p. 88, footnote 6; Cecil Woodham-Smith, *The Great Hunger* (London, 1962), p. 411.

[27] Jeffrey G. Williamson, 'Urban Disamenities, Dark Satanic Mills, and the British Standard of Living Debate', *The Journal of Economic History,* Vol. XLI, Mar. 1981, No. 1.

Williamson's data base is the 1908 Board of Trade Inquiry covering wages and cost of living in 72 towns, in 1905, and infant mortality as a surrogate for the quality of urban life. His conclusion is that it cost very little to bribe workers to move to the 'dark satanic mills' — a wage premium of a mere 2 per cent over the full half-century. Thus, he claims 'urban disamenities' were trivial. Indeed, if 'urban disamenities' can be thought to improve, they were improving. Williamson declares: 'There is no evidence to support the view that the quality of urban life as it influenced the common man [sic] was deteriorating following 1750, and plenty of evidence to support the contrary view.'[28] According to Williamson, the idea of deterioration in urban conditions in any period and place since 1750 was an upper-class Victorian myth.[29] Accordingly, Lindert and Williamson deduct a precise 2.5 per cent for 'urban disamenities' from their national indicator of the living standards of *all* workers in the period 1781—1851.

The difficulties of replying substantially to this claim within the compass of our journey from Dewsall to Camden Town are immense, particularly as Williamson's argument assumes that the question of 'the quality of life' is best resolved by speculation based on regression analysis, and by recourse to national averages designed to eliminate differences. Thus the mortality and infant mortality figures fed into Williamson's calculus assume an homogeneous, national population moving through homogeneous, empty time. Although he seems to have 'discovered' that 'urban disamenities appear to be class specific',[30] there are no classes, sexes, age-groups, and no specificity of time in his analysis. Just as there are no classes and only occasionally regional divisions in the population data analysed by Wrigley and Schofield and used by Williamson.[31]

Yet, what do the most recent population data show? The short answer is, at the level of national aggregates, mortality and infant mortality figures show little change over the period covered by Williamson's description. Reconstitution studies for 12 parishes show falls in infant mortality rates from 1700—49 to 1750—99, but show, too, that the overall rate in the latter period was higher than for 1550—99.[32] In any

[28] Williamson, ibid., p. 83.

[29] Ibid., p. 82.

[30] Ibid., p. 81.

[31] E. A. Wrigley and R. S. Schofield, *The Population History of England, 1541—1871: A Reconstruction* (London, 1981), chs. 6 and 7. For the effect of urbanization in a rural area on infant mortality rates, see the author's (*et al.*), 'Life and Death in Hillgrove 1870—1914', *Australian Economic History Review,* XXI:L Sept. 1981, pp. 91—113, and chapter 9 below.

[32] Ibid., pp. 248—9.

case, the decline in mortality in the late eighteenth century was arrested in the early nineteenth century. Thus, expectation of life at birth, which rose from 34.7 in 1781 to 40.8 in 1831, scarcely changed thereafter to 1871. It fell, in fact, to 39.5 in 1851, at which date it was no higher than in the late sixteenth century.[33] Moreover, the best evidence for the course of national infant mortality figures shows it to have remained at about 150:1,000 throughout the nineteenth century.[34] But English mortality experience in the eighteenth and early nineteenth centuries was also that of most countries in Western Europe. It has recently been argued that any fall in mortality and infant mortality in Western Europe, and the unfavourable levels of infant mortality in Eastern Europe, had more to do with the rise of absolutism in the West and the persistence of feudal production relations in the East than with urbanization *per se*.[35] The connection between a decline in infant mortality rates and urbanization, and, therefore, with 'urban disamenities' in this early period is tenuous indeed. (Perhaps I should remind Williamson that there are no causes in regression analysis, only in the theories one uses.)

Contemplation of these aggregate mortality figures merely blocks enquiry. A more disaggregative approach, comparing mortality rates in the nought to five age group in 21 healthy and 33 unhealthy (urban) districts for the years 1838—44, shows mortality in the unhealthy (urban) districts to be 124 per cent higher for males and 130 per cent higher for females. In Liverpool and Manchester, mortality was about five times as high as in the most healthy district in Northumberland.[36] Consequently expectation of life at birth in Liverpool was 17 compared with the national figure of 40.[37] Furthermore, mortality rates in Liverpool and Manchester rose from 1838—44 to 1861—70. They also rose in the following major urban centres: Birmingham, Blackburn, Bradford, Exeter, Halifax, Huddersfield, Newcastle, Sheffield, West Derby, West Ham, Walsall and York.[38] In Glasgow the crude death rate rose from 24.8:1,000 in 1821—4,

---

[33] Ibid., p. 230. See also *The Registrar General's Statistical Review of England and Wales,* 1955, Part III, p. 65, which shows no change from 1838 to 1854, and only slight improvement for males into the period 1871—80.

[34] Mitchell and Deane, *Abstract of British Historical Statistics,* pp. 36—7. The figures for Scotland show a rise 120:1,000, 1855—60; to 129:1,000, 1896—1900.

[35] Stephen J. Kunitz, 'Speculations on the European Mortality Decline', *The Economic History Review,* Vol. XXXVI, No. 3, Aug. 1983, pp. 349—64. See also, W. A. Armstrong, pp. 108—9, for some comments upon the relation between mortality figures and the standard of living debate.

[37]. *Report on the Sanitary Condition of the Labouring Population,* 1842, p. 219.

[38] *First Report of the Commissioners on The Housing of The Working Classes (England and Wales),* 1884—5, Vol. 2., p. 805.

to 39.9:1,000 in 1845—7.[39] Mortality rates also varied from ward to ward, and street to street, so that in the 1870s and 1880s there were rates as high as 50 to 60:1,000 in Glasgow, and 44:1,000 in Liverpool.[40] In Bath, in the 1830s and 1840s, mortality in the poorest districts was three to four times that in the most prosperous parts. Indeed, in the smallpox epidemic of 1837, the mortality rate in the Abbey Registration District was higher than that for Liverpool. How these ward, district and street rates varied over time is a subject for detailed local studies.[41] Yet, if mortality rates, particularly infant mortality rates, are accepted as surrogates for urban conditions and the quality of life, there is *prima facie* evidence that while, overall, the quality of life did not improve after the 1830s, the quality of life in many towns and parts of towns declined considerably. (See chapter 9 for a fuller discussion of infant mortality in a world/colonial context.) On the other hand, if mortality rates before the 1830s were a function of circumstances unrelated to urbanization, any improvements in them cannot be used as indications of improvement in Williamson's 'urban disamenities'. It seems that the question *is* rather more complex than Williamson allows, and that it cannot be resolved by regression analysis on 1905 data.

Nevertheless, there may be other, more direct evidence against which to test Williamson's very positive claim that there is plenty of evidence to support the view that the quality of urban life was improving after 1750. Since this claim pushes the argument back to 1750, it is imperative that comparisons be made taking that date as a base year. Although there is no such evidence in Williamson's paper (some might claim there is no evidence of any kind in it) there is some more direct evidence relating to housing that might be used. The most recent and comprehensive work in this field is C. W. Chalklin's *The Provincial Towns of Georgian England — a Study of the Building Process 1740—1820.* In this study of housing in 18 towns and cities, Chalklin summarizes his attempt to calculate the number of persons per house and per occupied house as some kind of measure of 'urban disamenities'. On the face of it, his assessment lends support to Williamson's assertion. He offers the following tentative conclusion:

[39] M. W. Flinn, *Scottish Population History,* quoted in Cage, 'The Standard of Living Debate', p. 180. See also, W. A. Armstrong, for Carlisle; and D. J. Oddy, for Lancashire.

[40] *The Second Report of the Commissioners on the Housing of the Working Classes, 1884—85* (Scotland), Evidence of Dr J. B. Russell, p. 45. *First Report,* p. 805.

[41] R. S. Neale, *Bath,* pp. 287—93.

On balance, it is likely that the secular pressure on living accommodation did not worsen in the industrial towns, and that in some it improved slightly. This is not to deny that there were severe temporary shortages. Although there were occasional short-term difficulties in the supply of capital for building, on the whole it was adequate, coming from the resources of a multitude of more substantial townsmen. Inhabitants of working-class districts of the centres of the Industrial Revolution probably suffered deterioration in living conditions in many ways as towns expanded: worsening sanitation, increasing isolation from the countryside and open spaces, and in some cases increasing housing density and poorer house construction. Yet the accommodation of the houses themselves did not worsen. In some instances they may have improved by the beginning of the nineteenth century.[42]

But, Chalklin's average figures, where they do point to improvement, reveal very little improvement: 5.8 persons per occupied house in Birmingham in 1751; 5.0 in 1821; 6.6 in Manchester in 1773; 6.5 in 1821; 5.8 in Liverpool in 1773, but 6.3 in 1821.[43] Overall, housing conditions as measured by occupancy improved between 1801 and 1821 in only nine out of his sample of 18 towns. His sample is misleading. Census figures for the whole of England and Wales show that occupancy of inhabited houses actually worsened, from 5.6 in 1801, to 5.7 in 1821. In 1831 the figure was again 5.6, in 1841, 5.4.[44] There were no comparable figures for Scotland, the instructions to collectors in 1841 not being clear. Nevertheless, the compilers of the census expressed the view: 'that the proportion which the population of Scotland now bears to the inhabited houses is rather above that exhibited in the Abstract of 1831.'[45] Clearly, there is not much evidence, even at the national level, to support Williamson's assertion for the first 40 years of the nineteenth century. Comparison over a longer period of time, where such comparisons can be made, also put Williamson's assertion to the proof. In table 6.6, I summarize evidence for those towns listed by Chalklin for which he gives occupancy figures for some year in the eighteenth century. According to these occupancy figures, housing conditions deteriorated, sometimes considerably, over periods of a century or more in six out of the ten towns identified by Chalklin.[46] If we bear in mind that the Birminghams and

[42] C. W. Chalklin, *The Provincial Towns of Georgian England: a study of the building process, 1740—1820* (London, 1974), p. 307.
[43] Ibid., Appendix VI. See also, P. J. Corfield, *The Impact of English Towns 1700—1800* (Oxford, 1982), p. 183.
[44] *Census of Population*, 1841, p. 6.
[45] Ibid., p. 7.
[46] *Census of Population*, 1881, p. 14.

Liverpools of the 1870s were very different from the places they had been in the 1750s and 1770s (they were bigger, more densely settled, more polluted), and that with the passage of time the average age of the stock of houses rose, it is difficult to read improvement in urban conditions into these figures. The argument would have to turn on improvement in the quality of housing. Such an argument would be difficult to sustain. Take the case of Scotland. In 1881, when Glasgow Corporation's specification was for rooms of 900 cu. ft (300 cu. ft per person), and when tenement rooms in Edinburgh measured 13 ft x 12 ft x 9 ft, 65 per cent of families

Table 6.6   Persons per house in selected towns, 1739—1871

	Date	Persons per house
Birmingham	1751	5.7
	1871	7.79
Leeds	1771	4.9
	1871	4.64
Manchester	1773	6.5
	1871	5.23
Nottingham	1739	5.6
	1871	4.84
Sheffield	1755	4.5
	1871	4.95
Liverpool	1773	5.4
	1871	6.29
Worcester	1782	5.3
	1881	4.72
Maidstone	1782	5.2
	1881	5.53
Chichester	1740	4.7
	1881	5.14
London	1801	6.9
	1871	7.79

Source: C. W. Chalkin, *The Provincial Towns of Georgian England 1740—1820*, pp. 338—40; and Census 1881, p. 14.

lived in two rooms or less, and 26 per cent of families (some 671,884 persons) lived in one room at an average density of 3.19 persons per room. In Glasgow in 1871, 72 per cent of the population of nearly half a million lived in houses or tenements of two rooms or less.[47] If these figures represent improvement over 1750, or some other time before 1800, Williamson has yet to demonstrate it. If he could, he would have only begun to *touch* upon the question of the quality of life.

Although the evidence and argument in this chapter are familiar to many economic and social historians it has been necessary to restate them because of the implications of Lindert and Williamson's method. It is a method according to which the authors isolate certain elements such as; male money wage rates, prices, mortality and unemployment, frequently from their relationships with each other, and always from other elements such as; lifetime earnings experience, women's earnings, family earnings, women's participation rate in paid employment, incidence of one-parent families, pauperism, old-age, conditions of employment, housing, water-supply, sanitation, air-pollution, cyclical and secular movements in the economy, and cultural change. Then, the authors remove some of these isolated elements from their position in time; infant mortality as a surrogate for urban conditions in 1905 and the results applied to the period before 1850, unemployment in 1851—92 as a surrogate for unemployment in earlier times, and they remove all elements from their location in space. (The authors would also like to isolate the 'economic' from the 'political', and, somehow, remove the Napoleonic Wars from the account.) The method also requires the assumption that there is some meaningful, rational, price-related way in which the gains of some (some male wage-earners) can be held to off-set the losses of others (infants dying under one year of age, the unemployed) — just as, in the past, Hartwell believed the benefits alleged to have accrued to women through the emancipation of women offset any ·losses experienced by earlier generations of male and female workers. Accordingly, the authors, working on the assumption that relations of production and human relations are reducible to relative prices, make commensurate the incommensurable, and add together the small number of elements previously isolated to

---

[47] *The Second Report of the Commissioners on the Housing of the Working Classes*, 1884—5 (Scotland), pp. 51—2 and Vol. 3, p. 501. See also, Anthony Sutcliffe (ed.), *Multi-Storey Living: The British Working Class Experience* (London, 1974), where it is shown that 'improvement' schemes in Liverpool exacerbated the housing problem such that by the late 1860s, 100,000 people were crowded into a shrinking and physically decaying stock of cheap pre-1840 housing, and mortality rates were higher than in the mid-1840s (pp. 41—81). Also in the first 40 years of the nineteenth century the 'backgreens' in Glasgow were built out and population densities rose to 1,000 per acre. Any improvement to housing came after 1850 (p. 214). For the effects of the Small Tenement;s Recovery Act, 1838, and for the housing problem as it persisted, particularly in London and Scotland in the 1860s and 1880s, see David Englander, *Landlord and Tenant in Urban Britain, 1838—1918* (Oxford, 1983).

produce the simple Benthamite calculus which is the basis of their proclamation of the 'final solution', when it is clearly no such thing. They have simply represented the past as progressing through homogenous empty time.

That is all their method allows. The method, with its ideological basis in the formulations of neo-classical (positivist) economics, is inherently incapable of generating descriptions of the varieties of human experience that would need to be incorporated in any attempt to describe the material and cultural experience of a whole population in the century or so after 1750. Their argument, wedded to the elusive concept of 'Industrial Revolution' as a causal factor, has no theoretical capacity to analyse causal relations between economy and culture (as a whole way of life) for any period. Perhaps it was, on the day Williamson set out from Loretto thinking he was in Rome, the people were out of town celebrating one of their many saint's days.

Lindert and Williamson's conclusion to their contribution to the standard of living debate has simply left it where it was. When they say that issues such as inequality, social injustice, social disorder, crime, alcoholism, and protest, not trends in absolute living standards should be the 'future battleground' about how workers fared under nineteenth-century British capitalism, they merely return the question to the point it had reached 20 years ago. What, I wonder, do Lindert and Williamson think the corpus of writing on class and class consciousness and culture over the last 25 years has been about? Where would they place popular newspapers, brass bands, the Small Tenements Recovery Act, 1838, and pig clubs in their analysis?

So to my fundamental objection to Lindert and Williamson's treatise on workers' living standards and the quality of their lives.

Lindert and Williamson believe that the question of living standards in the period 1780–1850, is politically charged. It is. And, in his paper on 'Dark Satanic Mills', Williamson signals that he thinks it has something to do with the ideas of Karl Marx;[48] which it has. Nevertheless, Lindert and Williamson's Karl Marx is a vague and shadowy figure, mostly understood through the writings of a handful of historians vaguely labelled 'pessimists'. Accordingly, in their bid for victory on the battleground of their choice, they use a scatter-gun rather than a precision rifle equipped with the latest aiming device. Consequently, nothing they have to say has any bearing upon the central arguments of the materialist conception of history. As I have emphasized strongly elsewhere, Marx, commenting about the consequences for social being and consciousness of the capitalist mode of production, was not only, or even mainly concerned with problems of distribution. On the other hand, everything Lindert and Williamson write

---

[48] Williamson, 'Urban Disamenities', p. 75.

about focuses on the distribution question. Consequently they miss the point of Marx's critique of the capitalist mode of production. Therefore, they miss the essential content of the political charge of the standard of living debate, at least as it is understood by Marxists. But they are not alone in this.

The core of Marx's critique is to be found in characteristics attributed to the capitalist mode of production subsumed in the concepts alienation and immiseration. While these concepts incorporate unequal distribution and the condition of the reserve army and the lumpen proletariat, they direct attention to more important issues. These are control of the means of production and appropriation, and those relationships between economic control and political and cultural power, which would prevent labourers (men and women) appropriating the product of their labour and realizing their human creative potential in conditions of freedom. While Marx on the income distribution effects of immiseration can be said to have argued in terms of absolute immiseration, there is much in his writing which suggests that he thought in terms of relative shifts in distribution, during different phases of the trade cycle, but within a developing and changing capitalist world system. With regard to the main thrust of his analysis, focusing upon the concepts alienation and immiseration, which are *not* reducible to Lindert and Williamson's 'urban disamenities', not yet to their 'quality of life', Marx was clear that it was power and control at one pole and unfreedom at the other, that was of paramount importance. Marx, writing on Lassalle and the iron law of wages, in *The Critique of the Gotha Programme*, dealt once and for all with the Linderts and Williamsons of his own day. His response to Lassalle in 1875 is still the most appropriate response to the economistic arguments of Lindert and Williamson in 1983. Although this point was made some two years before Lindert and Williamson published their novel findings, it seems appropriate to repeat it now. I wrote:

The essence of Marx's critical comment (on Lassalle) was that the real evil of the capitalist system lies in the unequal power relationship involved in the wage contract. In this relationship the worker parts with his/her labour power but receives in exchange just enough to subsist, or what Marx referred to as mere permission to live. It is a system of slavery and as such it is a power relationship. Indeed, capitalism is a system of 'slavery which becomes more severe in proportion as the social productive forces of labour develop, whether the worker receives better or worse payment'.a Marx emphasized that it is this slavery of the system that is at fault, not the fact that the slaves are poor. He concluded his critique of the Lassallean notion of the iron law of wages with the following words: 'It is as if, among slaves who have at last got behind the secret of slavery and broken out in rebellion, a slave still in thrall to obsolete notions were to inscribe on the programme of the rebellion: slavery must be abolished because the feeding of slaves in the system of slavery cannot exceed a certain low maximum!'b This statement alone should have convinced the German Social Democrats at Gotha, and all those who adopt an economist position, that Marx's critique of capitalism did not hang upon the fact that most were poor and likely to get poorer. As Marx made plain, it is essentially the authoritarian and alienating relations inherent in capitalism, relations subsumed and brought to their highest degree of antagonism in *class* relations, which he attacked, and which he believed would be removed through the mediation of the proletariat. Thus, while the Unity programme concluded by calling weakly for 'the elimination of all social and political inequality', Marx said it ought to have asserted the need for the abolition of all *class* distinctions, that is, property relations, for then 'all social and political inequality arising from them would disappear of itself.'[49]

Accordingly, there can be little doubt that the issues of central concern to Marx were; power, control, and the degree to which there was symmetry between the great technological productive capacity of the capitalist mode of production, on the one hand, and human freedom and equity, on the other, both in regard to decision-making (the exercise of control), and appropriation of the product. All this, of course, is to be explored in a world context. The claim is that capitalism and the capitalist state left to themselves concentrate subordination, alienation and immiseration at the one pole, and power, economic control and appropriation of the surplus product in the hands of a minority at the other. (Hence, in England a militarized police force and £200 million a year are used to break a strike, there is widespread famine in Africa and industrial catastrophe in Bhopal and absolute immiseration in both places relieved, if at all, only by charity. At the other extreme there are jogging harnesses for dogs, and dog kennels with thatched roofs to be bought for £600 each at Harrods.) This claim does not rest on the notion of some catastrophic departure from supposedly idyllic, pre-capitalist circumstances (as Hartwell seems to think it does). Nor does it stand or fall depending on calculations of national income per capita, national indices of real wages, nor yet the use of infant mortality rates as surrogates for urban conditions and the quality of life in limited cases. And it does not stand or fall according to a positivist/empiricist calculus of the additional items listed for research by

---

[49] R. S. Neale, *Class in English History, 1680—1850* (Oxford, 1981), pp. 36—7. The quotation (a) and (b) are from Karl Marx, *Critique of the Gotha Programme,* in Marx/Engels, *Selected Works,* Vol. II, pp. 27—8.

Lindert and Williamson. This is to say that the epistemological paradigm, within which Lindert and Williamson work, has no special status in dealing with these issues. Indeed, the notion that one can fragment the process of enquiry into the wholeness of human experience, attribute a 'price' to each fragment, make commensurate the incommensurable, and add up (or subtract) the fragments into a new national 'whole' of our own making, irrespective of the lived and felt experience of those whose lives we have fragmented, and do all this with a view of the past as homogenous, empty time, is itself an aspect of the problem to be studied — Lindert and Williamson *are* suitable cases for study. For my part, I merely decline to step inside their method, except as I have done in this chapter, to show that Lindert and Williamson are not even very good at their own business.

Unfortunately, those Marxist historians who entered the debate on the standard of living question in the post-war period, notably E. J. Hobsbawm and E. P. Thompson, did so on terms laid down by their positivist, empiricist opponents, and with only a weak or soft version of the materialist conception of history behind them. My own 'people's history' contribution in 1966 was also poorly theorized. Consequently it was never clearly argued that Marx's system was concerned with the alienating consequences of and possibilities for class formation within the capitalist mode of production, as it changed and was changed over time, not with the consequences of something called 'The Industrial Revolution'. The concept alienation was never used by Marxist historians, let alone placed in the forefront of the debate. (One of the alienating consequences, I believe, of the division of intellectual labour in our time.) Thus, it was not Marx's corpus of ideas — the materialist conception of history — that was at stake in the 1950s and 1960s. It is not that corpus of ideas that is at stake now, in the 1980s, only the reputations of some historians as history writers, and of some others as Marxists.

Nevertheless, because other Marxists have long recognized that that which is contained in the passage quoted above does represent the essence of Marx's case against capitalism, some of them have explored class formation and class consciousness in the eighteenth and nineteenth centuries for what they can tell us about human experience. And others, particularly from the moment of the Frankfurt School and of Gramsci, have sought to understand and account for the hegemonic incorporation of the working classes in industrial nations. And Raymond Williams has laboured to relate economy to culture, as a whole way of life and as creativity (the quality of life?) in ways seemingly beyond the comprehension of Lindert and Williamson, for the past 30 years. Over the same period, H. J. Dyos, making urban history his own, has expressed views about the quality of urban life and how it should be studied, wholly at odds with the concept and econometric short cuts adopted by Lindert and Williamson.[50] I agree with Dyos that in any historical construction there will be much that is left over. Compared with this work, Lindert and Williamson's, structured by their penchant for regression analysis using surrogate data in place of contemporary evidence, by the narrow bases of their general laws and Benthamite calculus, and by their poor specification of what they claim to measure, blocks enquiry and understanding. Steeped as they are in the idea of progress they merely demonstrate the poverty of positivism.

CONCLUSION

There can be no positivist 'final solution' to the questions Lindert and Williamson think they address; the standard of living and the quality of life. Their task at the aggregative level, as they understand it, is an impossible one (the national income approach does it better without pretending to describe reality), and one not worth the effort nor the econometric sleight of hand, nor yet the double think involved, namely, positing a simplistic theoretical (positivist) construction of the past and knowing it as such, yet believing that it represents the past as it really was. On the other hand, since the past (Britain in the period 1780—1850) can only be theoretically constructed it is probably better, because of greater content, to think of this past in terms of its complex articulation of modes of production and social relations, and uneven economic development. Therefore, we have to explore the tensions and conflicts, the gains and losses, material and immaterial, across a range of human experience, understand that there were class and regional differences in that experience, exacerbated and complicated by the sexual division of labour, and by religious and ethnic conflict, and remember that the winners never did compensate the losers.

As I approach this task, I prefer to replace Lindert and Williamson's idea of progress unlimited with Walter Benjamin's image of the angel of history:

[50] See, for example: E. P. Thompson, *The Making of the English Working Class* (London, 1963); R. S. Neale (ed.), *History and Class: Essential Readings in Theory and Interpretation* (Oxford, 1983), (see the Suggested Readings); Andrew Arato and Eike Gebhardt, *The Essential Frankfurt School Reader* (Oxford, 1978); Walter Benjamin, *Illuminations* (London, 1970); Raymond Williams, *Marxism and Literature* (Oxford, 1977); *Politics and Letters* (London, 1979), *Culture* (London, 1981); H. J. Dyos, *Exploring the Urban Past: Essays in Urban History* (Cambridge, 1982).

F

A Klee painting named 'Angelus Novus' shows an angel looking as though he is about to move away from something he is fixedly contemplating. His eyes are staring, his mouth is open, his wings are spread. This is how one pictures the angel of history. His face is turned toward the past. Where we perceive a chain of events, he sees one single catastrophe which keeps piling wreckage upon wreckage and hurls it in front of his feet. The angel would like to stay, awaken the dead, and make whole what has been smashed. But a storm is blowing from Paradise; it has got caught in his wings with such violence that the angel can no longer close them. This storm irresistibly propels him into the future to which his back is turned while the pile of debris before him grows skyward. This storm is what we call progress.[51]

The storm is also the passage of time. Among the debris left behind is evidence about standards of living and the quality of lives. As we recede into the future we can only build our images of the past theoretically (dialectically) and empathetically, relating structure to agency, barrowload by local barrowload; making an image here and an image there, always leaving something to our readers and to posterity.[52]

---

[51] Walter Benjamin, 'Theses on the Philosophy of History', in *Illuminations* (London, 1973), p. 259.

[52] Philip Abrams, *Historical Sociology* (Shepton Mallet, 1982), p. 318, wrote, 'The capacity to observe, describe, reconstitute or resurrect is not to be confused with the capacity to judge, interpret, explain and make sense. Yet just such confusion abounds in 'how it was' studies, compounded often by the dazzling sophistication of this or that newly found research procedure.' Although he wrote about Laslett and Le Roy Ladurie he might well have written about Lindert and Williamson. Abrams's general conclusion was that, 'the reality of the past is just not "there" waiting to be observed by the resurrectionist historian. It is to be known if at all through strenuous theoretical alienation' (p. 331).

7

Class and Urban History, and the Historian's Task

I wrote this chapter, and chapter 6, during the same period, taking time off from one to finish the other. There is no gap between them — the two most determined muleteers will also be encountered in this chapter. The two chapters cover much the same distance, from about 1780 (or 1750) to the First World War (or the 1930s), and they simply reach Camden Town by two different routes, and with different travelling companions. In chapter 6 our dealings were mainly with passive workers, mulishly experiencing and putting up with what was done to them. In this chapter some of the same workers, dressed in their Sunday best, are seen trying to take control of their lives in various ways, and becoming increasingly urban dwellers. But they are also joined by the middle-class (or some of them), and by women. The issue of the quality of lives, raised in chapter 6, becomes in this chapter a major question, and a question of theory. In this regard it brings our journey into our present, signalling the major theoretical concern of chapter 10.

* * *

The untimely death of H. J. Dyos in 1978 has led David Cannadine and David Reeder to evaluate the Dyos phenomenon and the phenomenon of urban history.[1] Their work is both panegyric and valediction. Reeder praises highly Dyos's work. But Cannadine, while acknowledging Dyos's entrepreneurship in the field of urban history asks; 'What, if anything, did it [urban history] stand for intellectually?' His own reply is; 'In fact it stood for very little.'[2] A view apparently expressed by Dyos himself. Urban history, according to Dyos: 'is a field of knowledge, not a single discipline

---

[1] David Cannadine and David Reeder (eds), *Exploring the Urban Past: Essays in Urban History by H. J. Dyos* (Cambridge, 1982).

[2] Ibid., p. 207.

Albion Rose or Glad Day (William Blake, c.1795: by kind permission of the Trustees of the British Museum)

in the accepted sense but a field in which many disciplines converge, or at
any rate are drawn upon. It is a focus for a variety of forms of knowledge,
not a form of knowledge itself.'[3] Accordingly, Cannadine tries to rescue
urban history from the intellectual void into which he cast it (and where
Dyos found it) by pointing to a myriad of new directions it opened up to
historical enquiry. He writes:

Nevertheless, what *could* be said in favour of urban history was that it had
made popular and respectable a whole variety of important subjects which
might not otherwise have been taken so seriously as objects of scholarly
endeavour. Sydney Checkland once listed them, and the catalogue is
impressive: housing, building, land use, land tenure, transportation,
administration, finance, politics, health, sanitation, food supplies, population,
family, social class, elites, power structure, sub-cultures, crime, conflict,
protest, philanthropy, welfare, architecture, spatial planning, the demands of
terrain, the aesthetics of the city, locational advantage, the industrial mix, the
commercial facilities of the central business district. Perhaps this list did not
really add up to anything coherent which could with intellectual conviction be
labelled urban history. But it did mean that, for the first time, many aspects of
city life were being taken seriously as objects of historical study.[4]

Notwithstanding the fact that Checkland was simply listing the thematic
contents of the *Urban History Newsletter* in 1966,[5] Cannadine's claim,
although qualified by the italicized *could*, asserts a certain historiographical
lineage. In the history of ideas, urban history beginning in the 1960s, was
a necessary catalyst for the serious scholarly study of subjects such as;
social class, elites, power structure, conflict, protest and politics. If this is
true (Checkland's own listing did not have this connotation), then it is an
indictment of the main stream of British empiricist historiography, and I
leave others to quarrel with it. But it is false and presumptuous with
regard to those outside the mainstream who, faced with the reality of
class, power and conflict over the past 200 years, have frequently devoted
a lifetime of scholarly endeavour to those very subjects.

The simple fact is that as objects of scholarly endeavour, class, politics
and power, with associated aspects of reality subsumed in the concepts,
class consciousness, social conflict and protest, did not wait upon the
burgeoning of urban history in the 1960s and 1970s. They derived their
scholarly significance from experience. Urban history, whether form or

---

[3] Ibid., H. J. Dyos, 'Urbanity and Suburbanity', p. 31.
[4] Ibid., p. 211.
[5] S. G. Checkland, 'Towards a Definition of Urban History' in H. J. Dyos (ed.) *The Study of Urban History* (London, 1968), p. 351.

field of knowledge, has no special claim to have advanced our knowledge of them. What has happened over the last 30 years or so, is that some historians, particularly that large body of post-graduate students studying the later modern period, have perforce studied these issues in urban contexts. At the same time, some practitioners of social history (a renewed discipline since the 1960s), with at least one foot in Marxist historiography, have begun to comprehend and accept the need for more theoretically based analyses of causation in historical explanation. This has led in turn to a need for greater clarity in identifying the content of concepts such as class and class consciousness, also frequently in local and necessarily urban settings.

More recently still, some observers, such as Frank Parkin[6] and Philip Abrams,[7] have seen urban history's claims as even more peripheral. They argue that relationships between structure and agency, which is the crucial issue in the study of class, is more a matter of theory than it is a question of urban empirical enquiry. Urban historians, on the other hand, believe they can demonstrate empirically the domination of agency over structure.[8]

In recent years, neither empirical urban historians, nor theorists of class and of history, nor yet both together, have had as much to say about urban history and class theory as Alan Bleasdale's *Boys from the Blackstuff*.[9] The way these plays, arising out of experience, relate agency to the mode of production in a real place and in real time, and return the argument to the people themselves, reveal academic squabbles and urban historians' failed attempts to describe urban life as it really was, trivial and insubstantial. Were it not for the primacy given by the intellectual world to the written word and the rapidly fading image of the television picture (none of 20 or so colleagues at a workshop at the University of New England had watched this series of plays), I would stop writing at this point. *Boys from the Blackstuff* explores relationships between classes in

---

[6] Frank Parkin, *Marxism and Class Theory: A Bourgeois Critique* (London, 1979). Apart from market reasons it is difficult to see why Parkin calls his book 'A Bourgeois Critique'. Parkin is not a bourgeois, at least in Marxist terms. Moreover, he concedes the relevance of Marxism to earlier periods (p. 9) and argues a case for restoring property to the centre of class analysis (pp. 53, 59). His might as well have been a 'Marxist Critique'. His point about 'closure' is an argument about agency. As far as I can tell, it has yet to enter urban or class history.

[7] Philip Abrams, *Historical Sociology* (Shepton Mallet, 1982) a more thoroughly historically based assessment of Marxism than Parkin's.

[8] See below the section on McLeod and McIntyre.

[9] Alan Bleasdale, '*Boys from the Blackstuff*' BBC, 1983.

an urban context more persuasively, and, I think theoretically, than any words of mine could do. But, I continue.

My purpose in this chapter is to comment upon connections between urban and class history, as related in (mostly) recent work in urban and class history and mainly in books, in order to explore relationships between theory and practice in historiography. The main points to be discussed are; (1) relations between structure and agency; (2) the importance and structuring effect of property relations in giving physical shape to towns and shaping social relations, and the consequent variety of forms of social protest; (3) the dissolution of the common-sense, three-class model of class, and the modification of traditional class theory brought about by studies in the consciousness of artisans, and of the role of sex, religion and nationality in class formation; (4) the question of urban historians' capacity to know what it *felt* like to live in towns and cities in the past; (5) the need for a new discipline linking (urban) culture to economy. And this leads to my second disclaimer. Although a survey of the use of class in history and of the part played by urban history in class history, this chapter is not one of those 'breathless reviews of the writing of urban history'[10] elegantly run by Dyos in 1966, and attempted by Cannadine in 1982.[11] Like all history it is necessarily selective. Its selection is dictated by my purpose and by space.

Class has been central to the materialist conception of history since Marx wrote *A Contribution to the Critique of Hegel's 'Philosophy of Right'* in 1843/44.[12] But it is well known that Marx claimed no originality in his identification of class as a proper object of scholarly enquiry — he acknowledged the prior claim of the Scottish school of political economists.

---

[10] H. J. Dyos, 'Agenda for Urban Historians' in H. J. Dyos (ed.), *The Study of Urban History* p. 42. This means that many important books, which bear only marginally on the question of class as I have treated it in this paper, have had to be omitted from the discussion. I list a few, which, in my view, could be incorporated in an extended study of class and urban history. Michael Anderson, *Family Structure in Nineteenth Century Lancashire* (Cambridge, 1971); Brian Jackson and Dennis Marsden, *Education and the Working Class* (London, 1962); Stefan Muthesius, *The English Terraced House* (New Haven and London, 1982); Antony Sutcliffe, *Multi-Storey Living: The British Working Experience* (London, 1974); Karel Williams, *From Pauperism to Poverty* (London, 1981); A. J. Youngson, *The Making of Classical Edinburgh* (Edinburgh, 1966).

[11] David Cannadine, 'Urban history in the United Kingdom: the 'Dyos phenomenon' and after', in Cannadine and Reeder (eds), pp. 203—21.

[12] Karl Marx, A contribution to the Critique of Hegel's 'Philosophy of Right', edited with an introduction by Joseph O'Malley, (Cambridge, 1970). A substantial extract is reproduced in R. S. Neale (ed.), *History and Class: Essential Readings in Theory and Interpretation* (Oxford, 1983), pp. 31—7.

What Marx did was to place class relations at the centre of historical development, give to class a definite location in the production process, and give a clearer and different content to the notion of *class* consciousness than that assumed by most of his contemporaries (for this usage see my Class in English History, ch. 1). They continued to use notions of class and class consciousness in a common-sense and ill-defined way, but in ways shaped largely by the notion of the three factors of production of classical political economy. Indeed, I would say that Marx's *The Eighteenth Brumaire of Louis Bonaparte* and *The Class Struggles in France 1848—1850*,[13] with their focus on class relations in Paris as well as among the peasantry, place him still in the forefront of urban historians using the concept class to explain political phenomena of the utmost importance. It was in the opening paragraphs of *The Eighteenth Brumaire* that Marx set out the conditions for relationships between structure and agency, emphasized the place of traditional culture in shaping the possibilities for present action, and drew attention to the importance of the existing range of images of self-perception in shaping the course of that action. In doing so, he laid down the outlines for a research programme in urban history which few urban historians have dared to tackle. Marx wrote,

Men make their own history, but they do not make it just as they please; they do not make it under circumstances chosen by themselves, but under circumstances directly encountered, given and transmitted from the past. The tradition of all the dead generations weighs like a nightmare on the brain of the living. And just when they seem engaged in revolutionizing themselves and things, in creating something that has never yet existed, precisely in such periods of revolutionary crisis they anxiously conjure up the spirits of the past to their service and borrow from them names, battle cries and costumes in order to present the new scene of world history in this time-honoured disguise and this borrowed language.[14]

Yet there were, and are, serious problems with *class* and *class* consciousness, and until the post-Second World War period, analysis of class by Marxists remained almost as simplistic as that of mainstream historians. There was a tendency to assume a national cohesion and homogeneity among the English working classes that was frequently

[13] Karl Marx, 'The Eighteenth Brumaire of Louis Bonaparte' and ' The Class Struggles in France 1848—1850' in Marx/Engels, *Selected Works, Vol. 1.* (London, 1950), pp. 109—311.

[14] Ibid., p. 225.

absent in practice, and a neglect of sexual, religious and national influences on class formation. The accepted Leninist wisdom was that structure alone was determining and that workers, left to their own devices, could scarcely get beyond a trade union consciousness. Indeed, the prevailing view was that the English working class and its leadership had been diverted from their anticipated revolutionary role by monopoly capitalism and imperialism.[15] In short, Marx's analysis of a process of alienation under capitalist development was mistaken for description of class structure in Britain at different points in the past and present. Taken in by Marx's prediction of the polarization of classes, and in the 1920s and 1930s, by the exigencies of Stalinist politics, and, of course, vastly outnumbered, English Marxists made no contribution to class theory. As Eric Hobsbawm writes, at the time of the formation of the Communist Party Historians' Group in 1946: 'There was no tradition of Marxist history in Britain.'[16] The common-sense model of three more or less homogeneous classes held sway.

This common-sense model is still important in the intellectual tool-kit of modern historians. Thus R. J. Morris, in *Class and Class Consciousness in the Industrial Revolution 1780−1830* (1979), a survey of the field of writers on class, claims that the three-class model, based on economic criteria such as income, source of income, or economic interest 'is the most natural way to think about class in an industrial society'. He also believes, that class models or explanations couched in class terms not, 'based on the sort of convergence of economic and ideological interest which is essential to class formation', and, presumably, found in the common-sense model, must be in 'error'.[17] An equally if not more important approach to class espoused by historians of modern urban society is eclectic and atheoretical. Like Arthur Marwick, in *Class: Image and Reality in Britain, France and the USA Since 1920* (1981), the devotees of this approach go out of their way to assert their atheoretical, down-to-earth use of ordinary language. Marwick writes: 'I prefer the "ordinary language". I prefer "class" to mean what people in every day life mean by it, rather than what Runciman or Weber tell me I should mean by it. . . . Class, perhaps, is too serious a subject to leave to the social

[15] See, for example, Lenin's argument about the effect of ' the parasitism and decay of capitalism' on the class structure and class consciousness of the English, in V. I. Lenin, *Imperialism the Highest Stage of Capitalism* (London, 1948).

[16] E. J. Hobsbawm, 'The Communist Party Historians' Group' in M. Cornforth (ed.), *Rebels and Their Causes* (London, 1978), p. 22.

[17] R. J. Morris, *Class and Class Consciousness in the Industrial Revolution 1780−1830* (London, 1979), pp. 32, 34.

scientist.'[18] A third approach to class, perhaps less common than it was, is that of historians who see no problems in the use of language, and assume that class and class consciousness are understood by their readers in the way they are understood by themselves. For this category of historians, urban or otherwise, words are signals.[19]

Probably, most British urban historians, when writing about class, use a mixture of these three approaches, and remain within the conceptual boundaries of the common-sense, three-class model of social structure. For, example, the debate on standards of living in Britain in the period 1780—1850 has troubled the hearts if not the minds of generations of English, Australian and now, American historians. Until 1966, the historians involved, Marxist and non-Marxist alike, mainly wrote as if their task was to determine the living standards and quality of life of a nationally homogeneous class of workers. The alternative approach, which seeks to establish limited truths about particular occupational groups mainly in urban contexts such as Bath, Birmingham, Carlisle and Glasgow, owes more to the traditional interests and practices of economic historians than to urban history or to urban historians *per se*.[20] However, even though at least one contributor to this alternative approach has worked within a broadly Marxist framework, it, too, is poorly theorized, at least from a Marxist point of view. Now, however, in 1983, P. A. Lindert and J. G. Williamson, in 'English Workers' Living Standards during the Industrial Revolution: A New Look',[21] have sought to override this alternative approach and to write a nationally derived 'final solution' to the standard of living question. They use econometric techniques derived from urban economics and urban history to make their case. Yet the

---

[18] Arthur Marwick, *Class: Image and Reality in Britain, France and the USA since 1930* (London, 1981), p. 15.

[19] See my discussion in R. S. Neale, *Class in English History 1680—1850* (London, 1981), pp. 100—19.

[20] R. S. Neale, 'The Standard of Living 1780—1844: A Regional and Class Study', *The Economic History Review* 2nd Series, Vol. XIX (1966), pp. 590—606. See also R. T. Gourvish 'The Cost of Living in Glasgow in the early nineteenth century', *The Economic History Review* 2nd Series, XXV (1972), pp. 65—80; G. J. Barnsby, 'The Standard of Living in the Black Country during the nineteenth century', *The Economic History Review* 2nd Series, XXIV (1971), pp. 120—39; W. A. Armstrong, 'The Trend of Mortality in Carlisle between the 1780s and the 1840s: a Demographic Contribution to the Standard of Living Debate', *The Economic History Review,* 2nd Series, XXIX (1981), pp. 94—114; R. A. Cage, 'The Standard of Living Debate: Glasgow, 1800—1850', *The Journal of Economic History,* Vol. XLIII, March 1983, No. 1. pp. 175—82; and D. J. Oddy, 'Urban Famine in Nineteenth Century Britain: The Effect of the Lancashire Cotton Famine on Working-Class Diet and Health', *The Economic History Review,* 2nd Series, XXXVI (1983), pp. 68—86.

concept — the standard of living — discussed by the authors is elusive. In their hands, the concept slides imperceptibly from standard of living, through standard of life, material well being, hardships faced by workers, workers' net gains to human gains and to quality of urban life. What is more, the authors employ the concept of 'all workers' (which is a concept of class), which excludes all domestic servants, all women workers, and all handloom weavers, and they use the wages of spinners as a surrogate for the wages of a whole class of textile workers. Their class of 'all workers' includes judges, lawyers and court officials! This work by exponents of the econometric method in urban history is the apotheosis of all stratificationist definitions of class based on source of income, and of all empiricist approaches to the study of class experience in urban history.

The taxonomy of historians' usage of class, set out in my *Class in English History 1680−1850* (1981),[22] and briefly outlined here, remains valid, but it seems that the threat to serious historical enquiry inherent in it is far greater than I imagined in the mid-1970s. Notions of class as generally used in urban history have little analytical power, and can rarely carry the burden of description and explanation placed upon them. It is time, therefore, to turn to more worthwhile theoretical approaches to the study of class in the context of urban history.

In the post-Second World War period, all but one of the theoretical or more clearly conceptualized approaches used in the historical study of class, whether or not they have been applied in urban contexts, derive from Marx or/and arose out of attempts to modify or combat some characteristic of his analysis. The exception I will call for the time being 'the Dyos approach'. But even that arose out of a concern to comprehend consciousness and agency in urban settings. The purpose of this 'Dyos approach' — to know what it was like to be alive, say, in Victorian London, which will be discussed later, is itself an aspect of the wider question of the relationship between agency and structure already placed on the agenda by the materialist conception of history. Therefore, as Dyos's question and approach seem to be the central concern of many urban historians, one might say that, heading the hidden agenda for urban history is the materialist conception of history and the meaning to be

---

[21] Peter H. Lindert and Jeffrey G. Williamson, 'English Workers' Living Standards during the Industrial Revolution: A New Look', *The Economic History Review* 2nd Series, XXXVI (1983), p. 24; and Jeffrey G. Williamson, 'Urban Disamenities, Dark Satanic Mills, and the British Standard of Living Debate', *The Journal of Economic History*, Vol. XLIII, March 1983, No. 1.

[22] R. S. Neale, 'The Standard of Living'.

attributed to its major determinist proposition: 'it is not the consciousness of men that determines their being, but, on the contrary, their social being that determines their consciousness.'[23]

When all qualifications have been made I think it true to say that the publication of E. P. Thompson's *Making of The English Working Class* (1963) marked a theoretical turning point in English historical writing about class and culture. Taking issue with the fixed categories of vulgar Marxism, classical political economy, positivist sociology and mainstream historiography, Thompson writes:

By class I understand an historical phenomenon, unifying a number of disparate and seemingly unconnected events, both in the raw material of experience and in consciousness. I emphasize that it is an *historical* phenomenon. I do not see class as a 'structure', or even as a 'category', but as something which in fact happens (and can be shown to have happened) in human relationships. . . . Class is defined by men as they live their own history, and, in the end, this is its only definition . . . class is a cultural as much as an economic formation.[24]

Accordingly, Thompson describes a lineage of self-conscious, sometimes militant working-class activity, each group contributing its mite to a developing working-class consciousness, rather in the way the Olympic torch is carried from one outburst of activity to the next. This idea of a non-class of labouring people making themselves, through experience and struggle, into a working class is developed in his 1978 paper in *Social History*.[25]

The revolutionary, and for many historians, the liberating effect of a work in Marxist historiography based on such a premiss is demonstrated by the quantity of critical and adulatory writing devoted to it and by imitation.[26] For example, very recently, R. W. Connell and T. H. Irving

[23] Karl Marx, 'Preface to a Contribution to the Critique of Political Economy', Marx/Engels, *Selected Works*, p. 329.

[24] E. P. Thompson, *The Making of the English Working Class* (London, 1963), pp. 9, 11, 13.

[25] E. P. Thompson, 'Eighteenth-century English Society: class struggle without class', *Social History*, 3 (2) (May 1978).

[26] See, for example, Perry Anderson, *Arguments within English Marxism* (London, 1980); Craig Calhoun, *The Question of Class Struggle* (Chicago and London, 1982); R. Currie and R. M. Hartwell, 'The Making of the English Working Class?' *The Economic History Review*, 2nd Series, 18, pp. 633–43; F. K. Donnelly 'Ideology and Early English Working-Class History: Edward Thompson and His Critics', *Social History*, No 2 (1976), pp. 219–38; Richard Johnson 'Edward Thompson, Eugene Genovese, and Socialist-Humanist History', *History Workshop*, 6 (1978), pp. 79–106;

have used Thompson's notion of class to underpin their own class analysis of the development of Australia, perhaps the most urbanized nation in the world by the end of the nineteenth century.[27]

The Making of the English Working Class is also a work in urban history necessarily using local illustration and urban examples to make its case, but it is not a work of urban history. Its central questions did not arise out of problems in urban history, but from Thompson's own experience in a particular conjuncture of national and world politics as shaped by an existing intellectual and cultural milieu. But the book has profoundly influenced the course of urban history and of history writing in general, giving it a culturalist orientation, muting the political thrust of the history of working-class response to the impact of industrialization and urbanization. The most recent culmination of this trend is Craig Calhoun, *The Question of Class Struggle* (1982). Calhoun uses social-anthropological theorizing about the structuring effect of community, in conjunction with empirical work on six urban communities in south-east Lancashire, and much of Thompson's own evidence, to maintain a sustained critique of *The Making of the English Working Class*, to show that what Thompson had actually identified was not class but community! Furthermore, he turns Thompson's notion of class on its head. He claims that the true significance of the real past, represented by Thompson's empirical work, may only be grasped if we shift our theoretical standpoint; if we relegate consciousness to its secondary role and concentrate on identifying those forms of social organization which determine the conditions or boundaries for social action. Hence the importance of community. The conclusion of his work is that 'There is a real and problematical sense in which [Thompson] chronicles not the making of the English working class but the rise and fall of the radical English artisanate.'[28]

F. K. Donnelly and J. L. Baxter, on the other hand, have maintained that something close to a 'working-class' and revolutionary tradition was already in the making in some urban areas. Writing of Sheffield, they say: 'We must assert that the revolutionary tradition was a significant factor

---

Gregor McLennan, 'E. P. Thompson and the discipline of historical context' in CCCS, *Making Histories* (Birmingham 1982); Also, E. P. Thompson, *The Poverty of Theory* (London, 1978), *New Statesman*, May—June 1980; and R. S. Neale, *Class in English History*, and, 'Theory and History: A Note on the Anderson Thompson Debate', *Thesis Eleven*, 2 (1981), pp. 23—9. This comment on E. P. Thompson is greatly expanded in my 'E. P. Thompson, the history of culture and culturalist history: a critique' in Diane Austin (ed.), *Creating Culture: Landmarks in Cultural Analysis*, to be published by George Allen and Unwin.

[27] R. W. Connell and T. H. Irving, *Class Structure in Australian History* (Melbourne, 1980).

(in the period 1791—1820) . . . it constitutes a proto-working class response to the advance of early industrial capitalism.'[29] And Mary Thale has recently reaffirmed that the records of the London Corresponding Society 'reveal a dangerous challenge to the established government' in London.[30] While one might doubt whether these were *class* conscious 'working-class' movements in Marx's sense, there is reason to suppose, taking into account the fact of uneven economic development, that Calhoun's views complement rather than displace Thompson's. In which case, one may hold that the concept 'working-class' may continue to serve as a shorthand term describing some aspects of the developing industrial capitalist mode of production in the eighteenth century.

The question of what Thompson had actually identified — a lineage of (working)-*class* consciousness, the populism of pre-industrial communities, or an artisanal consciousness, was already an issue when *The Making of the English Working Class* appeared. In the mid-1960s, J. R. Vincent, Harold Perkin, Peter Laslett, and I, the first and last partly working in urban history, attempted to describe aspects of social structure and of consciousness not explicitly recognized in the common-sense and Marxist, including the Thompsonian, models of class. Although with different intellectual and immediately theoretical antecedents, each one generated a model of class and a new terminology to encapsulate important but missing components in the social-structural images used by historians to describe their constructions of reality. Each one was also unconcerned with the work of the others, at least on the surface. Each author seems an island unto himself. But the debate between them, and between them and Thompson is no less real for being implicit. Their silences are eloquent.

Vincent, much influenced by Ralf Dahrendorf, in *Poll Books: How Victorians Voted* (1967), argues that industrialization did not simply produce two classes — employers and workers — who would inevitably

---

[28] Craig Calhoun, *The Question of Class Struggle: Social Foundations of Popular Radicalism during the Industrial Revolution* (Chicago and London, 1982), p. 14. John Dinwiddy in a recent survey of the Pentridge Rising has concluded, 'Still, one may well doubt whether the revolutionary impulse that did occur was at all formidable. . . . Nor was it very sustained. . . . These years are . . . important, it may be suggested, as a stage in the process whereby working men came to regard democratic control of the state as an essential means to improvement of their condition,' (An argument which also hinges on the notion of a lineage of class consciousness) 'Luddism and politics in the northern counties', *Social History*, 4 (1), 1979, pp. 333—63.

[29] F. K. Donnelly and J. L. Baxter, 'Sheffield in the English Revolutionary tradition, 1791—1820', *International Review of Social History*, XX, 1975.

[30] Mary Thale (ed.), *Selections from the Papers of the London Corresponding*

become polarized into the two great antagonistic classes, bourgeoisie and proletariat, as postulated by Marx. On the contrary he says:

As a working hypothesis which at least fits a number of phenomena which would otherwise be puzzling, it may therefore be suggested that while the Industrial Revolution produced some proletarians in some factory districts, over the country in general the economic growth with which it was associated worked for quite a long time in favour of a wider distribution of small property and a diminution of the relative power of large property.[31]

He identifies the essential division in society as one between the capitalist property owners of a highly concentrated agriculture on the one hand, and the small property owners in an urban system of petty production and exchange, on the other. He describes these urban petty producers as an urban 'free peasantry'.

My own work, 'Class and Class Consciousness in Nineteenth Century England: Three Classes or Five?' (1968) was also influenced by Dahrendorf. Although its immediate aim was to discredit the three-class structure of the still predominant common-sense model, my purpose was to enlarge not destroy Marx's schema. The urban stratum I tried to identify were not property owners as such, but artisans working in small workshops or on their own account, shopkeepers, and aspiring professional and educated men. I identified them as a 'middling class' individuated or privatized like the middle class, but collectively less deferential towards authority, and more concerned to remove the privileges and authority of the upper class in which, without radical changes, they could not realistically hope to share. They were a social class in the 1820s to the 1840s important for the understanding of urban politics and the politics of the nation. Indeed, their presence in towns such as Birmingham, Bristol, Bath and Brighton, and experience of urban riots such as occurred in Bristol in 1831, lent credibility to the Philosophic Radicals' claim that revolution was in the offing if no concessions were made in the proposed Reform Bill.[32]

Society 1792—99 (Cambridge, 1983), p. vii.

[31] J. R. Vincent, *Poll Books: How Victorians Voted* (London, 1967), p. 7.

[32] R. S. Neale, 'Class and Class Consciousness in Nineteenth Century England: Three Classes or Five?' *Victorian Studies,* Vol. 12, No. 1, Sep. 1968. Reprinted in R. S. Neale, *Class and Ideology in the Nineteenth Century* (London, 1972), See also Joseph Hamburger, *Intellectuals in Politics: John Stuart Mill and the Philosophical Radicals* (New Haven, 1965) and *James Mill and The Art of Revolution* (New Haven, 1963). For connections between the Bristol riots and riots in Bath see R. S. Neale, *Bath 1680—1880*, pp. 339—44. There is still no adequate modern treatment of the Bristol Riots.

Perkin, unlike Vincent and I, was not influenced by Dahrendorf.[33] His theoretical debt was to R. Aron and T. H. Marshall. He argues that in the course of the Industrial Revolution, English society changed from being a classless society, structured around vertically linked associations based on property and patronage, to become, early in the nineteenth century, a three-class society, based on sources of income. However, in a very short time, it was the 'ideals' these people held, couched in idealistic, particularly sectarian terms, which were to be the basis of social conflict, not income. Perkin also identifies a fourth class, the 'forgotten middle class'. These were professional men virtually 'above the economic battle' and able to choose their 'ideal' from the range available. But, they did have their own functional 'ideal' based on expertise and selection by merit. They were also the source of ready-made 'social cranks', men able to free themselves from their own class 'who could be relied upon to come to the aid of any class but their own'. Perkin, like Calhoun after him, draws attention to the violence which characterized some communities in early industrial England, and noted that conflict resolution by violence is the mark of an immature class society. Sometime around 1815–20, what he called a 'viable' urban class society began to emerge. In this viable class society, classes, although separated by deep objective and subjective differences (income, for example), managed to live in a state of peaceful coexistence under the general umbrella of a successful entrepreneurial ideal.

Although Laslett's work on class is important for historians of class and of pre-industrial urban society, and I mention it for this reason, it does not impinge upon the main area of British urban history, the nineteenth and twentieth centuries.[34] Therefore, I do not discuss it here.

What then, is the importance for our purpose of Vincent's, Perkin's, and my work? It is, I think, that each has tried to identify as classes groups of men (and women) important at different stages in the history of urban industrial society not comprehended within the limited categories of the common-sense or Marxian models. Certainly it seemed (and still seems) to me that the common-sense model restricts understanding and explanation within a conceptual straitjacket, as does Marx's analytical/heuristic schema when treated as description. In this respect it is important to note that Thompson's revision of Marxist class theory did not challenge the

[33] Harold Perkin, *The Origins of Modern English Society 1780–1880* (London, 1969).

[34] Peter Laslett, *The World We Have Lost* (London, 1971), Key passages from Neale, Perkin and Laslett are reproduced in R. S. Neale (ed.), *History and Class: Essential Readings in Theory and Interpretation* (Oxford, 1983). They are also commented upon more fully in my *Class in English History*.

categories themselves, merely the manner in which the classness of the working class was alleged to come into being. Consequently, I suggest, it was because he remained in the same atheoretical straitjacket as those who accepted the common-sense model, that Thompson did not pursue to the full the implications of experience in an economy characterized by uneven economic development, and therefore, failed to draw Calhoun's conclusion from his own penultimate paragraph in *The Making*, where Thompson writes: 'Hence these years appear at times to display, not a revolutionary challenge, but a resistance movement, in which both the Romantics and the Radical craftsmen opposed the annunciation of Acquisitive Man'.[35]

Other historians have developed some of the themes broached by Vincent, Perkin, and me. The five-class model has been taken up as part of a more generally applicable theory of social structural development by Frank Beckhofer and Brian Elliot in 'Persistence and change: the petite bourgeoisie in industrial society' (1976).[36] Iowerth Prothero, *Artisans and Politics in Early Nineteenth-Century London: John Gast and his Times* (1979), has, in a blow by blow account, explored the immediacy of experience of the London artisanate as the foundation for their independence and respectability. He argues: 'the anti-capitalist ideas which evolved in this period were those appropriate to artisans, not opposing all masters but condemning "merchant capitalism", the monopolist middle-men. It was a theory, not of exploitation within production, but of unequal exchange. And for most of those who held it, it was no "false consciousness" but an accurate analysis of the situation.'[37] Artisans, in short, were not proletarians.

Geoffrey Crossick also pursues the theme of a London artisanate generating its own independent and respectable culture and consciousness, in *An Artisan Elite in Victorian Society* (1978). Using a simple measure of mobility and marriages as a measure of social distance, he pushes the argument and the existence of a distinctive artisanal consciousness into the 1880s. Artisans, he argues, came to assume a position of particular importance in organized working-class activities during the mid-Victorian decades. Then he suggests four conditions for the emergence of a labour, as distinct from an artisanal, consciousness at the end of the century; changes in the work situation associated with the introduction of new

---

[35] E. P. Thompson, *The Making of the English Working Class*, p. 832.

[36] Frank Beckhofer and Brian Elliott, 'Persistence and Change: petite bourgeoise in industrial society', *European Journal of Sociology*, XVII (1), 1976, pp. 74—99.

[37] Iowerth Prothero, *Artisans and Politics in Early Nineteenth Century London: John Gast and his Times* (Baton Rouge, 1979), p. 336.

technology and management practices threatening the work status of artisans; the emergence of a non-manual lower middle class threatening their social status; a continuing process of residential segregation restricting relations between artisans and higher social strata; and increasing tactical conflicts with organized liberalism.[38] Crossick's and Prothero's accounts of London artisans, when juxtaposed with Gareth Stedman Jones's discussion of the lowest social groups in London, finally dissolves the common-sense model of class structure, at least in London.[39]

It does so without considering the position of women in London's class structure. In fact Prothero ignores the opportunity to take seriously an early example of the development of a women's oppositional consciousness. Thus, although he knows about Elizabeth Sharples he chooses only to draw his readers attention to her sexual role — she became pregnant by Richard Carlile and became his common law wife.[40] The fact that London and the Rotunda in Southwark and the radical artisanal milieu he writes about, were also the forcing ground and opportunity for the expression of a radical women's consciousness escapes him. But urban history generally has little place for women. Thus the index to the report of the first conference on urban history contains no entry under women, or feminism, or suffrage, and only two women are listed in the text as historical figures — Elizabeth Gaskell and Beatrice Webb. (But Marx, too, only gets one entry.) Cannadine's survey, while drawing attention to the importance of Asa Briggs's work and its emphasis upon 'civic consciousness', does not notice any work in which 'women's consciousness' is granted a significant place.

Work on women and women's consciousness has proceeded outside the mainstream of urban and class history. The last few years has seen a number of publications directly relating sex and class in specific urban settings, notably Leonore Davidoff's 'Class and Gender in Victorian England', and Barbara Taylor's 'The Men are as Bad as Their Masters; Socialism, Feminism and Sexual Antagonism in the London Tailoring Trades in the 1830s'. This work also contributes to a subtle dissolution of all existing class models of social structure, but reaffirms the determination of the capitalist mode of production. As the editors of *Sex and Class in Women's History* argue:

[38] Geoffrey Crossick, *An Artisan Elite in Victorian Society* (London, 1978), especially pp. 243–54. See for the lower middle class the same author's, *The Lower Middle Class in Britain* (London, 1977).

[39] Gareth Stedman Jones, *Outcast London: A study in the Relationships between Classes in Victorian England* (London, 1971).

[40] Iowerth Prothero, *Artisans and Politics*, p. 290.

the sexual division of labour is basic to an understanding of the way in which capitalism has maintained itself, for it has allowed capitalism to divide the workforce, to secure lower wages, to maintain a reserve army of inexpensive labour, and to ensure cheap maintenance and reproduction of the labour force. Feminist historians, moreover, have demonstrated in many different ways, that gender divisions have weakened and debilitated a mass working class movement by separating working-class men from working-class women.[41]

Something like the separatist artisanal consciousness noticed by Prothero and Crossick is also shown in the work of the contributors to Royden Harrison's collection on coal miners. Thus, colliers as small contractors and artisans were proudly independent rather than collectivist in places as far apart as the Forest of Dean, South Yorkshire and Lanarkshire. They derived their political significance from their self-generated, inborn conservative kind of liberalism.[42] On the other hand, J. A. Banks has shown that miners in Scotland did develop their own distinctive and collectivist class consciousness such that they were advocates of nationalization as early as 1892.[43]

Harrison's contributors, like Calhoun and Crossick, use the comparative method, applauded by the first conference on urban history in 1966, and much recommended to Ph.D. students.[44]

The upshot of these studies, some of them laborious micro-comparative

---

[41] Judith L. Newton, Mary P. Ryan and Judith R. Walkowitz, *Sex and Class in Women's History* (London, 1983), pp. 2—3. Also R. S. Neale, *Class and Ideology in The Nineteenth Century*, pp. 205—15; Barbara Taylor, *Eve and the New Jerusalem* (London, 1983); Zillah R. Eisenstein (ed.) *Capitalist Patriarchy and The Case for Socialist Feminism* (New York and London, 1979); Mary Evans (ed.) *The Woman Question* (London, 1982).

[42] Royden Harrison (ed.). *Independent Collier; The Coal Miner as Archetypal Proletarian Reconsidered* (London, 1978). See also the debate on 'Class Struggle and the Labour Aristocracy', in *Social History* 1 (3) 1976; 3 (1) 1978; 3 (3) 1978; 4 (3) 1979; 6 (1) 1981; 6 (2) 1981. Also, the labour process and labour history, and discussion in *Social History*, 8 (1) 1983; 9 (1) 1984.

[43] J. A. Banks, *Marxist Sociology in Action* (London, 1979), p. 127. Although not a work in urban history this book is an important contribution to class analysis of Victorian England. It is largely ignored by urban historians.

[44] H. J. Dyos. The comparative theme runs through the book and several of the papers are explicitly comparative in their structure. A recent work attempting to produce a typology for the comparison of eighteenth-century towns is P. J. Corfield, *The Impact of English Towns 1700—1800* (Oxford, 1982). The author says a little about a lot, but the comparative method is not well rehearsed. A book revealing the fragmented and fragmenting quality of comparative study is Dennis Smith, *Conflict and Compromise; Class Formation in English Society 1830—1914* (London, 1982).

studies, is to show that there was no 'working class'; something perhaps, that the working classes, members of the Labour Party, and some earlier historians always knew. In no movement were the consequences of the relatively slow and uneven economic development of Britain so important as in Chartism, frequently acclaimed as the first great 'working-class' movement to be born out of urban-industrializing society. Mark Hovell drew attention to this phenomenon in his classic study of Chartism in 1918.[45] Subsequently, the contributors to *Chartist Studies* in 1959 provided specific detailed urban examples to make a convincing case. Thus, the course of Chartism in Manchester, Leeds, Leicester and Glasgow was greatly influenced by the ways in which their different economic and social structures were affected by the varying incidence of economic fluctuations and unemployment, and, therefore, by their differing experiences of the Poor Law.[46] And Asa Briggs identifies the three major sub-groups of the English 'working class' as, the superior craftsmen (printers, tailors, shoemakers, cabinetmakers), factory operatives (mainly in textiles), and domestic outworkers (handloom weavers, framework knitters, nailmakers).[47] Recent work has confirmed and widened perceptions of the extent of variation in the support of 'working-class' communities for Chartism. In Oldham, Chartism competed with other movements favouring more direct industrial action, and there was little continuity among 'working-class' leaders across a spectrum of Chartist activity in 1838—41, the 1842 strike, and Chartist activity in 1848.[48] In London, the more militant East London Democratic Association (ELDA) soon ousted the Working Men's Association (WMA) from its initial position of Chartist leadership, so that the 'respectable' attitudes and values of the WMA no longer have to be accepted as the measure of London's Chartism.[49] In Bath, the radical artisanal component in its social structure made it an attractive base for Vincent of the ELDA to proselytize in the West Country, and in which to produce the Chartist newspaper the *Western Vindicator*.[50] Nevertheless, Chartism was also (and, perhaps, more significantly) a cultural as well as an economic and political

---

[45] Mark Hovell, *The Chartist Movement* (Manchester, 1918), pp. 8—27.

[46] Asa Briggs (ed.), *Chartist Studies* (London, 1959), Chs II, III, IV, and VIII.

[47] Ibid., p. 4. See also, David Jones, *Chartism and the Chartists* (London, 1975), and J. T. Ward, *Cahrtism* (London, 1973).

[48] John Foster, *Class Struggle and the Industrial Revolution* (London, 1974), pp. 154—9.

[49] Iowerth Prothero, *Artisans and Politics,* pp. 319—27. But see also, D. J. Rowe, 'The Peoples' Charter', *Past and Present,* XXXVI (April 1961), pp. 73—86.

[50] R. S. Neale, *Bath 1680—1850: A Social History,* pp. 329—80.

phenomenon.[51] While this might be generally acknowledged it has yet to be explored in any particular urban context, although F. B. Smith's *Radical Artisan* comes close to doing so.[52] Although Chartism was undoubtedly an expression of class struggle, it remains questionable whether it was a manifestation of a 'working-class' (a proletarian) consciousness.

The thrust of all this work is to show that experience structured by structures (modes of production) was determining, and these structures were different in different places and times as the economy lurched onwards unevenly and sporadically, sometimes with a modest rate of growth, but generally, over the last 100 years or so, with low and relatively declining rates of growth. One work which I think tries to relate structure and agency in these circumstances in a new way, is Bill Williamson's *Class, Culture and Community*. Through a study of the life of James Brown (1872–1965), a miner of Throckley in Northumberland, a man who never committed his thoughts to paper, and Williamson's grandfather, Williamson shows the independence of the man within the bounds of community: how he sought to carve a space for himself through the culture of his gardens; how he was respected and respectable although no leader; and how his liberalism turned to labourism as his experience changed, influenced by the growth of corporate enterprise, war, under-capitalization and world depression. James Brown was of his community and an agent in it. Although his choices were few, he tried to make himself in circumstances not chosen by himself. And there is much more about the making of working-class culture in the book.[53] Although Williamson does not use the comparative method in his own work, preferring to use a social anthropological method exploiting his advantage as an insider, it is possible to use his work to make comparison. For example, it may be compared with Margaret Ashby's *Joseph Ashby of Tysoe 1859–1919* (1961). Tysoe is a rural township in Warwickshire, and Ashby was the illegitimate son of a lady's maid and the lady's wealthy landowning husband. Within the limited choices available to him, he, too

[51] Y. V. Kovalev (ed.), *An Anthology of Chartist Literature* (Moscow, 1956); and P. Collins, *Thomas Cooper, the Chartist: Byron and the 'Poets of the Poor'* (Leicester, 1969).

[52] F. B. Smith, *Radical Artisan: William James Linton 1812–97* (Manchester 1973).

[53] Bill Williamson, *Class, Culture and Community: A Biographical Study of Social Change in Mining* (London, 1982). Another work seeking to link mode of production to (collective) social relationships is S. Yeo, *Religion and Voluntary Societies in Crisis* (1976).

made himself; agricultural labourer, small contractor, trade unionist, small farmer, parish councillor, secretary of the pig club, JP, contributor to the *Economic Journal*, and, like James Brown, liberal in politics.[54] The ambience of these stories of men and their families, and the reader's own role in reflecting on the influence on them of their different and changing relations to property in urbanizing and industrialized England, do more for our understanding than all the statistically comparative studies added together. And that brings me to the importance of property, which even Parkin agrees should be placed near the centre of discussion of class.

It is through discussion of property and relationships to it, that Avner Offer, in *Property and Politics 1870—1914* (1981), seems to pick up Vincent's theme of an urban 'free peasantry' in the 1830s and 1840s, to make a convincing case for a wider distribution of small property ownership in urban areas in the period 1870—1914 than previously acknowledged. He shows that wealthy landed proprietors controlled only 30 per cent of property by value of tenure, compared to 60 per cent in terms of acreage,[55] that land law was itself a property right, and that the clergy, corporations, estate agents and mortgagees all had a vested interest in property. Also there were more than a million house proprietors at the turn of the century. The national political, significance of this property interest was profound. It made and unmade governments as Liberals and Conservatives sought a wider distribution of small property to protect big property. In the end, this defence of property created a bureaucratic class managing society's collective capital at the local and national level, having appropriated many of the trappings of tenure. Offer wrote: 'Rousseau, in his vision of the strifeless society, did not forsee these prosperous and powerful offspring of the General Will.'[56]

David Englander, *Landlord and Tenant in Urban Britain 1838—1918* (1983) makes a case for another kind of significance for this mass of small urban property owners. Organized in Property Owners' Associations and armed with the Draconian measures of the Small Tenements Recovery Act 1838, they turned the question of urban rent into a battlefield. Thus house rent probably accounted for 5 per cent of GNP early in the nineteenth century and 9 per cent in 1901. Between 1880 and 1900, rents rose between 13 and 17 per cent. In the inter-war period, among the very poor, rent accounted for between a quarter and a third of income. Rent was thus a perpetual reminder of the fact of class and was a forcing

---

[54] Margaret Ashby, *Joseph Ashby of Tysoe 1859—1919* (Cambridge, 1961).
[55] Avner Offer, *Property and Politics 1870—1914: Landownership, Law, Ideology and Urban Development in England* (Cambridge, 1981), especially pp. 105—31.
[56] Ibid., p. 406.

ground for class consciousness in urban areas at least as important as experience in the work place and the presence of the workhouse. Accordingly, Englander describes the rise of Tenants' Defence Associations, the importance of rent in the rise of organized labour, and the rent agitation and strikes of 1912—18. He concludes that the struggle for tenants' rights between the wars was a radicalizing experience and that tenants associations played an important part in shaping social policy.[57]

Between them Offer and Englander reveal the importance of struggles over (urban) property rights for the transformation of the economic and socio-political structure of the national polity. Thus, rising urban rents, signifying conflict between property owners and house occupiers, particularly workers; and rising rates, signifying conflict between local authorities, and property owners and house occupiers in circumstances where the rate charge to meet the cost of poverty and other social problems was grossly unequal, led to unintended outcomes. Both the Conservative and Liberal parties, intent on preserving property, developed policies shifting the rate burden from local authorities and placing the charge on the central Exchequer. From such self-interested practices did the welfare state emerge — the product of class conflict structured by (urban) property rights. A further unintended outcome, revealed in our own time, is the power this now gives to a centralized state in a capitalist mode of production to eliminate local bases of countervailing power in the provision of welfare services and, of course, to destroy the welfare state itself.

The corollary of high house rent at the bottom end of the social spectrum could be great gains in rent income at the other. Yet it might well be true that the greatest gains in rent income were to be made where urban property development could be engineered to cater exclusively for the top end of the rental market. David Cannadine explores the conditions for just such a prospect in *Lords and Landlords: the Aristocracy and the Towns 1774—1967* (1980). He shows how Lord Calthorpe's income from the urban development of his Edgbaston estate rose from £3,566 (net) in 1810 to £27,734 (net) 100 years later, when it was the mainstay of his overall net income of £35,734. He shows, too, how the Duke of Devonshire's apparently expensive development of Eastbourne was in fact a self-financing exercise — the middle classes in their Sunday parades paid for their own esplanade and tree-lined avenues.[58] These two instances show that the wealthy business and professional classes, whether at work,

[57] David Englander, *Landlord and Tenant in Urban Britain 1838— 1918* (Oxford, 1983), p. 317. For the level of inter-war rents, see Margery Spring Rice, *Working-Class Wives* (London, 1939), p. 147.

on holiday, or in retirement, secured privileged (rented) access to space, thus heightening the barriers of class. (In Eastbourne, where there were too few artisans and disaffected poor tenants, it seems that it was the Salvation Army, insisting on banging their drums and shaking their tambourines on Sundays, who were in the vanguard of class consciousness.)

Cannadine also argues that the estate development plans of Landlords could only be realized where market forces (market relations embedded in modes of production) were also favourable.[59] I certainly would not quarrel with this view. The notion of the *totality* of urban space as socially organized and structured by class relations and competing interests, even in the most 'planned' of English cities, is also a theme of my *Bath 1680—1850: A Social History* (1981).[60]

Even as much of the previous work was in progress, John Foster in *Class Struggle and The Industrial Revolution: Early industrial capitalism in three English towns* (1974),[61] put forward a strong argument for the determination of structure, first, in the early development of something akin to Marx's *class* consciousness and secondly, in respect to the decline of that consciousness and its replacement by a liberalized consciousness by mid-century. All this occurred in Oldham. In *Class in English History*, I set out what seems to me to be the central argument of this book, and I make several criticisms of it, particularly with respect to the claim about the *class* consciousness of the Oldham spinners in and around 1842, and Foster's collapsing of Marxism into Leninism to explain the 'liberalization' of that *class* consciousness at mid-century. The point is, I think, that Foster's structural determination was *too* locally mechanistic, and therefore insufficiently Marxist. There was no tradition of the dead generations and almost no national or international context in Foster's discussion of

---

[58] David Cannadine, *Lords and Landlords: The Aristocracy and the Towns 1774—1967* (Leicester, 1980), pp. 83—135 and pp. 239—98. Although the book begins in 1774 it has very little to say about Lords and Landlords in the eighteenth century. The claim that there was some novelty in the use of 99-year building leases in 1776 (Preface and p. 31) may be true for London. In Bath, Wood built on 99-year leases in the 1730s, and Bath Corporation's first building development in the mid-1750s was on 99-year leases. By 1765—9, 95 per cent of all leases granted by Bath Corporation were for 99 years.

[59] Ibid., p. 401.

[60] R. S. Neale, *Bath 1680—1850: A Social History,* especially pp. 171—225.

[61] John Foster, *Class Struggle and the Industrial Revolution; early industrial capitalism in three English towns* (London, 1974). See also my *Class in English History,* pp. 441—5 and 111—14, and A. E. Musson's criticism and Foster's reply in *Social History* 1, (1976); John Saville in *Socialist Register* (1974) and G. Stedman-Jones in *New Left Review* (1975).

Oldham — certainly his judgement on working-class support for the Crimean War as a 'blocking out of class analysis' was not Marx's. Thus, while the Oldham spinners did succeed in politicizing the strike of 1842, and the Ten Hour Movement contributed to the liberalization of consciousness in Oldham, Foster's Eighteenth Brumaire of the Oldham Spinners is no match for Marx on Louis Bonaparte.

Despite this criticism, Hobsbawm's assessment of the book is still valid.[62] Foster does address himself to crucial issues of relations between class, struggle and movement (of structure and agency), and does attempt to clarify and provide analytical and quantitative methods for investigating class consciousness. He also emphasizes the importance of intellectual commitment for *class* consciousness, and of the agency of employers as they consciously sought to protect themselves by splitting the aristocracy of labour from the rest, in much the same way as national politicians sought to diffuse small property to protect big property. It is an important book.

Its importance is recognized by the fierceness with which an early version of it was opposed at that first conference on urban history in 1966. Thus, W. H. Chaloner denied that 70 or so families controlling 80 per cent of the means of production, and cut off from the rest of the community by social distance, marriage, and by their degree of interaction with the rest of the elite, were a 'ruling class'. Moreover, he thought the radicals 'were a bunch of anarchists', and that it was really not so difficult for men of working-class origin to rise to the status of mayor in Oldham in the nineteenth century.[63]

But the real issue was the place of theory in structuring historical enquiry. Some seemed to think that this meant that the task of historians was to prove theories or test hypotheses, others that theory generated questions, and others rejected theory entirely. At one stage the atmosphere in discussion seems to have become so tense that the young Foster broke off his discussion with the words: 'Probably nobody understands what I am saying anyway.'[64] Certainly nobody seems to have expressed the view that, like it or not, theory in one form or another permeates everything historians do, whether they know it or not. It was left to W. Ashworth on this occasion to express the down-to-earth view that 'whether we are doing urban history or any other kind of history, what we want is the history of

---

[62] Foster, Ibid., Foreword.
[63] II. J. Dyos, *The Study of Urban History;* W. H. Chaloner, Sixth Discussion, p. 341.
[64] Ibid., W. Ashworth, Final Discussion, p. 364.

the real world, and not to be lured into writing the history of Never-Never Land.'[65]

And that is how many urban historians approach the business of history writing. The mode of production and class, they say — even though they may not use these very words — were and are not determining and not really very relevant. They claim to show, empirically and ostensibly without theory, that religion and nationality were causes of social action cutting across any class determination. The 'economic' is denied any special role in causation. Urban history becomes a description of life in 'the real world' as it really was.

On the face of it, Hugh McLeod, *Class and Religion in the Late Victorian City* (1974) is about class and religion in urban history. There is a good deal in the book about class, thought of as three status groups based on occupation, and about the connection of these groups with secularism and with Church activity in London from about 1880—1914. We are told that the chief theme of the book is 'not the uniform impact of an "industrial society" or the adoption of an "urban way of life", but the division of a city into separate worlds, marked by radically different styles of life, and between which there was little communication.'[66] These status differences were particularly clear cut in the area of formal religious practice. Nevertheless, there was no clear fit between religious belief and commitment, and social status and class. As we have come to expect from books on London, there is also a good deal on respectability, but nothing on women. Although Bradlaugh figures significantly in the book there is no acknowledgement of his own expressed debt to Elizabeth Sharples,[67] and the opportunity to link free thought to women's consciousness is missed. (Perhaps, someday, someone will put all these books on London together and write a real history of London.)

It is not until we get to page 288 that the real object of the book is made clear. There McLeod writes: 'The obvious implications of these facts [in the book] is that however local patterns were moulded by social and political circumstances, *the primary source of the religious changes of the period must be sought in the flow of ideas rather than in situations peculiar to particular regions and countries.*[68] While this assertion rightly places religious belief in urban areas in a global context, and sees local communities affected by ideas brought in from outside, it does not

---

[65] Ibid., W. Ashworth, Final Discussion, p. 365.

[66] Hugh McLeod, *Class and Religion in the Late Victorian City* (London, 1974), p. 281.

[67] Hypatia Bradlaugh Bonner, *Charles Bradlaugh* (London, 1895), Vol. 1, p. 10.

[68] Hugh McLeod, *Class and Religion in the Late Victorian City*, p. 285 (my italics).

establish what McLeod seems to think it does, namely that 'ideas', flow at some kind of independent level of consciousness influenced only in a distant past by some (chance) political acts — in this instance, the Declaration of Indulgence in 1687 and the abolition of censorship in 1693 — and that this, in turn, means that class relations in changing modes of production (changing over nearly 300 years) were not crucial or perhaps, determining. This, I think, reflects a general weakness in these studies in urban history — they are not really historical. Many of the specifically urban studies I have commented upon deal with the short period, usually no more then 50 or 60 years, and often only 20 to 30 years. At the same time the micro-comparative method used in many of them inhibits attempts to write total history or to locate the short period study in its historical context. Consequently, in the absence of any broader theories about social action, the empirical data generated by these short-period, microcomparative studies takes on a cramped and static look. Their authors mistake short-term truths for eternal verities. So, while McLeod's proposition may be true, the evidence he adduces does not prove it. That would require a different kind of book. It could have been problems of conceptualizing and expressing complex ideas about such relationships between social being and consciousness within whole societies and over long periods of time, that caused Foster to break off his argument those many years ago.

The limitation on understanding brought about by urban studies set only in their local context is exemplified by P. J. Waller, *Democracy and Sectarianism: a Political and Social History of Liverpool 1868—1939* (1981). Waller is conscious of this problem but believes he resolves it by claiming that:

The structural integrity of this book . . . lies in the competition of four main parties, Conservative, Liberal, Irish Nationalist, and Labour, for the favours of the Liverpool electorate, and in the reflection of this scene against the national political background from time to time. Without the national quantity local history is parochial history; with it there is a chance that historians can truly measure political behaviour, for that, after all, takes place on the national and local stage at the same time, sometimes in collusion, sometimes in collision.[69]

So, Waller, with only narrative to help him (there is not one statistical table and only five unhelpful maps in the book), chronicles in minute

---

[69] P. J. Waller, *Democracy and Sectarianism; A Political and Social History of Liverpool 1868—1939* (Liverpool, 1981), p. xiv.

detail every national and municipal election in every electoral district in Liverpool from 1868 to 1939. The thrust of the narrative is that sectarian and national differences overrode class divisions to produce a predominantly conservative result in both local and national elections until the post-Second World War period. Furthermore, extra-political action, such as occurred in the strike of 1911, is described in words which demean the participants (adjectives substitute for analysis and argument). When he writes that: 'temperamental, not ideological, ascriptions best summarize the unrest (in 1911). Impatience was the prevailing mood and incontinent protest the form'[70] his words put an opaque gloss on the economic, social and political causes of 'impatience' and, conceal the conditions of 'incontinent protest'. These were: a still restricted franchise; the appeal of direct action; a strong military presence including a battleship and cruiser; and the general working-class experience of violent police action, which made Bloody Sunday a larger and more explosive version of daily experience. But that is how the book is structured — around the competition of four political parties for votes. It is absolutely removed from the structure of the economy (and modes of production) and from the social organization of space as they changed over time. All we have is agency constrained by sectarianism. It seems as if there is no way of relating sectarianism in Liverpool to modes of production. Thus, sectarianism is made to appear determining. I have little doubt that Waller's and McLeod's work will be used as further falsifactions of Marx — the exceptions that really put the rule to the proof.

Before that is done, however, it should be remembered that these urban studies like every urban study, whether comparative or not, *are* local studies. The terms of their construction are narrowly defined and confined, rather like the urban sociology at which so many urban historians turn up their noses. There are no *longue durées* in modern British urban history (or none that I have read).

The problem of localism in Liverpool cannot be overcome by locating it simply at the national political level. Liverpool, its commercial, industrial and social structure, its Irishism and sectarianism, and the long uneven struggle within its working classes towards a form of labour consciousness, has an historical, world and colonial context shaped by intricate relations between peoples locked in modes of production not of their own making, at least from a Marxist point of view. Sectarianism in Liverpool can only be comprehended holistically in an Irish context, Ireland can only be comprehended within its colonial relationship to England during the

[70] Ibid., p. 251.

European phase of primitive accumulation, and the significance of Irish Catholicism as a focus of Irish national culture can only be comprehended as an element in the sustained territorial (propertied) aggrandisement and cultural oppression of Ireland by English (and Scots) protestants. Then, the continuing significance of all this in nineteenth-century Liverpool can only be grasped with the help of something like Gramsci's notion of hegemony, coupled with an exploration of the *ways* in which the tradition of all the dead generations continued to weigh like a nightmare on the brains of those living in it in the nineteenth century. For it also has to be remembered that sectarianism in Liverpool was fought against, by people like the Bambers and Braddocks, for example, and that in the end sectarianism, even on Waller's admission, declined in significance.

Marx, himself, was clear if over-emphatic, on the importance of sectarianism and nationalism for the formation of British working-class consciousness.[71] But he set his account of the nationalism and divisive influence of the Irish and Ireland within a long historical perspective going back, at least to the fifteenth century. (I take up this theme in the next chapter.) Here it must suffice to say that for Marx Ireland was the paradigm of primitive accumulation and of uneven economic development under capitalism, and of the consequences of this in practice and in consciousness in Liverpool as elsewhere. In Marx, class in all its varieties and relations occurs within a 'total' set of circumstances, including the *longue durée*. My general point is that the materialist conception of history is an historical sociology. Urban history as it is currently practised, for all that its domain is the past, is not. And this revives the question, posed by Philip Abrams in *Towns in Societies* (1978), whether the town as such is a worthwhile or proper object of study, and whether relations within particular industrial cities and towns can be understood without some prior idea of the contradiction within the capitalist mode of production, such as that contained in the materialist conception of history.[72]

Stuart McIntyre's *Little Moscows: Communism and Working-Class Militancy in Inter-war Britain* (1980) is as different from Waller's *Democracy and Sectarianism* as chalk is from cheese. It is a celebration of

---

[71] Marx to Sigrid Meyer and August Vogt, 7 April 1870, in Marx/Engels, *Ireland and the Irish Question* (Moscow, 1971), pp. 293−4. Alan Campbell, 'Honourable Men and Degraded Slaves' in Royden Harrison, *Independent Collier: The Coal Miner as Archetypal Proletarian Re-comsidered,* pp. 75−113, also explores the effects of sectarianism within mining communities in Scotland.

[72] Philip Abrams and E. A. Wrigley (eds), *Towns in Societies: Essays in Economic History and Historical Sociology* (Cambridge, 1978), pp. 9−33.

the emergence of communist polities and culture in three communities: two mining townships, Mardy in South Wales and Lumphinnans in Fifeshire, and a cluster of textile townships in the Vale of Leven. The two mining communities were not unlike James Brown's Throckley in *Class , Culture and Community,* or those nineteenth-century townships described in Royden Harrison's *Independent Collier,* except that in the 1930s depression their people, or some of them, developed a mode of popular local control and a working-class consciousness more distinctive and convincing than anything Foster could find in Oldham 100 years earlier. Like some of the radical communities described in C. R. Dobson's *Masters and Journeymen: a Prehistory of Industrial Relations 1817 — 1800* (1980), and J. Brewer and J. Styles (eds), *An Ungovernable People* (1980), like those traditional communities discussed theoretically by Calhoun, and, like Prothero's London artisans, the people in the 'Little Moscows' were fighting for their community and lives. But they did so in a national and world context and an ideological milieu which gave a sharper political focus to their actions. McIntyre convincingly describes the forces making for their militancy; changes in the structure and relations of the workforce brought about by new technology; the growth of corporate capitalism; massive unemployment (80 per cent in the Vale of Leven 1931 — 5); limitation of poor relief; the repressive response of the state; the inability to cope with mounting distress by traditional means of co-operation and self help; a popular oppositional morality with Christian/humanist origins; the Russian example; and Communist leaders. Yet he, too, seems determined to deny the determination of the mode of production on social being and consciousness, and to raise 'leadership' almost to a position of accidental significance. He writes: 'We should resist the facile assumption that the radicalization of the three localities was a direct and inevitable consequence of the decline of their staple industries. That political process was the outcome of a number of factors besides the economic'[73] Yet, in his listing of the factors, a few pages further on, he also writes: 'It has been necessary to grapple with the complexities of relief in the Vale of Leven because unemployment was the primary determinant of the fluctuating tempo of local politics.'[74] And I wonder what to make of that, and of McIntyre's failure to distinguish 'the economic' from the concept 'mode of production'.

Although the immediate political reason for McIntyre's caution on the question of determination is understandable (his is a committed work)

---

[73] Stuart McIntyre, *Little Moscows: Communism and Working-class Militancy in Inter-war Britain* (London, 1980), p. 112.

[74] Ibid., p. 120.

there is no attempt to grapple with the problem of structure and agency, and the question of the agency of leadership is neither well-theorized nor explained. Why was there a cluster of 'leaders' in working-class communities in the 1930s? (There were many more Little Moscows than those described by McIntyre.) Why are there so few Little Moscows in the 1980s? Is it surprising that 'leaders' appear when communities fight for their lives? Is. 'leadership' really an isolatable factor? What are the conditions for leadership, which after all is a form of deviance? Historians, I think, and urban historians in particular, have no answers to these questions. For this reason they might have to turn to Philip Abrams, *Historical Sociology* (1982).

More urgently, they should study the conditions for and spontaneity of community involvement and action during the miners' strike of 1984. Miners' journals, the testimony of miners, miners' wives, miners' daughters, of groups such as Barnsley Women Against Pit Closures, and articles in the *Guardian* and *The Observer* are convincing evidence that 'Leadership' is not a problem. In the circumstances this is not to be wondered at. Government economic policy, here mediated by the NCB's issue of some very peculiar accounting procedures, and without any participation in decision-making by those most affected, destroys whole communities. It produces a growing class of the non-employed. At the same time, government social policy demeans people in those communities and the non-employed, and, in the end, all of the working class.

The government also deploys all the considerable coercive powers of the state to enforce its economic policy. A militarized, quasi-national but irresponsible police force, directed by a choleric and aggressive senior police officer, and acting contrary to the conventions and practice of the constitution (often outside the law), at a cost to the taxpayer of £200 million a year, creates conditions for police harassment and provocation of legal pickets, for assaults on peaceful citizens in their homes, and for police cavalry charges which evoke images of cavalry charges against the people in Tsarist Russia and at Peterloo. Orgreave, Armthorpe and Grimethorpe will surely be added to the list of violent acts carried out by British governments against the people in the interests of those with power and privilege within the capitalist mode of production throughout its history. There is, too, the partiality and pettiness of the law as it adds its dreadful weight to the coercion of the miners — obscure legislation from 1841 is invoked to exact heavier penalties for 'besetting workmen', and miners are heavily fined for the age-old practice of taking coal from slag heaps and for miaowing at a policeman's dog! At the same time the government, the NCB, the police, most newspapers and television stations have persistently encouraged miners to return to work without themselves having to face the personal consequences of such organized strike breaking. Biased media reporting has turned working miners into national heroes. The choleric senior police officer understands his function in law to stand between 'oppressors and oppressed' as he defines them, and children in school playgrounds in mining regions play 'police and pickets'. Is it to be wondered at that violence by striking miners sometimes breaks out on picket lines and people are beaten and sometimes killed? Is it surprising that women and men and children in hitherto peaceful mining communities have been politicized by harsh economic, political and social experience in ways anticipated by Marx, and that at the pressure points of class struggle no one has to lead anyone?[75]

Where structures of modes of production are similar and, therefore, similarly shaped by class struggle, it is appropriate to use our immediate experience of one such structure to inform our understanding of others lying beyond this experience.

It could be that McIntyre's emphasis on leadership springs from the

---

[75] Philip Abrams, *Historical Sociology* (Shepton Mallet, 1982). *Miner* and *Scottish Miner* throughout 1984; The Miners' Strike, session at Left Alive Conference, 3 Nov. 1984; *Women Against Pit Closures,* Barnsley Women (Barnsley 1984); the *Guardian,* 5—11—84, p. 10; 10—11—84, p. 2; 3—12—84, p. 15; 5—12—84, p. 2; 6—12—84, p. 4; 8—12—84, Letters; 10—12—84, p. 12 and Letters. *The Observer* 4—11—84, News; 16—12—84, p. 13. See also *Civil Liberties and the Miners' Dispute,* NCCL National Council for Civil Liberties (London 1984). Raphael Samuel, 'Friends and Outsiders', *New Statesman* 11—1—1985, and Michael Crick, *Scargill And The Miners* (Harmondsworth, 1985).

Two books about aspects of recent urban history and class, which appear likely to become source material for future urban historians writing of the search for human identity in the decaying urban environments in the mid-1980s, but which were published too recently for substantial inclusion in this chapter are: Peter Tatchell, *The Battle for Bermondsey* (1983) and Beatrix Campbell, *Wigan Pier Revisited* (1984). Both books tell shocking stories. But their themes are uneasily related to the history of class, to class politics, or to urban history. Accordingly their authors write about the power (or powerlessness) of human agency with only occasional glances towards the determination of class relations within specific urban economies experiencing massive technological and organizational change and located in a world capitalist mode of production. Thus Tatchell identifies the recent political (and personal) history of Bermondsey as marking a turning point in the history of labour politics in England, and believes that acts of will and of leadership can reverse the tide against labour. And Campbell, substituting a feminist perspective for class analysis, claims that the closed socialist imagination of the (men's) working-class movement in England was caused by something she refers to as 'the political settlement between men and women'. Accordingly, she calls for change in the attitudes of men as 'the condition of women's creative cooperation with the men's movement, and for socialism'. Campbell's analysis, published in the year of the miner's strike, not only did not predict it but excluded it, and its consequences for consciousness, as a possibility, and cannot account for it.

Orgreave: Lesley Boulton 1984 (John Harris, IFL)

two-fold purpose of his book; one 'to assess the meaning of the phenomenon (of Little Moscows) and to subject the legends that adhere to it to historical analysis', the other, 'to make an aspect of working-class history available to readers for whom the term 'Little Moscows' means little or nothing'.[76] McIntyre also recognizes the tension between these two objectives, and apologizes for the inadequacy of his literary powers and, therefore, his inability to do justice to the second objective. It seems to me that in this literary concern to return history to a constituency of (working-class?) readers, and, perhaps, to tell it as it was through an emphasis upon agency, understood as leadership, McIntyre places himself within the mainstream of urban historians and within the agenda laid down at that first conference on urban history.

In his wide-ranging opening address to that conference, Dyos, touched upon almost every aspect of urban history, but in commenting upon the achievement of Asa Briggs in his *History of Birmingham,* Vol. II. (1952), he said:

One of the major tasks of second-generation research in this part of the field must be to discover Birmingham's *private face* . . . most difficult of all is to unravel the common-or-garden domesticities of urban life, not merely to preserve a memory of its paraphenalia, but in order to find historically the patterns of behaviour and attitude which we have learned to recognise almost instinctively in our own experience.[77]

In the first evening's discussion, in which there was much earnest talk about the 'personality' of towns and how important it was to get this 'personality' right, Dyos intervened to insist on the importance of comparing life in one part of a city with another, and with other cities.[78] Checkland, in his summing up of the conference, also picked up this theme as one of the three principal approaches to the study of urban history to have emerged. Urban historians, he said, had raised a diffuse problem about the nature of urban life.[79] Dyos adverted to this theme again in 1969.[80] In 1982, Reeder again drew attention to this central thrust in Dyos's work.[81] Writing on the quality of urban life in 1969, Dyos referred to historians, inability to describe 'how good or bad it *felt* to be alive in the conditions of the time',[82] and said that only the creative artist,

---

[76] Stuart McIntyre, *Little Moscows,* Preface.

[77] H. J. Dyos, 'Agenda for Urban Historians', in H. J. Dyos, *The Study of Urban History*, pp. 30—1 (my italics).

[78] Ibid., First Discussion, pp. 63—4.

[79] Ibid., S. G. Checkland, 'Toward a Definition of Urban History', pp. 345—6.

[80] H. J. Dyos, 'Some historical reflections on the quality of urban life' in David Cannadine and David Reeder (eds.), *Exploring the Urban Past: Essays in Urban History by H. J. Dyos,* pp. 56—78.

[81] Ibid., David Reeder, 'H. J. Dyos and the urban process', pp. xi-xix.

[82] H. J. Dyos, *The Study of Urban History,* p. 58.

especially the novelist, could interpret that quality for us. Because this was so important to him he advocated the creation of a new discipline — 'The truth is that there can be no reliable *historical* chart to the quality of urban life without a new discipline for connecting the historical and literary traditions.'[83] Although Dyos did not produce such a discipline, or name it, something of what he had in mind is now quite common — I call it literary empiricism.

This impulse to *feel,* therefore, to know what the quality of life was in the past and to re-create that feeling in literary form, with the object of transferring that *feeling* to readers as an aid to understanding, is probably as old as the novel itself and modern historiography. It is certainly very strong in the mainstream of British empirical social history, for example, in the work of Best and Himmelfarb,[84] of Dyos himself, in Reeder's admiration for that work, in the views of a variety of critics of my own work, and now McIntyre's. Probably, too, this impulse lies behind the approach to class of that great body of historians, including urban historians, who prefer to use 'class' as they believe it was used by contemporaries, which, as Best says, is 'continually and confusedly' like mid-Victorian society itself, which 'was obsessed with class, and riddled with class consciousness, and generally not at all clear what it all meant.'[85]

This desire to feel and to know other lives also has intellectual antecedents in the 'philosophy of history'. It is not unlike the *Verstehen* of Historicism before Popper, and it is similar to Collingwood's preferred method, although without the latter's strong philosophic base in the 'Historical Imagination'.[86] And I need only refer to theoretical and analytical critiques of these approaches to show their limitations and impossibility.[87] Empathy, that yearning of isolated souls for community (the flipside of privacy) is a Will o' the Wisp, although just as entrancing. But I also know that such theoretical demonstrations could never persuade convinced empiricists of the error of their ways. Even E. P. Thompson

---

[83] David Cannadine and David Reeder (eds.), *Exploring the Urban Past*, p. 62.

[84] Geoffrey Best, *Mid-Victorian Britain 1851—76* (London, 1971), and Gertrude Himmelfarb, 'Social History and the Moral Imagination', in Quentin Anderson (ed.), *Art, Politics and Will — Essays in honour of Lionel Trilling* (New York, 1977), pp. 248—70. Reprinted in R. S. Neale, *History and Class; Essential Readings in Theory and Interpretation* (Oxford, 1983).

[85] Geoffrey Best, *Mid-Victorian Britain,* p. xv.

[86] R. G. Collingwood, *The Idea of History* (London, 1961), p. 243.

[87] See Patrick Gardener, *The Nature of Historical Explanation* (Oxford, 1961); W. H. Walsh, *An Introduction to Philosophy of History,* 3rd edn (London, 1967); R. F. Atkinson, *Knowledge and Explanation in History* (London, 1978); Arthur C. Danto, *Analytical Philosophy of History* (Cambridge, 1965).

believes that the facts can be made to speak in their own voices, and he writes as if they do. So that leaves me with a problem. How to reveal empirically the inadequacy of literary empiricism on the question of class feeling in urban society, and at the same time, say something worthwhile about the cultural dimension of class in urban history and the quality of lives?

I will begin by returning to two of the books already referred to to recover what I take to be attempts by their authors to meet some of the requirements of the Dyos approach — literary empiricism. Cannadine, in *Lords and Landlords,* has a chapter called 'The Belgravia of Birmingham'. In it he describes the outward appearance and content of houses, and mingles with his account literary description from the novels of Brett Young — the one is used to confirm the other. But, in this description there are no women, except as wives and daughters or landladies and maids, and no children, except they were in school. We are told a little of what went on in some heads — a list of things to do in a local periodical, *Edgbastonia,* is followed by the judgement: 'In short, its tone was quintessentially suburban.'[88] (In order to understand that we have to have prior knowledge of the meaning of suburban.) In short, 'The Belgravia of Birmingham' says little about what went on in people's heads in the form of ideas and, of course, nothing about feeling.

Waller, in *Democracy and Sectarianism,* uses diaries rather than novels to describe 'the Holt family as a mirror of change over generations in Liverpool'. And he tries to show how 'A style of life was at stake' by looking at the history of the Wellington Rooms. Apart from that, he lists the institutional participation and financial condition of the Holt's, father and son. Again, women are absent, except as wives and daughters, although Votes for Women does get one mention. Waller's conclusion from this foray into the culture of class is that as a mirror of change over generations in Liverpool, two features are outstanding;

One is a personal account. In Richard Holt there was too much consciousness about tradition for comfort, adaptation, and survival. The public service of the old Liberal Unitarian families was not so much exhausted as superannuated. The political world had left them behind. This announces the second conclusion, a commentary on post-war Party struggles. The historic Liberal party was no longer a contender for power in Liverpool.[89]

---

[88] David Cannadine, *Lords and Landlords: The Aristocracy and the Towns 1774—1967,* pp. 198—217, especially p. 207.

[89] P. J. Waller, *Democracy and Sectarianism,* p. 274—80, especially p. 279.

Which is but a powder-compact mirror of change over generations.

Whatever these historians' purposes might have been (and I cannot get inside *their* heads), Edgbaston and Sefton Park, two of the great suburbs in late Victorian and Edwardian England remain empty of people. There is no study of class culture, as a whole way of life, in either book. Nor is there a study of this kind in any other of the books surveyed in this paper, least of all in Lindert and Williamson's econometric calculus of the quality of urban life. And, of course, there is nothing about feeling.

Of the books I have mentioned, only *Ashby of Tysoe* and *Class, Culture and Community* have anything worthwhile on the culture of class. To these I should add Paul Thompson, *The Edwardians* (1975), for all its faults as given history; Robert Roberts, *The Classic Slum* (1971); Richard Broad and Suzie Fleming (eds.), *Nella Last's War: A Mother's Diary 1939—45* (1981); John Osborne, *A Better Class of Person: An Autobiography 1929— 1956* (1981); and the productions of those peoples' historians whose work is also urban history. But for a study of middle-class minds it would be necessary to look elsewhere, for example, in Richard Jenkyns, *The Victorians and Ancient Greece,* (Oxford, 1980). As for feeling, empiricist urban historians should steer clear of literary productions. Literary sources are not 'just like' other sources (even though other sources might be just like literary sources). For this reason they would require a different order of analysis and a greater knowledge of culture, theory, semiotics, and of relations between economy and culture than empiricist historians would appear willing to make. But they could study, fruitfully Norbert Elias, *The Civilizing Process (1939, 1978).* Elias argues for 'the continuous correspondence between the social structure and the structure of the personality, of the individual self'.[90] His account of the symbolism of social distance and, perhaps, the 'feeling', revealed in the long history of the knife and fork should be incorporated into any history of class, urban or otherwise. Historians could also test for themselves how well the 'feeling' of urban life might best be explored and revealed through similar studies of the minutiae of everyday life.

Because women and 'urban' sexual behaviour in a class context have so far been neglected in this discussion, because largely omitted from the works discussed, I would like to try to say something about the question of 'feeling' through an extended comment on an incident in a woman's memory, sharp with the sort of signification that Dyos would have us explore.

Those books referred to as having most value in relation to the question

---

[90] Norbert Elias, *The Civilizing Process* (Oxford, 1978), p. 191.

of the culture of class, are ones with some mixture of biography and autobiography, diaries and oral history. This is no accident. It is through works of this kind that historians can, as it were, listen in to people at work, in their homes and at play, take notes, notice bias, pick up signification that may not have been intended, and notice silences. It is as close as they can get to people even though class, culture and language still act as barriers to knowing (and to feling). It is not surprising, therefore that Vera Brittain, after toying with the idea of a novel and the conventional form of a history finally settled on her own story as the vehicle for a history of the experience of her generation. She writes: 'In no other fashion, it seemed, could I carry out my endeavour to put the life of an ordinary individual into its niche in contemporary history, and thus illustrate the influence of world-wide events and movements upon the personal destinies of men and women.'[91] The autobiography she finally wrote, *Testament of Youth* (1933), is both urban and class history.

How well Vera Brittain constructs her past. The ambience of life in her self-satisfied father's house in its respectable Buxton milieu is darkly drawn. She shows us 'Melrose' and its household as the little sub-culture it was, although the three maids and the garden boy seem merely shadowy figures. Perhaps they were. Yet her pen portraits of people in that world she lost are persuasive. Her father who, 'had never had a Trade Union man on the place . . . and . . . never expected professors to carry golf clubs'. Her mother, 'who had an agreeable soprano voice, took singing lessons; at musical parties, she sang "When the Heart is Young", "Whisper and I shall Hear", or "The Distant Shore" — a typical example of Victorian pathos which always reduced me to tears at the point where "the mai-den-drooped-and-died".' Mr, later Professor, J. A. Marriot, the Oxford University Extension Lecturer who, during one of his lectures on The Problems of Wealth and Poverty, 'was moved to tell his yawning listeners that Buxton did not strike him as *particularly* inquisitive'. Herself staying away from the first of these lectures to go to a dance, 'this far had I already fallen from grace!' Her friend, just after she 'came out' telling her, 'she was always afraid of going too far with men, because she really didn't know what "too far" was.' And the Headmaster of Uppingham who declared: 'If a man cannot be useful to his country, he is better dead.' But I see no point in trying to rewrite her writing to evoke feeling. *Testament of Youth* is there to be read. What I intend to do is rearrange some of her own memories in order to evoke a moment of feeling as a component in the quality of life. I will agree with Elias and Dyos that feeling is best

---

[91] Vera Brittain, *Testament of Youth* (London, 1933, 1979), Foreword.

recovered through the minutiae of everyday life (and that its recovery takes an unconscionable time). And I will express my doubt that this feeling is explicable by anything specifically urban, even though its environment is almost wholly urban. I will raise the problem of the 'literaryness' of her production, to suggest how much has to be left to the reader, and I will question whether feeling, as a component in agency, can be understood as other than specific to class, time and place, or apart from the historical location and consciousness of readers who have to become writers. That is, I raise again Roland Barthe's notion of the 'limpness' of history, and point to the inadequacy of theory as it now is. Yet, I also claim that theory is the best we have. Without it there is only the domination of empiricism and the econometrics of positivism.

Vera Brittain was an Edwardian middle-class girl in the upper industrial and provincial reaches of the designation. Her life was bounded by an urban childhood in Macclesfield and Buxton, and partially shaped by a period at a finishing school for girls at Kingswood in Surrey, under the direction of a dynamic woman, one of Miss Beale's 'ladies' from Cheltenham. After that she experienced several years of 'provincial young-ladyhood' back in Buxton again. In the fashion of the time she fell in love. The boy was Roland Leighton, a close friend of her brother's who she first met briefly at Uppingham School in June 1913. She was nineteen, he eighteen years old, the outstanding boy academically in his year, with the 'Oxford' accent of his class.

They met again in 1914, twice. For five days in April at Buxton and for three days in July at Uppingham. After their first April meeting, Roland sent Vera a copy of Olive Schreiner's *The Story of An African Farm* (1883). This book with its central character, Lyndall, played an important part in their relationship as they skirmished with each other, finding the other a strange and alien creature. (Her fascination with the book also shows the continuing problem posed to feminists by traditional religious belief.)

Roland told Vera that she was like the doomed heroine Lyndall, only 'sadder and less charmingly controversial'.[92] When she pressed him to know if he really thought she was like Lyndall: 'He replied, in spite of my saying that the Lyndalls of this world are few and far between, that he hoped and really thought I was, and as to the reason why, he supposed he was allowed to have intuitions occasionally too.'[93] And she records in her diary a

---

[92] Alan Bishop (ed.), *Vera Brittain's War Diary, 1913–17, Chronicle of Youth* (London, 1982), p. 30.
[93] Ibid., p. 94.

conversation she had with Roland's mother in August 1915. Mrs Leighton knew the Roland had sent *The Story of An African Farm* to Vera, and she said;

She felt instinctively that our fate was decided. That book, she said, had had such an immense influence on her life, but she never had thought it was going to be the same to us. She even told him a day or two ago that she was sure the book of Olive Schreiner's was responsible for all that had happened. Well it may be. The Lyndalls of this world are few and far between, and if Roland made her his ideal woman, and then when he met me felt, even after five day's acquaintance, that he had met her in real life . . . I should like to meet Olive Schreiner and tell her about it.[94]

By the end of the year (1914) Roland was a Second Lieutenant in the 4th Norfolks, and Vera at Somerville. They met the day after her twenty-first birthday for two days in London. She wrote in her diary: 'I felt then that I would give all I had lived or hoped for during the brief years of my existence, not to astonish the world by some brilliant and glittering achievement, but some day to be the mother of Roland Leighton's child.'[95] On 16 January 1915 Roland clandestinely met Vera at Leicester railway station to travel with her to Oxford. As the train pulled into Oxford, she put out her hand to say goodbye. She recalls in the *Testament of Youth* that 'With sudden vehemence he pressed it against his lips, and kept it there until the train stopped.'[96] In March, Roland, who had arranged a transfer to the 7th Worcesters, spent a few days embarkation leave in Buxton. Of their last evening together, she wrote:

We sat on the sofa till midnight, talking very quietly. The stillness, heavy-laden with the dull oppression of the snowy night, became so electric with emotion that we were frightened of one another, and dared not let even our fingers touch for fear that the love between us should render what we both believed to be decent behaviour suddenly unendurable.[97]

They met again in August. On 23 December 1915 Roland died of wounds near Hébuterne. Although they had written letters and poems to each other, they had walked and sat and talked together during a total of only 18 days. Yet that train journey to Oxford and that evening together at Buxton were even more electric with emotion than Vera could bring

[94] Ibid., p. 325.
[95] Ibid., p. 175.
[96] Vera Brittain, *Testament of Youth*, p. 123.
[97] Ibid., p. 131.

herself to remember, signifying as they did, such a depth of sexual tension and such a measure of Edwardian, provincial propriety and privacy, that the heart stops. We know this now because we can check her 'literary' reconstruction of her 'urban' life against the diaries she kept at the time, which have only recently been published.

The entry in her diary on the episode of the train journey to Oxford reads:

As the grey city began to surround us and the train slowed down I stood up, put out my hand and said good bye. He took it quite collectedly and then suddenly raised it to his lips and kissed it. Taken by surprise I resisted a little but quite unavailingly in his strong grip, and after all I did not really want to resist. I turned away from him and looked out of the window till the train stopped. I could not say any more but another brief good bye. I even did not thank him — but hurried away to see after my luggage.[98]

The entry on their last evening together at Buxton, some two months later, reads:

But we did speak of marriage a little; I said Mother was afraid I should become just an intellectual old maid, and that indeed was probably what I should become. 'I don't see why', he said. 'Simply because there will be no one left for me to marry after the war', I answered. 'Not even me?' he asked in a very low voice. . . . But it is useless to try to write about a fragmentary conversation which was really not a conversation at all but a fitful expression of emotions made up of a strange mixture of sorrow and the saddest kind of joy. At last I felt I could stand it no longer; when one is but prolonging something that must in any case end soon, the sudden need comes to end it quickly. I saw he was looking tired and rather worn, though I think he would have stayed up all night if I had let him, so I made him put the lamp out. *He took my hand and kissed it again as he did in the train once before — but this time there was no glove upon it.*[99]

When Roland was on leave from the front in August they kissed:

'You are a dear', he said, and gently drew my face down to him and kissed me.

Oh! I am glad his kisses come so seldom, for they mean so much that I could not bear the agonising joy of them often. They give me a thrill and a shock; they stir me in a way that the easy voluptuous oft-repeated kisses of a

---

[98] Vera Brittain, *War Diary*, p. 182.
[99] Ibid., p. 197. My italics.

sensuous man would never have a power to do. There, on that dark heather-covered cliff beside the sea, I realized the depth and strength of my own passion — realised it and was afraid.[100]

These episodes of two lives lived and felt took place in a provincial urban environment in 1914 and 1915: in the gardens of the school at Uppingham; in a first-class carriage in a train drawing into Oxford; on a sofa in the privacy of a room of a big semi-detached middle-class house in the Park in Buxton; in the bustle of London's shops; and in the restfulness of Lowestoft. As the measure of their generation and class we can learn from Vera Brittain and Roland Leighton what life 'felt' like at that moment in England's and the world's history, even though their moment may not also tell us how these things were done in a Glasgow tenement, nor in my grandfather's terraced house in Southall, nor yet in the home of Mullaway the wine merchant in Bath in 1774.[101] But, in the context of this chapter, we have to ask whether there was anything especially 'urban' in that moment, and whether any of its parts — *The Story of An African Farm,* Miss Beale's school at Cheltenham — are explicable in terms of urban history itself. And answer, No. Further, on the question of the urban historians' major responsibility to evoke 'feeling' as a condition for understanding and explanation, one must surely notice the (unconscious?) reticence of the literary autobiographical form, even of the diaries themselves, observe how long it takes to recover 'feeling', and finally what it demands of and leaves to the reader. For example, Clare Leighton, Roland's sister, after reading the diary for the first time in 1980, wrote: 'I found myself as emotionally destroyed as though my brother's death had happened but a short while before.'[102] A feeling, I am sure, that would be shared by many other readers of it. But how many share my response to the episode of the glove, which for me fills so many of the houses of Buxton, Edgbaston and Sefton Park with all the dead weight and inhibitions of privacy and social distance, the chronicle of which is told in *The Civilizing Process?* How many would believe with me that that episode forces privacy into the forefront of consideration more sharply than discussion of the layout of towns and the floor-plans of houses? How many would agree with me that the episode of the glove sharpens the focus of yet another fearful side of privacy, and another kind of response

---

[100] Ibid., p. 323.

[101] James Mullaway was the employer of a servant, Martha Abraham, twenty-eight years old in 1774, and the father of the child with which she was pregnant and the cause of her application for poor relief.

[102] Vera Brittain, *War Diary,* Preface.

to the strange and alien relation of the sexes nurtured inside the walls of nearly all the houses in the kingdom, revealed in another story, one that has haunted me for the last 25 years since I bought Mary Blathwayt's set of *Votes for Women?* The issue of the journal for 27 September 1912 carried a photograph of a young suffragette surrounded by a packed, milling, angry mob of cloth-capped and straw-boated men at Llanystumdwy in North Wales, her head forced backwards and her face marked by fear. The accompanying text reads:

I was on a level with Mr Lloyd George, and not more than fifteen feet away from him. He was speaking in Welsh, but was good enough to give me my cue in English, by ending an obviously sneering remark with 'personal chivalry' (I suppose there is no Welsh equivalent for these words). 'The Liberal treatment of political prisoners is a — —. A hand over my mouth choked the word 'disgrace', and I was dragged backwards off the form by as many men as could get hold of me at once.

A free fight over my body followed across the fifty yards or more that separated the platform from the roadway. Every man within hearing being anxious to obtain some fragment of my clothing, and if possible to leave his mark on me (in the latter endeavour they were largely unsuccessful), I did not have exactly an easy time, and in an extraordinarily short time my clothing was in shreds.

We crashed through the hedge and down a steep bank on the road. There a single policeman — most of the force were by now engaged in protecting the other women as far as possible — tried to fight his way through to me, but was swept aside by the crowd. It was an extraordinarily rough crowd, but two men who, I believe, got near me after I reached the road, saved me from what I suppose would have been brought in as 'accidental death', or possibly 'justifiable homicide'. I lost my footing once, and felt a vague curiosity as to how they killed you when they got you down. But I never went right down.

By the time the struggle had proceeded another fifty yards along the road I began to wonder how much longer it was possible for it to go on. Then the men who were fighting for me got me up a passage to some cottages, the first of which refused to open its door, though the people in the second were most anxious to afford me shelter.

By this time I was stripped of all clothing down to my waist. A thick blanket cloth coat was gone (pieces were returned to me later), a cloth skirt was literally in ribbons and more than half off, a strong linen blouse was utterly gone, and not a shred of underclothing remained on the upper part of my body. My hair had also been torn, but not so badly as those of the women with thicker and longer hair than mine.

Mr Lloyd George's 'chivalry' (Votes For Women, 27 Sept. 1912)

In the cottage the people were extremely nice to me — lent me clothes and gave me tea. All the local people told us that more than half the crowd was there not to see Lloyd George, but to see the Suffragettes and to give them a hot time.

Five of us were taken from Llanystumdwy in a motor-car, the only one the police could find to do the job, which meant driving through an exceedingly hostile crowd. When we thanked the driver he said, 'Well, you see, my wife happens to be a woman.'[103]

When I bring to my response to this text and photograph the signification of the episode of Vera Brittain's glove, I know that theorizing about class or about patriarchy and class or about urban history cannot give us this third dimension of the culture of Edwardian society, and that Dyos was right, but not only about urban history. I also know that these known moments in the texture of lives, like Lyndall in *The African Farm* 'are few and far between' — and that social being determines consciousness. Yet, like Dyos, I know that I cannot create a new discipline that could convincingly bring all the necessary elements together, and that something must be left to the reader. However, I do believe that such a discipline should not be one with a primary focus on connecting the historical to the literary traditions of scholarship. Rather we should persist in seeking ways of relating economy to culture and to consciousness and to the constricted lives as well as to the creative and human agency of people. This would involve understanding the complex articulation of modes of production as a process of uneven economic development in a world, as well as a national context. It would also involve attempts to discover the extent to which such changes were consequences of human agency, manifested in class relations and (political) struggles over property rights, modified as they undoubtedly were in different times and places, and to different extents, by sectarianism, nationality and sex, and by developments in technology. Jordi Borja set down the theoretical outlines for such a project in 1974. he writes:

The analysis of the urban phenomenon suffers, in its theoretical formations, from a particular difficulty in explaining *both* the urban structure and the urban movements. . . . The rupture, idealist in origin, between structures and

---

[103] *Votes for Women* 27 Sep. 1912. Note, the woman writing the text is not necessarily the woman in the photograph. The legacy of this relationship between the sexes in an urban setting is recorded for a large sample of London women in Ruth. E. Hall, *Ask Any Woman: A London Inquiry Into Rape and Sexual Assault* (Bristol, 1985).

practices paralyses dialectical analysis and develops an analytical dichotomy between a *theory of reproduction* ('the city of capital') and a *theory of change* of a historicist type (the city transformed by 'urban social movements'). The dialectical analysis conceives any structure as a contradictory reality in continuous change. These objective contradictions give rise to social conflicts that appear as *immediate agents* of change. There are no structures that are not something other than an ensemble of contradictory and conflicting social relations, more or less crystallized, but always in process of change. And there are no urban movements, in which all the social classes participate to different degrees, that are not situated within structures, expressing them and modifying them constantly.[104]

Nevertheless, the new-formed historical discipline I am looking for would also have to explore the changing cultural as well as political nature of class consciousness in these circumstances, and explore relationships of economy to culture, both as creativity and as a whole way of life. At present, Raymond Williams's cultural materialism, despite the idealism still inherent in it, is the best guide there is, at least for the apprentice urban historian dissatisfied with literary or any other kind of empiricism.[105] Then, the practitioners of this new discipline should strive to avoid the cultural power inherent in the language they use (they should not write like Borja or Williams). They should return the history they write to the people in such ways that they, too, may bring their own criticism and imagination to their reading of it, and in their reading, rewrite it. Only in this way may we come to understand how a generation of Rolands from all classes, and from all the cities and towns and villages in Europe and the Empire marched to their deaths with gloves waving and flags flying.

[104] Jordi Borja, 'Estructura urbana y movieientos urbanos', University of Barcelona (1974), quoted in Manuel Castells, *The Urban Question: A Marxist Approach* (London, 1977), p. 452.

[105] Especially, Raymond Williams, *Marxism and Literature* (Oxford, 1977); *Politics and Letters: Interviews with New Left Review* (London, 1981); *Culture,* (London, 1981); 'Culture' in D. McLennan (ed.), *Marx: The First 100 Years* (London, 1983). See also, Terry Eagleton, *Criticism and Ideology* (London, 1976), and my 'Cultural Materialisms; a critique', *Social History,* May 1984. A brilliant analysis along the lines suggested here, although not in the realm of urban history, is Francis Mulhern, *The Moment of Scrutiny* (London, 1981). A significant contribution to Marxist approaches to history writing is Richard Johnson, 'Reading for the best Marx: history-writing and historical abstraction' in Centre for Contemporary Cultural Studies *Making Histories* (London, 1982). See also Raphael Samuel (ed.), *People's History and Socialist Theory* (London, 1981). A work relevant to contemporary history is André Gorz, *Farewell to the Working Class: an Essay on Post-Industrial Socialism* (London, 1982).

8

Marx and Lenin on Imperialism

Although we have already arrived in Camden Town, this chapter takes us back to 1850 and to Brydges' world in the early eighteenth century. Then it brings us forward again to the First World War by yet another circuitous route, this time via France, Russia (and the Crimean War), India and Ireland. It provides a long view and a world context for Anne Phillips's 'three skewers and a lark spit', wages and employment in the Gloucestershire textile:trades, the Liverpool Irish, and Vera Brittain's glove. It is *the* chapter in the book which signals the breadth and compass of the materialist conception of history, and drags us away from the comfortable nest of Mansfield Park. It rubs against the grain of the minutiae, the local and the domestic, forcing the study of British economy, society and culture into the world arena where it properly belongs. And it is theoretical. It needs no apology.

*　　　　*　　　　*

It is a commonplace in recent writing on imperialism that Marx had nothing much to contribute to the subject. It is said that he never used the term, produced no theory or systematic view of it, and (worst sin of all) did not develop any perception 'that corresponds at all exactly to the concepts of imperialism advanced by later writers in the Marxist tradition'.[1] It is also alleged that his journalistic writings on colonization have richly embarrassed Marxists. As Shlomo Avineri puts it: 'Marx's views on imperialism can be painfully embarrassing to the orthodox communist.'[2] And Victor Kiernan, appropriately embarrassed, writes: '[Marx] may be said to have left a loop hole for an indulgent attitude to colonialism.'[3]

---

[1] Anthony Brewer, *Marxist Theories of Imperialism: A Critical Survey* (London, 1980), p. 27. See also Alan Hodgart, *The Economics of European Imperialism* (London, 1977), p. 21.

[2] Shlomo Avineri, *Karl Marx on Colonialism and Modernization* (New York, 1969), p. 13.

[3] V. G. Kiernan, *Marxism and Imperialism* (London, 1974), p. 6.

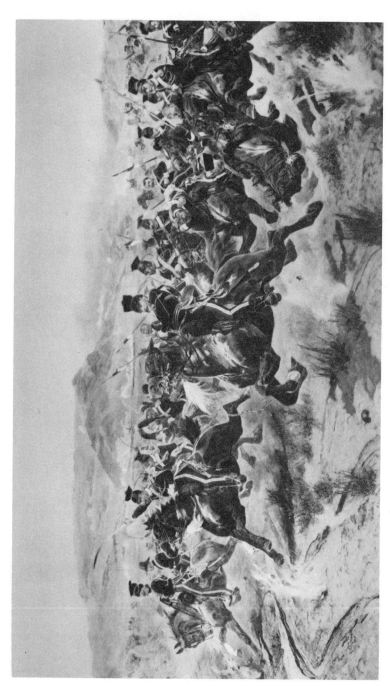

*The Charge of the Light Brigade (R. Caton Woodville RA:
Parker Gallery, London)*

Clearly the twentieth-century tale of Marx on imperialism is a sorry one, a litany of failure; it seems, in his account of Europe's relations with the rest of the world, that Marx rarely got things straight or straight enough to account for a world marked by monopoly capitalism, under-development, de-industrialization and wars of national liberation.[4]

While there is some truth in all this (not even a man of Marx's genius could be expected to analyse the complex articulation of modes of production which only came into the world after he had died), this recent twentieth-century view fails to do justice to Marx's own views about relationships between capitalist Europe and the rest of the world. Writers, such as those above, including the Marxists among them, obsessed, as they have a right to be, with the economic, social and political problems of the last quarter of the twentieth century, have neglected to place Marx in the context of the articulation of modes of production of his own time. Carried away by their blinkered pursuit of their own concepts of imperialism, and having failed to comprehend Marx's writings as historical products, they have failed as historians.

Marx *did* use the term imperialism. It may be true that his usage was not that of Marxist writing in the post Hobson—Leninist period, but he did write about imperialism and did so within the context of his systematic application of the materialist conception of history to the problems of his world. On the other hand, as should become clear in this chapter, the twentieth-century writer who remained closest to Marx's mid-nineteenth century usage was J. A. Schumpeter, an otherwise lively critic of Marx. Schumpeter defined imperialism as "the objectless disposition on the part of a state to unlimited forcible expansion'.[5] Finding it economically and socially rooted in earlier (pre-capitalist) relations of production, he identified imperialism as fundamentally atavistic.[6] In my discussion of Marx's account of relations between capitalist Europe, semi-Asiatic Russia and the rest of the world, I hope to show how Marx handled the atavistic characteristics of imperialism within the materialist conception of history.

Marx wrote about imperialism in the *Eighteenth Brumaire of Louis Bonaparte*. In this work he used the term twice. First, when writing about the *National*, the Paris organ of the bourgeois republicans who formed the

---

[4] Of the four authors referred to in footnotes 1—3, Brewer comes closest to representing Marx in the form of my own construction. However, even Brewer's representation is largely economistic (in spite of his acknowledgement of Marx's concern with the role of the state, p. 44), and he does not incorporate Marx's writing on Russia into the 'imperial' as discussed by Marx.

[5] J. A. Schumpeter, *Imperialism and Social Classes* (Oxford, 1951), p. 7.

[6] Ibid., p. 84.

official republican opposition to Louis Philippe between 1830 and 1848. On this occasion he referred to the "concealed imperialism' of the *National.*[7] Secondly, when writing about the peasant class. This was the class that had guaranteed the success of Louis Bonaparte's Eighteenth Brumaire. On this occasion Marx referred to, 'the empire sentiments [Imperialismus] of the peasant class'.[8] His argument was as follows: the successful suppression of the Paris proletariat by the bourgeois republicans during the 1848 June insurrection signalled the fact that 'The *bourgeois monarchy* of Louis Philippe can be followed only by a *bourgeois republic.*'[9] Which was to say that, whereas some of the bourgeoisie had ruled under the name of King Louis Philippe, now 'the whole of the bourgeoisie will . . . rule in the name of the people.'[10] Further, that the policies these bourgeois republicans pursued against the peasantry between 1848 and 1852 'forcibly strengthened the empire sentiments [Imperialismus] of the peasant class, it conserved the conditions that form the birth place of this peasant religion.'[11] It was this peasant 'Imperialismus' that guaranteed Louis Bonaparte's seizure of power. As Marx put it: 'The conditions of the French peasants provides us with an answer to the riddle of the general elections of *December 20 and 21*, which bore the second Bonaparte up Mount Sinai, not to receive the laws, but to give them.'[12] What then was imperialism?

In 1852, imperialism for Marx included the militarism and territorial expansionism of the first Napoleon, and signalled the despotism and nationalism of both Bonapartes. Associated with these elements was a belief that the atavistic conservatism of the French peasantry, locked as they were into a pre- or at best petty capitalist mode of production, was the source of the resurgence of French despotism. Marx wrote: '[This] ghost of the empire . . . represents not the enlightenment, but the superstition of the peasant; not his judgment, but his prejudice: not his future, but his past; not his modern Cévennes, but his modern Vendée.'[13]

This concept of imperialism (Imperialismus) in Marx was firmly located in his general theory of capitalism; in his perception of the world context in which capitalism grew and in which it existed as the only dynamic mode

---

[7] Karl Marx, the *Eighteenth Brumaire of Louis Bonaparte,* in Marx/Engels, *Selected Works* (London, 1950), Vol. I, p. 234.

[8] Ibid., p. 304.

[9] Ibid., p. 231.

[10] Ibid., p. 231.

[11] Ibid., p. 304.

[12] Ibid., p. 308.

[13] Ibid., p. 304.

of production in an overwhelmingly hostile, absolutist and militarily expansionist world. Thus, in Marx's system, in the middle years of the nineteenth century, capitalism, especially in its industrial form, was but precariously poised on the western fringe of Europe. Nevertheless, it was already firmly embedded in a world economic system in which Schumpeterian imperialism was rife; capitalism in Western Europe and industrial capitalism in England had their origins in a feudal mode of production in which a warrior class held property and power. It was not surprising, therefore, that war and conquest were present at the birth of capitalism, nor that the persistence of warlike and militarily expansionist traits accompanied it throughout its life. Up to Marx's time there was no pure capitalist mode of production; even in England in the first half of the nineteenth century the articulation of modes of production was complex. In these circumstances 'the tradition of all the dead generations' did weigh like a nightmare on the brain of the living, as they still do in England and in other countries.

As I have argued in chapter 4, English landowners, an ex-warrior class with strong vestigial warlike traits — hunting, shooting, support for a militia and opposition to a standing (professional) army — and driven by a constant enthusiasm for wars against France, played a key role in England's passage to capitalism.[14] But it is Marx's word for it not mine, that is under consideration.

Marx made clear, in at least two places, his views on the warlike and expansionist characteristics of the chief actors in the formation and expansion of capitalism. The first is in his discussion of primitive accumulation. The second is in his remarks about the scientific barbarians who took European capitalism and civilization to India. I take up the second point first, it links directly with my earlier observations about Napoleon, and about English landowners as an ex-warrior class with strong vestigial warlike traits throughout the eighteenth century, and during the early phases of industrial capitalism in England.

Within a year of completing his analysis of Louis Bonaparte's Eighteenth Brumaire, in which he drew attention to its atavistic ideology and the accompanying element of farce, Marx wrote a series of articles on India for the *New York Daily Tribune*. He began the third article with words signalling a connection in his mind between Napoleonic *imperialismus* and the activities of the British in India. He wrote: 'Napoleon said: "War is the Science of Barbarians." By means of that science, England has subjugated over one hundred millions of people or nearly all the East

---

[14] Eugene Kamenka and R. S. Neale (eds.), *Feudalism, Capitalism and Beyond* (Canberra and London, 1975), pp. 10–27 and 85–102; also, see chapter 3 above.

Indian Empire, and now must subjugate the rest.'[15] Marx then proceeded to argue that the 'cause' of this military conquest lay primarily in the persistence of institutions and traits generated in earlier pre-capitalist modes of production, but maintained by the immaturity of the capitalist mode of production in England, and by the consequent subordination of its agents to the power of a landed aristocracy. The thrust of this argument was as follows: work was despised by the nobility, consequently war, the science of barbarians, was one of the few employments permitted to sons of the nobility. Further, the plunder of war served the interests of this politically dominant class. Marx wrote:

Certain employments — all in a word, dissociated from Church and State — are deemed beneath the notice of noble families in England, or those founded in scientific barbarism. Hence the majority of the representatives of the noble families are scientific barbarians; and the wars of the White and Red Roses, of Scotland and Ireland, having ceased they must find employment in attacking distant nations.[16]

Therefore, while English traders sought to obtain markets, English governments aimed to provide employment for privileged orders. Accordingly, India suffered under 'the combined tortures of the Trade of War and the War of Trade'.[17]

'The trade of war' and 'scientific barbarism' were terms used by Marx to signal his perception that European capitalist expansion into Asia in the eighteenth and early nineteenth centuries was fuelled, perhaps inspired, by the interests of the landed aristocracy. Moulded by vestigial feudal institutions and traits, these interests were given free rein through the immaturity of the capitalist mode of production and its dependence upon and subordination to these same institutions and traits. Thus, the English aristocracy in 1853 was as atavistic as the French peasantry in December 1851. The chief difference was that the one class held power and had inherited an empire in India, while the other was without power and had lost its inheritance in 1815. Louis Napoleon was not Napoleon.

But it is in his discussion of primitive accumulation that one can discern the importance for capitalist development that Marx attributed to war, warlike and expansionist traits, and the acquisition of alien and overseas territory.

In an earlier work, *Feudalism, Capitalism and Beyond*, which might be

---

[15] Shlomo Avineri, *Karl Marx on Colonialism and Modernization* (New York, 1969), p. 81.
[16] Ibid., p. 81.
[17] Ibid., p. 82.

considered background reading for this chapter, I showed how Marx emphasized both the feudal and the agrarian origins of capitalism in Western Europe, particularly in England. I also drew attention to the importance he attributed to the coercive role of the state (the embodiment of the community), both at the point of the impact of the Germanic Military Constitution on Rome and at the point when the 'monied interest' accumulated a stock of money at the turn of the seventeenth and eighteenth centuries.[18] In highlighting certain aspects of this latter period, which I have described as the heroic age of primitive accumulation, Marx wrote: 'Force is the midwife of every old society pregnant with a new one. It is itself an economic power' . . . and . . . 'capital comes into the world soiled with mire from top to toe and oozing blood from every pore.'[19] What Marx meant, or alluded to so cryptically, was the Western European exploitation of the non-Western world, whereby 'the treasures obtained outside Europe by direct looting, enslavement, and murder, flowed to the motherland in streams, and were there turned into capital.'[20] Since this looting, enslavement, and murder were characteristic of the Spanish, the Portuguese and the French, as well as of the Dutch and the English, as they competed with each other for a share of the world, the modes of production in which they flourished were clearly pre-capitalist. In short, European pre-capitalist modes of production were essentially warlike in their social structures and purpose. Furthermore, in England by the end of the seventeenth century, all these elements: force, looting, enslavement, territorial expansion and war, had coalesced into the colonial system, created the conditions for the national debt and the system of taxation, and for national and international networks of credit. It was in this forceful fashion, given the conditions for the creation of free-wage labour, that the preconditions for capitalism had come into being. Thus, the concept of the stage of primitive accumulation places emphasis upon the importance for capitalist development of the following; an already existing network of international economic relations based upon the needs and practices of pre-capitalist modes of production; the practices of the ruling classes of pre-capitalist states as manifest in their control of their respective 'states' and legal systems; and the use by these competing ruling classes of warlike, coercive and murderous powers. Marx's scientific barbarians sprang from just such a milieu. They inherited all the economic conditions and ideological presuppositions of European pre-capitalist modes of production (under their respective nation states) in which imperial

---

[18] Eugene Kamenka and R. S. Neale, *Feudalism*, pp. 10—27.
[19] Karl Marx, *Capital*, Vol. I (London, 1962), pp. 833, 843.
[20] Ibid., p. 835.

aspirations of an atavistic and frequently objectless kind formed a considerable part. Outside the borders of these embryonic yet still precapitalist states of Western Europe, these characteristics loomed even larger.

It is important to comprehend these aspects of the materialist conception of history in order to understand the compatibility between Marx's general theoretical position and his mainly journalistic writing on relationships between the countries of Western Europe and the Balkans, Turkey, Russia, India and China: between the, as yet immature capitalist mode of production, with its accompanying uneven economic development, precapitalist institutions and traits, on the one hand, and non-capitalist modes of production on the other.

It is also necessary to have some acquaintance with the following: the concept mode of production, understood as a set of relations of production enveloping forces of production; relations of production understood as property relations and, therefore, as class relations; the classification of modes of production each identified in terms of its property relations (relations of production); the role of property relations, manifest in class relations, in bringing social change; the importance of different indigenous class (property) relations in non-capitalist modes of production for the shaping of the course of imported capitalist relations of production; the unevenness of capitalist economic development both as between nations and within them.

Therefore, I break my argument to share with you an intriguing montage between Marx's writing for the *New York Daily Tribune* on, for example, the Eastern Question, India and China and his general, more theoretical writing. The theoretical side of the montage is a passage on property in his notebooks, written between December 1857 and February 1858, subsequently published in the collection entitled *The Grundrisse.* This passage was written some two to five years after Marx had published numerous articles in the *New York Daily Tribune* on relations between bourgeois France and England on the one side and Imperial Russia on the other, during the Crimean War, but at the same time as he wrote for the *New York Daily Tribune* on the Indian Mutiny and England's relations with India. Some edited extracts from these notebooks are reproduced as an appendix to this chapter. I refer to the journalistic writing throughout.

In reading the passage in the Appendix, we can share in Marx's problem even if we cannot experience the urgency and sense of novelty with which Marx invested it; why, in the remote past, did some human societies experience significant change in their economic and social structures, and what did that change have to do with the kind of property relations which seemed to underpin the emergence of capitalism in Western Europe?

Marx himself posed the problem in the following way:

It is not the *unity* of living and active humanity with the natural, inorganic conditions of their metabolic exchange with nature, and hence their appropriation of nature, which requires explanation or is the result of a historic process, but rather the *separation* between these inorganic conditions of human existence and this active existence, a separation which is completely posited only in the relation of wage labour and capital.[21]

Marx believed that the question of *separation* was the important issue because he was fully aware of the role of community in giving life to the members of human groups in every respect; with regard to economy, society and culture. He was also conscious of the close links between individuals, tribes, clans and nature in all pre-capitalist societies wherever they appeared in the world and in whatever guise; Asiatic, Slavonic, Ancient Classical or Germanic. Thus, even in slave and serf societies, slaves and serfs were 'natural member(s) of the community . . . [and] participate in the communal property.'[22] In these circumstances, thought Marx: 'the only barrier which the community can encounter in relating to the natural conditions of production — the earth — as to its *own property* is *another community*.'[23] Therefore, for Marx, warfare was one of the earliest occupations of such communities as they sought to defend and obtain property. Warfare and conquest were also crucial in bringing about changes in forms of communal property, such as that involved in changes from slavery to serfdom. Wars of conquest and colonization were particularly important in this respect because the newly imposed secondary forms of property, consequent upon victory, frequently involved the creation of a more centralized or more perfect form of the original property arrangements (such as the English form of feudalism which turned out to be more conducive to the development of capitalism than the original French form). However, in the Asiatic mode of production, warfare and conquest had proved less effective in bringing about change. The long continuing characteristics of the Asiatic mode of production — the absence of private property and the self-sustaining unity of manufacture and agriculture (the absence of the first great division of labour between town and country), meant that the members of the communities were 'rooted to the spot, ingrown',[24] while the larger community was a great unchanging force of production. Therefore, the separation of humankind

---

[21] Karl Marx, *Grundrisse* (Harmondsworth, 1973). See Appendix to this chapter, p. 222.

[22] Ibid., Appendix, p. 222.

[23] Ibid., Appendix, p. 223. See also *The German Ideology* (Moscow, 1964), p. 34.

[24] Ibid., Appendix, p. 225.

from nature and community (the first necessary condition for the development of the capitalist mode of production) could only arise, in the Asiatic mode of production, 'by means of altogether external influences'.[25] Elsewhere in the *Grundrisse* Marx made the same point about Russia.[26] Also, in a letter to Engels in 1868, Marx indicated that while 'the Asiatic or Indian forms of property constitute everywhere in Europe the beginning', Russia alone of the European nations had failed to change or be changed. Thus, 'All that is left to them [Russia] is that they are still stuck today in the forms which their neighbours have long since cast off.'[27]

Notwithstanding the argument about the importance of warfare and conquest, the separation of the labourer from property and the community could and did occur as a result of indigenous development. Thus, communities, as they struggled to survive, changed their productive forces (including the community as a force of production) and, thereby, changed their relations of production. As Marx put it:

Until a certain point, reproduction, then turn into dissolution. . . . The development of the forces of production [by communities with existing relations between their members, property and nature] dissolves these forms, [relations between members, property and nature] and their dissolution is itself a development of the human productive forces.[28]

The point of all this is to argue that Marx was neither dogmatic nor simply contradictory about the place of internal or external forces in bringing change to pre-capitalist modes of production. For Marx, war and conquest and their accompanying brutality were not actions unrelated to internal changes. On the contrary they were inseparable from and inherent in the struggle for community survival. The fact that war and conquest

---

[25] Ibid., Appendix, p. 225.

[26] In commenting favourably on the development of the idea of labour as a general category, Marx wrote:

One could say that this indifference towards particular kinds of labour, which is a historic product in the United States, appears e.g. among the Russians as a spontaneous inclination. But there is a devil of a difference between barbarians who are fit by nature to be used for anything, and civilized people who apply themselves to everything. And then in practice the Russian indifference to the specific character of labour corresponds to being embedded by tradition within a very specific kind of labour, *from which only external influences can jar them loose. (Grundisse,* p. 105, my emphasis).

[27] Shlomo Avineri, *Karl Marx,* pp. 466–7.

[28] Karl Marx, *Grundrisse,* Appendix, p. 225.

had different consequences for different modes of production depended upon the nature of the articulation of modes of production in any social formation, and upon the relationships and contacts between dominant modes of production in different social formations. It depended upon empirical work to demonstrate connections and relationships in any concrete situation.

According to Marx, empirical history, theoretically constructed, showed that the internal dissolution of property relations and the development of human productive forces had developed first and most successfully in Western Europe. As I have already shown, in briefly restating his position, this process involved military force, state and class coercion, war, colonization, slavery — all the warlike and expansionist elements of primitive accumulation — as communities with different forms of property relations (modes of production) interacted and clashed with each other. Capitalism grew in a world context. The outcome, during the eighteenth century, and the first of its kind in history, was capitalism as a dynamic economic system with universalizing powers capable of dissolving all non-capitalist modes of production and creating class conditions for a general human advance towards enlightenment. The dynamic elements, as far as they affected relationships between the capitalist and non-capitalist modes of production, were: the competitive search for markets for the products of rapidly expanding sectors of the capitalist mode of production; but, above all, the search for cost-reducing sources of raw materials, minerals (including gold) and foodstuffs, all produced by cheap labour. Nevertheless, all of these factors, particularly in the eighteenth century, were subordinate to the interests of the Scientific Barbarians. Furthermore, the effect of these factors on non-capitalist modes of production, what one might call the trading effect, depended on the real-world form of the modes of production, their relations of production and class structures. In general Marx was sceptical about the alleged automatic development effects of trade. He argued that: 'The independent development of merchants' capital . . . stands in inverse proportion to the general economic development of society.'[29] He emphasized that:

Trade will naturally react back to varying degrees upon the communities between which it is carried on. It will subjugate production more and more to exchange value. . . . However, the dissolving effect depends very much on the nature of the producing communities between which it operates. For example, hardly shook the old Indian communities and Asiatic relations generally.[30]

[29] Karl Marx, *Capital* (London, 1962), Vol. III, ch. 20, p. 328.

Furthermore, because the capitalist mode of production was itself immature and characterized by uneven economic development, relations of production (class relations), and relations between classes and the state were even more complex in capitalistic states (modes of production) than they were in non-capitalist modes of production, even though the latter were subjected to wars of conquest and colonization and to the importation of secondary forms of property. Consequently, actual economic and political relationships between capitalistic nation states and other political formations could not be reduced to a single simple pattern of cause and effect relations. Each case had to be treated as in some sense unique although amenable to analysis within the general theory of the materialist conception of history. As we shall see, this was how Marx approached the day-to-day questions of politics, war, colonization and trade in his writing for the *New York Daily Tribune*.

RUSSIA

Marx's position on Russia is clear. Like Napoleonic France (in both its tragic and farcical disguises), Russia, in the mid-nineteenth century was an imperial power. It was, wrote Marx, 'far on the way to universal empire'[31] extending from the Baltic, through the Mediterranean, and into the Middle East. Needless to say, Russia's imperialism was not capitalistic, on the contrary it was atavistic. According to Marx, Russia was 'semi-Asiatic in her conditions, manners, traditions and institutions'.[32] It was this self-same semi-Asiatic conquering power that had stifled the revolutionary hopes of the bourgeoisie throughout Western and Central Europe in 1848. Marx wrote

Russia is decidedly a conquering nation, and was so for a century, until the great movement of 1789 called into potent activity an antagonist of formidable

---

[30] Karl Marx, *Grundisse,* p. 858. See also, *Capital,* Vol. III, ch. 20, p. 333:

The obstacles presented by the internal solidity and organisation of pre-capitalistic, national modes of production to the corrosive influence of commerce are strikingly illustrated in the intercourse of the English with India and China . . . (In India) this work of dissolution proceeds very gradually. And still more slowly in China, where it is not re-inforced by direct political power.

[31] Karl Marx, *The Eastern Question* (London, 1897), edited by Eleanor Marx Aveling and Edward Aveling, p. 18.

[32] Ibid., p. 21.

nature. We mean the European Revolution, the explosive force of democratic
ideas and man's native thirst for freedom. Since that epoch there have been in
reality two powers on the continent of Europe — Russia and Absolutism, the
Revolution and Democracy.[33]

According to Marx, the struggle between these 'two powers' was the
major international political issue about which nineteenth-century
socialists and communists had to make up their minds, especially as this
struggle related to the Eastern Question. This was because the struggle, in
its Middle-Eastern and world context, was clearly structured by the
existence on the border areas of Europe and Asia of two dominant modes
of production inherently antagonistic to, if not in permanent competition
with, each other, and by the unevenness of economic development between
and within these modes of production. By the mid-nineteenth century, the
antagonism between the 'two powers' was concentrated upon a region of
South-Eastern Europe believed to be important to both for commercial,
military and political reasons, but coming under the political sway of a
third power, the Ottoman Empire; hence the problem of Turkey in
Europe, and the Eastern Question.

In Marx's analysis, the Ottoman Empire was a ramshackle political
structure built on the decaying remnants of the Slavonic and tributary
semi-Asiatic modes of production, as modified by the importation of
secondary forms of property. Marx wrote, it was 'the living sore of
European legitimacy . . . [which] . . . has the misfortune to be inhabited by
a conglomerate of different races and nationalities, of which it is hard to
say which is the least fit for progress and civilization.'[34] Yet even in South
East Europe there were hopes for bourgeois, nationalist revolutions;
internal developments has already created conditions for the separation of
the direct producer from the soil and for the creation of free wage labour
(unlike in the Asiatic mode of production proper). Moreover, English and
other European traders were beginning to penetrate Asiatic as well as
European Turkey, fuelling the destruction of indigenous modes of
production. These circumstances seemed to indicate that sooner or later
Turkey in Europe would fall into the lap of capitalism. There was one
stumbling block, Turkish rule. Marx believed that the full potential for
capitalism in South-Eastern Europe would only be realized through the
forcible overthrow of the Turks. He wrote:

It is the Greek and Slavonic middle-class in all the towns and trading posts

[33] Ibid., p. 18.
[34] Ibid., pp. 2, 4.

who are the real support of whatever civilization is effectually imported into the country. That part of the population is constantly rising in wealth and influence, and the Turks are more and more driven into the background. Were it not for their monopoly of civil and military power they would soon disappear. . . . Remove all the Turks out of Europe, and trade will have no reason to suffer. . . . The fact is, they must be got rid of.[35]

This was easier said than done. There was a Russian bear in this Turkish bazaar. Marx described it in the story he told of two Persian naturalists examining a bear:

the one who had never seen such an animal before, inquired whether that animal dropped its cubs alive or laid eggs; to which the other, who was better informed, replied; 'That animal is capable of anything'. The Russian bear is certainly capable of anything, so long as he knows the other animals he has to deal with to be capable of nothing.[36]

Thus, Imperial Russia, a semi-Asiatic despotism, arising from an economic and social system virtually unable to generate within itself any new form of social relations (such as capitalism), but amenable to being organized for war and territorial aggrandisement in ways characteristic of such atavistic despotisms (modes of production), stood in the way. It was also erratic and unpredictable. Imperial Russia stood in the way not only of capitalistic penetration of South-Eastern Europe, but threatened the very life blood of Western-European Capitalism itself. It did so through the 'bread-screw which she can put on whenever the policy of Western Europe becomes obnoxious to punishment'.[37] Further, Imperial Russia blocked the spread of capitalism beyond the bounds of Mediterranean Europe into the Far East generally. Marx wrote:

The struggle between Western Europe and Russia about the possession of Constantinople involves the question whether Byzantinism is to fall before Western civilization, or whether its antagonism shall revive in a more terrible and conquering form than ever before. Constantinople is the golden bridge thrown between the West and the East, and Western civilization cannot, like the sun, go round the world without passing that bridge; and it cannot pass it without a struggle with Russia.[38]

---

[35] Ibid., p. 26.
[36] Ibid., p. 53.
[37] Ibid., p. 209.
[38] Ibid., p. 81.

While Marx could see the issues so clearly, the dominant classes in the capitalist nations prevaricated. This was partly because their diplomats 'knew no more about the real subject [of the Eastern Question] than about the man in the moon',[39] but, mainly because their internal class relations reflected their own immaturity as capitalist nations. In England, lack of harmony between the bourgeoisie and a landed aristocracy, who still held the reins of government (the abolition of the Corn Laws was a very recent memory), produced a lack of commitment to the real interests of capitalist Western Europe. A similar lack of commitment in France followed the accession to power of the second Bonaparte, mainly because of its own indigenous atavistic 'imperialismus'. Marx wrote, that while

The Sultan holds Constantinople only in trust for the Revolution . . . the present nominal dignitaries of Western Europe, themselves finding the last stronghold of their 'order' on the shores of the Neva, can do nothing but keep the question in suspense until Russia has to meet her real antagonist, the Revolution. The Revolution which will break the Rome of the West will also overpower the demoniac influences of the Rome of the East.[40]

According to this analysis Marx observed that it was only the English working class, some of whom, inspired by the Chartist, Ernest Jones, 'pledging the people to *war*, and declaring that before liberty was established peace was a crime',[41] saw dimly that the impending struggle over the Ottoman Empire was a class war — a continuation in 1853 of the revolutionary impulse set in train in 1789. Thus, wrote Marx: 'while the English Queen is, at this moment, [July 1853] feasting Russian Princesses; while an enlightened English aristocracy and bourgeoisie lie prostrate before the barbarian Autocrat, the English proletariat alone protests against the impotency and degredation of the ruling classes.'[42] Although one might doubt the validity of Marx's explanation of English prevarication over the Crimean expedition, there is little doubt that it was consistent with his general position on relations between the developing bourgeois nations of Western Europe and Russia.

RECAPITULATION

In Marx's system the industrial capitalist mode of production was

[39] Ibid., p. 21.
[40] Ibid., p. 81.
[41] Ibid., p. 63.
[42] Ibid., p. 62.

undoubtedly universalizing. Nevertheless, in the 1850s it was far from 'universal'. Indeed, it was by no means securely established anywhere in the world, not even in England. Industrial capitalism, its carrier states (and revolution) were only thinly spread and precariously poised on the Western fringe of Europe, especially prone to being thwarted at crucial moments by a despotic, atavistic and conservatively wooden Russia. Therefore, in spite of the optimism of the *Communist Manifesto's* argument for revolution in 1848, the growth of trade and the internal dynamic of industrial capitalism could not be expected to batter down 'all Chinese walls' unaided. On the contrary, in 1853 and 1854, Marx believed that the security and further progress of capitalism in the world depended on clear-sighted political and military intervention by Western (capitalist) governments to break up the Ottoman Empire and contain Russia. Further, because he always placed capitalism in a world context, Marx argued that there were connections between these distant 'Imperial' events and class struggles within the already most capitalistic of the Western nations. He believed that war against Russia over the Eastern Question would create conditions for the collapse of Bonapartist 'imperialism' in the West. As Marx, in his inimitable fashion, put it, in the final words of the *Eighteenth Brumaire*: 'when the imperial mantle finally falls on the shoulders of Louis Bonaparte, the bronze statue of Napoleon will crash from the top of the Vendôme Column.'[43] In short, Marx argued the necessity for political and military intervention to create conditions (relations of production) that would speed up the collapse of Asiatic and semi-Asiatic modes of production, and that the embroilment of partially capitalistic nations in 'imperialistic' wars would also fuel the process of their own dissolution by capitalism.

Clearly, Marx had no illusions about the speed with which the universalizing power of capitalism would bring about change in non-capitalist modes of production, or the inevitability of such changes. Therefore, just as he argued that war and conquest had been historical conditions for the break-up of communal property relations in pre-capitalist modes of production (and was a central condition for the success of primitive accumulation in England), he gave war and conquest a crucial place in his analysis of relations between capitalist and pre-capitalist nations and states in the mid-nineteenth century.

Marx did not use the term 'imperialism' to encapsulate any of these relationships. On the contrary, for him 'imperialism' signified the absolutism, despotism and militarism of Napoleonic 'imperialismus' and of Imperial Russia.

---

[43] Karl Marx, *The Eighteenth Brumaire of Louis Bonaparte*, p. 311.

INDIA

Marx's views on India and Indian relationships with England also fall within this general framework of analysis; hence his account is complex (some might say confused). In any case it is never dull.

In this account India, before the English conquest, was an Asiatic mode of production characterized by the absence of private property, by an undifferentiated association of agriculture and manufacture (little division of labour), and by the appropriation of the available surplus by tribute (taxation). Politically there were three departments of government: 'that of Finance or the plunder of the interior; that of War, or the plunder of the exterior; and finally, the department of Public Works.'[44] The maintenance of public works was a necessary condition for the preservation of the surplus to be plundered. However, India also had long established trading links with Europe. Marx wrote: 'From immemorial times, Europe received the admirable textures of Indian labour, sending in return for them her precious metals. . . .'[45] In short, India was a rigidly structured and coherent social formation whose limited trade relations with Europe had scarcely any effect upon its indigenous mode(s) of production. Like all Asiatic despotisms, it had a great capacity for war (and for being conquered) but no capacity for change. Accordingly, Marx believed it 'has no history at all, at least no known history.'[46] Its (pre)history (its changing) began with the English intrusion.

Marx linked the distinctive character of the English intrusion into India with the complex articulation of class relations in the period of the heroic age of primitive accumulation in England. (Remember Marx on the scientific barbarians.) He dated this intrusion from 1702, when the competing English claimants to Indian trade united into a single company. This was the epoch 'when the Whigs became the farmers of the revenues of the British Empire',[47] and when the 'old landed aristocracy having been defeated, and the bourgeoisie not being able to take its place except under the banner of moneyocracy, or the *haute finance*'.[48] The outcome of this set of class relations was 'the union between the Constitutional Monarchy and the monopolizing monied interest, between the Company

[44] Shlomo Avineri, *Karl Marx,* p. 90.
[45] Ibid., p. 91.
[46] Ibid., p. 132.
[47] Ibid., p. 99.
[48] Ibid., p. 99.

of East India and the "glorious" revolution of 1688. . . .'[49] Subsequently, Company and government were inextricably linked. The Company became a recognizable part of 'old corruption' and a source of employment (and plunder) for otherwise unemployable younger sons, the 'scientific barbarians' already referred to, who were atavistically committed to war as a trade. This linking of war and trade, especially after 1813, placed 'India under the combined tortures of the Trade of War and the War of Trade'.[50] During this period of a century or more, the plunder flowing back into England helped to consolidate the favourable financial conditions for the successful passage to industrial capitalism in England. Thus, just as Marx linked the heroic age of primitive accumulation in England to the despoilation of India, he linked the despoilation and destruction of India to the development of industrial capitalism in England. In doing so he identified the East India Company as a surrogate for the British state and its governance, as they in turn mirrored the interests of competing classes; the landed oligarchy of agrarian capitalists, the monied interest, the scientific barbarians, and traders.

In the East India Company's conquest of India, the jewel in England's 'Colonial Empire',[51] the Company appropriated the two departments of Indian plunder but neglected the department of government (public works). Instead, its agents attributed English notions of absolute property to the Indian systems of extracting tribute, and treated their institutions and human agents accordingly, and (but only latterly) swamped Indian domestic producers with cheap industrially produced cottons. Further, in Bengal, the Company decreed that land appropriated as 'private property' should be used exclusively to produce opium as a commercial crop. According to Marx, these activities destroyed the economic basis of the old mode of production without generating capitalism in India. Rather, by destroying indigenous producers they destroyed markets and destroyed a necessary condition for the development of capitalism. Consequently, after 1813, the Indian economy moved into deep crisis. Marx wrote:

Till then, the interests of the moneyocracy which had converted India into its landed estates, of the oligarchy who had conquered it by their armies, and of the millocracy who had inundated it with their fabrics, had gone hand in hand. But the more the industrial interest became dependent on the Indian market, the more it felt the necessity of creating fresh productive powers in India, after having ruined her native industry.[52]

    [49] Ibid., p. 100.
    [50] Ibid., p. 82.
    [51] Ibid., p. 101.

At this point, the 'Indian Question' became an English Question. However, the solution merely imposed an incompetent bureaucracy on India, compounding her problems.

According to Marx, the consequences of the English devastation of old India would be revolutionary. Ultimately they would create conditions for the regeneration of the Indian economy and society. Thus, political unity, an efficient native army, private property, a free press, a new educated class and improved communications between India and the rest of the world and within India itself, would make revolution possible. There was, however, nothing inevitable about this and nothing commendable about the processes involved. Marx wrote:

All the English bourgeoisie may be forced to do will neither emancipate nor materially mend the social condition of the mass of the people, depending not only on the development of the productive powers, but on their appropriation by the people. But what they will not fail to do is to lay down the material premises for both. Has the bourgeoisie ever done more? Has it ever effected a progress without dragging individuals and peoples through blood and dirt, through misery and degradation?[53]

Indeed, economic and social conditions in all colonies, wherever they existed, simply mirrored and threw into sharp relief the conditions created by private property and capitalist relations of production in capitalist Europe. For example, in the 'empty lands of Australia, New Zealand and Canada, the anti-capitalist cancer of the colonies threw into sharp relief capitalism's need for a property-less wage earning class as an absolute requirement.'[54] While, in the Indian colonies, the actions of the English demonstrated the

hypocrisy and inherent barbarism of bourgeois civilization . . . turning from its home, where it assumes respectable forms, to the colonies, where it goes naked. They are the defenders of property, but did any revolutionary party ever originate agrarian revolutions like those in Bengal, in Madras and in Bombay? Did they not . . . resort to atrocious extortion, when simple corruption could not keep pace with their rapacity? . . . The whole rule of Britain in India was swinish, and is so to this day.[55]

---

[52] Ibid., p.107.
[53] Ibid., p. 137.
[54] Karl Marx, *Capital,* Vol. I, pp. 716—24.

H

Because of this 'nakedness' of exploitation based on private property, even the development of modern industry based on the railwayization of India would not automatically benefit the mass of the Indian population. Marx wrote:

The Indians will not reap the fruits of the new elements of society scattered among them by the British Bourgeoisie, till in Great Britain itself the now ruling classes shall have been supplanted by the industrial proletariat, *or till the Hindoos themselves shall have grown strong enough to throw off the English yoke altogether.*[56]

Clearly Marx believed that the military conquest and plunder of India by England's scientific barbarians, the reorganization of India's systems of land tenure according to English notions of private property, and the opening of India to 'free trade' would destroy the 'ingrownness' of India's economic and social structures and create conditions for social revolution and revolution. That Marx also believed these conditions to be in the future is suggested by his analysis of the Indian Mutiny. According to Marx the Mutiny did not contain the seeds of revolution. Rather, its effect, had it been successful, would have been to halt the disintegration of Indian society and return the whole of the sub-continent to its pre-capitalist mode(s) of production and its pre-history. While the economic conditions for revolution in India were indeed developing, the necessary changes *were* in the future.

RECAPITULATION AND EMPHASIS

In Marx's system, Asiatic modes of production lacked the necessary conditions for the generation of change; they were without history. Therefore, change was the product of warlike intrusion from outside and the reduction of states to colonial status. Nevertheless, change was not automatic or inevitable. Responses to intrusion were conditioned by class relations in both capitalist and colonized nations, and by the timing of

---

[55] Shlomo Avineri, *Karl Marx,* pp. 137, 455. Marx to Engels, 14 June 1853. In this letter Marx gives an insight into his belief in the originality of his position on India, particularly with respect to the Sismondian views of Henry Carey, author of *The Slave Trade, Domestic and Foreign.*

[56] Ibid., p. 137 (my italics).

those relations. In the case of India the following conditions were important.

New relations of production in India were the result of changes in class relations in England during the period from the high point of the heroic age of primitive accumulation, to the emergence of the industrial capitalist mode of production (moneyocracy to millocracy); of the distinct bureaucratic/state form of the conquest and subsequent capitalist penetration of India; and of the accompanying level of technology (that is the different effects of the technology of cotton and railways). In Bengal, where the poppy was compulsorily grown at the behest of the bureaucratic state, these new relations of production were also embedded in international trade relations.

These new relations of production (secondary forms of property) were shaped by the prevailing English view about the nature and importance of absolute property in producing the wealth of nations, and also by the way these views shaped English perceptions about the nature of existing indigenous property relations. These two sets of inextricably connected perceptions shaped the views of the new bureaucracy about the changes in property relations necessary to generate the wealth of the nation and to maximize the extraction of surplus value (as in Bengal).

The effect of the introduction by force of new relations of production was also influenced by the actual property relations displaced, that is by the various forms of the Asiatic mode of production as it was fragmented among various states. In China, for example, the main factor influencing, in the sense of inhibiting market expansion for English goods was the combination of minute agriculture with domestic industry.[57]

Inherent in and necessary to all aspects of the introduction of new relations of production into Asiatic modes of production (to India) was force. This was necessary to coerce and/or persuade the indigenous ruling class to co-operate with the bureaucratic state. (It also had the effect of creating an educated and armed force as one of the ultimate conditions for resistance to foreign oppression.) According to Marx, England's problem in China compared with India was the absence of territorial power, China was unconquered. New relations of production were essential to destroy the economic base of Indian society and to release its true productive and creative potential. Nevertheless, until there was social revolution either in England *or* in India, there would be no improvement in the material or social condition of the mass of the population in India.

[57] Ibid., pp. 393, 398.

IRELAND

Marx's distant view of the world, taking in Eastern Europe, Russia, the Middle-East and India, and his view of the part played by the capitalist nations of Western Europe in it, did not prevent him from seeing things closer to home and closer to the bone. Ireland. Ireland for Marx was the paradigm of primitive accumulation and of uneven economic development under capitalism, and of the consequences of this in reality and in consciousness; things Irish *were* beyond the pale.

Marx's story of England's relations with Ireland shows as clearly as any other of his writings the part he saw that conquest and reduction to colonial status played in transforming property relations, the importance he attributed to the development of private property in land for the creation of free wage labour, and the acuteness of his perception about the unevenness of capitalist economic development and its significance for class consciousness. For example, following the first real subjugation of Ireland in 1545, and the subsequent legal thrust of the Act of Attainder against Shane O'Neill in 1570, more than half of Ulster went to the Crown. At the same time, the Lord Deputy in Council was empowered to issue re-grants under English tenures. (Subsequently the adoption of the title *the* O'Neill implied rebellion against English dominion.) In 1605, by a judgment in the King's Bench, gavelkind and tanistry,[58] as communal forms of property and inheritance, were again repealed and replaced by English laws of inheritance; all clan duties were converted into money rents. In 1608 Ulster was planted. By 1675, following the Cromwellian confiscations, some two-thirds of productive land was in the hands of the English, the Protestants and the Church (about 8.3 million statute acres according to Petty and 8.4 million acres according to Murphy). By 1699 a further 1.7 million acres had been escheated under William III. In short, by the early eighteenth century these various acts of war, conquest, and reduction to colonial status had created private property in land, mostly in the hands of absentee landowners, and turned communal rights into tenancies for terms of years. Those without property, either as owner or

---

[58] Gavelkind is a term from Kent used by English jurists to identify the Irish rules regulating the passing of the lands of a deceased clan member into other hands. In Ireland land was regarded as held on a temporary tenure. After death it was distributed among all free male kinsmen, including sons born out of wedlock. Tanistry is a system regulating inheritance of chieftainship in Ireland. The successor of the clan chief, the tanist, was appointed by election during the life of the chief from a family in the clan whose members were considered the 'eldest and worthiest' of kinsmen.

tenant, had only their labour to sell. Since, in the early eighteenth century, English industry was protected against imports from Ireland there were few employment opportunities outside agriculture; wages were depressed and lifestyles narrowly circumscribed. After the Act of Union in 1800, Irish industry, which had been re-established during the period of an Anglo-Irish Parliament 1783 — 1800, was subject to renewed competition from a modernized English industry, and virtually destroyed. Then, following the repeal of the Corn Laws in 1846, Irish agriculture (corn production for the English market) was replaced by a pastoral industry (also for the English market) requiring consolidation of holdings. The position of the remaining small tenants was further eroded. By the 1860s — by 1866 and the period of Fenianism — the result of this long drawn out epoch of colonialism was the reduction of Ireland to an economically backward region, owned and controlled by an English aristocracy and other absentee landowners. This dominant class regarded the indigenous people as inferior, trapped in an alien, Catholic culture. Despite the famine, and a million deaths by starvation, generated by this colonial system in the 1840s, Ireland was the source of an abundant supply of cheap labour, not only in England, but wherever world capitalism demanded it.

As a result of his study of Ireland, Marx became convinced that a necessary condition for the creation of *class* consciousness among the English proletariat was the repeal of the Act of Union. He believed that England's colonial relationship to Ireland, on its very doorstep, as it were, soured relations between English and Irish proletarians, turning all the English working class (with the exception of a few leaders) into unwitting agents of colonialism. Further, he believed that the authority of the English aristocracy could best be challenged in an independent Ireland by the Irish themselves. The benefit to England and to the English working class, with regard to the development of *class* consciousness and revolution, of such a challenge would be immense. Marx wrote:

But the English bourgeoisie has, besides, much more important interests in Ireland's present-day economy. Owing to the constantly increasing concentration of tenant farming, Ireland steadily supplies her own surplus to the English labour-market, and thus forces down wages and lowers the moral and material condition of the English working class.

And most important of all! Every industrial and commercial centre in England now possesses a working class *divided* into two *hostile* camps, English proletarians and Irish proletarians. The ordinary English worker hates the Irish worker as a competitor who lowers his standard of life. In relation to the Irish worker he feels himself a member of the *ruling nation* and so turns himself into a tool of the aristocrats and capitalists of his country *against Ireland*, thus strengthening their domination *over himself*. He cherishes religious, social, and national prejudices against the Irish worker. His attitude towards him is much the same as that of the 'poor whites' to the 'niggers' in the former slave states of the USA. The Irishman pays him back with interest in his own money. He sees in the English worker at once the accomplice and the stupid tool of the *English rule in Ireland*.

This antagonism is artificially kept alive and intensified by the press, the pulpit, the comic papers, in short, by all the means at the disposal of the ruling classes. *This antagonism* is the *secret of the impotence of the English working class*, despite its organization. It is the secret by which the capitalist class maintains its power. And that class is fully aware of it.

But the evil does not stop here. It continues across the ocean. The antagonism between English and Irish is the hidden basis of the conflict between the United States and England. It makes any honest and serious co-operation between working classes of the two countries impossible. It enables the governments of both countries, whenever they think fit, to break the edge off the social conflict by their mutual bullying, and, in case of need, by war with one another.[59]

Ireland, in short, was not only the paradigm of primitive accumulation and of its connection with the forceful creation of free wage labour, war, conquest, colonization and coercion; it was the outstanding example of the unevenness of capitalist development in a colonial context (the development of under-development). Therefore, for Marx, it was a key to his analysis of the interdependence of class relations and the development of *class* consciousness, both between as well as within, capitalist nations in a world context.

MARX: CONCLUSION

At the heart of the materialist conception of history lies the struggle over property rights, a struggle taking place between as well as within communities. Marx had no doubt that this struggle involved war and conquest as much as it did riot, rebellion and revolution. In the nineteenth century, the world in which this struggle occurred was not a capitalist one. Therefore, struggle (or conflict) frequently took place between states at different levels of economic development and sometimes, as in the Crimean War, involved at least three contending states, all at different levels of development. Because the tradition of all the dead generations in

---

[59] The account of Marx on Ireland is based on Marx—Engels. *Ireland and the Irish Question* (Moscow, 1971). The particular quotation is from Marx to Sigfrid Meyer and August Vogt, 7 April 1870, pp. 293—4.

this complex world system weighed like a nightmare on the brains of the living, it should not surprise anyone that Marx's writings were redolent with words, phrases, imagery and allusion — as in his story of the Russian bear — showing that the colonialism he knew and incorporated into his system was, for him, both rooted in the economic and social conditions of pre-capitalist relations of production, in the capitalist and non-capitalist regions of the world, as well as being a product of the expansionary economic forces of the still immature capitalist mode of production. His terminology alone shows this. Marx's use of language, as in 'the Trade of War and the War of Trade', in his case against the 'scientific barbarians', and in his references to the Bonapartes and 'imperialismus' is not merely colourful or extravagant. His juxtaposition of the terms 'Trade of War' and 'War of Trade'; 'scientific' and 'barbarian'; 'modern Cévennes' and 'modern Vendée', show more clearly than any long-winded argument of mine how much Marx was alert to the paradoxes of his day (and of history), and could write them into his system without damage to any of its parts. Consequently, Marx's 'Imperial' world picture at mid-century has the appearance of a painting by Picasso, and reads like a story by Laurence Sterne.

In India, a warlike and conquering bureaucratic English system, slowly at first and then more rapidly, had virtually destroyed the relations of production of its Asiatic mode of production. In conjunction with the then indigenous social changes, following the importation of secondary forms of property, these developments had begun to create conditions for social revolution. But that was still far in the future. In Ireland, similar circumstances had already put revolution on the agenda.

In China, on the other hand, the 'free-trading' interest of the instrument of the bureaucratic state, the East India Company, dictated that the economic penetration of China had been achieved through wars fought for the creation of a 'free' market in opium. Since the Chinese market, limited by the combination of minute agriculture with domestic industry, could not absorb both goods and drugs, legitimate trade had suffered; China was being incorporated into the world system only through a prolonged period of absolute demoralization. (The real 'imperial' beneficiary, both in 1842 and 1858, was Russia.)

In Turkey, Western-European capitalism in conjunction with the activities of a small but growing indigenous capitalist class, had created conditions for the destruction of its Slavonic and Turkish variants of the Asiatic mode of production. It only needed the defeat of Russia to complete the beginning of the end.

But Russia was still a successful absolutist and imperialistic state. At best it could only be contained and prevented from exercising counterrevolutionary force by a successful war launched against it by the otherwise competing capitalist states of France and England. These states, however, were either hamstrung or half-hearted about the need to contain Russia because of the still immature forms of capitalism they contained. Because their own relations of production were only imperfectly industrial-capitalist their political decision making was swayed by competing upper-class claims. Hence petit bourgeois France was imperialistic in the Russian (or Napoleonic) sense. In England, the class interests of the dominant class in the industrial-capitalist mode of production were badly served by the tradition of all the dead generations of the landed oligarchy, weighing like a nightmare on the brains of living industrialists. The Crimean War, in all its bloody, inept futility, was the measure of that nightmare. Then there was Ireland. (As the centrepiece of my Picasso-like version of Marx's world view I would place the Charge of the Light Brigade, including the 8th Kings Royal Irish Hussars, which lost 66 out of 104 men, and in which four VCs were won, none going to the Irish Regiment.)

Beyond these regions, in which states containing variants of the Asiatic mode of production were in contact with expansionist quasi-capitalist states, and also competing with a Russian 'imperialism' rooted in a non-capitalist mode of production, were the 'empty' lands: America (yet to become an industrial capitalist state) but itself already colonizing; Canada, Australia, New Zealand, South Africa. There, too, capitalist demands, mainly from England, exerted pressure for the search for more and cheaper raw materials and the protection of trade routes. In these countries, economic responses to demands coming from rapidly developing capitalist states had already virtually destroyed incipient peasant production — what Marx referred to as the anti-capitalist cancer of the colonies. On the basis of newly created private property rights, states in these 'empty' lands had recreated the conditions for capitalism. Accordingly, in 1858, Marx drew attention to the intricate network of international economic relations binding Australia to China, to England, to India and, therefore, to the opium trade, to the wars fought to guarantee its markets and to the necessity to contain Russia and destroy the Ottoman Empire, and, thereby drew attention to economic relations linking Australia to the futility of the Crimean War, which only some of the English working class dimly recognized as a class war.[60] In short, it was Marx's view, that even though every regional adaptation to capitalism was determined by indigenous relations of production, and by the degree to which indigenous ruling classes adapted to the fact of conquest and/or the disintegration of

---

[60] Ibid., pp. 386—7.

existing relations of production, no region of the world was immune to the universalizing and economically integrating effect of the uneven development of capitalism, almost everywhere backed by main force.

These picaresque stories in Marx's journalistic writings, and the Picasso-like canvas one could make out of them, are consistent with the principal general and theoretical arguments of the materialist conception of history. This conception of history, expounded at a time when both 'empire' and 'state' were necessary in fact for the existence of capitalism in Western Europe, incorporated the term 'imperialism' as Marx and his contemporaries knew it and comprehended it; as it related to Bonapartist France and Imperial Russia. That it was not a concept reflecting the interests and perceptions of some of his followers seemingly bent on transforming the intricate coherence of Marx's conception of history into a stage theory of history, is not a matter to regret. In Marx's materialist conception of history 'imperialism', thought of as the territorial expansion of rival national capitalisms throughout a non-capitalist world, never was the highest stage of capitalism; this characteristic was there all the time. Therefore, it should not come as a surprise to a Marxist historian to find that Marx on 'imperialism' was not a 'Marxist' — a fact which, for a Marxist, should be no cause for embarrassment.

Yet, even as I write, I pause, acknowledging a need to clarify the point I wish to make. What is the Marxist view of imperialism with which I compare Marx's writing on capitalism in a world context and his '*imperialismus*'? Is there any substance to my claim?

THE CLASSIC MARXIST THEORY OF IMPERIALISM

I confine my answer to the classic Marxist theory of imperialism generally attributed to Lenin in his pamphlet, *Imperialism, The Highest State of Capitalism.*

As Anthony Brewer has recently shown, Lenin's *Imperialism* was largely derived from the work of Rudolf Hilferding, N. Bukharin and J. A. Hobson.[61] This is undoubtedly true. The work is clearly structured by its dependence upon Hilferding and Bukharin, and flawed by its borrowing from Hobson — Lenin did lead Marxism up a wrong track. Nevertheless, it is also true to say that *Imperialism is* structured by Lenin's sense of the unity of the economic and the political in society, a sense which is riveted at the heart of everything Marx wrote, as if by a great bolt of lightning. Lenin did have a point to make. A point which Brewer seems to miss. This

---

[61] Anthony Brewer, *Marxist Theories.*

point is the urgent political purpose of Marxist economic (and historiographical) analysis. In this case the relationship of imperialism to, and its bearing upon *class* struggle in Eastern Europe and Russia. Therefore, although it will be necessary to digress for a while to set out the elements of Hilferding's finance capital, it is appropriate to concentrate upon Lenin's *Imperialism.*

Lenin on imperialism and Hilferding on finance capital were Marxists. Each in his own way understood something of the intricate coherence of Marx's conception of history, even though they sought to focus upon and develop certain aspects of it, Hilferding remaining closer to Marx than did Lenin. As Marxists, both worked with common assumptions and concepts. First, the concept mode of production, especially the capitalist mode of production characterized by changing relations of production, as exemplified by the development of joint stock company organization. Second, the assumption of the economically dynamic, therefore, universalizing nature of capitalism. Hence their consciousness of the importance of the fact of uneven economic development both in national and world contexts. Third, the notion that property relations and uneven economic development had an important part to play in forming class structures and in shaping political processes, for example, in South-Eastern Europe. Fourth, the associated idea that class structures and political processes were important for the shaping of *class* consciousness. Fifth, the concept of revolution as a necessary condition for the development of socialism on a world scale. Indeed, writing on the dynamic nature of world capitalism, Lenin echoed Marx. He wrote: 'Capitalism long ago created a world market' and 'colonial policy and imperialism existed before this latest stage of capitalism, and even before capitalism. Rome founded on slavery pursued a colonialist policy and achieved imperialism.'[62] Nevertheless, because they were Marxists, they both argued that twentieth-century imperialism was different, both from traditional colonialism and Roman imperialism. Developments within the capitalist mode of production had brought about a situation in which, Lenin wrote:

there are no unoccupied territories — that is, territories that do not belong to any state — in Asia and America . . . we must say that the characteristic feature of this period is the final partition of the globe — not in the sense that a *new partition* is impossible — on the contrary new partitions are possible and inevitable — but in the sense that the colonial policy of the capitalist countries have *completed* the seizure of the unoccupied territories on our

[62] V. I. Lenin, *Imperialism The Highest Stage of Capitalism* (London, 1948), pp. 83, 100.

planet. For the first time the world is completely divided up, so that in the future *only* redivision is possible; territories can only pass from one 'owner' to another, instead of passing as unowned territory to an 'owner'.[63]

Since the history leading to such an outcome was Hilferding's, it will be necessary to recount it here. Hilferding took up the theme of uneven economic development in Marx to show its particular significance, both in respect to the development of new relations of production — joint stock company organization — and the concentration of capital, for late developing countries, notably, Germany. Thus, while Marx had shown that both features were characteristic of mature capitalism in general, Hilferding argued, that in late developing countries modern technology and the need to create infant industries, in the face of competition from Britain, already entrenched throughout the world, had given a specially advanced form to company organization and the concentration of capital. According to Hilferding, financial requirements associated with the establishment of high (and new) technology industries in a mature capitalist world, in a backward country like Germany, acted as a forcing ground for the introduction of joint-stock company organization and for the setting up of big joint-stock banks; the latter able to invest directly in the capital goods industries, such as iron and steel, unlike in Britain. Also, in Germany, unlike in Britain, the state, called upon by industrialists (and by agriculturalists) to establish protective tariffs to protect infant industries, responded positively. The consequent restriction of competition in the domestic market, in a situation already marked by a high level of concentration of capital in joint stock companies, themselves with close relations with large corporate banks and finance houses — finance capitalism — facilitated further concentration of capital and production. Cartels became the order of the day. Cartellization, in its turn, led to the practice of dumping in foreign markets compensated by higher prices in the domestic market. By thus raising prices in the domestic market — and squeezing real wages — cartelization, the creature of finance capital, reduced domestic demand. This reduction in domestic demand (an elaboration of Marx's argument about a general tendency to under-consumption under capitalism), in circumstances of greatly increased productive capacity, restricted investment outlets. Hence there was a need to add economic territory to the existing national territory to provide investment outlets which would maintain world demand, especially for the products of the cartellized capital goods industries. This would further stimulate domestic investment. Thus, capital export became a necessity

[63] Ibid., p. 94.

for some sections of industry. In short, capital export, inherent in the uneven development of capitalism, and in those changes in the location and structure of the capitalist mode of production associated with it, which are subsumed in the concept 'finance capital', is central to the concept 'imperialism'. Furthermore, in the world economic context of the early twentieth century, by which time Britain had virtually established an imperial monopoly, and in which other large areas of the world were under the control of imperialistic powers in Marx's sense, such as Imperial Russia, circumstances would arise when essential capital export would be inhibited by the absence of territorial power over regions deemed suitable for investment. In such cases, economic penetration would have to be accompanied or followed by some kind of political control. Thus, competition between capitalist states, at different stages of capitalist economic development, over the question of access to regions with non-capitalist or only partially capitalist modes of production, brought about by finance capitalism's need for capital exports, was imperialism. As such it should be distinguished from Marx's usage, *Imperialismus,* although imperialism retained its connotation of aggressive nationalistic policies directed at foreign powers by absolutist or quasi-absolutist states. Thus, although early twentieth-century imperialism had opened up the Far East, Canada, South Africa and South America, its main battleground was Central, Eastern and South-Eastern Europe, and the chief participants were the great powers. It was in Europe, in the early twentieth century, that the imperial imperatives of finance capital were to work themselves out, not only between nations but also, and more importantly, within them, according to Hilferding.

As I have already indicated, Marxist analysis of the structures and processes of the capitalist mode of production always have as their objet the analysis of class struggle as a guide to the possibility of revolution. Hilferding's (and Lenin's) analysis of the conditions for and imperatives within finance capital and imperialism is no exception. (A point which academic debate on Marxist theories of imperialism frequently ignores.) According to Hilferding, finance capital and imperialism had united various classes — industrialists, financiers, agriculturalists, bureaucrats and a threatened petit-bourgeois — in opposition to the proletariat. It had intensified class contradictions within bourgeois society. Further, the concentration of economic power and the establishment of closer relations between those with economic power and the state had brought the power of the state out into the open — unlike in Britain. It had also proletarianized more members of other social classes. These developments, coupled with the intensification of conflict between capitalist and capitalistic nation states, meant that the proletarian revolution was on the agenda. Hilferding wrote:

Finance capital, in its maturity, is the highest stage of the concentration of economic and political power in the hands of the capitalist oligarchy. It is the climax of the dictatorship of the magnates of capital. At the same time it makes the dictatorship of the capitalist lords of one country increasingly incompatible with the capitalist interests of other countries, and the internal domination of capital increasingly irreconcilable with the interests of the mass of the people, exploited by finance capital but also summoned into battle against it. In the violent clash of these hostile interests the dictatorship of the magnates of capital will finally be transformed into the dictatorship of the proletariat.[64]

In linking finance capital and imperialism to conditions for class struggle, Hilferding wrote within the classic tradition of Marxism — class struggle *is* central to the materialist conception of history, and Marxism without class is *Hamlet* without the prince. As I hope to show, Lenin's imperialism was also cast in the same mould, the mould of *class* struggle.

Lenin's *Imperialism*, like Marx's *Eighteenth Brumaire*, was a response to a particular conjuncture of economic and political events providing possibilities for certain kinds of political action. It was written in 1916 to counteract the position of those capitalists and social chauvinist deserters in Russia who, in the event of a favourable outcome to the war, would be likely to support further territorial annexation by Russia. In order to demonstrate the cynicism with which Russian annexation of non-Russian territory was cloaked, and in order to get the pamphlet past the Russian censor, Lenin was obliged to write about Japan, of all places! As he pointed out in a later preface: 'The careful reader will easily substitute Russia for Japan, and Finland, Poland, Courland, the Ukraine, Khiva, Bokhara, Esthonia or other regions peopled by non-Great Russians, for Korea.'[65] It should be clear, therefore, that Lenin's purpose in *Imperialism* was to analyse Russian imperialism, which in many ways, was much the same as the Russian imperialism Marx had written about 60 years earlier although, by 1916, Russia had been brought into the mainstream of European capitalist development by its very economic backwardness, and

---

[64] Rudolf Hilferding, *Finance Capital, A Study of the Latest Phase of Capitalist Development* (London, 1981), p. 370.

[65] V. I. Lenin, *Imperialism,* Preface to the Russian edition.

an injection of finance capitalism. These developments made Lenin's task more difficult, namely to analyse the conditions for unifying the revolutionary aims of Marxist socialists with those of nationalist movements within Imperial Russia's annexed territories.

To do this Lenin followed Hilferding. He argued that imperialism was the monopoly stage of capitalism identified by five main characteristics. As set out by Lenin, these characteristics may be regarded as his summary of Hilferding's *Finance Capital* without Hilferding's analytical steps. They were:

1   The concentration of production and capital developed to such a high stage that it created monopolies which play a decisive role in economic life.

2   The merging of bank capital with industrial capital, and the creation, on the basis of this 'finance capital', of a financial oligarchy.

3   The export of capital, which has become extremely important, as distinguished from the export of commodities.

4   The formation of international capitalist monopolies which share the world among themselves.

5   The territorial division of the whole world among the greatest capitalist powers is completed.

Imperialism is capitalism in that stage of development in which the dominance of monopolies and finance capital has established itself; in which the export of capital has acquired pronounced importance; in which the division of the world among the international trusts has begun; in which the division of all territories of the globe among the great capitalist powers has been completed.[66]

Imperialism so described, with its stages analytically linked as in *Finance Capital*, brought Russia and its annexed European territories into the foreground, so to speak.

Lenin's Russia was an Imperial power (as it was for Marx). In Europe and in Asia it ruled over vast annexed territories — whereas Marx wrote of Russia that it was a conquering nation, Lenin wrote: 'The Great Russians in Russia are an oppressing nation.' But Russia, more economically backward than Germany, was itself a 'dependent' territory. Therefore, as finance capital from France and Germany was the key to the economic development of Russia and its annexed territories, it was both an imperial power (in Marx's sense) and a field for imperialism (in Hilferding's sense). Accordingly, as Lenin argued, this mélange of

[66] Ibid., pp. 108–9.

circumstance greatly enhanced the possibility of revolution in Russia — if only national movements could be linked to the movement for socialism, and if Kautsky, the major theoretician of 'opportunism' could be criticized out of existence. Hence the necessity of imperialism.

Lenin's challenge to Kautsky on the question of 'opportunism' and, therefore, his disagreement with Kautsky on the nature of imperialism and its significance for class consciousness and revolution, in 1916, was consistent with the position he had taken up in 1914 in *The Right of Nations to Self Determination*. In this pamphlet, Lenin had allied himself with Kautsky in opposition to Luxemburg. He referred approvingly to point 9 of the programme of the Russian Marxists, dealing with the right of nations to self-determination, and argued that independent nation states were a surer basis for capitalist economic development than heterogeneous states comprising many subordinate nations as colonies. As regards Russia in particular, he observed that the development of capitalism and the general level of culture were often higher in Russia's annexed territories than at the centre. Consequently, he wrote: 'everyone can see now that the best conditions for the development of capitalism in the Balkans are created precisely in proportion to the creation of independent national states in that peninsula.'[67] He made similar observations about Russia's Asiatic dependencies: 'it is precisely in the neighbouring Asiatic states that we observe incipient bourgeois revolutions and national movements, which partly affect the kindred nationalities within the borders of Russia.'[68] Lenin then drew the conclusion that the proletariats of both Russia and its annexed territories should fight side by side, in a dual fashion; to achieve equal rights as regards statehood (and the possibility of accelerated capitalist development), and to struggle against the nationalism of all nations in any form to preserve the unity of the international proletarian movement.

By 1916, however, it seemed to Lenin that Kautsky's views on imperialism, including his notion of 'ultra-imperialism', could encourage ideas according to which imperial powers need not act in a necessarily coercive and exploitative fashion with regard to their annexed territories. Indeed, Kautsky seemed to argue, capitalist nation states might *choose* not to have overseas territories to exploit in any way. If this were to be the case, not only would there be no intensification of exploitation within capitalist nations, but there would be no intensification of exploitation as between capitalist states and their dependent territories. Accordingly, there would be no necessary immiseration for Russia's proletariat, as the

---

[67] V. I. Lenin, *The Right of Nations to Self-Determination* (Moscow, 1951), p. 15.
[68] Ibid., p. 29.

victims of finance capital, nor for the proletariats in the annexed territories. *According to Kautsky such exploitation was a choice not a necessity.* Therefore, 'opportunist' rather than revolutionary policies would be the order of the day. Lenin's perception of these dangers, implicit where they were not explicit in Kautsky's views, made it necessary for him to use Hilferding, Bukharin and Hobson against Kautsky.

According to Lenin, Kautsky's mistake could be traced to his definition of imperialism 'as a product of highly developed industrial capitalism. It consists in the striving of every industrial capitalist nation to bring under its control or to annex increasingly big *agrarian* regions irrespective of what nations inhabit those regions.'[69] Such a definition, with its emphasis on the 'striving' of 'industrial nations', seemed to Lenin to turn imperialism into a policy option, a mere unexplained desire by industrial nations for agricultural territory. Furthermore, while Kautsky thought that imperialism as a policy option for industrial nations should be fought, with the intention of replacing it with some other option, it was more important to posit alternative options. One such future option envisaged by Kautsky was 'ultra-imperialism'. This was a form of imperialism in which the erstwhile competing imperialistic nation states would voluntarily cease making war on each other. Instead, through the evolution of peaceful democracy, they would engage in 'the joint exploitation of the world by internationally combined finance capital'.[70] The political implications of such an option, according to Lenin, were two-fold. First, the prospect of an embourgeoisement of *all* industrial proletariats similar to the English experience following that country's initial monopoly as the first industrial nation. Second, an ideological shift facilitating such an embourgeoisement, namely, the implementation of 'opportunist' rather than revolutionary policies on the part of working-class organizations. In short, 'ultra-imperialism' was English policy in Ireland and a divided working class (as in Marx), and the nationalism of Great Russians in relation to the peoples of the annexed territories writ large. Hence the importance of Hilferding's *Finance Capital*.

As we have seen, Hilferding's imperialism posited necessary, coercive relationships triggered by the demands of finance capital. Accordingly, wrote Lenin: 'German appetite for Belgium. French appetite for Lorraine'.[71] Furthermore, imperialism, violent as between capitalist nations and coercive towards non-capitalist nations, was the inevitable result of

[69] V. I. Lenin, *Imperialism,* p. 110.
[70] Karl Kautsky, *Die Neue Zeit,* 33, 1, 30 April 1915, p. 144. quoted in *Imperialism,* p. 114.
[71] Ibid., p. 111.

the equally necessary development of finance capital; imperialism was *not* a policy option. Therefore, the class struggle it would generate and the revolution that would follow was a necessity, not a choice; opportunism *was*, therefore, opportunism pure and simple.

In order to make good his case against Kautsky and to keep the proletariat to the sticking point, Lenin was obliged to show that the relentless, competitive penetration of exploitable territory by finance capital would intensify exploitation of the annexed territories. Thus, he had to show that the joint Franco-German, Great Russian exploitation and oppression of the non-Russian peoples of Russia's annexed territories, and of the Russians themselves, would be intensified. (Remember, throughout *Imperialism*, one had to read Finland, Poland, Courland, the Ukraine, Khiva, Bokhara, Esthonia for Korea!) It was at this point that Lenin expressed his preference for Hobson over Hilferding.

In the chapter entitled 'The Parasitism and Decay of Capitalism', Lenin wrote: 'One of the shortcomings of the Marxist Hilferding is that he takes a step backward compared with the non-Marxist Hobson. We refer to parasitism, which is a feature of imperialism.'[72] Thus, Lenin, following Hobson, Schultz-Gaevernitz, Lansburgh and others, argued that monopoly capitalism had an inbuilt tendency to stagnation and decay which, in conjunction with the general characteristics of finance capital and the export of capital, would concentrate money capital into even fewer hands. It would turn the most advanced industrial nations, such as Britain, into rentier states. Lenin wrote: 'The rentier state is a state of parasitic, decaying capitalism.'[73] To give weight to this assertion, for which there was some evidence in Britain's case, Lenin quoted Hobson. Writing in 1902 on the possible effect of a partition of China, Hobson commented:

The greater part of Western Europe might then assume the appearance and character already exhibited by tracts of country in the South of England, in the Riviera, and in the tourist-ridden or residential parts of Italy and Switzerland, little clusters of wealthy aristocrats drawing dividends and pensions from the Far East, with a somewhat larger group of professional retainers and tradesmen and a large body of personal servants and workers in the transport trade and in the final stages of production of the more perishable goods; all the main arterial industries would have disappeared, the staple foods and manufactures flowing in as tribute from Asia and Africa.[74]

Further, Hobson, foreshadowing Kautsky's 'ultra-imperialism', also wrote

[72] Ibid., p. 120.
[73] Ibid., p. 123.
[74] Ibid., p. 125.

of the possibility of a European federation of great powers which might 'introduce the gigantic peril of a Western parasitism'.[75]

According to Brewer, this argument about the parasitism of advanced capitalism was Lenin's great mistake. In following Hobson on the death throes of advanced industrial capitalism, Lenin led Marxists astray for a long time.[76] They were unable to explain capitalism's unexpected capacity not only to survive, but also to advance. One might add that in drawing upon Russian experience and emphasizing the development effects of capitalism in its dependent territories, Lenin also led Marxists astray in other ways — led them, as it were, to prefer Marx on India after the railways to Marx on Ireland.

Yet, Lenin was consistent as between Kautsky and Hobson. Although he embraced Hobson's notion of parasitism and decay, he remained committed to the general thrust of Hilferding's argument, which asserted the inevitability of the intensification of conflict between capitalist nations under finance capital. Therefore, he rejected Hobson's notion of a European federation of great powers living on tribute from Asia and Africa, just as he rejected Kautsky's idea of 'ultra-imperialism'. Rather, he chose to emphasize the point that parasitism, working in circumstances in which the great capitalist powers were already divided from each other by the unevenness of their own economic developments, would intensify conflict between them. The significance of this combination of parasitism and conflict for Russia was plain. It was that 'Opportunism . . . cannot now triumph in the working-class movement of any country for decades as it did in England in the second half of the nineteenth century. But, in a number of countries it has grown ripe, over ripe, and rotten, and has become completely merged with bourgeois policy in the form of "social chauvinism".'[77] According to Lenin, Kautsky was not only wrong, he was a class traitor.

CONCLUSION

Lenin's *Imperialism*, with its borrowings from Hilferding, Bukharin, Hobson and others, was without doubt, eclectic. Nevertheless, its central arguments and conclusions were unequivocal. Imperialism was not a policy option but an economic necessity leading, inevitably, to great power rivalry. Imperialism was parasitic capitalism. By the second decade of the twentieth century it had reached the point of decay as industrial capitalism

---

[75] Ibid., p. 125.
[76] Anthony Brewer, *Marxist Theories*, pp. 115—6.
[77] V. I. Lenin, *Imperialism*, p. 131.

at the centre had been replaced by rentier capitalism. Thereby, great power rivalry was intensified. Consequently, Kautsky's 'ultra-imperialism' was not a policy option. Therefore, political opportunism was not a viable course of action for Marxist socialists. Instead, revolution was at the head of the agenda.

Since Lenin wrote (as when he wrote) these conclusions have been challenged by Marxist and non-Marxist economists, and, seemingly, by events. Indeed, in the light of my account of Marx on capitalism in a world context, one might press this criticism further by asking how well grounded Lenin was in Marx's analysis?

There can be little doubt that Lenin's *Imperialism*, with its analysis of the mode of production as a key to understanding all aspects of societies, with its recognition of capitalism's growth in a world context, and with its emphasis upon the importance of economic analysis for understanding the conditions for class struggle and for laying down courses of political action, was recognizably a work of orthodox Marxism. Nevertheless, it differed from Marx's approach in two important respects. First, Marx's application of his own theoretical system was markedly superior to Lenin's, particularly with regard to their respective grasp of the significance of uneven economic development, of the existing articulation of modes of production, of class structures, and of technology, for the developmental potential of dependent territories, as was shown by Marx's writing on India, Russia and Ireland. Secondly, Hobson's and Lenin's notion of the rentier-like parasitism of finance capitalism and imperialism (and, therefore, the decay of industrial capitalism at the centre) was not in the spirit of Marx's analysis of capitalism. In my view, Hilferding on the dynamic nature of the consequences of uneven economic development within capitalism, and as between nation states, was more true to the spirit of Marx on capitalism in a world context than either Hobson or Lenin. For example, Marx envisaged industrial capitalism destroying itself through its successes in concentrating and accumulating capital, rather than on its failure to develop 'the main arterial industries'. Even so, industrial capitalism would only destroy itself in a relations of production (property relations) sense. Therefore, people under communism would inherit the achievement and technology of capitalism, not the money incomes of an effete rentier class. Indeed, as I showed in *Feudalism, Capitalism and Beyond*, Marx was so taken with the advance of knowledge and technology within the industrial capitalist mode of production, that he thought of labour stepping to the side of the production process, not in a new capacity as rentier, but as social producer and controller of the social product.[78] Lenin's argument

[78] Eugene Kamenka and R. S. Neale (eds), *Feudalism*, p. 25.

about parasitism was, therefore, not only a narrowing of Marxist perspectives but a misleading distortion of them.

On the other hand, Hilferding's analysis of finance capital, the export of capital, and imperialism, albeit carried out within a Marxist perspective on the mode of production and on the crucial importance within it of relations of production, was a substantial advance on Marx. (Only to the extent that Lenin followed Hilferding can *Imperialism* be thought of as an advance on Marx.) Accordingly, Hilferding's (and Lenin's) use of the term 'imperialism' was not Marx's, even though it still carried undertones of arbitrary, absolutist and despotic rule. But, it *was* Marx's imperialism and Hilferding's that did for the Rolands of Europe and of Empire — and gave us *Testament of Youth*.

APPENDIX: MARX ON PROPERTY, FROM THE GRUNDRISSE

The original conditions of production . . . cannot themselves originally *be products* — results of production. It is not the *unity* of living and active humanity with the natural, inorganic conditions of their metabolic exchange with nature, and hence their appropriation of nature, which requires explanation or is the result of a historic process, but rather the *separation* between these inorganic conditions of human existence and this active existence, a separation which is completely posited only in the relation of wage labour and capital. In the relations of slavery and serfdom this separation does not take place; rather, one part of society is treated by the other as itself merely an *inorganic and natural* condition of its own reproduction.

He [the slave or serf] . . . finds himself a member of a family, clan, tribe etc. — which then, in a historic process of intermixture and antithesis with others, takes on a different shape; and, as such a member, he relates to a specific nature (say, here, still earth, land, soil) as his own inorganic being, as a condition of his production and reproduction. As a natural member of the community he participates in the communal property, and has a particular part of it as his possession; just as, were he a natural Roman citizen, he would have an ideal claim (at least) to the *ager publicus* and a real one to a certain number of *iugera* of land etc. His *property*, i.e. the relation to the natural presuppositions of his production as belonging to him, as *his*, is mediated by his being himself the natural member of a community . . .

As regards the individual, it is clear e.g. that he relates even to language itself *as his own* only as the natural member of a human community. Language as the product of an individual is an impossibility. But the same holds for property. . . .

. . . . Communal production and common property as they exist e.g. in Peru are evidently a *secondary* form; introduced by and inherited from conquering tribes, who, at home, had common property and communal production in the older, simpler form such as is found in India and among the Slavs. Likewise the form which we find among the Celts in Wales e.g. appears as a transplanted, *secondary* form, introduced by conquerors among the lesser, conquered tribes. The completion and systematic elaboration of these systems by a *supreme central authority* shows their later origin. Just as the feudalism introduced into England was more perfect in form than that which arose spontaneously in France. . . .

. . . The only barrier which the community can encounter in relating to the natural conditions of production — the earth — as to *its own property* (if we jump ahead to the settled peoples) is *another community,* which already claims it as its own inorganic body. *Warfare* is therefore one of the earliest occupations of each of these naturally arisen communities, both for the defence of their property and for obtaining new property.

Property thus originally means no more than a human being's relation to his natural conditions of production as belonging to him, as his, as *presupposed* along with *his own being*; relations to them as *natural presuppositions* of his self, which only form, so to speak, his extended body. . . .

. . . A natural condition of production for the living individual is his belonging to a *naturally arisen, spontaneous society*, clan etc. This is e.g. already a condition for his language etc. His own productive existence is possible only on this condition. His subjective existence is thereby conditioned as such, just as it is conditioned by his relation to the earth as his workshop. (Property is, it is true, originally *mobile*, for mankind first seizes hold of the ready-made fruits of the earth, among whom belong e.g. the animals, and for him especially the ones that can be tamed. Nevertheless even this situation — hunting, fishing, herding, gathering fruits from trees etc. — always presupposes appropriation of the earth, whether for a fixed residence, or for roaming, or for animal pasture etc.)

Property therefore means *belonging to a clan* (community) (having subjective—objective existence in it); and, by means of the relation of this community to the land and soil, [relating] to the earth as the individual's inorganic body; his relation to land and soil, to the external primary condition of production — since the earth is raw material, instrument and fruit all in one — as to a pre-supposition belonging to his individuality, as modes of his presence. *We reduce this property to the relation to the conditions of production.*

The fundamental condition of property resting on the clan system (into which the community originally resolves itself) — to be a member of the clan — makes the clan conquered by another clan *propertyless* and throws it among the *inorganic conditions* of the conqueror's reproduction, to which the conquering community relates as its own. Slavery and serfdom are thus only further developments of the form of property resting on the clan system. They necessarily modify all of the latter's forms. They can do this least of all in the Asiatic form. In the self-sustaining unity of manufacture and agriculture, on which this form rests, conquest is not so necessary a condition as where *landed property, agriculture* are exclusively predominant. On the other hand, since in this form the individual never becomes a proprietor but only a possessor, he is at bottom himself the property, the slave of him in whom the unity of the commune exists, and slavery here neither suspends the conditions of labour nor modifies the essential relation.

It is now clear, further, that:

Property, in so far as it is only the conscious relation — and posited in regard to the individual by the community, and proclaimed and guaranteed as law — to the conditions of production as *his own*, so that the producer's being appears also in the objective conditions *belonging to him* — is only realized by production itself. The real appropriation takes place not in the mental but in the real, active relation to these conditions — in their real positing as the conditions of his subjective activity.

It is thereby also clear that *these conditions change.* . . . The aim of all these communities is survival; i.e., *reproduction of the individuals who compose it as proprietors, i.e. in the same objective mode of existence as forms the relation among the members and at the same time therefore the commune itself.* This *reproduction, however, is at the same time necessarily new production and destruction of the old form.* For example, where each of the individuals is supposed to possess a given number of acres of land, the advance of population is already under way. If this is to be corrected, then colonization, and that in turn requires wars of conquest. With that, slaves etc. Also, e.g., enlargement of the *ager publicus*, and therewith the patricians who represent the community etc. Thus the preservation of the old community includes the destruction of the conditions on which it rests, turns into its opposite. If it were thought that productivity on the same land could be increased by developing the forces of production etc. (this precisely the slowest of all in traditional agriculture), then the new order would include combinations of labour, a large part of the day spent in agriculture etc., and thereby again suspend the old economic conditions of the community. Not only do the objective conditions change in the act of reproduction, e.g. the village becomes a town, the wilderness a cleared field etc., but the producers change, too, in that they bring out new qualities in themselves, develop themselves in production, transform themselves, develop new powers and ideas, new modes of intercourse, new needs and new language. The older and more traditional the mode of production itself — and this lasts a long time in agriculture; even more in the oriental supplementation of agriculture with manufactures — i.e. the longer the *real process* of appropriation remains constant, the more constant will be the old forms of property and hence the community generally. Where there is already a separation between the commune members as private proprietors (on one side,) and they themselves as the urban commune and proprietors of the commune's *territorium* (on the other), there the conditions already arise in which the individual can *lose* his property, i.e. the double relation which makes him both an equal citizen, a member of the community, and a *proprietor*. In the oriental form this *loss* is hardly possible, except by means of altogether external influences, since the individual member of the commune never enters into the relation of freedom towards it in which he could lose his (objective, economic) bond with it. He is rooted to the spot, ingrown. . . .

. . . The original unity between a particular form of community (clan) and the corresponding property in nature, or relation to the objective conditions of production as a natural being, as an objective being of the individual mediated by the commune — this unity, which appears in one respect as the particular form of property — has its living reality in a specific *mode of production* itself, a mode which appears both as a relation between the individuals, and as their specific active relation to inorganic nature, a specific mode of working (which is always family labour, often communal labour). The community itself appears as the first great force of production; particular kinds of production conditions (e.g. stock-breeding, agriculture), develop particular modes of production and particular forces of production, subjective, appearing as qualities of individuals, as well as objective [ones].

In the last analysis, their community, as well as the property based on it, resolves itself into a specific stage in the development of the productive forces of working subjects — to which correspond their specific relations amongst one another and towards nature. Until a certain point, reproduction. Then turns into dissolution.

Property, then, originally means — in its Asiatic, Slavonic, ancient classical, Germanic form — the relation of the working (producing or self-reproducing) subject to the conditions of his production or reproduction as his own. It will therefore have different forms depending on the conditions of this production. Production itself aims at the reproduction of the producer within and together with these, his objective conditions of existence. . . .

All forms (more or less naturally arisen, spontaneous, all at the same time however results of a historic process) in which the community presupposes its subjects in a specific objective unity with their conditions of production, or in which a specific subjective mode of being presupposes the communities themselves as conditions of production, necessarily correspond to a development of the forces of production which is only limited, and indeed limited in principle. The development of the forces of production dissolves these forms, and their dissolution is itself a development of the human productive forces.

Empire Day, Hillgrove, NSW, 1908. The banner reads: 'Why are the Flags of Britain like the Stars of Heaven? Because No Power on Earth can Pull them Down.' (Historical Resources Centre, Armidale College of Advanced Education)

9
Life and Death in Hillgrove
1870—1914

Chapter 8 sketched Marx's view of imperialism on a grand and mainly theoretical scale. Chapter 9 brings us back to earth, although not in Camden Town (not even in Bath). It brings us back to earth in Australia, to offer such a prospect and diversion as would touch the imagination of Laurence Sterne. But it is a part of our journey, pointing as it does to the way in which the industrial capitalist mode of production creates itself anew, insisting that 'free' wage labourers follow in its wake, and suggesting how they struggle to make themselves in circumstances not chosen by themselves, with only the tradition of dead generations and their symbolic forms to help them. This local study of the minutiae of a few thousand Australian and British lives (their births, marriages and deaths), in what is now one of Australia's many 'deserted villages', also pulls the writing of a Marxist history of British society, economy and culture out of its local context. It rubs against the grain. But so did the lives of millions of Britishers; Scots, Irish, Welsh and English, as they thought they would find new worlds and better things outside Britain itself, taking their culture with them. In Hillgrove things did not turn out as many might have expected, and that is for the chapter to show. Then there are the thousands (like my grandmother's grandparents) who tried other worlds and didn't like them, and the millions (like my father) who thought about it once.

The geographical location of the community at Hillgrove was determined by a peculiarly disturbed geological formation, about two miles long and three-quarters of a mile wide, running North West to South East across the Baker's Creek gorge, located on the Great Dividing Range in Northern New South Wales. This line of granite upheaval contained rich supplies of stibnite, the ore of antimony. However, the nature and timing of the development of that community was determined by the demands of the industrial capitalist mode of production in its late nineteenth-century imperialist phase.

By 1867, when antimony was first noticed in the Baker's Creek gorge, it had many very important chemical and metallurgical uses. Its main chemical use was as a white paint base for enamelling and painting metalware and for paint used on ships. It was also used in vulcanizing rubber and in the manufacture of ammunition requiring the production of smoke, such as range-finding shells and tracer bullets. Its main metallurgical uses were as follows: as an alloy in type-metal, as an alloy in hardening lead used in the manufacture of bearings, cable-sheathings, pipes and traps, Britannia metal and pewter, and in the manufacture of shrapnel. In the 1880s the modern shrapnel shell was introduced into all modern armies. By 1914 the artillery units of the Great Powers were mainly equipped with them — an English eighteen-pounder used one pound of antimony. Then, between 1880 and 1905, Britain launched 63 pre-Dreadnought battleships. By 1912, 22 of those built before 1894 had been scrapped, 11 Dreadnoughts built and 11 were building. Between 1891 and 1912, Germany also built 30 battleships and was building ten more. The tons of shells, the miles of cables, the acres of paint, and the weight of bearings in this military build up is beyond my ability to compute. Yet it was this naval and military demand, as well as the increasing demand arising from the expansion of the world's merchant marines, that determined the sequence and pattern of economic and social development in Hillgrove, and, with the demand for gold, put that development out of phase with economic activity elsewhere in New South Wales. From 1880 to 1896 Hillgrove was a boom town, the creation of the industrial capitalist mode of production in Britain, as new technology and world imperialist competition increased world output of antimony eight-fold between 1886 and 1899.

Hillgrove's history captures a moment of time in which the mature capitalism of late nineteenth-century Britain and Europe swept into regions of recent British and European settlement, telescoping into a mere 30 years the passage from economic barbarism to the most advanced form of technologically based society.

*   *   *

Hillgrove is in northern New South Wales. It became a mining town in the last quarter of the nineteenth century. The records of births, marriages and deaths, now lodged in the Armidale Courthouse,[1] provide the basis for the present chapter. Althought the chapter is basically narrative in form, its structure is shaped by a theoretical perception about the capital/labour relationship in a peripheral region of a world capitalist economy.

---

[1] Records of Hillgrove Registration District hereafter referred to as RHRD and of Armidale Registration District hereafter referred to as RARD.

Hillgrove's rapid growth into a distinctively industrial and urban township was a response to a world demand for antimony and gold.[2] By 1890 Hillgrove was an urban-industrial island in a pre-industrial landscape. On three sides it was bounded by wild and spectacular gorges, inaccessible except if one climbed their thickly wooded and almost vertical slopes, a climb of some 1,800 feet. Only from the north was it possible to approach Hillgrove by road. And that ran for 22 miles through the characteristic pastoral but still wooded landscape of New England to Armidale, the only other place of any size within 80 or 90 miles. As recently as the 1920s it was a day's journey to Armidale for a wagon pulled by a team of 13 horses. The place was so isolated and insignificant that for many years it was known as Eleanora Township, after the antimony mine that for nearly a decade after 1876 was the sole reason for its existence. That you might think is little to be wondered at, for why else would anyone but a profit-hungry Victorian go there? Nor is it to be wondered at that its western suburb, perched on the other side of the gorge, was also first known as the Village of Sunlight, after the mine on that side, then West Hillgrove and, finally, Metz. Surely the place was a fortress. The battle it loomed over was one with nature.

In this struggle to wrest from nature the good things that people thought they needed in order to enjoy the fruits of their labour, people depended upon great advances in technology and massive infusions of capital. In technology there was steam power, about 500 hp in stationary and portable engines; hydro-electricity, the first of its kind in Australia; pelton wheels, steam-operated tramways, great stamping engines, advanced smelting plant, compressed air engines for drilling and winding and more besides. And capital. Moving nervously in search of ways of augmenting itself and making rich the possessors of other people's labour, capital seemed possessed of a life of its own. Yet the fact was, with the help of banks and Hillgrove stock exchange, it was carried to Hillgrove to buy this technology by local people, but above all by men and women from Sydney, South Australia and England.

The importance of capital and technology was more apparent than real. The mines, the stampers, the smelters, the engines, the tramways, all depended for their very existence and survival on the labour of men.

---

[2] We have sketched the outline of the economic history of the town in 'Hillgrove and its Associated Mines 1870—1920', a paper delivered to the Australian Historical Association conference on Regional History, Wagga Wagga, Feb. 1977. The present article is the group's second report on the Hillgrove project and the first part of a social history of the labouring population in the township. Research was made possible by an ARGC grant A75/15494 during the years 1976—9.

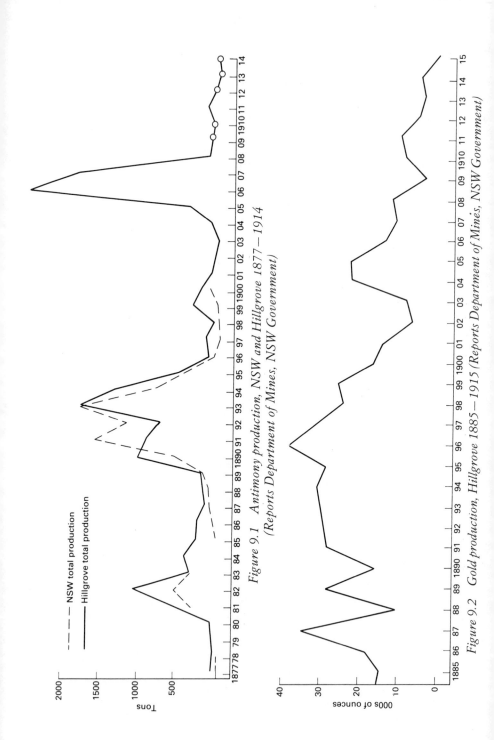

Figure 9.1 Antimony production, NSW and Hillgrove 1877–1914
(Reports Department of Mines, NSW Government)

Figure 9.2 Gold production, Hillgrove 1885–1915 (Reports Department of Mines, NSW Government)

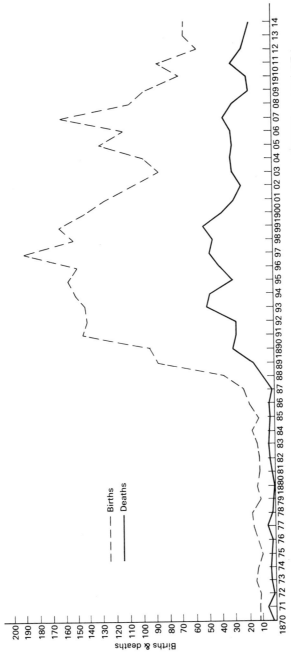

Figure 9.3   Annual births and deaths, Hillgrove Registration District, 1870 – 1914 (RHRD and RARD)

Through the institution of the family, which satisfied needs and kept the worker at work, they depended on the labour of women. It was labour that built Hillgrove, labour that sunk its mines and drove its adits straight as a die into the granite slopes of the gorges, labour that cossetted recalcitrant engines and put them in their proper places, labour that sought ways of solving technical problems, labour that developed new technology and labour that created capital and made its possessors rich. Labour is the theme of this article.

In 1870, before the transforming effect of labour, the place was scarcely more than Hillgrove pastoral station. Its population was so small that only 11 children were recorded as born in the district in 1870, five boys and six girls, and the only recorded death was of one of these babies, less than three months old. And so it went on. The even tenor of life from 1870 to 1876 was marked by an average of 11 births and two deaths each year. The only marriages in these years — a Wollomombi stockman to a Hillgrove house servant in 1870, a Hillgrove shepherd and a Hillgrove farmer to local women in 1871 and 1873, a Rockvale bushman to a Hillgrove house servant in 1874, and a Wollomombi labourer to a Hillgrove shepherd's daughter in 1876 — also testify to the pastoral life at Hillgrove. The first reference to a miner in our records was to a father in 1874.[3] Nevertheless, it was not until 1877 that antimony mining began in earnest. Then, as output from the Eleanora grew, there was a rise in births from 12 in 1876 to 17 in 1878. But it was a false start, both in the production of ore and of people. It was not until 1882/3, when the production of gold was added to the production of antimony, that there was a sustained rise in the number of births resulting from a continuous inflow of labour. Thereafter, stimulated by the gathering of war clouds in Europe and Asia, and by an incessant search after gold to prevent capitalism from destroying itself through its inherent contradictions, Hillgrove was born to become a community idyllic in the memory of people who were children there when they and the world they knew were innocent still.

In the census years of 1891 and 1901, the population of Hillgrove was recorded as 2,387 and 2,274 respectively.[4] However, calculations based on applying the crude birth rate in 1891 to the year of highest births (191 in 1897) suggest a total population in the region of 3,130. A similar calculation, applying the crude birth rate in 1901 to the years of next highest births (163 in 1899 and 160 in 1907), suggests total populations in these years in the region of 2,900 and 2,800 respectively. When all allowance is made for omissions in census taking, variations in birth rates

[3] RARD.
[4] *Census NSW,* 1891 and 1901.

and errors in calculations, we may well agree with contemporary opinion that the population of Hillgrove was close to 3,000 by 1890 and probably rising to well over that figure by 1897 and 1907. The social class composition of its population is suggested by the distribution of 1,255 fathers according to occupation as shown in table 9.1. By 1911 the population of Hillgrove had fallen to 1,581. By 1921 it was a mere 530.

Table 9.1   Distribution of 1,255 fathers in Hillgrove according to social class, 1870—1914[a] (percentages)

Class I	Graziers, capitalists, professionals, large shop owners, mine owners, manufacturers	12.3
Class II	Semi-professionals, small owners, clerks	13.0
Class III	Skilled workers, shop assistants	13.0
Class IV	Semi-skilled workers, including miners	49.5
Class V	Unskilled	11.9

[a]   A list of the occupations of these fathers is available on request from the authors.

Source: RHRD and RARD Note: This social class classification is based on the Registrar General's (UK) 1950 volume, *The Social Classification of Occupations,* and W. A. Armstrong's comment upon it in Appendix D of DEC. Eversley, Peter Laslett and F. A. Wrigley, *An Introduction to English Historical Demography* (London, 1966).

The growth and decline of Hillgrove as exemplified by annual totals of births and deaths is shown in figure 9.3.

Who were these people who came to Hillgrove and whose labour made it, for a time, the world's biggest single producer of antimony and the second most thriving mining community in NSW after Broken Hill? Where did they come from? What was their experience of life and of death? Fortunately, with the generous consent of the Registrar General of NSW it is possible for us to answer some of these questions for a single township like Hillgrove without depending upon the accidental survival of personal reminiscences, diaries or anecdotes. While our answers to aspects of these questions are not exhaustive, we do believe that the comprehensiveness of our sample gives an authenticity to our account not provided by any other source.

The birth records for the Hillgrove Registration District for the period 1888 to 1914 and for the Armidale District between 1870 and 1890 record 3,385 births at Hillgrove and provide information on 1,373 married couples and the mothers of 152 illegitimate children. The death records provide information on 931 Hillgrove people who died in the period

1870—1918. No doubt the usefulness of our sample of parents may be challenged as unrepresentative of a mining community more likely to be characterized by a majority of young, itinerant and largely unmarried males. Yet the sample can be defended by reference to the census of 1901. In this year, within a total population of 2,274, there were only slightly more males than females, 1,144 to 1,128. Of the 904 adults over twenty-one years of age only 206, roughly one in five were never married. The census shows that married adult males out-numbered never-married males by more than two to one, while married adult females out-numbered never-married females by a factor of seven to one.

Nevertheless, our sample does exclude young adults in the sixteen to twenty-one age group. In 1901 this age group was 9 per cent of the population and comprised 120 females and 91 males. In the group nine women and none of the men were married. Yet the census does lend support to our view that the adult population of Hillgrove was mostly married; in 1901 there were 312 married men and 370 married women. The discrepancy between the number of married men and women is probably accounted for by the absence of husbands looking for work or working elsewhere as local employment began to decline. The fact that Hillgrove had an exceptionally married population, rather like that of the Newcastle Coal Mining District (NCD) and different from country or metropolitan NSW, is shown in table 9.2.

Table 9.2   Proportion never married of the population aged forty-five to fifty-nine in 1901 (percentages)

NCD		Hillgrove		England and Wales		Sydney		Country	
M	F	M	F	M	F	M	F	M	F
8.8.	0.3	15.7	2.6	11.4	14.2	18.2	10.8	26.2	6.9

Sources: P. McDonald, *Marriage in Australia,* (1974), pp. 68, 96; Ellen McEwen, *In Australia 1888,* Bulletin, No. 4, p. 69; *Census,* NSW, 1901

Our question about the place of origin of the parents in our survey is answered in general terms in table 9.3.

With two out of three fathers and four out of five mothers Australian-born, Hillgrove was very much an Australian township, although to a lesser degree than the NSW population of parents in 1907, which shows 90 per cent of mothers and 82 per cent of fathers Australian-born.[5] A

[5] *NSW Vital Statistics,* 1907, p. 32, table 36.

Table 9.3   Birth place of parents of legitimate children born in Hillgrove 1870—1914 [a]

Birthplace	Fathers		Mothers	
	No.	%	No.	%
Australia	888	64.7	1140	83.0
UK	309	22.5	179	13.3
New Zealand	13	0.9	16	1.2
Other British colony	6	0.4	2	0.1
Europe	31	2.3	6	0.4
USA	5	0.4	—	—
China	2	0.1	—	—
At sea	3	0.1	4	0.3
No record	116	8.5	26	1.9
Total	1373		1373	

[a] Parents listed once only
Source: RHRD and RARD

further breakdown of the figures suggests also that the lower the occupational status the higher was the proportion of Australian-born. Thus, 71.5 per cent of miners, 75.4 per cent of labourers and 87.3 per cent of labourers' wives were Australian-born. Within the category Australian-born, the NSW contingent was by far the greatest: one half of fathers and two-thirds of mothers were born in NSW. The figures also show — and one might expect that they would — that many more men than women migrated over long distances. While only 25 per cent of Hillgrove fathers came from the New England district, 42 per cent of wives came from the local region. Of labourers and their wives, 39 per cent of husbands and 51 per cent of wives were local born. For miners and their wives the figures were 25 per cent and 39 per cent respectively.

Yet this evidence of the importance of local people, especially local women, for the populating of Hillgrove should not lead one to overlook the part played by immigrant labour. Immigrants were a significant minority of the population especially important as a source of semi-skilled and skilled labour in the earliest years of Hillgrove's development. Although the first of our sample of married miners identified in 1874 was born in NSW, as was his wife, the second miner, in 1880, was born in Wicklow in Ireland and his wife in Buckinghamshire. From that date until 1894, 37 per cent of miners who became fathers in Hillgrove were British-born: 59 in England, 14 in Ireland, 12 in Scotland and 1 in Wales

— in all 86. On the other hand, one-third of miners' wives before 1894 were local women from Armidale and the New England district. But once the town was fairly established, after 1895, the British-born were a very small minority, 15 per cent of miners and less than 10 per cent of wives. These proportions are very similar to the proportion of British-born fathers and mothers in NSW in 1907. Conversely, in the post-1895 period, the proportion of miners and their wives who were born in Hillgrove, Armidale, or the New England district was 35 per cent and 43 per cent respectively (118:338 and 145:338). The fact is, throughout the whole period 1870—1914, there were more local-born miners and miners' wives than there were British-born: out of a total of 568 miners, 140 were British-born and 144 local-born; of their wives only 79 were British-born but 221 were local-born, 70 of them being born either in Armidale or Hillgrove. It would seem that there was an abundance of local marriageable women and that immigrant working men, like soldiers in a foreign army, were able to find wives on their visits to neighbouring towns. Indeed, they seemed to find wives easily and at an early age, earlier than for NSW generally.

As Coghlan points out in *Wealth and Progress,*[6] information about age at marriage was not required in NSW until 1897. The earliest figures he records are for 1897—1900. They show the average age at marriage in NSW 1897—99 to have been 29.4 for men and 24.96 for women. These were quite high ages and reflected a response by the people of NSW to the economic malaise pervading the colony. But in Hillgrove, where the local clerk of the court began recording ages at marriage as early as 1889, the age at marriage of both men and women was substantially lower. In the whole period 1889 to 1918 it was 27.22 for men and 22.44 for women. Miners and their wives married slightly younger still: 26.17 for miners and 21.86 for their wives. In an attempt to be as accurate as possible we also scoured the Armidale registers for marriages of Hillgrove people. The combined figures from the Hillgrove and Armidale district registers for the years 1896—9 of ages at first marriage give the following results: men 26.63, women 21.64.

Although young workingmen as immigrants to Hillgrove were able to find young wives early in life, and thereby captured all the comforts provided by a Hillgrove miner's hut, fortune eluded them. One reason for this must be that after marriage children were born in quick succession and families were large. We have already noted that our sample of 1,373 married couples produced 3,385 children, an average of 2.46 births per

---

[6] T. A. Coghlan, *The Wealth and Progress of NSW,* Vol. 1895—6, p. 518.

couple during the period they lived in Hillgrove. Yet, because of the geographical mobility of many workingmen and the insecurity of their local employment, this average figure reveals little of the fertility of married women in Hillgrove. Fortunately it is possible, by using the birth records in the census years, to show that the crude birth rate in 1891, 1901 and 1911 was 55, 54 and 55.7:1,000 persons living respectively. It is also possible to relate the average number of births in the years 1900—02 to the census figures for 1901 to calculate a fertility rate of 225:1,000 women 16—44 years of age. (The highest number of births was 191 in 1897 which, when related to the census figures, gives a fertility rate of 396:1,000 women 16—44.) These figures, a crude birth rate of 55:1,000 and a fertility rate of 225:1,000 women 16—44 are extremely high rates of reproduction, higher than for NSW and Sydney in the period 1876—1900, and higher even than for the Newcastle coal mining district recently reported on by Ellen McEwen.[7] These high rates are the result of the high proportion of married couples in Hillgrove, the early age at marriage of new couples and high fertility within marriage. They also reflect a very high level of pre-marital sexual activity. For example, the Hillgrove birth registers 1890—9 record 291 first births to parents married in the Armidale and Hillgrove registration districts or to single women; 68 of these births were illegitimate and 79 took place within seven months of marriage. In the decade 1900—09 the figures were 222 first births, 62 illegitimate and 65 within seven months of marriage. We conclude, therefore, that 51 per cent and 57 per cent of first births in these two periods were the result of pre-marital sexual activity. A comparison of fertility in Hillgrove with fertility in selected places is shown in table 9.4.

Even these figures do not convey the full picture of fertility in Hillgrove, and the finer points can only be demonstrated for the census year 1901 when compared with similar rates for other regions. The appropriate figures are set out in table 9.5. It might be objected to the summary figures contained in it that without an analysis of female age structure the table is not very informative. We meet this argument here by a comparison of Hillgrove with NSW. Briefly the facts for Hillgrove, NSW and NSW Country Municipalities are as follows: 43 per cent of women in Hillgrove were in the age group 16—44 compared with 46 per cent in both NSW and NSW Country Municipalities; 61 per cent of women in the age group 16—44 in Hillgrove were married compared with 50 per cent in NSW. Moreover, only 14 per cent of females in Hillgrove were in the age group

---

Table 9.4   Fertility in Hillgrove compared with selected regions

	Live births per 1,000 population		Live births per 1,000 women (3 year average)
	1891	1901	1901
Hillgrove	55	54	255 (women 16—44)
Newcastle coal mining district	49	34 (1900)	—
Country NSW	34	29	—
Sydney	36	25	—
		1891—1900	
England and Wales	—	30	115 (women 15—44)

Source: As for table 9.2 and RHRD and RARD

21—9 compared with 17 per cent for NSW and NSW country municipalities generally. However in all age groups 21—44 the proportion married in Hillgrove was considerably higher than for NSW Country Municipalities. In the 21—9 age group the proportions were: NSW Country Municipalities, 47 per cent; Hillgrove, 71 per cent.

The rates shown in table 9.5 for legitimate live births per 1,000 married women 16—44 and for illegitimate live births per 1,000 unmarried women 16—44 of 402 and 37 respectively are extremely high. Occurring over a three-year period 1899 to 1901 they suggest that in any one year almost half of married women were pregnant while the other half nursed a baby less than twelve months old.

Unfortunately, the ultimate family size resulting from such a high rate of fertility per 1,000 married women cannot be shown for marriages contracted in Hillgrove. The average of 2.46 births per married couple already referred to is clearly no guide. Neither is the ratio of the number of children under sixteen to the number of married women. A better guide might be the ratio of the number of children under sixteen to the number of married women 16—44 which is 1:3.78 for 1901. Yet another calculation based on the records of family size of women dying in Hillgrove shows the following: the average completed family size of women who married before 1880 and died in Hillgrove (68 women) was 6.76 (the comparable figure for England was less than six);[8] for those who married

---

[8] *The Registrar General's Statistical Review of England and Wales,* 1958, Part III, p. 36.

Table 9.5   Live births per 1,000 women aged 16—44 by legitimacy

	All live births per 1,000 women 16—44	Legitimate live births per 1,000 married women 16—44	Illegitimate live births per 1,000 unmarried women 16—44
		3-year averages (1899—1901)	
Hillgrove (16—44) 1901	255	402	37
NSW (16—44) 1901	—	234	—
England and Wales (15—44) 1901	115	235	9
Ireland 1901 (15—44)	—	289	—
Colyton, Devon (15—44) 1560—1629	354	—	—
Mysore (India) (15—44)	188	—	—

Source: Registrar General's Statistical Review of England and Wales 1958 Part III,
p. 28; E. A. Wrigley, *Population and History,* p. 91; *NSW Vital Statistics,* 1906, p. iii and
RHRD and RARD

after 1880 and died in Hillgrove (51 women) it was 4.0. The contrast
between these two figures of family size suggests, and it can do no more
than suggest, that a younger generation of married couples in Hillgrove,
as elsewhere in NSW, were aware of the domestic economic consequences
of high fertility and did make some effort to limit the burden of large
families. Nevertheless, the high fertility rate per 1,000 married women at
the turn of the century is evidence that they were not particularly
successful.

Another manifestation of high fertility among Hillgrove women was
the average size of the household as shown in the census for 1891. In
Hillgrove it was 4.17, in West Hillgrove 3.54. The size of the Hillgrove
household is remarkably similar to that found in England during the last
400 years. However, this average conceals the presence of 148 single
male households out of a total of 504 households, and the presence of
many large households with more than eight persons and several very
large households — there were two with 31 members, which could only
have been hotels or lodging houses. The distribution of households is
shown in table 9.6.

Table 9.6 shows that about two-thirds of households had less than four
persons. But only one-third of the population lived in these small

Table 9.6   Size of household in Hillgrove, including West Hillgrove, 1891

Size of household	Number	Per cent of households
1	153	26
2	93	16
3	73	13
4	50	9
5	67	11
6	48	8
7	29	5
8	23	4
9	16	3
10	10	2
11	5	0.9
12 and over	17	2.9

Source: Census Records, 1891.

households. Most people in Hillgrove lived in larger households containing between five and ten persons. No doubt these high fertility rates and consequent large family size were the reasons why attendance at the three public schools in the Hillgrove district rose sharply, from 17 in 1885 to 464 in 1900, 336 in Hillgrove alone.

A more dramatic consequence of the growth of population and its greater density coupled with high fertility and large married households was a sharp rise in infant mortality. In this section of the paper we will argue that these circumstances, themselves the consequence of a mode of production requiring high labour mobility, in conjunction with an institutional failure, also embedded in the structure of the mode of production, meant that the gains and losses of the labouring population were not merely to be measured in terms of levels of wages and employment. The true cost is to be seen in levels of infant mortality which not only reflect the influence of immediate environmental factors but also longer term factors influencing the physical well being of mothers. They are very sensitive indicators of social welfare. Judged by these standards the human costs of the development of antimony and gold at Hillgrove were borne not only by wage labourers wandering rootless over the face of the earth, but by infants conceived, born and dying in avoidable squalor.

The general trend of infant mortality in Hillgrove when compared with infant mortality elsewhere in NSW is shown in table 9.7.

If we recall that Hillgrove grew from a sheep station in the 1870s to a

Table 9.7   Infant mortality: deaths under 1 per 1,000 live births [a]

	Colony	City	Suburbs	Country	Hillgrove[a]
1871—75	103	175	138	83	36
1876—80	115	179	160	93	45
1881—85	124	185	167	99	47
1886—90	115	172	148	93	99
1891—95	111	160	131	97	102
1896—1900	114	136	128	105	148
1901—05	97	119	105	92	79
1906—10	77	109	80	73	48

[a] The sample size for Hillgrove 1871—75, 1876—80, 1881—85 was small and we place little weight on the figures recorded for these years.
Source: *NSW Statistical Register,* 1888, 1900, 1910; RHRD and RARD

township with rather more than 3,000 people by 1900, then the figures in table 9.7 show that as the town grew infant mortality also rose. This rise was contrary to the downward drift from the 1880s elsewhere in NSW, including Sydney. Consequently in the five-year period 1896—1900 the Hillgrove rate, 148:1,000 (112 deaths: 795 births) was substantially higher than for the colony and for Sydney. Annual rates 1890—1910 are shown in table 9.8.

Infant mortality rates of the order of 140—160:1,000 are high. In the nineteenth-century context they are very high; they are comparable to the rate for England in 1900 (150:1,000) and the worst for that country in the nineteenth century, although well below Sydney's maximum of 210:1,000 in 1880. Indeed, in terms of birth and infant mortality rates throughout the 1890s, Hillgrove was closer to a pattern of relationships more characteristic of underdeveloped countries in the 1970s than the developed countries at the turn of the century. See Table 9.9.

In order to explore the question whether, in spite of the employment prospects that attracted people to Hillgrove in the first place, these figures of infant mortality may be said to indicate a deterioration in well being, it will be necessary to look in detail at the causes of death among infants. At the outset we emphasize that this is not an easy task. First, the evidence we collected was originally classified under nineteenth century classifications, but we now find that medical classification is not a helpful way to organize the evidence.

For example, late nineteenth-century medical statistics still used a classification 'miasmatic' for a group of infectious diseases including typhoid but excluding other diseases such as TB. It also excluded from another category 'diarrhoeal' such water- and food-borne diseases as typhoid and tuberculous meningitis. Secondly, the question of diagnosis, always a difficult one, was then more problematic. Hence we find, in the nineteenth century, convulsions classified under diseases of the nervous system and dentition (teething) under diseases of the digestive system, whereas medical historians regard the true cause of death under these headings as air-borne infections. Because of these problems we have chosen to follow Thomas McKeown, and to reorganize the evidence under four broad categories:[9] air-borne diseases, water- and food-borne diseases, other diseases due to micro-organisms, and conditions not attributable to micro-organisms. Air-borne diseases include tuberculosis (respiratory), bronchitis, pneumonia, influenza, whooping cough, measles, scarlet fever, diphtheria, smallpox and infections of the ear, pharynx and larynx. Water- and food-borne diseases include cholera, diarrhoea, dysentry, tuberculosis (non-respiratory), typhoid. Other diseases due to micro-organisms include convulsions, dentitions, syphilis, appendicitis, puerperal fever.

Conditions not attributable to micro-organisms include prematurity, congenital defects, cerebro- and cardio-vascular diseases, cancer, diseases of the digestive system, old age and violence. In Hillgrove, death from violence was the biggest single cause of death among those one year and over, 91 out of 610. This figure includes 8 suicides, 2 homicides, 12 drownings, 23 fractures and 13 deaths in mine accidents, 11 of which were concentrated in the 1890s at an average rate of one death each year. There were also 24 deaths in childbirth. This is equivalent to a rate of 7.09:1,000 live births. The NSW average for the period 1875—1907 was 5.69 and 7.3 for the decade 1895—1904.

The average age at death of those who died over one year of age was 39.50 for men and 34.23 for women. However, more than a third of all deaths were of children under one year.

As is shown in table 9.8 the contrast in the incidence of infant mortality was greatest between the periods immediately before and after 1900. The discussion, therefore, will focus upon the periods 1890—9 and 1900—09.

In the first ten-year period there were 1,496 births and 183 deaths amongst children under one year of age, a rate of 122:1,000 (cf. 1896—1900 = 148:1,000). In the second ten-year period there were 1,163 births and 86 deaths under one, a rate of 74:1,000. The number of deaths in each of the four categories listed is shown in table 9.10.

It may be seen in table 9.10 that the chief causes of infant mortality 1890—9 were in two broad groups: those attributable to micro-organisms,

---

[9] Thomas McKeown, *The Modern Rise of Population,* (London, 1976).

Table 9.8   *Infant mortality: deaths under 1 per 1,000 live births*

	NSW	Hillgrove	Sydney
1890	105	154	155
91	119	41	188
92	106	70	154
93	115	161	170
94	109	139	154
95	106	96	133
96	121	107	147
97	102	147	132
98	122	166	162
99	119	141	129
1900	102	142	111
01	104	63	134
02	110	57	117
03	110	105	145
04	82	92	110
05	81	85	89
06	75	36	97
07	89	50	97
08	76	37	88
09	74	73	125
1910	75	44	136

Source: as for table 9.7

mainly air-, water- and food-borne, and those not so attributable, although one may suspect that diagnoses in the latter category were really 'don't know'. The table also shows a halving in the number of deaths attributable to micro-organisms over the two periods 1890—9 and 1900—09. In the category of air-borne disease the principal decline was in bronchitis and

Table 9.9   *Birth rates and infant mortality rates*

	Birth rate (per 1,000 population)	Infant mortality rate (per 1,000 live births)
Egypt 1970	35	116
Haiti 1970	37	146
Hillgrove 1896—1900	54 (1901)	148

Source: Thomas McKeown, *The Modern Rise of Population*, p. 42; RHRD, RARD and NSW Census, 1901.

Table 9.10   Infant mortality in Hillgrove

| | 1890—9 | | 1900—9 | |
	No.	Rate/1,000 live births	No.	Rate/1,000 live births
Air-borne disease	32	21: 1,000	11	9: 1,000
Water-and food-borne disease	32	21: 1,000	10	9: 1,000
Other diseases due to micro-organisms	25	17: 1,000	8	7: 1,000
Conditions not attributable to micro-organisms	94	63: 1,000	59	47: 1,000
	183	122: 1,000	86	74: 1,000

Source: RHRD and RARD

pneumonia, from 27 to 7. In the water- and food-borne category the principal decline was in the diarrhoea, dysentery and cholera group, from 25 to 8. In the third category, other diseases attributable to micro-organisms, the principal declines were in meningitis, 6 to 0, and dentition and convulsions, 17 to 5. In the fourth category, deaths not attributable to micro-organisms, the principal declines were in premature birth, 33 to 14, atrophy, debility and inanition, 21 to 5. There was an increase in deaths attributable to starvation from 5 to 10.

These changes in the incidence of death cause for infants clearly admit no simple explanation of the rising rate of infant mortality in the 1890s nor of the quite dramatic fall in the first decade of the twentieth century. Since the main areas of decline were in the categories of air-, water- and food-borne disease and in other diseases due to micro-organisms, a number of possible explanations arise. First is one to which we have already alluded, namely, that as more people with a low marriage age and high fertility migrated to Hillgrove, the size and density of the infant population at risk grew. The corollary is that as the infant population and fertility declined after 1900, and as Hillgrove began to lose population, the risk of infection also declined. To this explanation for the category of water- and food-borne disease must be added the possibility of a deterioration in water supply, sanitation and community cleanliness, a deterioration overcome some time after 1900. The weight of this possibility may be judged by the decline in deaths from infantile diarrhoea, dysentery and cholera from 25 to 8, and by a decline in deaths from typhoid from 16 to 7 between the period 1890—9 and 1900—9. On the other hand, we cannot overlook the possibility of changes in relations between infective agents and their hosts.

The sort of changed relationship we have in mind would be similar to those noted by medical historians as occurring in England and the USA during the nineteenth century, which antedated any significant medical contribution.[10] Thus, in England and Wales, deaths from bronchitis, pneumonia and influenza peaked in 1901 and fell rapidly thereafter, well before the introduction of sulphapyridine in 1938. Deaths from scarlet fever and whooping cough plummeted from the 1870s, some 70 or 80 years before the introduction of sulphanamides and immunization. Deaths from measles began to decline in the 1890s, 80 years before immunization. Only in the case of diphtheria is there a possibility that the decline in mortality was connected with the introduction of antitoxin in 1898. However, in Hillgrove, this group of diseases, with the exception of bronchitis and pneumonia, had negligible influence on mortality. In the whole period 1870—1918, deaths were as follows: influenza, 13; diphtheria, 12; whooping cough, 9; measles, 5; scarlet fever, 5. Among infants 1890—1909 there were only three deaths from whooping cough and one from scarlet fever. The one exception, bronchitis and pneumonia, deaths from which among infants declined from 27 to 7 from the 1890s to the 1900s and, thereby, matched the decline in England and Wales from the turn of the century, suggests that some changed relationship between infective agent and host may have been influential. However, these diseases continued to take the same relative toll among all other age groups in Hillgrove: 28 out of 228 deaths in the 1890s and 27 out of 211 deaths in the 1900s. This suggests that whatever factors were at work, they were selective. Perhaps what was at work among infants in the 1900s was lower maternal fertility, smaller family size, less overcrowding, and a better level of general health associated with relief from the debilitating effects of the diarrhoeal and dysenteric diseases, which were at their worst in the hot summer months. (Bronchitis and pneumonia were winter diseases.) If this is the case, then the incidence of mortality and hence morbidity in the category of food- and water-borne disease is doubly important.

Food- and water-borne disease accounted for 32 out of 183 infant deaths in the 1890s. There were also 20 deaths from typhoid at all ages over one between 1893 and 1903. In the first decade of the twentieth century, infant mortality in this category fell by more than half. In the ten years after 1903 there were only five deaths from typhoid. As elsewhere

[10] Ibid.

in the world, the general causes of improvement lay in advances in water supply and sanitation and in developments in dairying favouring pathogen-free milk in a fresh, condensed or dried form. Nevertheless, there were several local factors which help to account for the high level of infant mortality from food- and water-borne diseases in Hillgrove in the 1890s, and the very delayed response to what was seen by contemporaries to be a most pressing social evil.

These local factors were intricately related to the production relations which characterized the industrial/capitalist structure of the local economy. The mines, many foreign-owned, were great consumers of water. Any interruption in water supplies would bring about a temporary closure of mines and an immediate loss of earnings for miners. The local business community would be affected in their turn. The 1890s were generally years of low summer rainfall, either in November/December or in January/February.[11] But the whole period 1890—1900 was a prosperous period for gold, and 1893 was a spectacular boom year for antimony. Therefore, throughout the 1890s, industry was in competition with people for water at a time of water shortage, especially in the worst years of summer rainfall, 1893, 1894, 1897, 1899 and 1900. Further, in response to the mining companies' demands for labour, Hillgrove had grown haphazardly in a fairly confined space on the edge of the gorges on its southern, eastern and western boundaries. To the north it was hemmed in by Hargraves' freehold land. In this space it had grown as a mining encampment without the benefit of municipal government. Consequently, until it was incorporated in 1899, Hillgrove in relation to water supply, sanitation, roads and public works generally was in a position similar to many industrial areas in England during their early industrialization, and until the Municipal Corporations Act of 1835. Meanwhile, for close on 15 years before 1899, the mining companies carried out no public works that were not mainly of benefit to the companies. The town had to depend on a series of *ad hoc* Progress Committees to agitate for, and attempt to regulate, essential services without which the companies could not function — water and timber supply mainly, but also the construction and maintenance of roads, sanitation and the control of public nuisances.

Therefore, it is not surprising, in periods of low summer rainfall, when miners could expect to be unemployed, that mortality, especially infant mortality was so high. These were also periods when water was short, when pools of stagnant water and decaying refuse lay in gutters, when day by day night soil was heaped uncovered on the noxious reserve, when

---

[11] Bureau of meteorology, Station 057019, Hillgrove Public School, 1889—1917.

cattle, horses, and geese drank freely from declining water supplies intended for human consumption, when butchers plied their trades in the main street almost without benefit of water. As these things happened no one had powers to co-ordinate the control of nuisances and no body had powers to tax mining companies, banks, butchers and all the rest to provide much-needed water and sanitation. What little authority there was was either divided among various government agencies, such as the mine warden's court and the police, with only limited legal powers to act in these matters, or vested in Progress Committees with only moral powers. It is not surprising, therefore, that mortality from infantile diarrhoea, dysentery, diarrhoea, enteritis, gastritis and, above all, typhoid was highest in years of low summer rainfall — when God as it were, refused to clean up the mess that people, or should we say, the mining companies, had made — 1893, 1894, 1897, 1899 and 1900. It seems that all the waste and detritus associated with the need for labour at Hillgrove was only ever flushed away after a good downpour of rain. This you might say is merely an historian's fancy built around a skeleton of figures and fleshed out with preconceived notions and prejudices. And it may be so — an observer's jaundiced account. So, let us ask the actors what they thought — or some of them at least.

Water shortage was recognized as a problem in Hillgrove as early as 1887. In these early days this shortage sometimes worked to the advantage of local landowners, as in 1889. In that year there were outbreaks of diphtheria and typhoid which the Progress Committee for the time being attributed to pollution of the town's water supply. They recommended that it be not used.[12] Hargraves of Hillgrove Station was asked to supply water. He responded by selling the townsfolk casks of fresh water at 1s each.[13] Because the town was unincorporated, it became the Progress Committee's task to obtain a better water supply. There was talk of asking the Government for a grant of £200 to build a tank at the Springs, but the needs of the mining companies and the community could not be met from such a modest undertaking.[14] Eventually, after three years' lobbying by the Progress Committee and the companies, and in response to questions in the Legislative Assembly, the NSW Government finally acted.[15] It resumed land from Hargraves and the Eleanora Company along the Swamp Creek, and at no cost to the companies or the local

[12] *Armidale Express,* 17 Sept. 1889, p. 4; 24 Sept. 1889, p. 8.

[13] Ibid., 11 Oct. 1889, p. 7.

[14] Ibid., 11 Oct. 1889, p. 7; 5 Nov. 1889, p. 4; 20 Dec. 1889, p. 8.

[15] Ibid., 20 Dec. 1889, p. 8; *NSW Parliamentary Debates,* Session 1890, pp. 4284, 4450.

community (although the local community is reported to have promised to bear the cost) constructed a reservoir to hold 2.5 million gallons over 16 acres, installed an engine to pump water to a summit level tank, and provided a water main servicing seven fire plugs and five standpipes in the township. The people of Hillgrove received their first piped water in December 1891.[16] The problem of unincorporation was then overcome by the establishment of a Water Trust for local control and distribution of water. Nevertheless the final authority remained vested in the Department of Mines and Agriculture in Sydney.[17]

This first Progress Committee also sought the extension of the Towns Police Act to Hillgrove, and in 1891 was still attempting to use powers under that Act forcibly to control nuisances and to help it in its campaign to replace cesspits with the dry earth system. But in these years the Progress Committee was as much if not more concerned to improve communications by road to Armidale and West Hillgrove, and to get a better postal and telegraph service as it was to control nuisances and agitate for an improved water supply. Consequently, at the end of the century, the 800 people in Metz were still without water, and Hillgrove's supply, with the dam silting up and the mining companies ever demanding more water, was precariously dependent on regular rainfall. Indeed in 1898 the officer in charge of the water works reported that the existing main was insufficient to supply both the town and the mines.[18] At the same time the mining companies were actively seeking an augmentation of the reservoir and a better main's supply. They even offered to underwrite the interest at 4 per cent on £1,500 to·build a new 6 inch main.[19] At the end of 1898 and early in 1899, after the driest year for ten years, things were so tight that a reporter on the *Hillgrove Guardian* wrote:

It seems opportune now to contemplate the very important part the water supply takes in the government of our local temporal welfare. Had the weather not broken as it did on Easter Monday, the Baker's Creek Mine could not have resumed work until the weather did break or until Mr Brown finished his work on Tuesday 18th, 175 men would have been idle for over a fortnight, involving a dead loss of wages amounting to nearly £900 without counting what might at the same time have happened at the Eleanora, the

[16]   Ibid., 11 Dec. 1891.

[17]   Ibid., 11 Dec. 1891. For scale of charges see *Journal of the Legislative Council,* 1894–5, Vol. 53, part 3, p. 443.

[18]   *Hillgrove Guardian,* 20 Aug. 1898.

[19]   Ibid., 22 Oct. 1898; 21 Jan 1899.

Sunlight, the Consols and the Proprietary. In place of this, through the opportune rain, the £900 wages was earned and during the interval mentioned, the Baker's Creek mine alone produced over £2,000 worth of gold imperishable.[20]

The article concluded by calling for a duplication of the pumping engine and a raising of the height of the dam. A few months later, however, there was still only one month's supply of water in the dam, and the local community was acutely aware of the problem. Without a better water supply the industries and people of Hillgrove could not long survive. The community was also alert to the fact that unless the water was pure, and until cesspits and uncontrolled dumping of raw sewage in the night soil depot were banned, Hillgrove would continue to be a dangerous place to live in. But those most aware, the members of the Progress Committees, were powerless. Conditions would have to get much worse before public opinion could be mobilized for change.

The first step in this direction was a major outbreak of food- and water-borne diseases in 1893 and 1894 which resulted in 21 deaths: nine from typhoid, two from dysentery and ten from infantile diarrhoea. The Hillgrove correspondent of the *Armidale Express* wrote:

I hope that this malady [typhoid] will soon run to the end of its tether and leave us. Hillgrove should not to have this disease in its midst, for with the natural facilities for drainage which it possesses, combined with a very small outlay of capital, I am convinced that Hillgrove would be the sanitorium of the New England district. Surrounded by an immense gorge 1,800 feet deep and a fall from nearly every house or yard in the town there is nothing to prevent a thorough sanitary system, and until this matter is taken up in a practical way Hillgrove will continue to suffer from typhoid, which is the national [sic] outcome of bad sanitary arrangements.[21]

A year later he wrote:

Fever has made its appearance here again, and though an unwelcome guest certainly does not come uninvited for some of the people in Hillgrove have very crude notions of sanitary laws. The pity of it is that the punishment so often falls on the wrong shoulders. What a boon an inspector of nuisances would be.[22]

[20] Ibid., 22 April 1899; see also ibid., editorial, 16 April 1898.
[21] *Armidale Express,* 20 March 1894.
[22] Ibid., 26 April 1894.

A second serious outbreak of food- and water-borne diseases occurred in 1897—8. This time there were 18 deaths including four from typhoid, seven from infantile diarrhoea and six from enteritis/gastritis. In 1898 there were 25 deaths of infants under one year and 151 births. Infant mortality, therefore, was at a rate of 166:1,000 live births which was higher than for Sydney and 36 per cent higher than for NSW generally. This outbreak of disease provoked the *Hillgrove Guardian* to say:

Were the most ordinary sanitary precautions observed the town should be the healthiest in Australia, but with an increasing population and no system of local government, we must expect, until the place is incorporated, an increased amount of sickness, busy and anxious times for our doctors and steady work for our undertakers.[23]

Two local doctors, Harry M. Massey, the Government Health Officer, and Cooper Hardcastle were so concerned that they organized a petition to the Colonial Secretary. It read:

We the undersigned residents of Hillgrove respectfully beg to bring under your notice a matter of most dangerous importance to the people of Hillgrove, and pray that such means may be taken by the Executive as may be deemed adequate to its removal. We beg to lay before you the following statement of facts: Bracken, the main street, being situated on the crown of a ridge the debris and filth from the principal tenements is carried to Brereton Street, one of the chief thoroughfares, there stagnating and creating along its sides a veritable fever bed. This latter street leads to one of the most thickly populated outskirts of the town, to the hospital and places of worship. The nuisance therefore remains a standing menace to the health of the people. The cost of its removal would be very small and considering the town contains a population of about three thousand inhabitants and its revenue-producing status, may we not humbly beg you to cause enquiry to be made with a view to remedying the evil of your petitioners in duty bound will ever pray.[24]

Public concern about health was helped by the mine managers' growing concern about the shortage of water for the mines (1898 with only 25.6 inches was the year of lowest rainfall between 1889 and 1902). The upshot was, in August 1898, the Progress Committee resolved to seek incorporation for Hillgrove.[25] Even so there was still no sense of urgency. The movement for incorporation had to wait for the election of a new Committee in January 1899 for the initiation of a petition in favour of

[23] *Hillgrove Guardian,* 25 Feb. 1899.
[24] Ibid., 25 June 1898.
[25] Ibid., 20 Aug. 1898, p. 3.

incorporation. But it seems that there were as many people in Hillgrove opposed to incorporation as in favour of it. Early in the year there were two petitions circulating in Hillgrove, one for and one against incorporation.[26] The issue was a particularly divisive one. A citizen's Committee came into existence strongly in favour of incorporation. The Progress Committee, with a vocal minority opposed to incorporation, was bitterly divided and voted itself out of existence. The opponents of incorporation found a champion in the editor of the *Armidale Chronicle*. Citizens issued backyard challenges to each other, and public meetings ended in uproar.[27]

It is not easy to identify the reasons influencing the anti-incorporationists. One factor undoubtedly weighing in their minds was the cost in rates to be paid coupled with the fact that the unimproved value of town allotments was thought to be unduly high. This fear was probably linked with a general feeling that local government was an expensive and undesirable burden — Hillgrove could do without government.[28] This feeling may have been particularly strong in Hillgrove because it was feared that once incorporated the new Borough of Hillgrove would be required to take over the debt contracted by the NSW Government in constructing Hillgrove's water supply, and, thereafter, become responsible for bringing the system up to the standards necessary to meet the increasing demands of the mining companies. According to the editor of the *Hillgrove Guardian*, it was this fear added to apathy which had frustrated all earlier attempts at incorporation and kept Hillgrove in a chronic state of ill health.[29] But in 1899 this fear had momentarily been laid low by the emergence of another belief that there was something to be got from the new Government.[30] Even so migratory miners and tradesmen, alienated from their fellow workers, had little to gain from incorporation. Those in favour were: 'the business people and settled miners who had made comfortable homes for themselves and their families and hope to live in comfort and live long, enjoying health and die when their time came from natural causes and not be harried into eternity by a beastly epidemic.'[31]

Our analysis of support for and opposition to incorporation leaves no doubt of an overwhelming social class basis for opposition to it. Thirty-four per cent of professed supporters of incorporation were drawn from

[26] Ibid., 4 March 1899, 18 March 1899, 15 April 1899; *Armidale Express,* 4 April 1899; *NSW Government Gazette,* 2 Jan 1899 and 29 March 1899.

[27] *Hillgrove Guardian,* 1 Oct. 1898, 22 April 1899, p. 3, 29 April 1899, pp. 2, 3.

[28] Ibid., editorial, 12 March 1898.

[29] Ibid., editorial, 26 Aug. 1899.

[30] Ibid., editorial, 9 July 1898, 20 Aug. 1898, 1 Oct. 1898.

[31] Ibid., editorial, 22 April 1899.

social classes 1 and 2 (see table 9.11) compared with 8 per cent of opponents to it, whereas 70 per cent of opponents were from social classes 4 and 5 compared to 43 per cent of supporters in these two social classes. Miners alone made up two thirds of opponents but only one third of supporters of incorporation.[32] The breakdown of signatories of the two petitions according to social class is given in table 9.11.

Table 9.11   Signatories of Petition for and against the incorporation of Hillgrove 1899 (percentages)

Social class	For incorporation	Against incorporation
1	9 ⎫	1 ⎫
2	25 ⎬ 54	7 ⎬ 20
3	20 ⎭	12 ⎭
4	39 ⎫ 43	67 ⎫ 70
5	4 ⎭	3 ⎭
occupation not specified	3	10

Source: NSW Government Gazette, 21 Jan. 1899 and 29 March 1899

While the township waited for the result of their petitions, a new Progress Committee was frustrated by the cost of burying all the night soil on the noxious reserve, and by Senior Constable Cook's report that he had no powers to prevent people burying night soil in their own gardens. Yet they also decided to take no action to repair a defective drain on the road leading to the hospital pending incorporation.[33] So the year ran on with more deaths from typhoid, enteritis/gastritis and infantile diarrhoea. In all this time the people of Hillgrove were assured by newspaper advertisers that they could protect themselves against dysentery and diarrhoea by taking D. E. Williams Pink Pills for Pale People and Bile Beans for Biliousness!

The first step towards incorporation was a meeting at the Court House on 20 July 1899, called to test the validity of signatures on the petitions for and against incorporation; 225 people had signed the former, 229 the latter. The presiding magistrate, W. F. Parker, found that 30 people had signed both petitions and declared that their names be struck off the petition against incorporation. Then he declared invalid a further 50

[32] *NSW Government Gazette,* 21 Jan. 1899 and 29 March 1899.
[33] *Hillgrove Guardian,* 24 June 1899.

names on that petition against 12 invalid on the pro-incorporation petition. With that done he retired to Armidale to write his report. The result was that Hillgrove was proclaimed a borough on 29 September 1899. The first meeting of the newly elected council was held early in January 1900.[34]

Almost immediately the council set about putting Hillgrove's house in order. They called for tenders for emptying pans and cesspits, appointed a committee of four to supervise the contractor and appointed Alderman Sydney Smith as acting inspector of nuisances. In May, they appointed Mr Cranston, the sanitary contractor, as their first part-time salaried inspector of nuisances at a salary of 10s per month. They also declared Wednesday to be early closing day.[35]

Within a year or so sanitary controls were fully established, typhoid became sporadic rather than endemic and epidemic, and infant mortality fell to the national average. Even as these things came to pass, one by one the mining companies closed down. Within seven years of incorporation Hillgrove was in decline as a place of production and reproduction. The fear that the borough would have to take over the water supply was realized. In 1907 the people of Hillgrove were saddled with a debt of £4,000 repayable over 50 years at 3.5 per cent. Yet the population of the place was already in decline, and the rateable capacity of the borough was insufficient to service the debt. Consequently by 1922, Hillgrove was indebted to the extent of £3,905 2s 11d on its capital account and for £1,347 6s 3d interest — a total debt for the water supply system of £5,252 9s 2d. In the same year the council spent £640 14s 10d on current account (an over-spending of £15 18s 8d), £180 of this was spent on the sanitary service and £283 on the water supply, including £115 as interest on the outstanding debt.[36]

So it came about that a water supply system built to service the needs of antimony and gold mining companies and the labour force they brought into existence, originally paid for by the NSW Government out of general revenue, became a charge on the people of Hillgrove as their livelihoods disappeared. Moreover, the fear that this would happen with the advent of incorporation had fuelled the clearly social class-based hostility to incorporation. This social class-based hostility to incorporation coupled with the failure of that same system of water supply to come up to

[34] Ibid., 8 July 1899, p. 3, 15 July 1899, p. 4, 22 July 1899, p. 3, 20 Jan. 1900, p. 2.

[35] Ibid., 10 Feb. 1900, p. 2, 17 March 1900, p. 2, 12 May 1900, p. 3.

[36] A collection of Council papers relating to the Borough of Hillgrove currently in the author's possession but to be deposited in the Archives at the University of New England.

expectations as the township grew, meant that Hillgrove lacked all sanitary controls, and was without adequate water supply. Therefore, throughout the 1890s, Hillgrove experienced high and rising levels of infant mortality. The social costs of mining were borne by these infants, by families bereaved through typhoid and by countless workers weakened by endemic dysentery, diarrhoea and other food- and water-borne diseases. Subsequently, the financial costs were borne by the remnants of a community unable to pay because the mining companies had gone elsewhere; by 1922, £373 of rates were in arrears. In the end the outstanding capital debt was extinguished by the Country Towns Water and Sewerage (reduction of debts) Act 1922, and the borough was merged with Dumaresq shire in 1924.

Thus capitalist relations of production, as they spread outwards in consequence of Europe's industrialization, created Hillgrove in Britain's image. For a while these relations of production attracted a hard-working and fertile labouring population to the district, and added to the world's output of minerals. They also created a class structure and social conditions that killed babies. In the end, those capitalist relations of production destroyed the township and the community itself, leaving only debts, the debris of abandoned technology, and memories fading into myth. Hillgrove today is as much a monument to Australia's past and to its making as a nation in conflict, as any of the country's war memorials; it should be a national shrine. Its ANZAC day should be 29 March, the day of the publication of the petition against incorporation in 1899.

10

Cultural Materialism: a Critique

With this chapter on cultural materialism, our journey has come a long way beyond Camden Town and Hillgrove, and some 300 years from our starting point, whether in Dewsall or Norwich or Wincanton. Yet we have encountered its central problem — the problem of determination and of structure and agency throughout the book. Although I attempt to resolve the question in general, theoretical, terms as a problem for today and, therefore, for tomorrow, the instances deployed tie this end of our journey to our start, at the turn of the seventeenth and eighteenth centuries, and to Bath. The chapter and the argument works at three levels in relation to the rest of the book and the book itself. First, at the level of a perception of the materialist conception of history which emphasizes relations of production (property relations), class relations, and the creativity of labour; which comprehends cultural productions as aspects of (class) consciousness and, therefore, as determined by perceptions of class relations structured within a complex articulation of modes of production. Second, at the empirical level of what this means in particular cases. Thus, class consciousness, cultural (mainly literary) production, aspects of culture as a whole way of life, and the book itself, as a cultural production and product of class culture, may be located and examined within its compass. Finally, at the level of history; Raymond Williams and cultural materialism *are* part of a Marxist history of British society, economy and culture since 1700. This chapter brings that history into 1984.

*   *   *

Cultural materialism, developed in recent years by Raymond Williams,

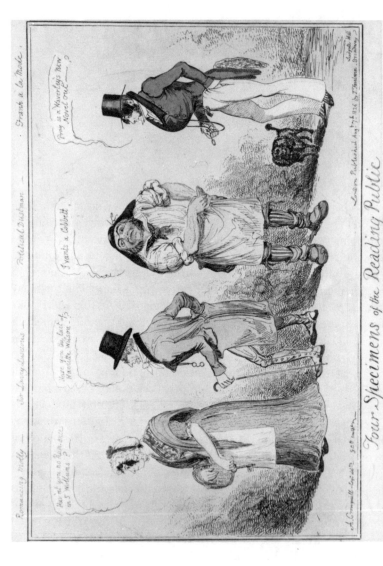

Four Specimens of the Reading Public (A. Crowquill, 1826)

notably in *Marxism and Literature*, claims to be a Marxist critique of 'criticism' and of 'Marxism'. It affirms, against literary 'tradition', the materiality and constructedness of cultural practice, including 'literature', but devalues (denies) the determination of the economic in general. As he struggles against the vulgar Marxism of the 1930s, Williams argues that culture is not merely a reflection of economic reality, 'the base', nor an expression of process in it. Accordingly he acknowledges a determining and controlling power in 'literature', especially in its manifestation as 'tradition' and 'criticism' (noting at the same time that 'aesthetics' and 'criticism' are products of a market society). But he sets against this determination of 'literature' the constitutive and produced nature of language and its literary derivatives. Williams believes that this places all literary production within the general arena of production and leads him to the view that that which is produced is determining *because* it is produced. Williams writes:

What is fundamentally lacking, in the theoretical formulations of this important period [the classic period of marxism] is any adequate recognition of the indissoluble connections between material production, political and cultural institutions and activity, and consciousness. . . . Thus . . . it is not 'the base' and 'the superstructure' that need to be studied, but specific and indissoluble real processes, within which the decisive relationship, from a marxist point of view, is that expressed by the complex idea of determination. . . . Determination of this kind . . . is in the whole social process itself and nowhere else: not in an abstracted 'mode of production' nor in an abstracted 'psychology' . . . it is wholly beside the point to isolate 'production' and 'industry' from the comparably material production of 'defence', 'law and order', 'welfare', 'entertainment', and 'public opinion' [castles, prisons, workhouses, theatres, printing presses]. In failing to grasp the material character of the production of a social and political order, this specialized (and bourgeois) materialism failed also, but even more conspicuously, to understand the material character of the production of a cultural order [schools, printing presses, art galleries]. The concept of the 'superstructure' was then not a reduction but an evasion.[1]

Williams, in his alternative, indigenous English cultural Marxism, emphasizes the productive (creative) nature of labour and the constitutive nature of language (language as practical consciousness), and therefore insists upon the fundamental material nature of literary production. Also derived from labour and language, he identifies literary counter-cultures,

---

[1] Raymond Williams, *Marxism and Literature* (Oxford, 1977), pp. 80, 82, 87, 93. The words in square brackets are my additions.

growing in the interstices between and within modes of production. All of these material literary productions are to be thought of as codetermining with all other economic (material) determinations. Marxist literary criticism circulating around these central ideas is cultural materialism.

Whatever the value of cultural materialism — in challenging 'literature' as a revered object of contemplation for traditional criticism, and restoring Marxist critical theory's centrality — we have to ask how far it offers an adequate understanding of Marx or of relationships between culture and economy. It could be that Williams's production, his contribution to culture, is as influential as it is said to be, less because Williams is a socialist (let alone a Marxist) and more because he has interpreted Marx for English students of 'Literature and Society' such that their reading of Williams (rather than of Marx or of other Marxists) preserves for them the romantic culturalism — and the moment of *Scrutiny* — to which Williams appears so deeply opposed.[2]

BASE/SUPERSTRUCTURE

Williams's difficulty with Marx is that which faces all Marxists. It is the nature and structure of 'the mode of production' and the determinate role claimed for it in relation to law, politics, the state and, most importantly for Williams, 'culture'; the question, that is, how best to understand and express the relationships implied in Marx's proposition, 'It is not the consciousness of men that determines their being, but, on the contrary, their social being that determines their consciousness.'

Williams's solution to this Marxist puzzle is structured (and limited) by his long-standing quarrel with the mechanism of the base/superstructure model of vulgar Marxism. In this model, the base (the mode of production) is the place where material production occurs; where the technology of the forces of production exerts irresistible pressure on the relations of production (property relations, position in the production process), and is determining. The superstructure is held to be the place where the determination of the material forces of production (in the mode of production) is revealed in forms of consciousness; in 'culture'; the superstructure mirrors of reflects production. In this model determination means causation.

Williams challenges such formulations of Marx's system. He does so by claiming, and rightly so, that 'culture' (hereafter, in this chapter, 'literature')

[2] See the brilliant analysis of *Scrutiny* in Francis Mulhern, *The Moment of 'Scrutiny'* (1981), especially pp. 305—11.

should always be understood through its own necessary (inescapable) materiality; literary products in all their variety are to be understood as productions, rather than as expressions. Furthermore, and fundamentally, language, the medium through which 'literature' is produced, is also the chief means through which people understand and interpret for themselves the world they have made through production; it is through language that people make themselves as conscious of themselves. Therefore, language is not a given structure (as in Saussure) and is not determining, and is not a mere reflection of material production (as in vulgar Marxism). Language is an activity, a series of acts of production, practical consciousness (as in Marx and Volosinov). Accordingly, Williams says, language and its productions as 'literature' ought properly to be placed within the forces of production, within the mode of production, within the base. Then, because 'literature' is produced, the arena in which it is produced within the mode of production must be deemed to be just as determining as any other arena in which commodities, such as cars, are produced. (As Williams says, 'it is wholly beside the point to isolate "production" and "industry" from the comparably material production of "defence", "law and order", "welfare", "entertainment and public opinion".')[3] Clearly such a location for literary production cuts across and destroys the dualism base/superstructure. The conclusion is equally transparent; literary production, 'literature' as well as language, must be thought of as determining. In Williams's homely example, literary production is at least as important and determining as car production. Indeed, if we take structuralism and semiology seriously, as Williams would have us do, then the structure of the verbal signs in *Marxism and Literature* can be said to show that Williams actually believes in the primacy in determination of 'literature', both as ideology and as counter-culture. For example, the arrangement of chapters and argument within chapters gives a power to the theme of the book which the argument itself frequently lacks. Thus the first three chapters are entitled 'Culture', 'Language' and 'Literature'. And they state the following propositions, giving these concepts a place and priority that the argument has yet to justify.

(1) At the very centre of a major area of modern thought and practice . . . is a concept 'culture'. . . . Yet . . . the concepts, as it is said, from which we begin, are suddenly seen to be not concepts but problems, not analytic problems either but historical movements that are still unresolved. . . . We have only, if we can, to recover the substance from which their forms were cast.[4] (2) A

---

[3] Williams, *Marxism and Literature,* p. 93.
[4] Ibid., p. 11.

definition of language is always, implicitly or explicitly, a definition of human beings in the world.[5] (3) The special property of 'literature' as a concept is that it claims [a] kind of importance and priority. . . . Thus it is common to see 'literature' defined as 'full, central, immediate human experience' . . . [consequently] other concepts . . . are downgraded, as mere hardened outer shells compared with the living experience of literature.[6]

However, the final chapter 'Creative Practice' emphasizes that 'At the very centre of Marxism is an extraordinary emphasis on human creativity and self creation.'[7] Accordingly, Williams claims that creative practice is of many kinds, transcending the content and boundaries of the concepts evolved by humankind, transcending, that is, the concept 'literature' and requiring a definition of language, and therefore of human beings in the world, as constitutive. Further, although Williams argues that conceptual problems are really unresolved historical movements, his elliptical accounts of the problems circulate around the theme of the historical development of relations between words and concepts as if they do have a life of their own. He does so in a context which sees these words and concepts as socially constituting. The structure of the book is beguiling. Consequently, the mode of production fades into the background. Rough edges and silences in the argument are thereby passed over. The medium does become the message.

Williams's belief, that 'literature' as material production is relatively autonomous and should be granted a parallel and equal status with other productions in the mode of production, is, as I have said, structured and limited by his quarrel with vulgar Marxism. It depends, in the first instance, upon a whimsical view of the structure, relations and role in the determination of consciousness of the mode of production; a whimsy apparently shared by *New Left Review*. Yet, as their *Politics and Letters* shows, this view is inhibiting for any serious discussion of relationships between cultural production and the mode of production, and of base and superstructure.

New Left Review challenges Williams for rejecting 'the whole distinction between base and superstructure', and for writing cloudily of 'a single and indissoluble real process simultaneously integrating economic, social, political and cultural processes'.[8] Yet it too is limited by the trap of vulgar Marxism into which it was lured by Williams's quarrel with it.

---

[5] Ibid., p. 2.

[6] Ibid., p. 45.

[7] Ibid., p. 206.

[8] Raymond Williams, *Politics and Letters: Interviews with New Left Review* (1981), p. 351.

New Left Review argues that if Williams's dissolution of the base/superstructure distinction in favour of the idea of 'a single and indissoluble real process' is accepted, it is also necessary to agree with him that a political order is a material production consisting of palaces, churches, prisons and schools, and, therefore, that the political order is, like the mode of production, determining. This, says *New Left Review*, is plainly not so. 'It is not the buildings which themselves constitute a political system, it is the uniformed and civil agents of the ruling order who operate them that define their function.'[9] Therefore, *New Left Review* seems to say, the buildings — the material productions, as it were, of a political system — do not give a determinate role to politics like that properly attributed to strictly economic production. Economic production, says *New Left Review*, 'permits cultural production in a way which is not symmetrically true of the relation of cultural production'.[10] *New Left Review* believes it clinches the argument by employing another homely example. Its case goes like this. While a capitalist legal system can dispense with specific structures such as law courts and prisons, and can use other structures such as ships and hotels as prisons and law courts, the same relation is not true of 'the great factories and machine complexes of an industrial economy'.[11] What is more, the same prisons can be turned into schools as well as into law courts. The point seems to be that these material structures in the political/cultural arena are flexible in the use to which they can be put and are, therefore, not determining. But, demands *New Left Review* — implying that here lies the crucial test and proof of the primary determinate property of the economic and of 'the base' — 'could steel mills become law-courts?'[12]

Although the anticipated answer to this rhetorical question is 'No', I cannot see why a steel mill or part of one might not be used as a law-court. Nor can I see why I might not rephrase the question, and bringing *New Left Review* up to date, ask, 'Could computer buildings, powerhouses, Cal. Tech., stock exchanges, banks, warehouses, or woolsheds become law-courts?' And answer 'Yes!'

My point; this homely argument and example has no bearing on the essential question — the relation of cultural production to the mode of production. Neither has Williams's response to it.

Williams concedes primacy in determination to basic production only; the production of food and shelter and of the means of producing these

[9] Ibid., p. 351.
[10] Ibid., p. 351.
[11] Ibid., p. 352.
[12] Ibid., p. 352.

commodities. (He concedes nothing to the production of cars.)[13] In making and not making these concessions, Williams entraps the argument deeper into notions of a hierarchy of production and of parallel, although unequal, cause and effect relationships. He seems to argue that while the production of 'literature' may be less determining than the production of food, it is clearly more determining than the production of cars. The tragedy of this exchange in *Politics and Letters* is that it shows both emperors without clothes. It trivializes a fundamental theoretical question. This exchange reduces the base/superstructure argument to a sort of architectural determinism, evades the challenge to cultural materialism represented in the work of such English-speaking theorists of Marxism as Cohen and Shaw, and mistakenly focuses critical attention on the materiality of production as the crucial issue in the problem of the determinate core in the materialist conception of history.

LANGUAGE/THE 'FOUR MOMENTS'

Williams's argument about 'language', 'literature' and 'culture', and their central place in cultural materialism, although structured by his quarrel with vulgar Marxism, depends for its very life on two other streams of thought. One flows from Volosinov's and, by derivation, from Williams's confrontation with Saussure and the question of the arbitrariness of verbal signs. The other flows from Williams's encounter with the 'four moments' of *The German Ideology.*

Volosinov (Bakhtin) first. Williams writes:

Volosinov accepted that a 'sign' in language has indeed a 'binary' character ... That is to say, he agreed that the verbal sign is not equivalent to, nor simply a reflection of, the object or quality which it indicates or expresses. The relation within the sign between the formal element and the meaning which this element carries is thus inevitably conventional (thus far agreeing with orthodox semiotic theory), but it is not arbitrary and, crucially, is not fixed.[14]

Williams concurs, adding that while Volosinov agreed that verbal signs are not images of things he also believed that they are not arbitrary in the sense of being casual or random. More importantly for his argument, Williams agrees with Volosinov's insistence upon the fact that verbal signs are not signals; verbal signs are polysemic and their signification

---

[13] Ibid., p. 353.
[14] Williams, *Marxism and Literature,* p. 36. See also V. N. Volosinov, *Marxism and the Philosophy of Language* (New York, 1973; first published 1929).

changes over time. Therefore, argues Williams, 'conventional' rather than 'arbitrary' best describes the status of verbal signs, because conventions, while binding, are only more or less binding. They may be changed by and through human social activity. Therefore, language should be thought of as activity; constitutive and rooted in material practice, rather than structured. Williams writes, 'Signification, the social creation of meanings through the use of formal signs, is then a practical material activity; it is indeed, literally, a means of production. It is a specific form of that practical consciousness which is inseparable from all social material activity.'[15]

The notion that verbal signs are conventional, therefore constitutive rather than arbitrary, is central to Williams's argument. So, too, is the notion that language as practical consciousness is inseparable from all social material activity; a notion flowing from Williams's encounter with the 'four moments'. The relevant passage in *The German Ideology* reads:

Only now, after having considered four moments, four aspects of the primary historical relationships do we find that man also possesses 'consciousness', but, even so, not inherent, not 'pure' consciousness. From the start the 'spirit' is afflicted with the curse of being 'burdened' with matter, which here makes its appearance in the form of agitated layers of air, sounds, in short, of language. Language is as old as consciousness, language *is* practical consciousness that exists also for other men, and for that reason alone it really exists for me personally as well; language like consciousness, only arises from the need, the necessity of intercourse with other men.[16]

Williams argues that in this passage and in the 'four moments' Marx emphasizes the constitutive nature of language and the simultaneity and social nature of the whole production process as men and women laboured to satisfy needs. Rightly so, all Marxists might agree.

But no Marxist can stop at this point, resting his or her case on the concept of man. Marx certainly did not. Man, although initially an organizing concept in Marx's thought, is rarely so later. Rather, Marx's thought is marked, some might say scarred, by his perception of the socially separating and abrasive effect of the division of labour and the division of humankind into classes. Thus, while practical consciousness (language) was at first merely 'a sheep-like or tribal consciousness', it was fractured, one might say, at the outset of the 'four moments' by the division of labour in the family and between the sexes. Yet, says Marx, the

---

[15] Ibid., p. 38.
[16] Karl Marx and Friedrich Engels, *The German Ideology* (Moscow, 1964), p. 41.

full consequences of the division of labour for consciousness appeared only with the division between material and mental labour. It is necessary, therefore, having followed Williams through the 'four moments', to follow Marx into the two paragraphs after the key passage above — critically commented upon by Williams in his discussion of ideology but omitted by him in his analysis of language — in order to grasp adequately Marx's position on the fate of practical consciousness and of language.

The passage reads:

Division of labour only becomes truly such from the moment when a division of material and mental labour appears. From this moment onwards consciousness *can* really flatter itself that it is something other than consciousness of existing practice, that it *really* represents something without representing something real; from now on consciousness is in a position to emancipate itself from the world and to proceed to the formation of 'pure' theory, theology, philosophy, ethics etc.[17] [And, I add, 'literature' and 'culture'.]

The argument continues; consciousness, practical consciousness incorporating and mediated by language, is divided by the division of material and mental labour, therefore intellectual and material activity is allocated to different individuals. So, too, writes Marx, 'enjoyment and labour, production and consumption, devolve on different individuals'.[18] Which is to say that consciousness becomes a proprietorial and privileged category over and above those employed (as labourers) in material or practical activity. It is at the point of the division of material and mental labour, Marx argues, that the forces of production, the state of society and consciousness (incorporating language), which hitherto produced a tribal (community) consciousness (incorporating language), 'must come into contradiction with each other'.[19] In short, and this is crucial, Marx links all further development of consciousness (incorporating language) to the division of labour and to the accompanying development of classes; thereafter consciousness, incorporating language, like capital becomes a class instrument. It becomes ideology. (But ideology, even when considered hegemonic in Gramsci's sense, is not primary or determining.) Restoration of consciousness to the labourer, the proletariat, is the subject of Marx's analysis of capitalism and the subject of the myth of Marxism from Sorel

[17] Ibid., p. 43.
[18] Ibid., p. 43.
[19] Ibid., p. 43.

to E. P. Thompson and Raymond Williams. Explanation of Marx's failure with *his* subject has been the subject of Marxist analysis throughout the twentieth century.

CLASS/RELATIONS OF PRODUCTION

The point of this exegesis is not that I seek the authority of a text, imperfectly used by Williams, to make my case against cultural materialism. Rather is it to show that Marx, in *The German Ideology*, was already thinking in *class* terms, relating the development of consciousness (incorporating language) to the growth of the division of labour in the production process;[20] and to give point to my proposition that, 'Marx without *class* is like *Hamlet* without the Prince.'[21] Then to contrast Marx's *class* position with the almost classless account of Marxism given by Williams in *Marxism and Literature*. Williams does not naturally think in *class* terms, or so it seems. In his key chapter on language the word *class* (or class) is absent except, as I read him, when he rejects the role of *class* in language. (This *is* surprising since *class* figures conspicuously in *Keywords*.[22]) Rather, when Williams writes of language as activity and practical consciousness rooted in production, he gives it a social location, using words shimmering with ideas of community and wholeness. Williams, like his mentor Volosinov, is inclined to see practical consciousness as some sort of homogeneous (collective) phenomenon resulting, it is true, from activity between real individuals, but individuals all more or less equally active in developing and creating (producing) language and contributing to practical consciousness in a classless sort of way. But in Marx it is not material production *per se* that matters; it is not simply that things, language and consciousness (culture) are produced, but that they are produced within certain kinds of relationships. These relationships are those property relationships in the mode of production which, in turn, generate *class* relationships.

Williams, on the other hand, does not write of language and the social processes creating meaning and contributing to practical consciousness as

---

[20] See also Karl Marx, *A Contribution to the Critique of Hegel's 'Philosophy of Right': Introduction,* edited with Introduction by Joseph O'Malley (Cambridge, 1970), pp. 137—42, reprinted in R. S. Neale (ed.), *History and Class: Essential Readings in Theory and Interpretation* (Oxford, 1983), pp. 30—7.

[21] R. S. Neale, *Class in English History 1680—1850* (Oxford, 1981), p. 17. My use in this paper of the italicized *class* is in accordance with the practice I advocate in this book.

[22] Raymond Williams, *Keywords* (1976), pp. 51—9.

taking place between real individuals distinguished by sex (as the original of *classes* in Marx) and by *class*. Consequently much of the argument in *Marxism and Literature* has an air of remoteness from the material base in which Williams so clearly wishes to locate it. For example, Williams makes no reference to the work of Basil Bernstein nor to that of the post-Second World War generation of teachers of English in primary and secondary schools, whose material practice has been to try to facilitate the production of language within material and *class* conditions rooted in the mode of production, which stunt the production of language.[23]

Only when Williams discusses 'hegemony', some half way through the book, does it begin to appear that *class* might be central to his claim about 'literature'. Even so, his main argument about 'hegemony' is that it too is always an active process and in any social formation 'hegemony' is not hegemonic.[24] There are always some areas of human perception left over from earlier social formations and some areas of human experience untouched by an otherwise hegemonic ideology. Also, there are the cultural productions of the dominated class. Therefore, says Williams, because of these residual, emergent and biologically determined continuities in human experience, there is always room for the production of counter-cultures.[25] This emphasizes the importance of the constitutive nature of literary production. In short, Williams claims that literary production draws upon sources of energy outside the social system and beyond the reach of ideology and presumably, therefore, outside relations of production and *class* relations. And yet, just as *class* haunted Marx to the very last pages of *Capital*, it sits unacknowledged and neglected on Williams's shoulder throughout his confrontation with Saussure over the arbitrariness of verbal signs.

So, from Marx and the 'four moments' back to Volosinov (Bakhtin). This time, however, with a consciousness of the central and theoretical place of *class* in Marx and with the voice of sex, as the original of class, and with memories of the language of class echoing through our inner speech.

The 'truth', that verbal signs are not signals, also applies to the terms of

---

[23] Basil Bernstein, *Class, Codes and Control* (St Albans, 1973), and, for example, J. W. Patrick Creber, *Lost for Words* (Harmondsworth, 1972). It should be recognized, however, that many of the attempts to teach language have been attempts to teach conventional or hegemonic language. This may be an additional reason for failure and for the suppression of the capacity among working-class children actively to construct language.

[24] Williams, *Marxism and Literature*, pp. 112—13.

[25] Ibid., chs 6—9 and the essay on 'Culture' (see footnote 39).

this discourse; 'conventional' and 'arbitrary' are not signals. 'Conventional' always means somebody's — some group's — conventional. However, whenever one asks about the source of the conventional — whose convention? whose conventional? — answers are generally couched in and obscured by words and phrases denoting perceptions arising from notions of social cohesion and the wholeness — the community — of society; 'social convention', 'social processes', 'social relationships', 'social compact', 'social contract' (as in Williams). Yet, if one looks to the history of 'conventional', it will be heard resonant with its origin in the calling together of *selected* persons to settle issues and reach agreements and, as in England in 1660 and 1688, to appoint monarchs following military coups d'état. 'Conventional', says the *OED*, refers to a general agreement, 'arbitrarily and artificially determined'. In which case 'conventional' masks real social relationships; social relationships which would be better encapsulated in the word 'arbitrary' because there is a meaning of 'arbitrary' not touched upon by Williams/Volosinov.

In contemporary usage 'arbitrary' often, if not generally, refers to the decisions and actions of those in positions of authority and power. According to the *OED*, the word is surrounded by an aura of dependency upon will and upon the unrestrained exercise of will; arbitrary carries with it notions of the despotic — hence the conventions of 1660 and 1688 and their conventions. Therefore, as 'arbitrary' signifies 'power' and 'conventional' signifies 'social contract', the first, like the language of *class,* identifies division within society, the other agreement and consensus, like the language of community to which it belongs.

Furthermore, Saussure accompanied his notion that the signifier is arbitrary with the more revolutionary notion that that which is signified is arbitrary.[26] In which case, 'arbitrary' appears twice rooted in relationships of authority and subordination; why Man? Why not Woman? Why seminar? Why not ovular? Why pork? Why not pig? Why conventional? Why not arbitrary? Surely it is the challenge to codes of social relationships embodied in words such as these that gives point to Freud's venerable story. A feudal lord, travelling through his domains, noticed a man in the cheering mob who looked remarkably like himself. He summoned him over and asked, imperiously, 'Was your mother ever employed in my castle?' 'No, my Lord', the man responded, 'but my father was.' If we could unfold the sources of such joking challenges we would understand much about the constitutive nature of language and of creativity. Yet we

[26] Ferdinand de Saussure, *Course in General Linguistics* (1960); Jonathan Culler, *Ferdinand de Saussure* (Harmondsworth, 1977).

K

would have to set against such knowledge Saussure's pertinent observation that in the question of language, and therefore in the matter of literary production, 'The masses have no voice in the matter.'[27]

If the language we use is to encapsulate the real position and relations of a people, then the language men and women are born to use (in their *classes*) and the objects and relationships to which those words direct their attention are best thought of, like the mode of production into which women and men are born (in their *classes*), as arbitrary and determining for any cohort of men and women (in their *classes*). Which is to say that both *class* position and *class* language are determined by relations of production in the mode of production. Such a use of language would be consistent with Marx's account of society as structured by property relations (relations of production) and, therefore, as fissured by *class* relations such as those in the following pairs: propertied/propertyless, capital/labour, mental/material labour. Only with such a use of language will it be possible to understand the relationship of language to labour as practical consciousness, and offer a Marxist account of the relationship of 'literature' and of 'culture' to the 'base' in the capitalist mode of production.

I agree with Williams that human labour is inextricably meshed with the human capacity to produce language as practical consciousness; language *is* always mixed with labour in production — but we differ in our conclusions. In short, *because* language is mixed with labour in production, one might say, under capitalism, and as labour power has two elements — necessary labour and surplus labour — language, as practical consciousness, may also be thought to contain two elements, necessary language and surplus language. In both instances, which are really the same instance, the surplus is appropriated and transformed into a product which stands over and above the labourers (women and men) who possess only a stunted life and a stunted necessary language of labour and everyday life. Marx's concept of alienation encompasses the latter pole, ideology and Gramsci's concept of hegemony the former. And this is to say quite simply that language, like capital, *is* an instrument of domination, a carrier of cultural power.

Therefore, while one may regard language as constitutive and mixed with labour at every moment of production (Marx/Williams), it is also proper to think of verbal signs as arbitrary (in both senses, Saussure) and determining in the strong sense of the word, for any cohort of people in their *classes*. Language is both arbitrary and constitutive. While its

---

[27] De Saussure, *ibid.*, p. 71. See also Arthur Koestler, *The Act of Creation* (1964).

arbitrariness may have its roots in the very structure of a language, in any mode of production, it will be determined by *class* relations; that is, by the necessary enveloping nexus which binds together the relations and forces of production in any mode of production. It is in this sense that the mode of production (the economic), perceived as a whole structure rather than as the home of material production, is of primary importance in the determination of consciousness. This argument is also to be found in the 'four moments' of *The German Ideology*, Williams's most preferred of Marx's texts.

In the 'four moments' Marx begins with men and women with physical needs, just like animals, but, unlike animals, endowed with the capacity to satisfy those needs through labour as an imagined and constructed, rather than as a random and instinctual activity. As men and women satisfy their physical needs for food, shelter and clothing, and for the reproduction as well as the production of labour, through their labour, which is necessarily *social* labour, they create new needs, but not in the sense of a hierarchy of needs. Furthermore, in the process of material production, to satisy needs and for reproduction, women and men produce language and consciousness. Thus needs, satisfaction of needs through production, production of new needs, production of language, production of social organization, production of consciousness, reproduction, as these occur and reoccur at every moment and over time, possess their quiddity in labour. But in Marx, labour, the basis of all material production, is always cribbed, cabined *and* liberated by the enveloping nexus between forces and relations of production in the mode of production. Within this nexus labour is *always* fragmented by the division of labour, itself the result of a division of control and appropriation. The division of labour (and of control) starts in the family and continues with the division of material and mental labour and the division between town and country (between manufacture and agriculture). It is unceasing in its development and consequences. Therefore, while relationships between all these elements are simultaneous, recurring, complex and difficult to demonstrate empirically, they can never be reduced to a hierarchy of orders of relatively autonomous material production, nor to an equality of parallel, vertical and interlocking factors. They have their collective quiddity in labour. In the capitalist mode of production, this is infinitely fragmented by the division of labour but is also structured by the characteristic property relations of the capitalist mode of production. Thus, it is not the fact that production is material that is fundamental, but the fact that production itself is not 'relatively autonomous' at all that is crucial.

HOMOLOGY/ARCHITECTURAL DETERMINATION/BATH

The degenerate analogy of architectural determination used by Williams and *New Left Review* is inadequate for their purpose. Nevertheless, the notion of 'architectural determination' may be used homologically to reveal the emptiness of the notion — that a belief in the indissolubility of the social process leads inevitably to a conclusion which emphasizes the determining role of 'literature' and of 'culture', and leads to a rejection of the idea of the determination of the mode of production.

Architecture, like 'literature', is art. It is culture. It is material production. It differs from 'literature' in that its materiality and constructedness is immediately apparent, but the extent to which it embodies language as practical consciousness is less obvious. Yet, from the first 'four moments', when men and women began to build, they developed symbolic languages of architecture. These languages as well as the structures themselves did incorporate language as practical consciousness. With the passage of time these symbolic architectural languages were translated into verbal signs. Today, with the aid of both languages, we can still appropriate or absorb buildings in moments of private contemplation (as we absorb 'literature' when reading). More importantly for analyses of relations between culture and economy it seems that most people absorb their buildings, their architecture, in the very process of living, as Walter Benjamin puts it, in moments of distraction (as they do television); yet the buildings, although material products, are not determining.[28] For example, the city of Bath was the greatest public work of art in eighteenth-century England constructed at a cost of some £3 million. It was built within an architectural tradition emphasizing order and harmony.[29] At the centre of this work of art many hundreds of houses were built within this tradition by John Wood. Wood also added to the tradition his own culturally derived system of signs. And he created (constructed) architectural setpieces to emphasize that his construction of order and harmony derived, through the Judaic/Christian tradition, from God. Wood expected the citizens of Bath and visitors to it to absorb these historically determined Christian values of order and harmony and community, in moments of distraction, and to be shaped by them.[30]

---

[28] Walter Benjamin, *Illuminations* (1970; first published 1955), pp. 241−2.

[29] This section is based on R. S. Neale, *Bath 1680− 1850: A Social History* (1981).

[30] John Wood, *The Origin of Building: or, The Plagiarism of the Heathens Detected* (1741), *An Essay Towards a Description of Bath* (1742 and 1748), and *A Dissertation Upon the Orders of Columns* (1750).

However, in my book on Bath I argue that while there were many Christian sects in the city, some order, and a little harmony, there was no community. Different classes in Bath absorbed Bath differently. Among the labouring population violence and disorder was threaded through the fabric of life. Bath, I argue, was a valley of pleasure and, for the poor, a sink of iniquity. In the end, at least by the 1830s and 1840s, sufficient of the labouring population absorbed a message from its architecture and their experience of life within it to generate a class consciousness threatening the destruction of the order and harmony represented to them by Palladianism and Wood's construction of it.

If art in Bath, striving to evoke responses to it by absorption rather than by contemplation — like film and television — was not able to determine, at least in the manner expected of it, what was it that played the greater part in the determining of consciousness in Bath?

Bath as material production, as architecture, as a workplace and as art as distraction was determined, in the strong sense, by the relations of production of the agrarian capitalist mode of production. But what does this mean?

Around 1700, in Bath and its surrounding countryside, the material forces of production in their forms as land, labour and capital, for all intents and purposes, were inert. In this corner of England the autonomous, progressive thrust of the forces of production (Cohen, Shaw) was absent. There it was the relations of production that determined (set boundaries to and made possible) responses to the attractions of the market. To cut a long and interesting story short, Wood's constructions, his great contribution to eighteenth-century culture, were determined; determined by the size and nature of the market for Bath, by the entailing of its surrounding estates, by the kinds of building leases entailed estates could generate, by the structure of credit built upon those leases and the funds made available by the bill of exchange, by the legal and territorial powers of the corporation, and by incessant competition for the factors of production set in train within that set of relations of production characteristic of the agrarian capitalist mode of production. Without these conditions Wood's creations would have remained in miniature on paper. Moreover, the social organization of space in Bath, including the contributions that Wood was allowed to make to it, was marred by the contradictions inherent in those relations of production. In the end there was little order and harmony and no meaningful Christian tradition. Thus, those relations of production which made Wood's constructions possible also made it impossible for his expressed cultural purpose to be achieved; everything Wood did as an entrepreneur to make his production contribute to order and harmony contributed to disorder. In the hands of his son his firm went bankrupt.

But the hardest cut of all was that few of Wood's contemporaries could read his signs. As they absorbed his architecture in their *class* moments of distraction, they gave to his Bath their own readings of it; readings that did little to stem the flood of irreligious and economically and socially disruptive forces against which Wood, quixotically, set himself. Then subsequent generations lost all knowledge of his signs as Wood's constitutive contribution to architectural signification was not so much forgotten as ignored, dismissed by the epigones of architectural history as a farrago of nonsense. Instead, different *classes* in different periods 'absorbed' other messages from his material production. Now, in the twentieth century, historians and others attribute their own twentieth-century interest in 'town planning' to John Wood, and a visit to Bath is contemplated as a way of passing time or doing homage to that other voice of culture, Jane Austen.

Bath as construction, as architecture, as art, as an aspect of practical consciousness, as an homology for 'literature' and 'culture' was undoubtedly the product of an indissoluble process. Nevertheless, the determination of the relations of production in the mode of production is clear, clearer by far than any determination that may be claimed for the constructions themselves, despite their evident materiality and the possibility that their origins lay in residual areas of human experience untouched by the ideology of early eighteenth-century England. Yet it should also be clear that Wood's art was no mere reflection of the economic in the mode of production. His buildings, constructed at a moment in which the agrarian capitalist mode of production, during the heroic phase of primitive accumulation, was firmly in its ascendant, yet poised to collapse through the emergence of a more socially diffused entrepreneurial class, were utopian as well as ideological products: one might say that the utopian moment of *Scrutiny* was anticipated by Wood in the moment of *The Origin of Building*. But that moment, coterminous with the 'four moments', is repeated throughout English history; it is the product of the painfully slow and uneven development of capitalism in England. In short, architecture in Bath was not determining. Neither was it a reflection — what could it reflect? It was a crystallization of a moment in the historical process, a moment at the apogee of the heroic age of primitive accumulation — a dialectical image casting an uncomprehended shadow on the future; an image of fear.[31]

That is as it may be, you might say, determined as you may be by

---

[31] The idea of 'dialectical images' was a development of the Frankfurt School, most notably propagated by Adorno and Benjamin.

'literature', but, Bath, and its architecture cannot serve homologically for 'culture' or for 'literature' because 'literature' and 'culture' are precious and different. 'Literature' is the 'full, central immediate human experience'. But architecture! Architecture is about building duplexes! And, for the sake of peace and quiet, if Raymond Williams has not been able to persuade you about the materiality of cultural practice, I might agree. I might agree to look at 'literature' in the eighteenth century, if only the eighteenth century could be got to agree that it had one. Alternatively, I could agree to look at some aspects of its literary production. For example, I could ask how Bath appeared in such literary production because, try as you might in the eighteenth century, it was not possible to escape from Bath, at least, not for very long. Indeed, I am willing to bet — about a million to one — that in the eighteenth century, more people talked of Bath than thought of the Industrial Revolution! To put it briefly, Bath was a place for making and losing money, for health and illth, for seeking pleasure and finding boredom. In these various guises Bath made many appearances in literary production. Early in its life, as it was in the period before it was disciplined by John Wood and Jane Austen, it took the fancy of Daniel Defoe. Defoe wrote about Bath in *The Tour Through England and Wales*, a major source for all economic and social histories of eighteenth-century England, and in *Moll Flanders*, which like Samuel Pepy's *Diary*, is a necessary text for the study of sexual mores in the period. My question here is, are versions of and opinions about Bath in these eighteenth-century literary productions to be thought of as determining, whether in an ideological or constitutive sense? And, are these versions and opinions to be thought of as more determining than the architecture of the 'real' Bath because, like the 'real' Bath, they, too, may be thought of as having been produced? Or, can I find in Defoe's Bath a cultural meaning similar to that I find in Wood's Bath, namely a dialectical image of fear, bringing into sharper focus certain economic, social and cultural relationships otherwise obscured by appearance, but which was neither reflecting, determining nor yet constituting, precisely because its image was dialectical?

In *The Tour*, Defoe had little to say about Bath — for all his renowned powers of observation, Bath's economy seems to have eluded him. 'The best part (of its life) being but a barren subject, and the worst part meriting rather a satyr than a description'.[32] But then, in *Moll Flanders*, he had already written that satire, or something like it. In *Moll Flanders*, Defoe had written Bath for what it was; like his Robinson Crusoe it

---

[32] Daniel Defoe, *A Tour Through England and Wales* (London, 1948), Vol. II, p. 34.

embodied 'the abstracted spirit of improvement and simple economic advantage'.[33] We have Raymond Williams's word for it — although Williams also claims that these novels are defective because they fail to, 'consider their underlying social reality'.[34] This 'fact' Williams finds ironic because of the 'social reality' allegedly described by Defoe in *The Tour*. Yet, just as there is no 'social reality' of Bath in *The Tour*, there is more, much more, than a study of 'simple economic advantage' in *Moll Flanders*. The book and its main character are the paradigm of the market-place during the heroic age of primitive accumulation when absolute property and absolute self-interest, the twin pillars of market society, finally stripped away the velvet masking the spreading points of the 'cash nexus'.

Moll Flanders, who takes and is given the name of a parcel of lace, personifies free wage labour, she has nothing to sell but her labour. First she sells her body. Although at the outset she is uncertain about the true value of her labour — her asking price for her virginity was four or five guineas, a sum equal to the annual wage of a domestic servant — she learns quickly. As her career in prostitution unfolds, and in order to keep poverty at bay, she sells her person as well as her body. She commits adultery, bigamy and incest, and abandons her children. Subsequently she lies, cheats and steals. She steals from shopkeepers and the rich, but also from children and fellow workers. In the competitive world which she inhabits as an unskilled and marginalized worker, she becomes so isolated in her work that she rejoices at the hanging of one of her colleagues. Thus, throughout her life, whether in or out of work, she is alone, isolated, friendless and afraid, even when most happy. She says: 'Even in the greatest height of satisfaction I ever took, yet I had the terrible prospect of poverty and starving, which lay on me as a frightful spectre, so that there was no looking behind me.'[35]

It will probably surprise no one if I mention that Moll reached this 'greatest height of satisfaction' in Bath, nor if I add that it is in Bath that the tensions in her life are agonizing in their felicity.

Defoe allows Moll Flanders to arrive in Bath on her return from Virginia without virginity and virtue, and almost equally financially bankrupt. There, in Bath, she is 'entirely without friends' and, by drawing upon her little stock of capital, slowly 'bleeding to death'. Clearly for Defoe, Bath is, symbolically, the one place in England least suited to Moll's needs but best adapted to her abilities; it is a place where, 'Men find

---

[33] Raymond Williams, *The Country and the City* (St Albans, 1975), p. 81.
[34] Ibid., p. 81.
[35] Daniel Defoe, *Moll Flanders* (Harmondsworth, 1978), p. 128.

a mistress sometimes, but rarely look for a wife',[36] a market place for sexual labour wholly divorced from any constraints that might be imposed by a 'moral economy of sex'. Moll in Bath is alone, without resources (other than her labour) and in constant fear of approaching poverty. She is in a state of terror. So much so that she must make a quick sale or go under. Therefore, for the first time in her life Moll Flanders willingly and knowingly enters into a contract — as a whore. Hitherto, as the guarantee of a more or less just price for a sale, she had had or, thought she had, an offer of marriage. She thought she could live under the protection of the moral economy of sex. Therefore, the symbolism of this contract in Bath — whether Defoe intended it or not — is that Bath *was* a market place pure and simple; in it Moll Flanders sold her labour, John Wood his, prostituting himself in the dirt of the Avon cut. Yet, as with the final outcome of John Wood's work, Moll Flanders' new relationship in Bath, was dressed in benevolence. So we find, in Bath, that Moll who is not a wife acts like a wife, and that Moll who is a whore does not act like a whore — it is an accident when she does. So she lives for six years, much of it in Bath, gay but melancholy, neither wife nor whore, neither happy nor unhappy. In Bath appearance masks reality. Finally the approach to and retreat from death's door of the nameless man involved leads him to strip the aura of benevolence from the contract, revealing Moll Flanders to herself for what she is in reality — a free wage labourer — a whore with a broken contract and no recourse to the law, thrown back into the reserve army where she has been before and will be again, increasingly estranged from her fellow humans and without even the aura, the benevolence of the 'moral economy of sex' to protect her. In the not too distant future she will steal from the man she beds with and rejoice at the execution and transportation of her comrades. In short, the tension that is in Wood's Bath is there, too, in Defoe's *Moll Flanders*; thus Bath and Moll Flanders in Bath are dialectical images of the heroic age of primitive accumulation in England.

This notion of a dialectical image suggests that what should matter for a Marxist concerned with the relationship of 'literature' and 'culture' to economy *is* the determination of relations of production in the mode of production, and therefore the determination of *class* relations. The concept suggests that a possible alternative to the indissoluble processes of Williams's cultural materialism is not the base/superstructure model of vulgar Marxism with its emphasis on material production, nor yet that of Cohen and Shaw's representation of it. This possible alternative is a

---

[36] Ibid., p. 117.

L

materialist conception of history at the core of which lies the concept 'mode of production', incorporating forces of production enclosed and permeated by relations of production, *and* giving rise to *class* relations, and in which cultural productions as manifestations and productions of consciousness are located not as reflections of reality but as perceptions of reality, shaped by contradictions between forces and relations of production as experienced and perceived by men and women in actual *class* positions. These women and men give expression to their experiences using languages which are arbitrary and therefore, at least for the dominated *class*, alienating; and in which ideology *is* hegemonic. In fact, hegemonic ideology seems to be so pervasive and absorbent that non-ideological constitutive constructions tend either to disappear from memory or to become reincorporated into ideology; Brecht's and Beckett's drama become good box office, marxology good business, Bath a tourist attraction. Only in this sense may these counter-cultural products be thought of as 'determining', not because they are produced, but because they become reincorporated into an already 'determined' hegemonic ideology. It takes *class* consciousness to see them differently.

CONCLUSION

Cultural Materialism is Raymond Williams's answer to a fundamental question in Marxist studies; namely, how best to understand and express the relationships implied in Marx's proposition, 'It is not the consciousness of men that determines their being, but, on the contrary, their social being that determines their consciousness.' In his solution, Williams argues for the relative autonomy of 'culture' and claims for it and for literary production an equality with all other (material) determinations in the determination of consciousness. His argument flows along two apparently unrelated modes of thought. In the first he emphasizes the material nature of cultural production and seeks to locate its determinate qualities in that materiality. In the second he locates the determinate qualities of cultural production in areas of human experience untouched by an otherwise hegemonic ideology, in residual and emergent cultural practice and in human responses to biological continuities. Consequently, he denies that the mode of production has any general overriding determination. He writes, 'Determination of this kind . . . is in the whole social process itself and nowhere else: not in an abstracted "mode of production".' But tensions in the argument tend repeatedly to destroy its coherence.

Williams tries to hold these two strands of thought together through his argument about the conventional, therefore the constitutive nature of language — language is mixed with labour in every arena of human activity. Nevertheless, this reader is drawn uneasily from one pole of the argument to the other. A challenge to the idea of the conventional/constitutive nature of language, which suggests that language is best thought of as both arbitrary *and* constitutive, and is, therefore, an instrument of class and cultural power as well as of *class* consciousness, and which, thereby, brings cultural production of all kinds back within the relations of production and *class* relations in the mode of production, threatens the coherence of Williams's system. It shows the two modes of thought as the uncomfortable bedmates they are; a vulgar materialist Marxism on the one side, an idealism in the mould of the Young Hegelians on the other.

This inherent instability in cultural materialism may be overcome, and Williams's valuable insights into the processes of cultural production be preserved for Marxism, by stepping outside the limitations of the base/superstructure model. This would make it possible to abandon the structural imagery and terminology, and break free of the notion that it is the materiality of production that constitutes the determinate qualities of the mode of production. In which case the alleged determination flowing from the perceived materiality of cultural and literary production would have no status. Rather than deny the general overriding determination of the mode of production, through giving unwarranted attention to the materiality of production, a truly comprehensive Marxist analysis of 'indissoluble' relationships between economy and culture should give a central place to the production relations characteristic of various modes of production and sub-sets of modes of production. Thereby, it should also give due weight to *class* relations, which are poorly represented in cultural materialism. And it should employ a more complex and sophisticated *class* analysis than that characteristic of much Marxist cultural history.

What are required are analyses and descriptions of modes of production which can show how the residual, the emergent and the biological continuities, as they are manifested in specific social and cultural forms, may be related to what may well be a complex articulation of modes of production. This is no easy task. I do not pretend to have settled the problem through my account of relationships between the agrarian capitalist mode of production, architecture and the social organization of space in Bath, only briefly outlined in this chapter. Yet I believe that the notion, 'dialectical image', best encompasses and expresses the nature of relationships between economy and culture most likely to be identified in such Marxist analyses.

Such analyses and descriptions of the articulation of modes of production would be able to incorporate cultural production in all its forms —

architecture to literary production — as creative responses to the tensions and conflicts in *class* societies, as dialectical images. These are made images which bring certain relationships within any social formation or articulation of modes of production into sharper focus, or into the forefront of human consciousness, not as reflections of 'reality' but as multiple-faceted (at last two-sided) images. As products of human experience and consciousness these images are also elements in 'reality'. But they should not be mistaken for it. (As I have argued elsewhere, reality may only be theoretically constructed.) Accordingly, it may not be claimed that these images are determining in a strong sense because, as Williams rightly observes, they are material productions. They enter 'the indissoluble process' as images reinforcing or enhancing determinations located elsewhere in the articulation of modes of production or, sometimes, appear as challenging and critical appraisals of dominant *classes* and of ideology, as is the materialist conception of history itself. But they are always subject to alternative readings and to incorporation into an already determined hegemonic ideology. Because cultural materialism, through the significance it attributes to the evident materiality of cultural practice, threatens to prise loose determinate relationships between modes of production and cultural production, cultural materialism is itself on the way to such incorporation.

At this point I think I should draw attention to the greater importance given to class by Raymond Williams in a more recent book, *Culture* (1981), and to statements which suggest that he now acknowledges the determination of social relations.[37] Nevertheless, Williams continues to write of the residual, the emergent, biological continuities, relative autonomy, relative distance and of free-floating cultural movements in ways reminiscent of *Marxism and Literature*.[38] Moreover, in his recent essay on 'Culture' in *Marx: the First 100 Years* (1983), and although he again appears to concede more to Marx's theory as I have outlined it, Williams remains committed to his idea of the significance for a Marxist cultural theory of the materiality of cultural production. He writes: 'It is only from the most active senses of the material production of culture and of language as a social and material process that it is possible to develop the kind of cultural theory which can now be seen as necessary, and even central, in Marx's most general theory of human production and development.'[39] And he chides Marx for not developing such a materially

---

[37] Raymond Williams, *Culture* (1981), pp. 74, 103, 107, 201 – 3.

[38] Ibid., pp. 202 – 3, 204, also the essay on 'Culture', and footnote 39.

[39] Raymond Williams, 'Culture', in D. McLellan (ed.), *Marx: the First 100 Years* (1983), p. 54.

based cultural theory and criticizes other Marxist formulations, 'that actually blocked the inquiry'.[40] But this capacity to block Marxist enquiry, as I have said, is a characteristic shared by cultural materialism, at least as it is presented in his major work, *Marxism and Literature* and defended in *Politics and Letters*. Williams's critique of the concept, mode of production, and his substitution of the notion of the material and, therefore, the determining nature of cultural production, his emphasis on language as conventional and socially constitutive in a classless sort of way, and the relative autonomy which, in the absence of close analysis, he frequently allocates to cultural production, have the capacity to domesticate the materialist conception of history and perpetuate the moment of *Scrutiny*.

[40] Ibid., p. 55.

PO/X 122993 (September 1944)

11

PO/X 122993

The gap between the last chapter and this last one, and the rest of the book, is as impassable as the Grand Canyon, according to some I take to be writers of Marxist history. In their view, the historical terrains or either side of the divide have almost nothing in common. On the one side lies the barren waste of professional, given history. On the other the arcadian world of popular memory. In the wastelands, predatory ugly historians and sociologists gobble up the people's yesterdays. They tell 'us what our explanations *should* be, fitting *our* "facts" to *his* theories, presenting our experience back to us, sometimes in unrecognisable forms'.[1] They write a (Marxist) history of the past (rather than the present) in which 'there is little or no evidence that the historian's theorization of "the people" was actually adequate either for a contemporary politics or for a historically informed explanation of their own conjuncture.'[2] On the arcadian side are the people, their popular memory realized in community history, popular autobiography, properly reconstructed oral history, and working-class writing generally, creating conditions for 'the formation of a popular memory that is socialist, feminist and anti-racist'.[3] Sometimes I wonder whether there is any point in trying to build even the most rudimentary bridge to push my mule across, or in trying to scramble a way through, the massed cohorts would hammer at my fingers even as I clawed my way towards a tolerable straight line.

Popular memory is a poor thing. It appears in many guises. From the standpoint of writing Marxist history it may be perverse; conservative, nationalistic, individualistic, self-deprecating, racist, sexist, and always myopic and full of silences.

---

[1] Centre for Contemporary Cultural Studies, *Making Histories: Studies in History-writing and Politics* (London, 1982), p. 240. See also p. 222.

[2] Ibid., p. 74.

[3] Ibid., p. 214.

One June evening in 1981 I drove from Norwich to Cambridge. It was getting late when I gave a lift to a truck driver who was on his way to pick up a truck for delivery back to Norwich. He told me his story. He was an ex-soldier, married with three children. Since leaving the army, 12 months earlier, he had been made redundant twice, the last time from BRS. To make a living, he and two mates had set up in the highly competitive business of delivering trucks to buyers. The only way they could make it pay was to hitch free rides to the pick-up points. Tomorrow, he said, the three of them would hitch from Norwich to Bristol then deliver three trucks back to Norwich. It would take them all day to get to Bristol, and they would gross £50 each. They had no other jobs lined up but lived from day to day waiting for telephone calls — hence the lateness of the pick-up. I sympathized with him and talked about his plight as symptomatic of England under Thatcher. 'Yes', he said, 'but if the socialists get in I'd rather emigrate to Australia.'

The advocates of popular memory know all this, so they say. Consequently they urge us to theorize about it. It is, they say, 'more a question of whose problems you set out to study and resolve [for then] . . . the decisive question is the standpoint of projects and the connections they require.'[4] Even so, the problem remains, 'how to organize such a connection politically, how to generalize skills of secondary analysis and how to connect this popular education to other daily struggles'.[5] To this practical and theoretical question popular memorists have no non-interventionist answer. Ugliness has many appearances, and they are as bad burnt as scalded. You either give 'the people' a made history (which they may read as they wish), or, if you are a Marxist of sorts, you give them the theoretical code for making their own. In which case their 'people's history' could become a cabbage planter's line. Clearly the problem of cultural power, of intervention by determined muleteers; writers, teachers, intellectuals (whether women or men, Marxist or non-Marxist) cannot easily be resolved. No matter how you dress it up, or at what stage it occurs, intervention *is* intervention. In practice, in writing Marxist history, the mulishness of writers, teachers and intellectuals, can only be eased by the quality of human relations involved, by leaving the final form and content to the history writer, the worker or the shop floor, as it were, whether that worker be a people, a student, or even an 'ugly' professional. And a thousand flowers may bloom. There is nothing peculiarly Marxist about such a practice.

---

⁴ Ibid., p. 251.
⁵ Ibid., p. 251.

On the other hand, such history writing may claim no privilege. Popular memory as the basis for *class* consciousness would have to be recognized for what it is, barely 60 years old at any time and structured by an already determined ideology and cultural practice. The tradition of the dead generations does weigh like a nightmare on the brains of the living. This is true of my own fragment of autobiography. Consequently it has no privilege and is subject to interrogation, like the rest.

Popular memory has no privilege on two grounds other than its possible perversity. The first is, it has more than a touch of the genetic fallacy about it. Take my 'given' history of 'people' in Bath as an example. I began it, I now discover, labouring on what is referred to (with approval) as a 'people's history'. Although I was then a teacher, I was also recently a marine, a labourer in a bakery, and a navvy — still 'a people' entitled to write 'a people's history'. Then I wrote as a part-time student at Bristol University — still a teacher, and, presumably, still 'a people'. But, I finished it professionally engaged as a professor of economic history. That, I gather, turns me into an ugly historian and renders my work suspect and of doubtful value — what *is* the point of given history? Better to have remained 'a people' (as in 1944—7). Except that I only began to learn about *class* and *class* consciousness *after* 1947, as a student of economic and social history with an FETS grant the award of which hinged on that one year in sixth form I remember later in this chapter. The writing of Marxist history was a question of time.

The second objection to granting privilege to popular memory is the 'presentism' inherent in its brevity — a 'presentism' characteristic of Hindess and Hirst's *Pre-Capitalist Modes of Production.* Yet to castigate those who try to write Marxist history for writing about the past rather than the present, and to press the immediacy and primacy of popular memory and its 60 years, is to favour both a short journey *and* a straight line. It turns the materialist conception of history into an historical convenience. Marxism and Marxist history writing are nothing if they are not both historical (in the long sense) and theoretical. And I claim that my yesterdays are historically and theoretically structured, even when told as stories, and it is their substance that should be interrogated. It is these things (and the eating) that should create value in Marxist history writing, not the author's status as a people or a professor (even though one may be both), nor the assumed primacy of popular memory.

The body of this chapter is a fragment of popular autobiography. It is based almost entirely on memory, a little reflected upon. It is shaped by my understanding of the materialist conception of history and the idea of determination as it has arisen throughout the book, and in the previous chapter, but, I hope, not too obtrusively. It touches the earlier parts of the book through its connection with the historical journey towards my today, which I unknowingly began in 1947. It brings my private yesterdays close to my historical ones. As they rub shoulders, history becomes memory, memory history. Although the mode of apprehension varies, I experience them all in one lifetime and today. There is no divide (and no privilege). As their images jostle and tumble for expression, like cherubs in a Thornhill painting, *all* are my yesterdays: Anne Phillips's three skewers and a larkspit; Vera Brittain's glove; Mary Blathwayt's collection of *Votes for Women*; my mother's belly button; Moll Flanders, and my family of 'free wage' labourers; Chandos's twitchings; John Wood's illusions and bad drains; Clarke's reason and revelation; the dead at the Battle of Wincanton; Fort George, and Adam Smith on property and education; a bourgeoisie barely out of nappies; Jane Austen and the proprieties of Mansfield Park, and Antigua; Martha Abraham's wages and bastard child, and alienation; London artisans; 'Charlie's' Clarion Cycling Club; Marx on imperialism and Ireland; the McKendrys — my wife's family, who went from Scotland to Ireland in the seventeenth century and returned to England, during the 'Troubles', through marriage to a sergeant in the Seaforth Highlanders; Hillgrove, its antimony, water supply and dead babies; Cheltenham Workhouse; the unemployed man and his dog; war and Hong Kong, and sacks of grass; Little Moscows; Ginger, and Bacon's Excelsior Emulation Ladder; Raymond Williams on Marxist theory, and structure and agency, (even *New Left Review*); Achnacarry; Orgreave. When they insist on having their say I usually let them have their way, making the best I can of them as they flash up in memory making a long journey and a circuitous one. This last chapter is end and beginning of that journey, and part-fulfilment of a promise made to external students enrolled in a history writing course, and I have scarcely begun its telling.

As I finished this last chapter, an unsolicited book arrived in my pigeon-hole (sent by a capitalist publisher), presumably because one or more of a trio of sociologists thought I needed to be told, because they had 'proved' the 'dominant ideology thesis' to be false, that there were no ideological or educational or intellectual processes involved in the incorporation of the working classes into the capitalist mode of production. In their view, ideology only did something to or for the dominant class.[6] This event invites me to make explicit that which I hoped would remain implicit in this fragment of autobiography. The story I have to tell (in my round about way) is about my own incorporation through family, school,

---

[6] Nicholas Abercrombie, Stephen Hill, Bryan S. Turner, *The Dominant Ideology Thesis* (London, 1984).

nationalism, and war. Some aspects of this process were very deliberate indeed, done to me through a web of social institutions.

The story I tell in the rest of this book is part of my attempt through writing Marxist history, to throw off the worst theoretical, linguistic, intellectual and emotional inhibitions of that incorporation. And I am still incorporated. Although, in this chapter, I do not claim to speak for a generation, I do believe my experience was far from unique. I guess it was shared in general, if not in its particulars, by all pre-war working-class scholarship boys and girls, and by many who became grown-ups during the war. Indeed, my wife's experience of educational and ideological incorporation from her unskilled, Midland, working-class family and background, is far more startling than mine. She has yet to write her own story. I can only say to the capitalist publisher (contributing his mite towards incorporating Marxology as good business), and to the authors, experience is against you.

My own yesterdays begin with the humiliation and sexual ignorance of my mother, Alice Amelia Johnson, the skill of my father, Horace Stanley, and the political memories of my grandfather, Charlie. My mother's story is an unhappy one. She was born in Cheltenham in 1900. Her mother, Mary Ann, died when she was about five years old. Her father, a builder's labourer, remarried and the family was broken up. What love remained was stretched to its limits. Unlike another, happier Alice, Alice and her younger sister were forcibly tumbled out of a familiar world into one entirely brillig, in which slithy toves did gyre and gimble, in which the borogroves were mimsy and the mome raths always outgrabed. As they plummeted into darkness, some of the events in Alice's life were caught by the fine mesh of procedures for enforcing the principle of less eligibility, decreed by the Government of England in the Poor Law Act of 1834, and laid down by the Board of Guardians of the Cheltenham Poor Law Union. As a result some of the 'facts' of her working-class experience may still be found in historical records. These 'facts' do not speak for themselves. Even my arrangement and interrogation of them is barely enough to squeeze a murmur of hurt and protest out of them. Their meaning was locked away in my mother's heart for the rest of her life, their voices unheard outside the walls of our house, uncomprehended even there.

On the afternoon of Saturday 27 April 1907, Thomas Johnson stepped out of his house, number 4, Hereford Court, in the meanest part of Cheltenham. With him were his two daughters, Alice Amelia, aged seven and Ellen May, aged four. The three of them walked to the Porter's Lodge at the Cheltenham Workhouse in Swindon Road, just up from St Pauls, the men's teacher-training college. (What the girls prattled about as they walked is not recorded.) At five past two the porter, on an order from the Board, admitted the two girls, entering their names in his black bound *Admissions and Discharge Book*, along with those of two other children and 11 aging and mostly homeless paupers for the fifth week of the quarter ending Midsummer 1907. Then the Workhouse door closed on them.[7]

The two girls were probably taken directly to The Elms, the Union's home for children, standing in the workhouse grounds. Probably, too, they were to be clothed in the black of the Union soon to be decided upon by the House and Visiting Committee: black dress, black woollen stockings, black cape, and, for the younger women, a black sailor hat relieved only by coloured ribbons.[8] Not until March 1908 was the matron to report that the children were to be given a second suit of clothes so that they would not have to wear their best (and only) suit of clothes at play.[9] So, when she went to school, Alice and everyone around her was reminded of her pauper status by the big WH burnt black into the sides of the boots they gave her to wear. The humiliation remained with her 50 years later. Ellen May (always May to my mother) was too young to go to school. Children her age were kept in a separate nursery. According to the Board's instructions this had to be, 'dry, spacious, light and well ventilated.' And 'In no case should the care of young children be entrusted to infirm or weakminded inmates' they said, 'unless young children are placed under responsible supervision they cannot be said to be "properly taken care of", and the committee should never fail to make careful inquiry under this head.'[10] Yet, in 1905, the House and Visiting Committee had refused Mrs Grayton at The Elms extra paid assistance to cope with an increase in the number of children. They were, 'satisfied that Mrs Grayton could manage to do the work with the pauper assistance the Matron undertook to supply'.[11] A few months after the committee had turned down Mrs Grayton's appeal, an inmate complained that an inmate helper had smacked one of the children and used bad language. The committee decided there were no grounds for the complaint and left the matter in the hands of the

[7] All dates and entries are to be found in the *Porter's Admission and Discharge Book 1906—1090*, G/CH 92, Gloucestershire Record Office.

[8] *House and Visiting Committee, Minute Book, 1903—1912*, 8 June 1907, G/CH 8c 4, GRO.

[9] Ibid., 9 March 1908.

[10] *Cheltenham Union Handbook*, 1904, G/CH—3/3, GRO.

[11] *House and Visiting Committee, Minute Book.* 15 July 1905.

matron.[12] It was likely, therefore, that May was put in the care of a pauper inmate. And scarce any visiting allowed — two hours twice a month. May's diet, according to the Workhouse dietary, was half a pint of milk, 4 ounces of bread and half an ounce of cheese in every eight-hour period. Alice, as a grown-up seven year-old was given the same diet as for women: 6 ounces of bread and 1 pint of gruel at breakfast and supper, 6 ounces of bread and 1½ ounces of cheese, or 5 ounces of bread and 1 pint of soup for dinner.[13] The senseless weight and wonderland of the Government's and the Board's insistence on the principle of less eligibility (and all the Victorian virtues) is revealed in a comparison of Alice's diet with that given to all Poor Law Officers in 1905. What tea parties there must have been in the Workhouse! What room for Alice at the table? What and whose the crime?

House and Visiting Committee Minute Book[14]
9th September 1905

Officers Dietary

3. The Committee Resolved to recommend the adoption of the following revised Dietary for the Officers of the Workhouse.

Officers Weekly Dietary

	Male Officers	Female Officers
Bread	6 lbs	5 lbs
Meat (including Veal, Pork, Fish, rabbit, or sausages)	5 lbs	4 lbs

	Male & Female Officers
Bacon	1 lb
Butter	½ lb
Cheese	½ lb
Tea, Coffee, or Cocoa	6 oz
Lump Sugar	1 lb
Moist Sugar	½ lb
Rice, Sago, Tapioca, or Cornflour	½ lb

---

[12] Ibid., 2 Nov. 1905.
[13] *Cheltenham Union Book*, 1904.
[14] *House and Visiting Committee, Minute Book, 1903—1912*, p. 114, 9 Sept. 1905.

Suet	¼ lb
Flour	1 lb
Currants & Raisins	½ lb
Jam & Marmalade	½ lb
Eggs	4
Salt, Pepper, Vinegar, Mustard & Pickles	
Potatoes and Vegetables as required	
Milk	7 pts

Extra for each Night Nurse
2 oz tea   ½ lb Sugar weekly
Mutton chop or 1 egg per diem

On 6 July at 5.10 p.m., the two girls were discharged by their aunt, Mrs Sexton, and taken to her house at 65 Rutland Street, only minutes away from the Workhouse. But at 11.30 on the morning of Monday 26 August she took them back to the Workhouse again. A month later, on Monday 23 September, they were again discharged, this time by their father. May was then five years old. The time 9.35 a.m. After Christmas 1907, the two girls, deserted by their father in Grove Street, were taken to the Porter's Lodge by their aunt and admitted to the Workhouse for a third time. It was 11.00 on the morning of Monday 30 December. Four days later the Board of Guardians resolved, 'That Mr T. Lloyd, Relieving Officer, be instructed to obtain a warrant against Thomas Johnson for deserting his two children Alice Amelia and Ellen May Johnson and allowing them to become chargeable to the Union.'[15] On 25 January 1908, Thomas Johnson collected the girls from the Workhouse. Alice was eight years old. The Porter's Admission and Discharge book, extant only from 1906—09, shows no further re-admission of the girls.[16]

After the girls had been taken from the workhouse for the third time, May was taken and brought up by little 'granny' Salt and Alice went into her aunt's family where, she said, 'there were always more mealtimes than meals.' After the war had started and as soon as she could, Alice borrowed her cousin Gwen's birth certificate in order to join the Women's Royal Army Corps. As a cook or cook's assistant 'Gwen' Johnson met my father, then 26 years old and a sergeant in the RFC. They married at the war's end. My father called my mother 'Gwen' for the rest of his life.

In 1919 my older sister was born, my mother believing until the last that the baby would appear out of her belly button. Surprised by labour

[15] *Cheltenham Union Minute Book,* 28 June 1906 to 30 Jan. 1907, p. 422, G/CH, 8a/38, GRO.

pains and alarmed at the failure of her belly to open, she finally asked the visiting midwife where the baby would come out. 'The way it went in', said the midwife. My mother's belly button, Vera Brittain's glove, the Suffragette's story — these say all that needs be said about sexuality and sexual relations in the world in which I was about to be born.

My father was a carpenter and joiner. As a sergeant in the RFC he had flown as a passenger at the front and across the channel, testing by feel and sound, the frames of aeroplanes newly delivered or repaired after combat. When I was ten or eleven I sensed his pride in his skill, and I believe I knew that he was exploited. His skill as a craftsman was made plain to me in the furniture he crafted for our front room, and in the evenings he spent setting out patterns and estimates for timber to be used in building a circular staircase and oriel windows for a job in London. He was the firm's setter-out, possessing a rare and valuable skill. He knew it. The firm knew it. His only payment beyond his weekly wage was a travelling allowance when he went to London to supervise the work on the staircase and oriel windows. His reward was pride in his skill and the work he turned out. Yet, in his lifetime, his trade declined from bowler hat to cloth cap, and he never thought to turn me into a carpenter. Sometimes I met him from work or took him a meal when he worked overtime. The timber smells of his workshop, remembered in pine furniture shops and Australian timber mills, remind me of what I might have been. My father always refused to take the foremanship offered him, preferring the fellowship of his workmates, and to sack no one. When he told me this I think I must have loved him, but never told him so. He died too young, when I was historically immature. I never did find out where he built the circular staircase. But I kept his tools.

---

[16] There is an epilogue to this story. In February 1907 a submission by the Cheltenham Board of Guardians to the Royal Commission on the Poor Laws and Relief of Distress stated:

> The Workhouse has ceased to be deterrent to certain classes of the community. The standard of comfort in Poor Law Institutions has steadily risen in recent years and the Workhouse Test is consequently weakened as the condition of the pauper is now gradually being made more eligible than that of the independent poor.
>
> Poor Law relief is now often applied for with no further motive than the settlement of family disputes and disagreements.

Since the case of Thomas Johnson and his family seems to confirm the opinion expressed in the second paragraph, Alice and May, you might say, have a place in history after all. The reader may judge whether the opinion expressed in the first paragraph was relevant to their predicament.

My father was one of three brothers, all carpenters and joiners, sons of a cabinet maker. Their father and my grandfather, Algernon (Charlie) Neale was born at 42 Chester Street, Lambeth, in 1864. According to the 1861 Census his father, Gregory, came from Norwich and his mother, Julia, daughter of a shoemaker, from Bermondsey. In 1861 she was already, at thirty-two, the mother of six children.[17] Gregory, like his father before him, was a coachmaker. He had built coaches for Prince Albert, according to my grandfather, after completing his apprenticeship with a two-year spell in France. After migrating to London Gregory seems to have built up his own business. My grandfather remembered his father going to work in top hat and frockcoat, changing into his working clothes at his workshop. In 1873 the business closed down (could it have been a result of the agricultural crisis of the 1870s and the consequent contraction of landed income?). Algernon was sent to work at nine years of age, subsequently becoming a cabinet maker. Because of his belief in his Scots origin and his life in London, in Lambeth and Camden Town, he once described himself to me as 'neither Jew nor Gentile', but he was a Londoner through and through. When, as a twenty-one year old student of economic and social history, I began to know him as a person, he was Charlie Neale, a big, stiff, eighty-three year old, usually to be found on a Sunday morning in the bar of his local, where he had been every Sunday morning of my childhood, when we called on my diminutive grandmother, who always welcomed us with Dairy Milk Toffees from a bowl standing on a table draped to the floor with a plush green tablecloth. Charlie was lived history, part of the yesterdays I had scarcely begun to recover through the accident of economic and social history.

When still a young man Charlie attended meetings of the Battersea branch of the Social Democratic Federation. He told me of sessions addressed by Tom Mann and of a seeming acquaintance with Eleanor Marx Aveling (and was surprised and delighted that I knew anything at all about them). And he read Dickens. Towards the close of the century, in Camden Town, he was a member of a *Clarion* cycling club distributing the socialist message of Blatchford's *Clarion* as far afield as Brighton. ('His excuse' said my grandmother.) As I read Blatchford's *Merrie England* today, I reach back to Charlie.[18]

About this time Charlie seems to have sensed the writing on the wall for his craft being etched by new technology. Having moved as a cabinet-maker from Lambeth to Wandsworth, where my father was born in 1892,

---

[17] My grandfather told me his parents were Scots.
[18] *Merrie England,* By Nunquam (London, 1893), pp. 15—16.

MERRIE ENGLAND

THE problem of life, Mr Smith, is, 'Given a country and a people, show | how the people can make the most | of | the | country and themselves.' Before we go on, let us try to judge how far we in Britain have succeeded in answering the problem.

The following are facts which no man attempts to deny:—

1. Large numbers of honest and industrious people are badly fed, badly clothed, and badly housed.

2. Many thousands of people die every year from preventable diseases.

3. The average duration of life amongst the population is unnaturally short.

4. Very many people, after lives of toil, are obliged to seek refuge in the workhouse, where they die despised and neglected, branded with the shameful brand of pauperism.

5. It is an almost invariable rule that those who work hardest and longest in this country are the worst paid and the least respected.

6. The wealthiest men in our nation are men who never did a useful day's work.

7. Wealth and power are more prized and more honoured than wisdom, or industry, or virtue.

8. Hundreds of thousands of men and women, willing to work, are unable to find employment.

9. While on the one hand wages are lowered on account of overproduction of coal, of cotton, and of corn, on the other hand many of our working people are short of bread, of fuel, and of clothing.

10. Nearly all the land and property in this country are owned by a few idlers, and most of the laws are made in the interests of those few rich people.

11. The national agriculture is going rapidly to ruin to the great injury and peril of the State.

12. Through competition millions of men are employed in useless and undignified work, and all the industrial machinery of the nation is thrown out of gear, so that one greedy rascal may overreach another.

And we are told, Mr Smith, that all these things must remain as they are, in order that you may be able to 'get a living.'

What sort of a living do you get?

Your life may be divided into four sections: Working, eating, recreation, and sleeping.

As to work. You are employed in a factory for from 55 to 70 hours a week. Some of your comrades work harder, and longer, and in worse places. Still, as a rule, it may be said of all your class that the hours of labour are too long, that the labour is monotonous, mechanical, and severe, and that the surroundings are often unhealthy, nearly always disagreeable, and in many cases dangerous.

Do you know the difference, Mr Smith, between 'work' and 'toil'? It is the difference between the work of the gardener and the toil of the navvy—between the work of the wood carver and the toil of the wood chopper.

We hear a good deal of talk about the idleness of the labouring classes and the industry of the professional classes. There is a difference in the *work*. The surgeon, or the sculptor, following the work of his *choice*, may well work harder than the collier, drudging for a daily wage.

An artist loves his work, and sees in it the means of winning fame, perhaps fortune; an artisan sees in his toil a dull mechanical task, to be done for bread, but never to be made to yield pleasure, or praise, or profit.

As a rule, Mr Smith, your work is hard and disagreeable.

Now, what are your wages?

I don't mean how many shillings a week do you get; but what *life* do you get as the reward of your toil?

You may get fifteen shillings a week, or a pound, or twenty-five or thirty-five shillings, or two pounds; but the question is how do you *live*? What will your money *buy*?

As I have shown already, you do not get enough leisure, nor enough fresh air, nor enough education, nor enough health, and your town is very ugly and very dirty and very dull. But let us go into details.

I have often seen you, Mr Smith, turn up your nose with scorn at the sight of a gipsy. Yet the gipsy is a healthier, a stronger, a braver and a wiser man than you, and lives a life more pleasant and free and natural than yours.

Not that the gipsy is a model citizen; but you may learn a great deal from him; and I doubt whether there is anything he could learn from you.

And now let us see how you live. First of all, in the matter of food. Your diet is not a good one. It is not varied enough, and nearly all the things you eat and drink are adulterated.

I am much inclined to think that a vegetarian diet is the best, and I am sure that alcoholic liquors are unnecessary. But this is by the way. If you *do* drink beer and spirits it would be better to have them pure. At present nearly all your liquors are abominable.

But there is one thing about your diet worse even than the quality of the food, and that is the cookery. Mrs Smith is an excellent woman, and I hereby make my bow to her, but she does not know what cookery means.

John Smith, it is a solemn and an awful truth, one which it pains me to utter, but you never ate a beef steak, and you never saw a cooked potato.

God strengthen thy digestion, John, 'tis sore tried. Oh, the soddened vegetables, the flabby fish, the leathery steak, and juiceless joint, I know them, John. Alas! Cookery is an *art*, John, and almost a lost art in this country; or shall we say, an art unfound?

Poor Mrs Smith gets married and faces the paste-board and the oven with the courage of desperation, and the hope of ignorance. She resembles the young man who had never played the fiddle, but had no doubt he could play it if he tried. And sometimes he *does* try, and so Mrs Smith tries to cook.

From food we will turn to clothing. Oh, John, John Smith, it is pitiful. Do you know the meaning of the words 'form' and 'colour'? Look at our people's dress. Observe the cut of it, the general drabness, grayness, and gloom. Those awful black bugles, John, those horrific sack coats, those deadly hats and bonnets, and they do say, John that crinoline—Ah, heaven! That we should call these delicate creatures ours and not their fashion plates. John, the dresses, but especially the Sunday clothes, of the British working-classes are things too sad for tears.

Costume, John, should be simple, healthy, convenient, and beautiful. Modern British costume is none of these.

This is chiefly because the fashion of our dress is left to fops and tailors, whereas it ought to be left to artists and designers.

But besides the ugliness of your dress, John, it is also true that it is *mean*. It is mean because hardly anything you wear is what it pretends to be, because it is adulterated and jerry-made, and because it is insufficient. Yes, John, in nearly all your houses there is, despite our factory system, a decided scarcity of shirts and socks and sheets and towels and table linen.

Come we now to the home. Your houses, John, are not what they should be. I do not allude to the inferior cottage—*that* is beneath notice. Here in Manchester we have some forty thousand houses unfit for habitation. But let us consider the abode of the more fortunate artisan. It has many faults. It is badly built, badly arranged, and badly fitted. The sanitation is bad. The rooms are much too small. There are no proper appliances for cleanliness. The windows are not big enough. There is a painful dearth of light and air. The cooking appliances are simply barbarous.

Again, the houses are very ugly and *mean.* The streets are too narrow. There are no gardens. There are no trees. Few working-class families have enough bedrooms, and the bathroom is a luxury not known in cottages.

In fine, your houses are ugly, unhealthy, inconvenient, dark, ill-built, ill-fitted, and dear.

thence to Camden Town, he retrained as a wood-working machinist and moved to Southall, then a semi-rural working-class suburb in West London, and into factory work in 1905. By the time he retired, and unlike my father, he was foreman at his workplace. Even so, for many years, the house in which he brought up his three sons and two daughters was a three-bedroomed tunnel-backed terraced house. It had a bay window on the front ground floor and a small railed-in front garden. There was a built-in coal fired copper in the scullery, an outside lavatory, and a tin bath hanging on the outside wall in the backyard. At the bottom of the narrow back garden of 45 Lea Road, was the high brick wall of the 'Tube' factory. When my grandfather moved to better things, sometime after 1927, my parents left the cramped flat where I was born and moved into number 45. I lived the first nine or ten years of my life in Lea Road.

Charlie put all of his sons to the trade of carpenter and joiner and all three joined the RFC in that capacity during the First World War. One died in the Middle East. My uncle Arthur was badly injured swinging the propeller of an airplane to get it started. My father served in England and France, as I have said. My grandfather also expected his sons to develop some creative or performing talent apart from their work. The uncle who was killed was put to wood-carving, uncle Arthur developed as a water colour painter — I have a water colour of his lions to this day — and my father and my aunt Winnie learned the piano. The piano was my father's claim to a leading place in the family at Christmas time, at work on work's outings, and among a circle of friends in Lea Road, the Garretts up the street, the Browns across the way, window-cleaners both. The piano was parties and singing and laughter. My father was always in demand. Photographs show him as a young man wearing a jaunty bowler. Until his family grew too big and times too hard he ran a motor-cycle and side car. My older sister, Gwen, remembers rides into the countryside. In the end, by the time I and my brother Eric were born in 1927 and 1932, the motor-bike had been replaced by a bike, the jaunty bowler by a cloth cap.

Four generations of 'free' wage labourers (Prothero's and Crossick's London artisans), and a family of builder's labourers from Wales, marked in my mother by the stigma of the Workhouse, were my family yesterdays. All shaped in their experience by the vagaries, crises, and technological change in the capitalist mode of production. Unlike Moll Flanders and those she represented, their 'freedoms' were inhibited by respectability (although Gregory and Julia remained unmarried for three years after the birth of their first child) and constrained by their pride in skilled labour. Charlie Neale, whose watch I possess, whose name lives in my second son, who appropriated Dickens as his own, and who came as close to Marx as an English artisan could, was their epitome.

In the 1920s and 1930s I knew none of this. My small world was bounded by house, street, school, Sunday school; occasional exciting visits to London for pantomime and Jubilee; trips down the river to Southend; Sunday school outings, and summer camps with the Church Lads' Brigade at Bognor. Mostly there was the street. It was where we lived. I remember little of school up to the age of ten, except the streets along the way. According to season we marbled our way to school along the gutters, skipped and hop-scotched along the pavements, conkered in groups at street corners, and whipped and topped along in the streets themselves. When nothing was in season, or we tired of what was, we hung daring from the backs of trucks and carts to shouts of 'Whip-behind' from those less fortunate or nimble than ourselves. School for me was all success. There I was, eight years old, at Clifton Road Junior Boys', standing at the top of Bacon's Excelsior Emulation Ladder, the Union Jack in my right hand and a pennant in my left, inscribed, 'RONALD NEALE 139/150'. At the bottom were 38 F. HITCHCOCK ab and 37 K. MOSES 25/150ab. At eight, the process of separation was already at work, authenticated by W. A. Bennett, classteacher, and G. C. J. Butler, headmaster. For me there were no tensions, no traumas, no canings. None that I remember. No memory either of the celebrations when Southall became a borough and I was chosen from all the schools to present a bouquet to the first mayoress, except a photograph tells me so. A scrubbed, shining cherub. I must have liked school and school smiled on me. They certainly worked on my dropped aitches and glottal stop.

The journey from school was much like the journey out, only there were hundreds and thousands, sherbet dabs, liquorice sticks, spanish wood and coloured gob-stoppers, bigger than your gob, all to be bought with pennies and ha'pennies, or lusted after through shop windows buzzing with flies. Out of school and after tea there was Shipman's corner. Shipman's was the corner shop where, every Monday dinner-time, I bought two-penny worth of mustard pickle and pickled cabbage to eat with our cold meat and mashed potatoes. Monday was washing day. Yellow and red, the pickles were kept in great stone storage jars and ladled out into bowls to be carried home, and dipped into. Monday's dinner! Shipman's corner was our theatre. Two Garretts, three or four Neales, a bevy of Dairys, and others I cannot remember gathered there for charades. Charades was a performed word game involving honour, organization and co-operation across all age groups. One team went round the corner out of sight and sound of the other, agreed on a word or phrase or film title, and settled on how to mime it in three or four acts. Then they reappeared to give their performance. When the rival team correctly guessed the word or phrase, it was their turn to go round the corner. Periodically we would overflow from Shipman's corner into the street to play skipping with the longest rope you ever saw, British Bulldog, Re-leaso, Tin Can Copper, Kingy, and more sedately, cricket.

On special occasions we organized fairs. At our end of the street, up against the 'Tube' wall we set out fag-cards to be won by flicking them down with other fag cards flicked at them from a pavement width away. The winner also taking those flicked cards which had failed in the attempt — it paid to have a heavy smoker in the family, or 'Giz a fag card, mister' outside tobacconist shops or in picture queues. There, too, we had hop-scotch and marbles and whips and tops and conkers and fives and skipping. We had an exchange for fag-cards and comics, skipping contests, hand stands against the wall, roller skates, and rides in wheel barrows. When bonfire night came along there were other uses for wheel barrows, as guys were wheeled everywhere — 'penny for the guy, mister?' On the day itself there were bonfires, tin hand-warmers swung on wires, potatoes burned in their jackets, and fireworks. As winter came there were slides in the street and on the cut. Saturday mornings there was the 'twopenny rush', pictures at the 'Gem': Laurel and Hardy, Superman, Tarzan, The Three Stooges, Tom Mix, The Bowery Boys — all the heroes and situations for a life-time of street games. Saturday afternoons there were the grown-up pictures; two full length pictures and a half-hour live show for sixpence — half price for children, hand out-stretched, holding money, 'Take us in wiv yer mister?'

My special friend in all this was Ginger. Ginger must have been down a step or two from us in social status. He lived in a council house. And was seen as a bad influence. I suspect, now, that he was probably well down the rungs of Bacon's Excelsior Emulation Ladder, although I can't remember his name to find out. Across the road from Shipman's was another corner shop much grander than Shipman's. We never shopped there. Alongside one of its great expanses of shop window was a street gas lamp. One late afternoon, a Sunday, I think, me and Ginger did one of our 'dares'. We tossed a housebrick to each other, over the top of the gas lamp. The risk and the joy were immense and inseparable, not only was there the gas lamp but the shop window, too! What we had in mind happened. One of us missed going over the top, and we ran like the wind with the shopkeeper after us. Ginger escaped over a fence into his own garden. I was trapped. Then came the police and a talking to, and a beating from my father urged on by my mother. Ginger got off scot-free. 'Silly old nosey-bugger' he said his father said when he heard that the shopkeeper had told the police of Ginger's part. Even then, I think, I felt the weight and unfairness of respectability!

Respectability had also affected me hardly in the affair of Jean Dairy's garden shed. Surrounded by cardboard boxes, an old mattress and this and that, Jean Dairy and me played doctors. We took off our clothes and put clips and pegs all over each other, on our nipples and between our legs. Engrossed in our sensations we didn't see my sister peering through the window as she called for me to come home. 'They're doing dirty things! They're doing dirty things!' she danced. When the story got back to my parents my father beat me. The only other beating I remember; my mother urging my father to lay on heavily and looking sour. Jean Dairy, like Ginger, wasn't punished, or so she told me. But, then, the Dairys were never quite us. After that I kept my distance. I am sometimes tempted to understand these two occasions, vivid in memory, as instances of my parents' internalization of the values of respectability and their unconscious perpetuation of the two proprieties, property and sexual privacy and shame, upon which their society depended for its very existence. But my feelings at the time were simply fear and unfairness. I would have preferred to have been Ginger and Jean. I would need to know them now to know whether I have any greater respect for property and privacy than they, and how these things affected our lives.

The street was also where I played at work. Milk was delivered in our street from a heavy three-wheeled push-cart gleaming with brass fittings — ladles, churns, wheel-hub caps, hinges and padlocks — operated by the local Co-op. From about the age of eight or nine, I worked our local streets, Saturdays and Sundays, with our milkman. Thick creamy milk in half-pint, pint and fat quart bottles, or ladled from our brass churn into bowls and jugs were our mainstay, with eggs and butter sold from the zinc-lined box at the front of the cart. I learned the trade and was nearly as quick as the milkman himself, I thought.

But life was not all street and milk. One washing day I mangled the index finger of my left hand. I had my tonsils out in London. Then we had diphtheria. One sister and my younger brother Eric were whisked away and the house sealed and fumigated. Swabs taken from me proved positive and away I went, too, to the Fever Hospital to spend a glorious two weeks surrounded by diphtheria and scarlet fever, in and out of the wards, but never a positive swab again. So they let me out. And my brother and sister recovered. Bronchitis was less kind to me. My family tell me I nearly died, but I have no memory of it except some kind of hot wool wrapping or poultice around my chest, and sitting up in bed reading.

In this first ten years of life I had no sense that things could be other than they were. I did not feel deprived or poor. Everyone had a tin bath in the backyard, everyone ate meat and pickles on Mondays, everyone played marbles in the gutter, and everyone said 'Giz a fag card mister'. The 'them' and 'us', so frequently attributed to working-class cultural experience, made no impact. Everyone I knew was 'us': at school, in the street, pushing the milk-cart, in hospital. The only 'thems' were angry shopkeepers and grown-ups objecting to house bricks and noise. But Ginger and Jean Dairy were only just 'us', or so I came to learn. Yet the economy and the Education Act of 1902 were already at work changing the circumstances in which I would make my own history.

Caught up in the housing boom of the mid-1930s we moved to the other side of the 'Rec' in 1937. Number 66 Greenland Crescent was the end house of a terrace of 10 or 12 recently built houses, not quite new. It was, therefore, semi-detached. We now had a bathroom, indoor lavatory, and a kitchenette with a gas boiler instead of the old copper. The fire in the kitchen had a back boiler and we had running warm water. We had a front garden. Our next door neighbour, Mr Erie was a civil servant with a pension due on retirement. My mother and Mrs Erie were gloomy over cups of tea. This change of street meant a change of school. I lost Ginger, my milk round, and saw the last of Jean Dairy.

At Western Road Junior School in a class of 50 we did Reading, Composition, Handwriting, English, Recitation, Dictation, Arithmetic, Mental Arithmetic, History, Geography and Science to a total of 180 marks. In December 1937 I scored 164 to come third out of 47 in a class of 49. Miss Drayton, the headmistress, was a formidable woman. She summoned my father to her office to tell him that I should take a scholarship examination for entrance to Southall County School, one of those modern co-educational grammar schools set up under the Act of 1902. It would give me a real education and turn me into a 'County Cad'. Gwen, my older sister, had already been to the County School but at fourteen had been taken away and put to work for 12s 6d a week in the office of the 'Tube' behind 45 Lea Road. The family needed the money. So, partly at her expense, and with no say in the matter, I was to be allowed to go to the County School (so I found out later) to School Certificate level, and then put into the Civil Service and a pension — my mother was very taken with our neighbours, the Eries. So, in 1938, three children out of a class of 50, passed the Scholarship examination, me and two girls. One of them didn't take up her place and the other, like Gwen, left before taking the School Certificate. Consequently, only one out of 50 (two per cent of the working class population of Southall) was to complete the School Certificate, at least by the direct route, and he was destined to leave school at fifteen or sixteen. I remember one boy, not dressed in second-hand clothes, promised a bicycle by his father if he passed the scholarship, getting a beating for failure. For my part I was a reluctant, although not a resisting, scholarship boy. I would have preferred to stay with my friends, maybe meet up with Ginger again, but I did the tests as I always did, with no thought to deliberately fail the examination as I read others claim to have done. As I have said, then I had no great sense of 'them' and 'us'.

So began my separation from family and street and (eventually) my unintended discovery of myself, and *class*, and my yesterdays.

Southall County School was a mile or so away, on the other, the posh, side of town. I got there in the mornings on an 82 bus but could save 1d on the return journey by walking. Walking meant passing the Featherstone Road Elementary School where the failed scholarship takers and Ginger would have gone. My friends had guaranteed me protection in this hazardous undertaking, but, dressed as I was in black blazer, black school cap and bulging satchel, I doubted their capacity to ease my passage, rather than their good will. After all, they were at the bottom of the school. So I usually managed to go the long way round, or pass by well after school was out. In either case I saw less of my old street friends, and homework and the Church Lads' Brigade kept me off the streets, except at the weekends, when my mother's 'Gotcher nose in a book again. Why n't yer go out and play like the others do', drove me to despair and into the street. Then there were new school friends. Tom who lived only a few streets away with a family much like mine, only Catholic — the reason we had never met before — and Alan, living in a modern detached house close to the park and school. Dropping in to his house going or coming from school was my first glimpse of another mode of living. And there were Empire Days dressed in Church Lads' Brigade uniform around the Cenotaph, and a half-day holiday.

After the first term at the County School I was placed in the Remove. There, while I sometimes scored a B+, I never made an A, and mostly recorded Cs — 'Satisfactory'. For English I was told 'more energy needed'. My overall report said: 'Good on the whole, but he must be more alert.' Clearly the competitive struggle for incorporation was on in earnest. One of 4 per cent of my class to get there in the first place, placed in the

Remove, then told I was still only 'Satisfactory' and not alert enough: poor old Ginger! Not that these things worried me then. I won five events in the junior school athletics, and recall a boisterous game on top of a heap of builder's rubble, in which a boy I wrestled off the top broke an arm as we fell, and I had my first interview with a remote and awesome headmaster. We weren't meant to do those things at the County School.

Above all, 1939 and 1940 stand out in memory for the life of crime Tom and me and others got into. I think it began as we walked home from school. Me and Tom used to pass a Home and Colonial grocery shop that displayed some of its goods, including eggs, on the pavement, just past the Dominion cinema. Our dare was to walk past without stopping and to collect an egg or two on the way. Every so often we had one or two eggs to get rid of. Since we couldn't take them home or do anything useful with them, we dropped them off in suitable places — people's front doorsteps and in other shops. Our favourite place was a long narrow hallway and flight of stairs in the Territorial Army Drill Hall. The length of the passage was a challenge. Tom and me (like me and Ginger) ran like the wind. We were never caught. From this pointless stealing of eggs we moved into the organized stealing of sweets and chocolates on sports days. It was a sports day when we heard the news that France had fallen — we stole some sweets and played leap-frog all along the Broadway. We graduated to stealing items of stationery; rulers, compasses, pens, pencils, rubbers, pencil sharpeners, mostly from Woolworths, with the purpose of selling them to friends at school. Then we stole toy soldiers, model aeroplanes, and ships from toyshops. For a time, in the summer of 1940, our selling of stolen items became an obsession. We even began to steal to order. Challenged, we always protested our County School status, crowding the shops with our presence, and we were never caught. The excitement ran very high. And so were the stakes; expulsion from school almost certain and some kind of reform school, likely. With such a record I could never have known Charlie.

War was my salvation, in 1940 and again in 1944. Because of the war my father's factory closed. Since he had always looked down his artisan's nose at the prospect of mere carpentering on building projects — hammer and nails men were anathema to him — he applied for a job as civilian instructor in the RAF and was posted to the big RAF training camp at Hednesford in Staffordshire. He was a failure as an instructor and would have spent a most unhappy war, but someone recognized his skill. He spent the rest of the war making scale model aircraft for training in aircraft recognition. His wooden and brass models were perfect. So, early in November 1940, we moved to the Midlands. I had no wish to go. The blitz on London and the Battle of Britain were spectacles both night and day, and they disrupted school as we spent most of our half-day's attendance in the air-raid shelters. I would lose my friends.

Hednesford was a terrible place. A decaying mining township, ugly and old-fashioned. It was poor, poor by any standards I had experienced in Southall. As I delivered Christmas mail in the winters of 1942 and 1943 I experienced the shock of the sight and smell of houses and people poorer and less respectable than us. I was entitled to compare, I thought, because, in spite of my life of crime, I had worked on Fridays and Saturdays delivering greengroceries in the streets about ours in Southall. Compared to Hednesford, Southall was posh. We were not as they were. Our house, a semi-detached, was out of town backing on to Hednesford Hills, then strewn with great pieces of timber to prevent the Germans landing. I spent my time on the Hills with my dog Gyp, fantasizing heroic resistance to German paratroopers from all the secret places I found. I wished they would come.

Five miles from Hednesford was Rugeley Grammar School. We got there by train. It was a very different place from Southall County; smaller, narrower in its range of subjects, and more given to meeting the standards of farmers' sons whose fathers paid for their education. There were no girls. Big, boisterous and rosy-cheeked, the girls went to Queen Mary's in Walsall from the opposite platform. Rugeley Grammar seemed to lack the edge of Southall County. Its staff had been badly disrupted by the war, and, although they were generally friendly and helpful and competent teachers, no one seemed interested in working-class scholarship boys. The school lost the brightest boy in my class before he took School Certificate, and no teacher thought to mention to me or my family that I might continue my education beyond school level. After School Certificate, working-class boys were channelled away to apprenticeships with GEC in Stafford. It seemed the proper thing to do. Boys who went into the sixth form were almost invariably from middle or lower middle-class families. Only the war changed that. There were friends, too. Blockley, Cartwright, 'Fas' Smith, and 'Bonker' Bennison. We sported hammer and sickle badges. I read the first volume of *Das Kapital*, mystified. With them crime was out. Fun and foolishness was in. 'Bonker' pretended madness or an epileptic fit. He drooled at the mouth, contorted his whole body and face as in extreme pain, and writhed on the ground. We held him down, propped him up, carried him along. 'Hold him, Block! Mind his head.' 'Excuse me Sir! Would you not mind crowding round our friend — he's sick.' 'Thank you, Sir.' 'Hey, Cartwright, ask if we can rest Bonker in that house.' 'Excuse me, madam, our friend is sick with a fit. We need somewhere warm to keep him until he comes round. Could we use your front room? Or a blanket?' 'Go away you boys! Go away! Leave me alone!'

The door would slam. We exploded in laughter. And so it would go on. I also learned to play hockey.

But the war. I enjoyed every moment of it. In Southall I had already dug two air raid shelters, one before and one after the Anderson given to us by the Government. When war was declared and the siren blew on that first day, we took our Sunday dinners and ate crouched in the confined space. At night, when the blitz was on, I stood at the entrance, entranced. At Rugeley, Mr Toye, the history master and the geography teacher, organized a company of Army Cadets. Mr Toye 'Massachusetts' or 'Chuss' was short, thick-set, and black-haired. About 38. He taught a very conventional history, from *Piers Plowman,* which I read in my first week: ''04, '06, '08, '09, Blenheim, Ramillies, Oudenarde and Malplaquet.' He used to read us some of his own writing and his poetry. We sniggered and laughed, of course, but his love for his subject and the genuineness of his interest in us took the edge off our feigned amusement and boredom. 'Chuss' was an affectionate nickname. Anyway, he formed the Cadet Company and I joined. It was my element. We map-read and judged distances. We marched and camped. We fought mock wars. We practised regularly at the rifle range at the local Drill Hall, under the eye of a regular Sergeant Major, and I went to an Army Physical Education School in North Wales to qualify as a Physical Training Instructor in the Cadets. I was made sergeant and then under-officer. At a regional cadet camp I commanded a whole long column of army cadets as we marched through the streets of Uttoxeter. In that year, too, when I was sixteen, I tried for the Indian Army. Nothing too soon or too distant to get away from the future planned for me. I wore my father's Sunday jacket for the interview at Chester, and knew as soon as the interview was over that I was not acceptable, in spite of Mr Toye's recommendation. But I was determined. I discovered the 'Y' scheme. Under this scheme, volunteer recruits from grammar and public schools were invited to join the Royal Marines at seventeen and a half. Recruitment into a 'Y' squad for a period of initial training of about four months would be followed by appearance before a War Office Selection Board (WOSB) for entry into officer cadet training school. I wore the 'Y' scheme badge on my cadet uniform and walked tall. I think that a preferred condition of entry was admission direct from school — at seventeen and a half. In any case, having joined the scheme, I set about persuading my parents, using that argument. I also argued that I might as well stay at school because no one would give me a job for such a short time — and what short period jobs were there? And, if I didn't go at seventeen and a half, I would be called up at eighteen anyway, without any choice of service and no prospect of officer training. At the end of fifth form Mr Toye had written on my report under Physical Exercises; 'Cert A

(PT) [passed with an A mark] VG A1. Is capable of running a gym class. PT1 in Cadets. *Cadets.* Is an Under Officer and has splendid word of command. The type for future promotion.' So I stayed at school. That year in the sixth form, with Blockley, 'Bonker', Cartwright and 'Fas', studying English, History, Geography and French at the subsidiary level of the Higher School Certificate was a reprieve from a life sentence. At the outset, according to Rodwell, the English master called back from retirement because of the war, I seemed 'to want to mark time for a year'. 'Probably has likes and dislikes', he wrote, 'We may discover his likes some day.' (This was when we were doing *A Midsummer Night's Dream*, and I had my eyes on the Marines and on the war I wanted to get into!) But I improved. I passed the four subjects at the year's end. That year in the sixth form, and those four passes, were to be the key to my yesterdays, my todays and my tomorrows. For the time being they served to keep me out of the Civil Service. On 14 August 1944, for 3s a day and all found, I joined the Royal Marines at their depot in Deal.

DEAL

'PO/X 122993, Neale, R. S., Marine, Y4 Squad, Deal, Sah!' Enthusiastic soldier. Good right marker. Ram-rod straight. Bright as a button. Fit as a fiddle. Creases sharp as razors. Blanco like a baby's bottom. Backs of brasses polished like mirrors. Boots to eat your dinner off.

'You play ball with me — I'll play ball with you!'
'Stand still! Wait for it! Never mind them buzz-bombs!'
'I'll have yer guts for garters!' 'Stand still that man!'
'Fixing bayonets on the march — fix bayonets!'
'Down -2-3, Up -2-3, Over -2-3.' 'As you were!'
'Wakey, Wakey!' 'Squad, halt!'
'You're not bleeding Bootnecks, you're a bunch of Guardsmen, mother's boys! What are yer?'
'Mother's boy's, sarn't!'
'Bootnecks, sarn't.'
'Fit for officer training, sarn't.'
'Right then Royal, off to WOSB. At the double, march!'

WOSB

'I say, you've landed by parachute in the only tree in a field surrounded by wolves. How do you reach the rest of your unit without giving your position away?'

'Here's two short planks and a barrel. Get across that ditch so you can't be followed.'

'Take this box across that assault course with these men without touching the ground in three minutes. Go!'

'On the wall map show me the position of Hong Kong!'
'I want you to do this test. You have 30 minutes. Start on the word go. Go!'
'I say, you meet the CO in the Officers' Mess for drinks at 1900 hours.'

Result NY three months. As I remember, only two members of Y4 Squad, both from minor public schools, passed WOSB at that first go. The rest of us merged with others to become S2 Squad, sent to Portsmouth barracks to complete initial training.

Sergeant 'Tiny' Head was a regular NCO, big, affable, likeable, efficient, occasionally drunk. He turned hours of parade ground drills at Pompey into a game. Intricate manoeuvres lasting minutes at a time, were performed on one word of command from start to finish — a sort of massed military ballet. He found spots in the drill sheds where our marching time and the slightly loosened butt-plates of our rifles were 'music to his ears' — and to ours. Our 'eyes right' to passing Wrens, who fluttered around him, were crisper than for the Adjutant himself. And he marched us off to the serious business of our training. Winter mornings were the worst, putting on wet uniforms and full fighting order to swim lengths of the baths and float for minutes on end. Drop anything — a boot, a helmet, trousers and back you went. And the ranges; rifle, Vicker's heavy machine gun, mortar and automatic weapons. And assault courses. All in deadly earnest, and fun. Earnestness was emphasized by jungle warfare training on the downs behind Portsmouth in March 1945. We knew then, that while the war in Europe might be beyond our reach, the Far East would still be our killing ground. I shot my 'oppo'. We unloaded Tommy-guns at the end of our run through the jungle warfare track. As I removed the magazine, a round lodged in the breech, fired and Jack Colston dropped to the ground — a .45 bullet passed through both buttocks, a hairsbreadth from his spine.

The time came for the NY3s to return to WOSB. But the war was getting away from us. Almost to a man (boy) some six or eight of us volunteered for Commando training, preferring the Combined Operations Badge and a green beret to a second doubtful chance. So we took a train for Towyn in North Wales, hence to Achnacarry in Scotland.

Cader Idris and the mountains behind Towyn were our playground. A captain, the only marine officer I remember with respect, led us on our first cross countries. He set a sharp pace through bog, over rock, up hill, down slopes — he never tired. It was my first experience. As he enjoyed every mile and aspect of the march he showed me the pleasures of mountain walking. As the others straggled out behind, I stuck to him like a leech. He carried a walking stick. We were in full fighting order. Except to give an order, he never spoke. For the rest, it was the NCOs — 'Tiny',

'Tarzan', 'Bomb Happy' who trained us. The election of 1945, with its promise of a brave new world, passed us by.

To a London boy, who had lived in the Midlands (with only Towyn to compare), Achnacarry, its mountains, lochs, rivers, skies, was a paradise of space. Achnacarry was that first six-mile speed march down from Spean Bridge into nowhere, followed by a sloped-arms approach through the avenue of trees lined by mock graves marked by skull and crossbones, each warning against some 'idiocy' — 'Lit a fag at night', 'Fired his mortar under a tree'.

Achnacarry was the wire bunk and a blanket for a bed.
Achnacarry was the end of the seven day week.
Achnacarry was the champion boxer, fear frozen on a rock face.
Achnacarry was that infinity of time stepping into space for a first absail down the castle wall.
Achnacarry was the right moment for release on the death slide.
Achnacarry was striving for a perfect score with pistol, rifle and sub-machine-gun, heart pumping and sweat running after a speed march.
Achnacarry was 30 miles across country in a day.
Achnacarry was the massed swarm of midges settling on every exposed part — hands, wrists, neck, nose, ears, eyes — at every morning and evening parade, and 'Stand still that man'!
Achnacarry was an abomination. Its discipline was freedom. I return to Scotland and its mountains whenever I can.

So we marched, speed-marched, ran, swam, climbed, absailed, canoed, learned unarmed combat and how to use a knife, set up booby traps and identified them, stormed houses, rode the deathslide, humped our weapons, fired them, did assault courses, blacked our faces, lived on survival packs, slept rough, read our maps, worked as a troop, and lived with our 'oppos'. Jack Colston shot, I took up with 'Pilly' (Pilsworth). And they made me a Lance Corporal. At the end of it all and about 12 months after joining at Deal, those of us who had stayed with it won our green berets. Trained as we were sure no troops had ever been trained before, we were immortal — and out of place.

The productive capacity of the American capitalist mode of production, its science, technology and geo-political interests overwhelmed our insignificance. August 4th mocked our efforts. At the highest point of our achievement it robbed us of our glory. The people of Hiroshima were vapourized, the concentration camps spewed out their dead, the world rejoiced. We crumpled our new green berets making them worn. 'Fuck!'

By the end of the year Dick Shephard and I were new squaddies in 'E' Troop, 45 Royal Marine Commando. The Troop seemed full of seasoned warriors, long-service marines and HO marines with time in — and Walcheren. Captain Loudon, the Troop CO, thought our Lance Corporal status too grand for these conditions and demoted us — two ex-grammar school boys, failed WOSB, back with the class to which I belonged!

Early in the New Year we sailed for Hong Kong. Dick and I privileged beyond belief. Our fresh faces, the sharpness of the creases in our battledress, and the marks of education turned us into orderlies, Dick to the CO, me to the 2IC. Our job was to follow them on the rounds of the ship and carry messages. No parades, no scrubbing out the mess, no chores. Privileged. They, too, never spoke to us except to give an order. Embarrassed, perhaps (we were Indian Sepoys who almost spoke the language), even on the hockey field. Somehow Dick and I got into the Commando hockey team. The rest were officers. I can see Captain Loudon, breathing hard, charging along, making a 'mess of things; refusing to admit that I was faster and in a better position to score than he was. The sort of calls that make a team work were just not possible. We were ball boys. And we had to change in a separate room. In Hong Kong we had to make our own way to and from the playing field. Privileged!

In Hong Kong I learned four things. First, already alluded to, I was not officer material — not of the officer class. My preference for Commando training over WOSB was not sour grapes. I had come to realize, I think, that the 'Y' scheme, with its lure of upward social mobility for gullible working-class grammar-school boys, was a fraud. I believe now that it was simply a war-time extension of the more general fraud of educational upward social mobility held out to working-class children. It successfully incorporated us (me) into the military machine as well educated 'quality' recruits, but kept the middle-level rewards (officer status) for middle-class, minor public school boys. I was not even middle-class material.

Weekend leave in London was a delight to the marine from Bermondsey. He would rush home, change his clothes and join his mates, the 'Bermondsey Bashers', for a good piss-up and punch-up. 'Aggro', I think they call it today. 'Bermondsey Bashers'; drinkers, skivers, swearers, prostitute-beaters, punch-up lovers, cluttered the nissen huts, tents and barrack rooms of 45 Royal Marine Commando, wherever they were in Hong Kong. Language was a 'fucking' bludgeon and everything defiled. Thought was at a discount. To the 'Bermondsey Bashers' I must have seemed a prudish, puritan of a boy. I didn't drink or get drunk. I never went out on a Saturday night punch-up. I was repulsed by their prostitutes and those who passed them from bed to bed, spewing them out in the morning with bloody noses and black eyes. I stayed away from them. The second thing I learned — I was not a 'Bermondsey Basher'. Marked by the respectability of my artisan background and separated by education, I kept my distance. And they kept theirs; perhaps because I was bigger and stronger than most, for all their bluster, and better at many of the skills of Commando life they admired. I could look after myself. And there were enough like me around to give support to each other. It could only have been Dick Shephard's and my respectability that earned us the two-week visit to Macau, sponsored by its Portuguese rulers as gesture of goodwill to the British and their Tommies. No 'Bermondsey Bashers' for them. A pleasant surprise for us.

So, while I was now pretty sure about 'them', I was not so sure about 'us'. I hope Ginger never joined the 'Bermondsey Bashers', although the mode of production was against him.

The third thing I learned was poverty. And the third and a half, you might say, was how easy it is to exploit it and to become part of the exploitative system; how difficult not to be incorporated. Dick Shephard and I soon got back to our Troop. On Hong Kong island we did police duties in the western districts, always patrolling in pairs. In day time we carried the handles of entrenching tools as batons. At night we carried loaded rifles and were ordered to stay on the main roads. On these patrols we had no right of arrest, only powers of intervention. We had to call on the Hong Kong police to make arrests. Since every bank and counting-house had an armed Sikh on guard, we felt redundant, at least as far as property was concerned. As for offences against persons, who cared? During the day poverty was fairly well behaved, it stayed out of sight except for the 'Cum Saw. Cum Saw!' of scores of outstretched hands, children mostly, but adults, too, although they seemed to know that when we were on patrol it was not on. At night poverty was king. Poverty commanded the streets. In their hundreds and thousands, along our beat, people and their babies and their aged spread newspapers and rags on pavements thick with spittle, urine, and vegetable and animal waste (in summer we longed for the rains to break), and slept uncovered, packed like sardines in an enormous decaying, crumbling tin. Off from the pavements, the gutters were lined with rickshaws, each with its sleeping 'boy' curled in the seat, like cats, waiting for a fare. Then we could only patrol in the middle of the street.

One day we thought we had a riot on our hands. In a side street there was a swarm of people. In its middle an upturned rickshaw and two 'boys' pulling, pushing, shouting over it, one more loudly and violently than the other. The quieter one seemed to plead with us for help. The noisy one was noisy. We recalled seeing two members of the Hong Kong police a short while before. My 'oppo' went to fetch them. So all eyes were on me and the two 'boys'. The noisy one started boxing me, feinting with both hands and feet. He looked very tough. The quieter one dragged around at my side. I had no idea what the problem was, or who had rightful claim to the rickshaw. I was a Solomon in a Chinese tower of Babel. Out of nowhere, it seemed, came a frail old man with a whisp of white beard and perfect, although inflected English. He explained that the noisy one, drunk on rice wine, had taken the rickshaw from the quieter one. That the quieter one was reluctant to claim his title too strongly in case the noisy one broke the rickshaw. In fact he would rather the noisy one take it than break it. That was my problem. Then he disappeared. (A gentle moment of sensibility suspended in time.) I knew what needed to be done. The problem was how. The crowd seemed to have got much bigger and I was carrying all the white man's burden. The noisy one became more aggressive. As he jumped and flicked his legs and arms at me I sensed the power of a rickshaw 'boy' in every kick. He was very tough — 'a tough bastard', I thought, as I shuffled around in the boots you could eat off and my scrubbed gaiters. I judged that I would get one go at him and if I missed I'd had it. I intended to go for the artery on the side of his neck, one sharp chop with my entrenching tool handle should do it. So I watched and waited. At my moment of decision he left. Just left. Tired of the game he just danced away into the maze of streets and markets beyond our beat. We righted the rickshaw. The quieter one fondly walked it away. The crowd dispersed. It was a draw. My 'oppo' never did find the Chinese policemen. I never saw the frail, white bearded Chinese again. The homeless were back on the pavements that night.

At Lo Wu railway bridge, on the frontier with China, there was a sick old man. Discharged as incurable from a Hong Kong hospital he wanted to get back to China to die in his native village. But the Chinese wouldn't let him re-enter the country. So he crept back to die on our side of the bridge, his testicles swollen to his knees, putrid and alone. The only people who would touch him were the two Chinese we paid to dispose of his body.

On our 'medical' rounds of the villages in the New Territories, villagers were glad of mepacrin and aspirin for any ailment our sickbay attendant was able to diagnose. They gave us tea in return.

At Lo Wu, as everywhere in Hong Kong, our job was to search out smugglers of UNRRA supplies; flour, rice, salt, tinned milk, kerosene, and military stores. The big operators, Chinese traders in Nationalist China and in Hong Kong, tried everything. One time we found several railway truck loads of peasant women, all with babies on their backs. But the babies weren't babies. They were small sacks of flour. The women wept when we off-loaded them to confiscate their 'babies', and we beat their arms and hands with batons and the flats of bayonets to make them let go. It was a futile act. We never caught one of the entrepreneurs who paid the women a few cents to get the flour through, and to weep. Nor did we know what happened to the confiscated goods when they got back to our headquarters or to the local police station.

Salt was generally smuggled openly by peasant women with carrier poles and baskets. Once we caught ten or twelve of them, confiscated the salt, and locked them away. Someone gave the order to destroy the carrying poles. We did. The women wailed. Today, I still have a section of one of the poles turned into a baton. As British workers deprived Chinese peasant women of their means of livelihood, capitalists got away.

The bus station at Yuen Long had been used by the Japanese to carry out executions. It was where we decided to join the smugglers. At the bus station check point we had to prevent goods being smuggled into Hong Kong from the New Territories. Instead we merely counted what went through; barrels of kerosene, sacks of salt and flour, cases of milk, and, when we could identify it, opium. Then we presented our bills at the agreed rate, sometimes on the spot to the travelling agent, generally in the village at week's end. We decided to 'squeeze' the local business community further. Two of us and our interpreter penetrated the inner sanctum (so we thought) of Yuen Long's opium and gambling dens. We were invited to sit, to take tea, to discuss terms. We asked for a share in their profits, pointing out that our duty required us to act against all illegal activity, and that we really thought the smuggling past the bus station should be stopped. They appreciated our predicament. They would like to oblige, they said, but they already paid a sergeant at headquarters and a police inspector. Wouldn't we agree, they said, that the harvest was not yet in and farmers were not spending as much as they would in a few weeks' time. If they cut us in — and they recognized our just claim — the drop in their margin of profit would force them out of business. Then who would benefit? Perhaps we could wait until the harvest was in? We agreed — who wants to kill a golden goose? By the time the harvest was in we had been moved elsewhere in the New Territories, and had to start again. The capitalists of Yuen Long knew that the sergeant at headquarters and the police inspector were permanent.

On our side of the railway bridge at Lo Wu, one morning, we kept a desultory watch on the people coming and going. It was about 10.30, well after the morning train had gone, and tea-time. Two coolies wearing only shorts and flip-flaps came by carrying a sack bulging with who knew what. My 'oppo' gestured for the coolies to drop the sack, and prodded it several times with his rifle and bayonet. He told them to pass, waving them on. But, as we took up our tea-drinking again they got very angry. One of them picked up a large piece of ballast. From a distance of about ten feet he hurled it at me. In no time at all I doubled over to take the force of the rock in my stomach. At the same time, with outstretched arms, as I bent double, I shot my nearly full mug of hot tea over him. Then we made threatening gestures with our rifles and kicked the sack in their direction. 'Fuck off', we said. And they did. But not for long. They returned leading a threatening crowd of coolies.

With the help of our interpreter we gathered that the two coolies were members of Chang Kai Chek's 30,000 strong 90th Airborne Commando on their way back to their side of the river with a sack of newly-cut grass for their horses. (We had an agreement with them about cutting grass.) They considered they had been hardly done by and the agreement flouted. We said we were sorry, but how were we supposed to know they were soldiers, they wore no uniform and had offered no identification. And they had resorted to violence. That wasn't the point, they said, we had insulted them and caused them to lose face before other Chinese on the bridge. The only way, they said, to make amends would be for us to carry the sack into China for them. We refused. At this the crowd, which had grown considerably, got very angry. They dragged and pulled at our interpreter, threatening to hang him as a traitor to China. They were joined in their anger by some of our men, one of whom in a trembling fury threw off several of the Chinese attacking the interpreter. At which another Chinese had to be forcibly prevented from cutting down the would-be rescuer with a machette. By this time our sergeant with the rest of the section had appeared. He ordered us to load our rifles. The ragged opening and closing of rifle-bolts had the desired effect. The 90th Airborne Commando gave us back our interpreter and retreated to their side of the bridge, all the time shouting abuse and throwing stones. Our interpreter said they had gone to fetch their commander and reinforcements. We decided to do the same.

That day, for some reason, the road track to Lo Wu bridge was impassable. Consequently our reinforcements, led by the second-in-command of the Commando, in his private scout car festooned with wireless aerials and machine-guns, would have to travel along the railway line. They would be some time in coming. So we set about preparing our defences (there were about a dozen of us). We placed a single concrete sleeper across the line (in case the afternoon train would lead the first attack). We stretched a single strand of barbed wire across the width of the bridge (to stop all foot traffic). And we unpacked a greasy Vickers .303 machine gun left behind in the station block house by the Hong Kong police. We cleared off most of the grease from the firing mechanism and mounted the gun on its tripod in the middle of the track, just behind the concrete sleeper and the strand of barbed wire. Then we found that the recoil mechanism did not work (the Hong Kong police *did* have their wits about them). So there it was. A very thin red (green) line — one sten gun,

10 or 12 rifles, a strand of barbed wire, and a broken Vickers (no Victor McLaghlan that day), and 30,000 Chinese. As we waited in the hot sun, the grease dripped off the useless machine-gun, and rocks and stones from the other side whomped and skittered at our feet. By this time, one or other of our Troop officers had arrived. All through the afternoon there was much to-ing and fro-ing and some negotiating with a Chinese officer. The upshot was, we carried the sack to the centre of the bridge, they carried it over their half. They at least, saved face. And the end of the affair? The second-in-command arrived on foot. He had broken the back axle of his scout car driving at speed along the railway track. Border incidents, I knew about! But the Civil War in China?

And the fourth thing I learned? One day at Victoria Barracks I had·to take a message to some place outside the barracks. To get there I had to walk up the hill that looked down on to the main parade ground set in a sort of amphitheatre cut into the hillside. As I marched up the slope I became aware of a press of Chinese — men, women, children — pushing up against the wire fence and looking down into the amphitheatre, and laughing. I stopped, looked down and saw my troop going through its parade ground paces, not as polished as Y4 and S2 squads, but high stepping as they marked time, kicking up little spurts of dust. In a flash, like that rock at Lo Wu, it struck me, the Chinese were laughing at me down there on the parade ground, and I saw me as a manikin among automatons. As I watched myself through, what I thought, were Chinese eyes, but not quite laughing, I was outside myself.

Then it was time to go home.

Since then I have lived that sensation of being outside myself on several occasions; as a teacher, watching me teach, and increasingly as a history writer, watching me seize hold and shape images of my yesterdays as they flash up, in moments of danger, threatening to escape for ever. This book captures some of those images. It meets some of those dangers. It is a beginning. And you may still agree with Yorick.

Index